RADICAL EVIL

For Agnes

RADICAL EVIL

A Philosophical Interrogation

Richard J. Bernstein

polity

First published in 2002 by Polity Press in association with Blackwell Publishing Ltd.

Reprinted 2003, 2004, 2005, 2006, 2007

Polity Press
65 Bridge Street
Cambridge CB2 1UR, UK

Polity Press
350 Main Street
Maldon, MA 02148, USA

Library of Congress Cataloging-in-Publication Data

Bernstein, Richard J.
     Radical evil : a philosophical interrogation / Richard J. Bernstein.
          p.   cm.
     Includes bibliographical references and index.
     ISBN: 978-0-7456-2953-7
     ISBN: 978-0-7456-2954-4 (pbk)
     1. Good and evil—History.   I. Title.
BJ1406 .B47 2002
170—dc21

                                                                                    2001007377

Typeset in 10.5 on 12 pt Baskerville
by Ace Filmsetting Ltd, Frome, Somerset
Printed and bound in Great Britain by Marston Book Services Limited, Oxford

This book is printed on acid-free paper.

For further information on Polity, please visit our website :http://www.polity.co.uk

Contents

Preface

My understanding of philosophic inquiry, shaped when I was an under-
graduate at the University of Chicago in the early 1950s, has always been
Socratic. By this I mean that I have always believed that the deepest
philosophic perplexities have their roots in our everyday experiences, and
ought to help to illuminate these experiences. Looking back over the
horrendous twentieth century, few of us would hesitate to speak of evil.
Many people believe that the evils witnessed in the twentieth century
exceed anything that has ever been recorded in past history. Most of us do
not hesitate to speak about these extreme events – genocides, massacres,
torture, terrorist attacks, the infliction of gratuitous suffering – as evil. We
have an intuitive sense that there is a difference between radical evil and
more common forms of immoral behavior. But when we stop to think and
ask what we mean by evil and what we are really saying when we call a
person, act, or event evil, our responses are frequently weak and diffuse.
There is a disparity between the intense moral passion that we feel in
condemning something as evil and our ability to give a conceptual account of what we mean by evil. If we turn to moral philosophy as it has
been practiced in the twentieth century, we do not find much help. Moral
philosophers are far more at ease talking about what is right and wrong,
good and bad, just and unjust, than in speaking about evil. "Evil" appears
to have been dropped from the vocabulary of most moral philosophers,
even though it is still very much in evidence in our everyday experience
and discourse.

This inquiry – this series of interrogations – began from the perplexity
concerning the disparity between our readiness to classify and condemn
phenomena as evil and the apparent lack of intellectual resources with

which to clarify the meaning, varieties, and vicissitudes of evil. The original stimulus was the thinking of Hannah Arendt, one of the very few twentieth-century thinkers to grapple with what was distinctive about twentieth-century evils. Reflecting on her contribution, I was led to ask, what can we learn about evil from the modern philosophical tradition? This book is the result of the intellectual journey taken in seeking to answer this question. In the Introduction, I explain why I begin with Kant's understanding of radical evil, and why I have chosen the particular thinkers that I focus on in this inquiry. The manuscript for the book was finished a few weeks before September 11, 2001. But the events of that infamous day confirm some of the main claims of this book. Few would hesitate to name what happened on that day as evil – indeed, the very epitome of evil in our time. Yet, despite the complex emotions and responses that the events have evoked, there is a great deal of uncertainty about what is meant by calling them evil. There is an all too familiar popular rhetoric of "evil" that becomes fashionable at such critical moments, which actually obscures and blocks serious thinking about the meaning of evil. "Evil" is used to silence thinking and to demonize what we refuse to understand.

I completed this book during a magnificent year (2000–2001) as a fellow at the *Wissenschaftskolleg zu Berlin*. This Institute of Advanced Study is an academic utopia. Everything is done to facilitate one's thinking and research. It is not only the detailed attention to taking care of one's material needs, but the extraordinary welcoming and generous spirit of the entire staff that make it such an unusual place to work. Not the least of the benefits of the *Wissenschaftskolleg* was the intellectual stimulation and collegiality provided by the fellows working on the most diverse problems in an enormous range of disciplines. Many new friendships were formed in the course of the year, but I want to acknowledge especially the helpful philosophic suggestions and conversations with my co-fellow, Dieter Henrich. Berlin, an exciting city that is in the process of becoming a major cosmopolitan center once again, is probably the most self-consciously historical city in the world. The past, especially the troubled past of the twentieth century, is always vividly present even in its silences and absence. Berlin turned out to be an appropriate site to explore the abyss of twentieth-century radical evil.

I want to make a brief comment about the use of masculine pronouns in the book. Originally I tried to adopt one of the new linguistic strategies for avoiding sexist language. But frankly, none of them seemed to work without stylistic awkwardness. All of the major thinkers examined in the book use masculine expressions when speaking about human beings in general. For stylistic reasons – albeit with a few exceptions – I have followed this practice.

The chapter, entitled "Radical Evil: Kant at War with Himself" is based on an earlier version of a paper published in *Rethinking Evil*, edited by Maria Pia Lara (Berkeley: University of California Press, 2001). The chapter, entitled "Levinas: Evil and the Temptation of Theodicy" is based on an earlier version published in *The Cambridge Companion to Emmanuel Levinas*, edited by Robert Bernasconi and Simon Critchley (Cambridge: Cambridge University Press, 2001).

I want to thank my research assistant, Laureen Park, for her care and diligence in preparing the manuscript for publication. I am also grateful to Jean van Altena who edited the manuscript with sensitivity and good judgment.

For the past twelve years I have benefited from the stimulation of my colleagues and students in the Graduate Faculty of the New School of Social Research. We have a lively, intense, engaged philosophic community. Discussing, arguing, and working closely with my colleague Agnes Heller, for whom philosophy is a living passion, has been a primary source of the joy and intellectual excitement that I have experienced teaching at the New School. This book is dedicated to her.

Introduction

In 1945, when the Nazi death camps were liberated, and the full horrors of what had happened during the war years were just beginning to emerge, Hannah Arendt declared, "The problem of evil will be the fundamental question of postwar intellectual life in Europe."[1] Later, when Arendt was asked about her first reactions to the rumors about the extermination camps (which she first heard in 1942), she said that it was as if an abyss had opened. "Something happened there to which we cannot reconcile ourselves. None of us can."[2] Arendt, like many others − especially the survivors of the camps − felt that what happened in the camps was the most extreme and radical form of evil. "Auschwitz" became a name that epitomized the entire Shoah, and has come to symbolize other evils that have burst forth in the twentieth century. We might also mention Cambodia, Rwanda, Bosnia − names and sites so very different, yet manifesting horrendous events that we desperately try to understand, but to which we cannot reconcile ourselves. Yet there is something extraordinarily paradoxical about the visibility of evil in our time − a visibility that can be so overwhelming that it numbs us. Andrew Delbanco acutely observes, "a gulf has opened up in our culture between the visibility of evil and the intellectual resources available for coping with it. Never before have images of horror been so widely disseminated and so appalling − from organized death camps to children starving in famines that might have been averted. . . . The repertoire of evil has never been richer. Yet never have our responses been so weak."[3] We have been overwhelmed by the most excruciating and detailed descriptions and testimonies; nevertheless the conceptual discourse for dealing with evil has been sparse and inadequate. What do we really mean when we describe an act, an event, or a person

as evil? Many of us would agree with what Arendt once wrote to Karl
Jaspers: "There is a difference between a man who sets out to murder his
old aunt and people who without considering the economic usefulness of
their actions at all . . . built factories to produce corpses."[4] But what is this
difference? How is it to be characterized? What are we really saying when
we speak of *radical evil*?

Philosophers and political theorists are much more comfortable speaking about injustice, the violation of human rights, what is immoral and
unethical, than about evil. When theologians and philosophers of religion
speak about "the problem of evil," they typically mean something quite
specific – the problem of how to reconcile the appearance of evil with a
belief in a God who is omniscient, omnipotent, and beneficent. Even this
discourse has become specialized and professionalized, and remote from
the lived experiences of ordinary people. In much of this literature, there
is a litany of the usual examples of evil: Nazi horrors, willful sadistic acts,
gratuitous murders, humiliating tortures, the extreme suffering of innocents, and the traditional Christian catalogue of sins. Frequently these
examples are treated as if they were unproblematic. The main issue of the
so-called problem of evil is not really the characterization of evil and its
varieties. It is rather the problem of how to reconcile evil (however it is
described) with religious beliefs and convictions. It is almost as if the
language of evil has been dropped from contemporary moral and ethical
discourse. We might try to explain this in a variety of ways. There certainly has been a loss of the grip of traditional religious and theological
discourse on people's everyday lives. Traditionally, evil has been closely
associated with religious, especially Christian, concerns. But today, there
is a prevailing sense of the irrelevance of theodicy. If we think of theodicy
in a broad sense as the attempt to find some "justification" for the evil and
useless suffering that we encounter, we might say, with Emmanuel Levinas,
that we are now living in a time after the "end of theodicy." "The philosophical problem . . . which is posed by the useless pain [*mal*] which
appears in its fundamental malignancy across the events of the twentieth
century concerns the meaning that religiosity and human morality of
goodness can still retain after the end of theodicy."[5] In 1982 Levinas, who
spent several years in a Nazi prisoner of war camp, and who lost most of
his family at Auschwitz, wrote: "This is the century that in thirty years has
known two world wars, the totalitarianism of right and left, Hitlerism and
Stalinism, Hiroshima, the Gulag, and the genocides of Auschwitz and
Cambodia. This is the century which is drawing to a close in the haunting
memory of everything signified by these barbaric names."[6] Since 1982,
the list of new "barbaric names" has grown at an alarming rate.

There is another reason why philosophers are reluctant to speak about evil. In our popular culture there is a subterranean current of "vulgar Manichaeism." By this I refer to the ease with which the world gets divided into good and evil forces. Evil (as Nietzsche had already taught us) comes to represent everything that one hates and despises, what one takes to be vile and despicable, which is to be violently extirpated. This vulgar Manichaeism can take deadly forms in fanatical ideologies. Today, it is the most ideological and fanatical groups that still employ the language of evil to identify what they despise and want to destroy.

Yet the problems concerning evil come back to haunt us. There is an increasing anxiety that we can neither prevent nor anticipate the bursting forth of ever-new evils. We need to gain some comprehension, some conceptual grasp of these evils – what we even mean when we label something evil. We lack a discourse that is deep, rich, and subtle enough to capture what has been experienced. This is the problematic – the felt difficulty – that forms the background for my present inquiry.

The immediate occasion for writing this book arose from my study *Hannah Arendt and the Jewish Question*. Arendt is among the few post-World War II thinkers who sought to explore what is distinctive about twentieth-century evil – as epitomized by totalitarian regimes – and to do so in a manner that does not rely on religious or theological descriptions of sin and evil. In my study of Arendt, I dedicated two chapters to her explorations of evil, radical evil and the banality of evil.[7] I argued there – as I will also show later in this study – that she was extremely insightful in her questioning. But, despite her perceptiveness, Arendt (as she realized) raised many questions concerning evil that she did not address. Specifically, the comment she made about Kant in *The Origins of Totalitarianism* led to my own interrogations. In introducing *her* concept of radical evil, she said that Kant – the philosopher who coined the expression "radical evil" – must have suspected the existence of a phenomenon that "confronts us with its overpowering reality and breaks down all standards we know." (I have cited the entire passage at the beginning of chapter 1.) Later, I will explore what Arendt meant by radical evil. But it was this reference to Kant that aroused my interest and curiosity. What did Kant, who many consider to be the most important modern moral philosopher, mean by radical evil? What might we still learn from Kant, and from those post-Kantian thinkers who have probed the meaning of evil?

There is another reason why Kant is important for my investigation. In 1791, two years before the publication of *Religion within the Limits of Reason Alone*, Kant wrote a little known, but extremely important, essay entitled "On the Failure of All Attempted Philosophical Theodicies."[8] The very title of this essay is significant. Kant is declaring that theodicy is not a task of science, but a matter of faith. If theodicy is conceived as a *science* or a discipline that can yield *theoretical knowledge*, then it is *impossible*. Consequently, not only do all attempted philosophical theodicies fail; they *must* fail. Theodicy as a science presupposes that we can have some theoretical *knowledge* (no matter how partial and limited) about God. But the thrust of Kant's entire critical philosophy is to call into question this possibility. We cannot have theoretical knowledge of what transcends the bounds of possible experience. This claim is epitomized in Kant's famous declaration in the *Critique of Pure Reason*, "I have therefore found it necessary to deny *knowledge*, in order to make room for *faith*." Kant is the modern philosopher who initiates the inquiry into evil without explicit recourse to philosophical theodicy. In this respect, Kant is especially important for the way in which I want to examine the post-Kantian vicissitudes of our understanding of evil. (Actually, as we investigate the philosophical reflections on evil since Kant, we shall see how the specter of theodicy still casts its shadow.)

Before presenting an overview of this inquiry, I want to clarify the interpretative stance that I have adopted. This study consists of a series of *interrogations*, a series of critical dialogical encounters. I agree with Hannah Arendt, Hans Jonas, and Emmanuel Levinas (and many others, including Theodor Adorno) that Auschwitz signifies a rupture and break with tradition, and that "after Auschwitz" we must rethink both the meaning of evil and human responsibility. Although we should not underestimate the rupture that has occurred, we can still interrogate and learn from earlier thinkers who have grappled with trying to understand the meaning of evil. I am inquiring into this modern tradition from our contemporary horizon – from "after Auschwitz," with all the treacherous ambiguities of this phrase. But throughout, I seek to avoid being anachronistic. It would be unwarranted to expect that thinkers who lived before Auschwitz should have anticipated it. But it is certainly not anachronistic to ask whether they can help us to think through the relevant issues concerning evil. I approach these thinkers in the spirit of seeking to learn from them. I have tried to be sensitive to their distinctive strengths, but also to engage them critically. There are important insights to be gleaned from each of the thinkers I examine, but there are aspects of their thinking that need to be criticized, and even rejected. Thus, in my discussion of Kant, I first explore what I take him to mean by evil and radical evil, and what role these concepts play in his moral philosophy. I then try to highlight unresolved tensions and conflicts in what he says about radical evil. I argue that Kant is at war with himself. But I am not primarily interested in critiquing Kant. I explore *why* Kant seems to contradict himself, and what this reveals about his moral philosophy. Pursuing this line of thought takes us to the very heart of Kant's deepest insights about morality and human responsibility.

The book consists of three parts. In the first part I examine Kant, Hegel, and Schelling. In the second, I take up the reflections of Nietzsche and Freud. And in the third and last part, I explore the thought of thinkers whose lives were dramatically altered and deeply affected by the Nazis, and who struggled with the meaning of evil and human responsibility "after Auschwitz." Although I deal with these thinkers in roughly chronological order, my purpose is not to write a history of modern reflections on evil, and certainly not to survey what has been written about evil since the end of the eighteenth century. It is always difficult to justify one's selections of certain figures for detailed examination and one's neglect of others. And in the course of writing this book, I have frequently been asked why I didn't also examine one or another philosopher. Given my fundamental problematic − the search for some clarity about evil from our contemporary perspective − the thinkers that I selected have something vital to contribute to the ongoing discourse of evil, even when I think they are mistaken.

I have already indicated my reasons for beginning with Kant. He coined the expression "radical evil" to designate what he took to be an innate human propensity to evil. Questioning Hegel and Schelling then follows, for both these thinkers not only stand in the shadow of Kant, but their entire philosophical projects can be conceived of as appropriations, responses, and critiques of Kantian motifs. Nowhere does this become clearer than in the manner in which they deal with the nature of evil. We will see how Hegel relates the problem of evil to his distinctive understanding of the dialectic of finitude and infinitude, and to his critique of the way in which Kant conceives of the relation of the finite and the infinite. There are deep, systematic ambiguities in Hegel's philosophy. Evil turns out to be a *necessary* stage in human development and the development of the Spirit; but at the same time there is a *necessary* sublation (*Aufhebung*) of this evil. Hegel's judgment about evil is epitomized in his declaration, "The wounds of the Spirit heal, and leave no scars behind."

Schelling is a philosopher who is barely known or discussed by Anglo-American philosophers. And even among continental philosophers he is frequently viewed as a transitional figure between Kant and Hegel. But here, I show how Schelling's reflections on evil provide a transition from classical philosophical approaches to evil to a much more modern treatment of the moral psychology of evil. The possibility of good and evil is integral to human freedom. Schelling strongly resists any account of evil that diminishes its brute reality − a brute reality that defies any dialectical sublation. Although he relies on a theological vocabulary in his characterization of human evil, he opens the way to a more penetrating moral psychological analysis of evil. He thereby provides a bridge to the two great modern moral psychologists of evil, Nietzsche and Freud.

Many treatments of Nietzsche focus almost exclusively on the meaning of evil that Nietzsche introduces in his *On the Genealogy of Morals*, where he contrasts the good/bad mode of evaluation characteristic of aristocratic nobles and the reactive good/evil contrast of the priestly class. I argue that we gain deeper insight when we understand this contrast dialectically. Nietzsche is a dialectical ironist, and from his perspective, evil is closely associated with *ressentiment* as he analyzes it. Many commentators have noted the similarities between Nietzsche and Freud. But the differences between them are both subtle and profound. Freud was at one and the same time attracted by the psychological insights of philosophers, but deeply skeptical about philosophy as an autonomous discipline. Yet I will argue that Freud's fundamental claims about the nature of psychological ambivalence must be taken into account in any adequate treatment of evil.

The three thinkers whom I examine in part III were roughly contemporary, and were all Jewish. Each of them – Emmanuel Levinas, Hans Jonas, and Hannah Arendt – identified strongly with their Jewish heritage, although Judaism as a religion was far more significant for Levinas and Jonas than it ever was for the more secular-oriented Arendt. Jonas and Arendt, both born in Germany, met when they were students of Heidegger in the early 1920s. A few years later, Levinas, who had left the great center of Jewish learning in Lithuania to become a university student in Strasbourg, went to Freiburg to study with Husserl and Heidegger. Levinas, who became a French citizen in the 1930s, was primarily responsible for the introduction of phenomenology into France. All three were influenced by phenomenology, and especially by the turn taken by existential phenomenology with Heidegger. Although "Jewish" issues were always important for these thinkers, they nevertheless stressed that their philosophical views (and in the case of Hannah Arendt, her political thinking) should be judged independently of their Jewish concerns. Each of their philosophical projects can be viewed as a response to Heidegger, especially in light of Heidegger's failure to respond to twentieth-century evil and human responsibility for this evil. Their struggles with twentieth-century evil shaped their philosophical orientations. Although each followed a different pathway, collectively, they enrich our conceptual discourse of evil.

In characterizing my inquiry as a series of interrogations or critical dialogues. I want to make it clear from the beginning that my aim is not to develop a new "theory" of evil. Frankly, I am deeply skeptical of the possibility of the very idea of a theory of evil. Rather, I think that our situation is one of an open-ended hermeneutical circle – one that defies any closure or completion. I agree with Hans Jonas when he says, "the perception of the *malum* is infinitely easier to us than the perception of the *bonum*; it is more direct, more compelling, less given to differences of opinion or taste, and most of all, obtruding itself without our looking for it. An evil forces its perception on us by its mere presence."[9] But, of course, even if we experience what we take to be evil, this is just the beginning of any inquiry. The task, then, is – to the extent that this is possible – to develop a conceptual understanding of what we mean by evil. This requires sorting out just what we take to be insightful, misleading, and even false in accounts of evil. As in any critically hermeneutical inquiry, there is a to-and-fro movement in such thinking, whereby we seek to enlarge our understanding, testing it against the phenomenon of evil that forces itself upon us. I do not believe that there is, or can be, any finality to this process; we must always be wary of thinking that we have reached a final resting place. There is, so I shall claim, something about evil that resists and defies any final comprehension. Levinas makes this point when he characterizes evil as an excess that cannot be synthesized adequately, and consequently comprehended by us. His distinctive phenomenological manner of stressing this "transcendence of evil" is to say that "evil is not only the nonintegratable, it is also the nonintegratability of the nonintegratable."[10] But even if we agree with this, it does not follow that we cannot enrich our understanding of the many facets of evil. In this spirit, I will conclude my interrogations with a series of theses about what we have learned in the course of this journey.

Part I

Evil, Will, and Freedom

1

Radical Evil: Kant at War with Himself

It is inherent in our entire philosophic tradition that we cannot conceive of a "radical evil," and this is true both for Christian theology, which conceded even to the Devil himself a celestial origin, as well as for Kant, the only philosopher who, in the word he coined for it, at least must have suspected the existence of this evil even though he immediately rationalized it in the concept of a "perverted ill will," that could be explained by comprehensible motives. Therefore, we actually have nothing to fall back on in order to understand a phenomenon that nevertheless confronts us with its overpowering reality and breaks down all standards we know. . . . . Totalitarian solutions may well survive the fall of totalitarian regimes in the form of strong temptations which will come up whenever it seems impossible to alleviate political, social, or economic misery in a manner worthy of man.

Hannah Arendt, *The Origins of Totalitarianism*

It was really as if an abyss had opened . . . . *This ought not to have happened.* And I don't mean just the number of victims. I mean the method, the fabrication of corpses and so on – I don't need to go into that. This should not have happened. Something happened there, to which we cannot reconcile ourselves. None of us ever can.

Hannah Arendt, "What Remains? The Language Remains"

I have begun with these two epigraphs from Hannah Arendt because they help to orient my discussion of Kant. The first quotation is from the closing remarks of *The Origins of Totalitarianism*; and the second is from a television interview that she gave in 1964 in which she recalls her shock

when she first discovered what was taking place in Nazi death camps.[1]
Ever since Kant used the expression "radical evil" (*radikal Böse*) in *Die
Religion innerhalb der Grenzen der blossen Vernunft*, it has been a source of
fascination and perplexity: fascination, because it has struck many of his
readers (including Arendt) that Kant was dimly aware of a type of evil
that exceeds our traditional conceptions of evil; perplexity, because it is
not clear precisely what Kant means by "radical evil," or how it fits (or
does not) with his moral philosophy. I want to probe the meaning of "radical evil" for Kant, the philosophic context in which he explores its significance, and how radical evil is related to his moral philosophy. Is it true, as
Arendt suggests, that Kant suspected the existence of a type of evil that calls
into question our traditional ways of understanding evil? Is it true, as Arendt
claims, that he "immediately rationalized it in the concept of a 'perverted ill
will' that could be explained by comprehensible motives"?

It would be anachronistic to expect that Kant anticipated the horrors of
the twentieth century. But Kant is certainly a thinker who has transformed the way in which we think about morality in the modern world.
Despite the many critiques of Kant's conception of morality, he has not
only inspired subsequent thinkers, but we are presently living through a
resurgence of interest in, and novel appropriations of, Kant's moral philosophy. So it is eminently appropriate to ask whether Kant's reflections
on morality and radical evil can help orient our own thinking about the
evil we have witnessed in the twentieth century. It is in this spirit that I
approach Kant and interrogate him.

The primary analysis and discussion of radical evil is to be found in
Religion within the Limits of Reason Alone.[2] The opening sentences of the
preface reiterate Kant's fundamental conviction that "for its own sake
morality does not need religion at all."

> So far as morality is based upon the conception of man as a free agent who,
> just because he is free, binds himself through his reason to unconditioned
> laws, it stands in need neither of the idea of another Being over him, for
> him to apprehend his duty, nor of an incentive other than the law itself, for
> him to do his duty. At least it is man's own fault if he is subject to such a
> need; and if he is, this need can be relieved through nothing outside him-
> self: for whatever does not originate in himself and his own freedom in no
> way compensates for the deficiency of his morality. Hence for its own sake
> morality does not need religion at all (whether objectively, as regards will-
> ing, or subjectively, as regards ability [to act]); by virtue of pure practical
> reason it is self-sufficient. (*Rel.* 3; 3)

Kant not only asserts the independence of morality; but it is also clear
from this passage that human beings are fully accountable and completely

responsible for what they do as free moral agents – whether they do their duty and obey the moral law or whether they fail to act in accordance with the moral law. If we are to understand what Kant means by radical evil, then our first task is to understand what Kant means by evil. Kant tells us that good or evil must "lie only in a rule made by the will [*Willkür*] for the use of its freedom, that is, in a maxim" (*Rel.* 17; 19). This is extremely important, for we will soon see that neither our natural inclinations nor our reason is the source of evil, but only our will. Just as Kant singles out the will as the primary locus of what is good, so it is the will that is the primary locus of evil. Consequently, we can say that good and evil have reference to the *maxims* of human volition.

We can already see how the *Religion* clarifies a troubling ambiguity in Kant's moral philosophy. This concerns his understanding of the will. In the *Groundwork*, Kant appears to identify the will with practical reason. But if this were a strict identity, then how would it be possible for someone to commit an immoral or evil act? His younger contemporary, Reinhold, already criticized the identification of the will with practical reason during Kant's lifetime, and this objection has been reiterated over and over again by many subsequent critics of Kant.[3] But the *Religion* makes it eminently clear that Kant has a more complex and subtle understanding of the faculty of volition. This is indicated by the distinction that he introduces between *Wille* and *Willkür* (which unfortunately are frequently both translated as "will" in English).[4] Although Kant is not always consistent, in general, when he refers to the will as the capacity to choose between alternatives, he calls it *Willkür*. The human *Willkür* (as distinguished from the *Willkür* of brute animals) is the faculty of free spontaneous choice. Or, more accurately, it is that aspect of the faculty of volition that involves unconstrained free choice. As Kant tells us, "the freedom of the will [*Willkür*] is of a wholly unique nature in that an incentive can determine the will [*Willkür*] to an action *only so far as the individual has incorporated it into his maxim* (has made it the general rule in accordance with which he will conduct himself); only thus can an incentive, whatever it may be, coexist with the absolute spontaneity of the will [*Willkür*] (i.e. freedom)." (*Rel.* 19; 23).[5] The *Willkür*, the name we give to the capacity to choose between alternatives is neither *intrinsically* good nor *intrinsically* evil; rather, it is the capacity by which we freely choose good or evil maxims. In the *Religion* it is clear that *Wille* (in its more technical, narrow sense) does not act at all; it does not make decisions. *Wille* refers to the purely rational aspect of the faculty of volition. Henry Allison states the point succinctly when he writes: "Kant uses the terms *Wille* and *Willkür* to characterize respectively the legislative and executive functions of a unified faculty of volition, which he likewise refers to as *Wille*."[6] And John Silber gives a lucid description of the relation of the *Wille* to the *Willkür*.

> Unlike *Willkür*, however, *Wille* does not make decisions or adopt maxims; it does not act. Rather it is the source of a strong and ever present incentive in *Willkür*, and, if strong enough to be adopted by *Willkür* into the maxim of its choice, *Wille* "can determine the *Willkür*" and then "it is practical reason itself." *Wille* expresses the possibility of autonomy which is presupposed by transcendental freedom. The *Wille* represents the will's own demand for self-fulfillment by commanding *Willkür*, that aspect of the will which can either fulfill or abnegate its freedom, to actualize its free nature by willing in accordance with the law (and condition) of freedom. The most important difference between *Wille* and *Willkür* is apparent here. Whereas *Willkür* is free to actualize either the autonomous or heteronomous potentialities of transcendental freedom, *Wille* is not free at all. *Wille* is rather the law of freedom, the normative aspect of the will, which as norm is neither free nor unfree. Having no freedom of action, *Wille* is under no constraint or pressure. It exerts, instead, the pressure of its own normative rational nature upon the *Willkür*.[7]

It is vital to see why Kant makes this all-important distinction between *Wille* and *Willkür*. When he introduces the categorical imperative in the *Groundwork*, we are left with an awkward consequence. If the will is completely identified with practical reason, then it is not clear where choice enters into making a moral decision. But Kant's account of morality presupposes that we are agents who have the capacity to choose freely to obey or disobey what is dictated by the moral law. Moral responsibility requires this capacity. To have the capacity to choose does not mean that we are indifferent. On the contrary, to the extent that we respond to what the *Wille* as the moral norm − as the law of freedom − dictates, we are autonomous. Furthermore, the moral law can be a *sufficient* incentive for us to do what duty requires. But, as Silber properly emphasizes, we must also be able to make heteronomous choices. Nothing determines the *Willkür* unless the *Willkür* chooses to be so determined. In this sense, to be a finite rational agent is to be radically free − that is, to be an agent who can choose good or evil maxims.

Evil maxims

But what precisely is an evil maxim? Before addressing this question directly, I want to emphasize that Kant is perfectly clear that it is not our natural inclinations that are the source of evil. On the contrary, he does not even say that the existence of natural inclinations is neutral (neither good nor evil), but rather, that they are actually *good*! (Later we shall consider in what sense they are good.) Kant declares: "Natural inclinations, *considered in themselves*, are *good*, that is, not a matter of reproach, and it is not only futile to want to extirpate them but to do so would also be harmful and blameworthy. Rather, let them be tamed and instead of clashing with one another they can be brought into harmony in a wholeness which is called happiness." (*Rel.* 51; 60).

He explicitly repudiates the caricature that is so frequently drawn of him. He is frequently, but mistakenly, criticized for allegedly claiming that it is our natural inclinations that are the source of human evil. This caricature is misleading, because it obscures what is fundamental for his understanding of freedom and morality – that human beings, by virtue of their faculty of volition, are completely accountable and responsible for the good and evil maxims that they adopt. In *this respect*, there is no original sin or evil, just as there is no original moral goodness. To put the point positively, all sins, vices, and virtues originate in a (free) *Willkür*. The primary issue for Kant is always how we *choose* to respond to different, and sometimes conflicting, incentives.

> Man *himself* must make or have made himself into whatever, in a moral sense, whether good or evil, he is or is to become. Either condition must be an effect of his [*Willkür*]; for otherwise he could not be held responsible for it and could therefore be *morally* neither good nor evil. When it is said, Man is created good, this can mean nothing more than: He is created *for good* and the original *predisposition* in man is good; not that, thereby, he is already actually good, but rather that he brings it about that he becomes good or evil, according to whether he adopts or does not adopt into his maxim the incentives which this predisposition carries with it ([an act] which must be left wholly to his own free choice). (*Rel.* 40; 48)

Yirmiyahu Yovel emphatically makes Kant's point: "Kant insisted in the *Religion* that evil too originates in freedom. This principle bars the view that when acting immorally we are causally determined by natural inclinations, and makes responsibility for evil possible. Nature cannot generate evil; only the free human will can."[8]

In order to clarify the nature of duty and the moral law in the *Groundwork*, Kant focuses on those situations in which there is a conflict between our natural inclinations and our moral duty. In his famous (and sometimes misleading) examples, he tends to suggest that the paradigmatic examples of acting morally occur only when there is an overt clash between what we naturally desire and what we recognize as our duty, what we ought to do. This is the source of another persistent caricature of

Kant: we are only truly moral when we are acting *against* our natural inclinations. But here too, the *Religion* repudiates this caricature, and helps to clear up this misunderstanding. The basic issue for Kant in determining whether a maxim is good or evil is not whether it "contains" the incentive to follow the moral law *or* our natural inclinations. Rather, the issue is how these incentives are ordered – which incentive is primary and which one is secondary, that is, *subordinated*.

> Hence the distinction between a good man and one who is evil cannot lie in the difference between the incentives which they adopt into their maxim (not in the content of the maxim), but rather must depend upon *subordination* (the form of the maxim) i.e., *which of the two incentives he makes the condition of the other*. Consequently man (even the best) is evil only in that he reverses the moral order of the incentives when he adopts them into his maxim. He adopts, indeed, the moral law along with the law of self-love; yet when he becomes aware that they cannot remain on a par with each other but that one must be subordinated to the other as a supreme condition, he makes the incentive of self-love and its inclinations the condition of obedience to the moral law; whereas on the contrary, the latter, as the *supreme condition* of the satisfaction of the former, ought to have been adopted into the universal maxim of the will [*Willkür*] as the sole incentive. (*Rel.* 31–2; 38)

As Allen Wood declares:

> *all* maxims of finite rational volition (be they good or evil) contain *both* the incentives of moral reason and of sensible inclination; every maxim must contain both these incentives if it is to be the principle from which a finite rational subject acts, since both incentives belong to the predisposition of such a subject. . . . The maxim of the good man differs from that of the evil man only in that the former conditions the incentives of inclination by those of duty, whereas the latter reverses the moral order of incentives and makes it a rule to do his duty only on the condition that it be consistent with the pursuit of inclination.[9]

Consequently I can, and frequently do, act morally in a manner that is consonant with my sense of what is morally required and with what I naturally desire to do. I do not frustrate my natural inclinations. The moral worth of an agent depends exclusively on how these different incentives are ordered in the maxim that he adopts. But, of course, as Kant has noted already in the *Groundwork*, I may be mistaken about what really is my primary incentive, and whether a genuinely moral incentive has motivated the adoption of a maxim.

Although this understanding of the difference between a good and an evil maxim clears up a persistent misunderstanding about the role of inclinations in our maxims and our actions, it does have some strong (Kant would say "rigoristic") consequences. If we consider the example from the *Groundwork* of the shopkeeper who feigns honesty because this is the most advantageous and profitable policy, we can well understand how in his maxim there is an ordering such that his primary incentive is to maximize his profit rather than to do what is morally required. He may act in accord with duty, but not for the sake of duty. But consider the more difficult example of the person whose primary motivation is his sympathy for his fellow human beings. Kant tells us that there are persons "so sympathetically constituted that without any motive or vanity of selfishness they find an inner satisfaction in spreading joy and rejoice in the contentment of others which have made this possible." Although actions performed on this basis are "dutiful and amiable" and "deserve praise and encouragement," they do not evince moral worth, because they are not done from duty. Christine Korsgaard has given a very sensitive and insightful analysis of this example.[10] She notes that Kant clearly distinguishes this example, where one acts "from direct inclination (perform an action because one enjoys it)" from the shopkeeper example, where one acts "from indirect action (performs an action as a means to an end)."[11] Explicating what Kant means, Korsgaard writes:

> Therefore, when Kant says that the difference between the sympathetic person and the dutiful person rests in their maxims, the contrast he has in mind is this: although the sympathetic person and the dutiful person both have the purpose of helping others, they have adopted this purpose on different grounds. The sympathetic person sees helping as something pleasant, and that is why he makes it his end. The morally worthy person sees helping as something called for, or necessary, and this is what motivates him to make it his end.[12]

I think that this is exactly right, although Kant in the *Religion* gives another reason for placing greater moral weight on the person who acts for the sake of duty rather than out of the motivation of sympathy.

Consider the consequence of Korsgaard's explication when we put it together with Kant's analysis of good and evil maxims in the *Religion*. Korsgaard tells us that "Duty is not a different purpose, but a different ground for the adoption of a purpose. So Kant's idea here is captured by saying that the sympathetic person's motive is *shallower* than the morally worthy person's: both want to help, but there is available a *further* stretch of motivating thought about helping which the merely sympathetic person has not engaged in."[13] Korsgaard's interpretative suggestion is eminently reasonable, but she ignores a consequence of Kant's rigorism. For she describes the motivation of "the merely sympathetic person" in a way that clearly indicates that the individual is giving priority to his sympathy (a natural inclination) rather than to what his moral obligation requires. And this is the paradigm of what Kant takes to be an *evil maxim*. Indeed, Kant himself explicitly makes this point in the *Religion*.

> For when incentives other than the law itself (such as ambition, self-love in general, yes, even a kindly instinct [*gutherziger Instinkt*] such as sympathy) are necessary to determine the will [*Willkür*] to conduct *conformable to the law*, it is merely accidental that these causes coincide with the law, for they could equally well incite its violation. The maxim, then, in terms of whose goodness all moral worth of the individual must be appraised, is thus contrary to the law, and the man, despite all his good deeds, is nevertheless evil. (*Rel.* 26; 31)

The person who (self-consciously) gives priority to his sympathetic feeling in his maxim is not just "shallower" than the moral person; he is evil. He is adopting an evil maxim.[14] Yet Kant does not flinch from drawing this conclusion. In the *Religion*, he endorses such a rigorist analysis. He tells us that we call a man evil not because he performs actions that are evil, "but because these actions are of such a nature that we may infer from them the presence in him of evil maxims" (*Rel.* 16; 18). Furthermore, Kant accepts the exclusive disjunction that "*Man is* (by nature) *either morally good or morally evil*" (*Rel.* 17; 18). Kant admits that although "experience actually seems to substantiate the middle ground between the two extremes," nevertheless, it is "of great consequence to ethics in general to avoid admitting, so long as it is possible, of anything morally intermediate. . . . Those who are partial to this strict mode of thinking are usually called *rigorists* (a name which is intended to carry reproach, but which actually praises)" (*Rel.* 18; 21). Whoever incorporates the moral law into his maxim and gives it priority is morally good; and whoever fails to do this, but gives priority to other nonmoral incentives (including sympathy) is morally evil. And to drive home his point, Kant affirms: "Neither can a man be morally good in some ways and at the same time morally evil in others. His being good in one way means that he has incorporated the moral law into his maxim; were he, therefore, at the same time evil in another way, while his maxim would be universal as based on the moral law of obedience to duty, which is essentially single and universal, it would at the same time be only particular; but this is a contradiction" (*Rel.* 20; 23). Allison provides a clear statement of Kant's grand either/or – his rigorism. He tells us:

Starting with the premise that respect for the law is an incentive, Kant reasons that since the freedom of the will (*Willkür*) entails that an incentive can determine the will only if it is "taken up" into a maxim, it follows that the failure to make it one's incentive, that is, the failure to make the thought of duty or respect for the law the sufficient motivation for one's conduct, must be regarded as resting on the adoption of an alternative principle of action. But since the adoption of an alternative principle involves an explicit deviation from the law, such an act must be characterized as "evil".[15]

So, following out the logic of Kant's rigorist analysis, there does not seem to be any way to avoid the conclusion that a benign sympathetic person (who gives the incentive of sympathy priority over the moral law in his maxim), Hitler, and even Eichmann (whose maxims presumably did not give priority to respect for the moral law) are *all* morally evil. Kant would certainly acknowledge that there are differences among them. Despite his "official" doctrine, he recognizes such differences. Nevertheless, given the exclusive rigorist disjunction – good or evil – we must judge them to be evil. What they have in common is "the failure to make the thought of duty or respect for the law the sufficient motivation for one's conduct."

Radical evil

Thus far, I have been addressing the question of what Kant means by evil, specifically what constitutes a morally evil maxim; but I have not yet said anything about radical evil. How does Kant's understanding of radical evil supplement what he has told us about evil maxims? More generally, we want to know how radical evil is compatible with his moral theory.[16]

Why did Kant (so late in his career) feel the need to introduce the concept of radical evil? There are several reasons. There is no doubt that he wanted to extract and defend what he took to be the moral rational core of Christian religious faith. But I also think that there is a deeper philosophical reason. Without compromising his moral stance that human beings are responsible for their good and evil maxims and deeds, Kant's understanding of human nature is that we are neither angels nor devils. He rejected the idea that we are born morally good and become corrupted, as well as the idea that we are intrinsically morally evil, that we are born sinners, and consequently cannot escape from actually sinning. His understanding of human nature as intrinsically neither morally good nor morally evil also has significant consequences for his understanding of human history and progress. Kant seeks to walk a fine line. On the one hand, he is skeptical of the idea of moral progress whereby human beings can (and will) achieve human perfection. On the other hand, although human beings can never escape from the propensity to evil – a propensity constitutive of their species nature – there can be moral progress in history insofar as human beings can become actually good by virtue of their freedom. Kant's faith in (limited) moral and political progress is played out against a dark background, a realistic appraisal of "crooked humanity." In this respect, Kant departs significantly from some of the more naïve and optimistic Enlightenment conceptions of human progress (for example, Condorcet). Many of the tensions and problems in Kant's conception of radical evil can be traced back to his attempt to reconcile the claim that human beings are, by their very nature, evil with the claim that, despite this propensity to evil, human beings (even those who are wicked) can become morally good.

Despite the striking connotations of the term "radical," Kant is not speaking about a special *type* of evil or evil maxim. He would not agree with Arendt when she declares that radical evil is a phenomenon that "confronts us with its overpowering reality and breaks down all standards we know."[17] And he certainly does not mean anything like what Arendt means when she claims that "radical evil has emerged in connection with a system [totalitarianism] in which all men have become equally superfluous."[18] But what does Kant mean? And why does he introduce this tantalizing concept? The answer to this question is complex, and we need to introduce a number of important distinctions in order to answer it.

To set the context for our analysis, we must first consider briefly the sharp distinction that Kant makes in his Critical Philosophy between phenomena and noumena. This distinction, which is so central to Kant's understanding of human freedom, has proved especially troublesome. There are many passages in Kant that seem to suggest a "two-world" theory in which there is no (and can be no) interaction between the two. If this were really so – if phenomena and noumena referred to two "ontologically" different worlds – then there would be no way to make coherent sense of his moral philosophy. Recently, a number of sympathetic commentators have argued that there is a more adequate way of interpreting (and/or correcting) Kant which shows that he is not committed to a rigid ontological distinction between two entirely different realms or worlds. Although they approach the relevant issues in a variety of different ways, these commentators, who include Silber, Allison, Wood, and Korsgaard, present a strong case for the claim. Thus Silber: "Although he [Kant] asserted that the two realms exist 'independently of one another and without interfering with each other,' he found it impossible to speak of moral problems without presupposing their complete interaction. . . . The experience of moral obligation is a prime example of thorough interaction. If the same human being (and, therefore, the same *Willkür*) were not both moral and natural, existing fully and simultaneously in both realms, moral experience would be impossible."[19] Korsgaard argues that the confusions regarding the two-world theory stem from "a failure to appreciate the radical nature of Kant's separation of theoretical and practical reason, and of their respective domains of explanation and deliberation. When these domains are separated in the way that Kant's philosophy requires, the problems about responsibility disappear, and we see that Kant's theory of freedom does not commit him to an ontological dualism."[20] Although these commentators have not cleared up all the problems that arise from the distinction between noumena and phenomena, I do think that they have been successful in showing that Kant is not committed to an extreme ontological dualism, and that Kant does have a unified conception of the human agent who is both free and conditioned by natural causality.

In the *Religion*, Kant does not abandon the noumena/phenomena distinction, but he plays down its significance. In the preface to the second edition, he says:

> To understand this book in its essential content, only common morality is needed, without meddling with the *Critique of Practical Reason*, still less with theoretical Critique. When, for example, virtue as skill in *actions* conforming to duty (according to their legality) is called *virtus phaenomenon*, and the same virtue as an enduring *disposition* towards such actions from *duty* (because of their morality) is called *virtus noumenon*, these expressions are used only because of the schools; while the matter itself is contained, though in other words, in the most popular children's instructions and sermons, and is easily understood. (*Rel.* 12–13; 15–16)

The reason why it is so important to see that Kant is not committed to a two-world theory is because his analysis of radical evil presupposes the intelligibility of speaking about a "human nature" which cannot be identified simply with our phenomenal nature (or with our noumenal selves).

"Nature" and "human nature" are used in the *Religion* in a manner that is strikingly different from the typical use of these terms in the *Critique of Pure Reason* and the *Critique of Practical Reason*. Human nature encompasses what we are as phenomenal and moral beings. This becomes evident when, for example, Kant tells us that human nature possesses three predispositions [*Anlagen*] to good. To be more precise, these are three divisions, or elements "in the fixed character and destiny [*Bestimmung*] of man: (1) the predisposition to *animality* in man, taken as a *living* being; (2) the predisposition to *humanity* in man, taken as a living and at the same time a *rational* being; (3) the predisposition to *personality* in man, taken as a rational and at the same time an *accountable* being" (*Rel.* 21; 25). It is perfectly clear from this passage that Kant is speaking about "human nature" (*der menschlichen Natur*) in a way that encompasses what he has previously classified as phenomena and noumena. When Kant speaks of "man" here, he is not referring to individual men. He is referring to man – or rather human beings – as the human race or species. He tells us, "The man of whom we say, 'He is by nature good or evil,' is to be understood not as a single individual (for then one man could be considered as good, by nature, another as evil), but as the entire race" (*Rel.* 21; 24–5). We must be careful not to misinterpret what Kant is affirming. We may be tempted to think that these three divisions of the original predisposition to good are constituents of a predisposition to be *morally* good. This temptation may be especially strong in the case of the predisposition to personality, because this is "the capacity for respect for the moral law as *in itself a sufficient incentive of the will* [*Willkür*]" (*Rel.* 23; 27). But the *capacity* for respect is not to be identified with the *actual* (moral) *exercise* of this capacity by the *Willkür*. We, as human beings, may have a *predisposition* to become morally good, but it is only by exercising our free will (*Willkür*) that we *actually* become morally good (or evil).

> Man *himself* must make or have made himself into whatever, in a moral sense, whether good or evil, he is or is to become. Either condition must be an effect of his free choice [*Willkür*]; for otherwise he could not be held responsible for it and could therefore be *morally* neither good nor evil. When it is said, Man is created good, this can mean nothing more than: He is created *for good* and the original *predisposition* is good; not that, thereby, he is already actually good, but rather he brings it about that he becomes good or evil, according to whether he adopts or does not adopt into his maxim the incentives which this predisposition carries with it ([an act] which must be left wholly to his own free choice). (*Rel.* 40; 48)

But if this is so, then in what sense can we say that the original predisposition is a predisposition to and for *good*? Wood is helpful in clarifying what Kant means.

> These predispositions all belong to "human nature" in the sense that they are "bound up with the possibility of human nature." They are predispositions *to good* in the sense that they are considered in themselves "not a matter of reproach" and that through them man is created "for good.". . .
>   No man is *actually* good or evil on account of his possession of these predispositions. Hence, if man is to be said to be "by nature" good or evil, this goodness or evil cannot consist in the predispositions bound up with the possibility of human nature. The very concept of morally good and evil involves, rather the actual use man makes of his capacities, and prevents us from regarding these capacities themselves as morally good or evil.[21]

It would have been clearer if Kant had simply said that although human beings have a predisposition to become morally good, they are not actually born morally good. They become morally good only if they freely choose to act so that they incorporate the moral law into their maxims.

Before turning explicitly to what Kant means by radical evil, we must first clarify what he means by disposition (*Gesinnung*) and propensity (*Hang*). For they are the basis for understanding radical evil. These concepts are not to be confused with what he calls a predisposition (*Anlage*).[22] Silber claims that "the development of [the concept of *Gesinnung*] is, perhaps, the most important single contribution of the *Religion* to Kant's ethical theory, for by means of it he accounts for the continuity and responsibility in the free exercise of *Willkür* and for the possibility of ambivalent volition, as well as the basis for its complex assessment."[23] We can appreciate why Silber makes this strong claim. On the basis of the *Groundwork* and the *Critique of Practical Reason*, it is not entirely clear how Kant deals with the continuity of moral agency. In part, this is because he has focused primarily on the role of maxims in making moral decisions. But the individual who adopts maxims and makes choices is not simply a collection of discrete choices and maxims. Nor is he simply a timeless noumenal self. As Silber perceptively notes, "The disposition [*Gesinnung*] is thus the enduring aspect of *Willkür*, it is *Willkür* considered in terms of the continuity and fullness of its free expression. It is the enduring pattern of intention that can be inferred from the many discrete acts of *Willkür* and reveals their ultimate motive." And he adds: "Continuity in disposition [*Gesinnung*] is essential to moral self-identity."[24] This helps to clarify the work that the concept of *Gesinnung* is intended to perform, and why it is so essential to Kant's analysis of moral agency.

As long as we stay at this general level of abstraction, we do not encounter any difficulties. But the more closely we examine the details of what Kant says about *Gesinnung*, the more problematic this concept becomes. Initially we might think that Kant is finally coming to acknowledge the importance of what Aristotle recognized long ago, that he means something that closely approximates what Aristotle called *hexis*, an acquired disposition to act virtuously, a disposition that requires a proper upbringing and education. But Kant explicitly says that "this disposition [*Gesinnung*] itself must have been adopted by free choice [*Willkür*]" (*Rel.* 20; 24). The passage from which this comes is even more perplexing, because Kant says that, although this disposition is acquired, it "has not been acquired in time."

To have a good or evil disposition [*Gesinnung*] as an inborn natural constitution does not here mean that it has not been acquired by the man who harbors it, that he is not the author of it, but rather, that it has not been acquired in time (that he has *always* been good, or evil *from his youth up*). The disposition, *i.e.*, the ultimate subjective ground of the adoption of maxims, can be one only and applies universally to the whole use of freedom. Yet this disposition itself must have been adopted by free choice [*Willkür*], for otherwise it could not be imputed. (*Rel.* 20; 24)

This is an extremely perplexing and obscure passage, and we will have to keep it in mind as we proceed. But, for all its obscurity, there is no ambiguity regarding what Kant is saying about a good or evil disposition (*Gesinnung*) being "adopted by free choice." This, perhaps, is the most significant difference between a predisposition (*Anlage*) and a disposition (*Gesinnung*); a *Gesinnung* is adopted by free choice, but an *Anlage* is *not* chosen; it is a constituent of human nature, and it is bound up "with the possibility of human nature." This freely chosen character of *Gesinnung* has led one critic to suggest that it is an unstable combination of Aristotelian *hexis* and a Sartrean "*projet fondamental.*"[25] We can see how radically Kant's notion of a *Gesinnung* departs from any ordinary or traditional concept of a disposition when he tells us that "it has not been acquired in time," and that this *Gesinnung* must itself be conceived of as a maxim – a supreme maxim that orients the moral life of an agent viewed as a whole (even though it is possible to alter this disposition).[26] One might think that here Kant comes close to being incoherent. He seems to get himself ensnared in a vicious circle: a good or evil disposition (*Gesinnung*) is adopted by free choice (*Willkür*), but *Willkür* itself presupposes this disposition.

Without underestimating these problems, I do think that we can give an account of *Gesinnung* that at least *approximates* what Kant wants to say (and is compatible with much of what he actually does say). For the moment, let us set aside the problems arising from the noumena/phenomena distinction and from what is and is not "acquired in time." We frequently do distinguish persons with good and evil dispositions. There are persons whom we can trust or count on to do the right thing (what the moral law requires) in difficult moral situations. They exhibit an overall pattern of commitments, beliefs, intentions, and actions that provides a basis for our (fallible) judgment that when they confront difficult moral situations, they will do what duty requires. Or, to phrase this point in a Kantian manner, they will adopt good maxims, maxims that incorporate and give priority to the moral law. Of course, there are persons who are so selfish or narcissistic that they are likely to do anything to achieve their ends and to avoid acting for the sake of duty. There is no difficulty in drawing a distinction between a person's disposition or overall moral character and the specific maxims he adopts and the actions he performs. Although his pattern of action is the basis for making judgments about his character, we recognize that it is this character that informs his specific choices. The relation between moral character and the specific actions performed is neither strictly causal nor strictly logical. A person with a good disposition may occasionally act out of character and adopt a maxim that subordinates the moral law to natural inclination. And a moral scoundrel may occasionally do what duty requires (honor among thieves).

Viewed in this manner, we can understand why such a disposition may be characterized as the subjective ground for the adoption of specific maxims. For such a disposition *informs*, but does not (causally) determine the maxims that are adopted in specific situations of moral conflict. We can also understand the sense in which we are responsible for our dispositions or characters. It is not that at a specific moment in time we "choose" this disposition. Nevertheless, our disposition is the result of free moral decisions that we make and the maxims that we adopt. We are not born morally good or evil; we *become* morally good or evil by virtue of the choices we make.

If we press further and ask why one person develops a disposition or character that leads him to adopt good maxims and someone else adopts evil maxims, there is much that we can say about their background, social circumstances, and education; but we cannot give an ultimate answer to this question: it is inscrutable. For such an answer would require us to be able to give a *theoretical* account of human freedom. And this is precisely what the Critical Philosophy shows us to be impossible. To claim that a free choice is inscrutable is not to say that it is *mysterious* – as if, in principle, we should be able to give necessary and sufficient reasons for why someone makes the choices he does make; it is only to insist that the choice is *free*. Ultimately, we cannot *know* why one person chooses to follow the moral law and another person does not. Nevertheless, from a *practical* point of view, we can (and must) postulate freedom, and assert that moral agents have the capacity to choose freely good or evil maxims. We are responsible for our individual choices and for our overall moral character.

Furthermore, this disposition is not something fixed and unchangeable. A good person can become evil, and an evil person can become good. "For man, therefore, who despite a corrupted heart yet possesses a good will (*Wille*), there remains the hope of a return to the good from which he has strayed" (*Rel.* 39; 47). We can even demystify what seems so counterintuitive, that a *Gesinnung* "has not been acquired in time." We have to distinguish *two* different senses of being acquired in time. Kant is certainly not denying the obvious fact that we commonly specify the *time* when a moral decision is made. All of the examples that Kant gives in the *Groundwork* presuppose such a temporal location. We make our moral decisions in concrete situations at specific times and places. For example, *tomorrow*, I may be faced with a terrible moral dilemma in which I will be confronted with a choice about what I ought to do. But there is a more *technical* sense of something happening in time that is explored in the *First Critique* when Kant gives his analysis of causality. *In this sense*, to say that something happens in time is to say that it is causally determined, and consequently not free. When Kant tells us that a *Gesinnung* is not acquired in time, he is telling us that it is not (naturally) causally determined but, rather, issues from our freedom.

I do not want to suggest that this understanding of *Gesinnung* clears up all the problems and difficulties that Kant's discussion involves; but it does help to show the plausibility of the idea of a *Gesinnung*, the sense in which it is a disposition, and yet freely chosen, and why such a notion is so important for a robust understanding of human agency. There is, however, one *major* difficulty with my analysis that cannot be avoided. Ironically, this points up one of the most troubling features of Kant's conception of radical evil. If my description approximates what Kant means by a *Gesinnung*, then it is applicable to *both* good and evil dispositions, or characters. And most of the time, Kant writes in a manner that would lead us to think that there are good and bad dispositions. Yet, when Kant turns explicitly to the notion of radical evil, and characterizes it as a propensity (*Hang*), he neglects the symmetry between good and evil dispositions. Most of the time he writes as if there is no significant difference between a disposition (*Gesinnung*) and a propensity (*Hang*), but he *never* speaks about a propensity to good, but only a propensity to evil.[27] He explicitly tells us that "man is evil by nature" (although we will see that this does not mean quite what we might think it does). Kant also insists that although "the character (good or evil) distinguishing man from other possible rational beings . . . is *innate* in him. . . we shall ever take the position that nature is not to bear the blame (if it is evil) or take credit for it (if it is good), but that man himself is its author" (*Rel.* 17; 20). In short, what Kant calls a propensity (*Hang*) cannot be identified with a disposition (*Gesinnung*), yet he fails to clarify what distinguishes these two concepts. He never explains why the disposition (*Gesinnung*) of human beings can be good or evil, whereas there is a propensity (*Hang*) *only* to evil.

Although there are certainly many obscurities and difficulties in Kant's characterization of *Gesinnung*, we can begin to appreciate why Kant gets himself entangled in these difficulties. They spring from one of the most admirable and central features of his moral theory. The many caricatures of him, notwithstanding, Kant certainly acknowledges that temperament, background, social circumstances, moral training (and even geographical location) of persons influence their moral character and choices. But the primary issue for Kant is always the individual's accountability and responsibility. Our moral freedom is never compromised by external events or by our natural inclinations. We can make Kant's point even more forcefully by asserting that we alone are ultimately responsible for the individual moral choices that we make and for our moral character. Kant even seems to be aware of the awkward way in which he has described a *Gesinnung*. For he characterizes it as "the ultimate subjective ground of the adoption of maxims," and then immediately adds, "But the subjective ground or cause of this adoption cannot further be known (though it is inevitable that we should inquire into it)" (*Rel.* 20; 24).

We are finally in a position to turn explicitly to the concept of radical evil. On the basis of what we have learned about "the original predisposition [*Anlage*] to good in human nature," we at least know what radical evil is not. Radical evil is not, in any way, to be identified with natural inclinations. Radical evil is not to be identified with our phenomenal sensuous nature. The body, with its needs and desires, is not the source of evil. Nor is radical evil to be identified with any *intrinsic* defect or corruption of human reason. It is related solely to the corruption of the will. We can locate an essential clue about the meaning of radical evil, and why Kant introduces this concept, by returning to his analysis of the third division of the original predisposition (*Anlage*) to good that is inherent in our human nature. Let us consider again what Kant says about the predisposition to *personality*.

> The predisposition to *personality* is the capacity for respect for the moral law as *in itself a sufficient incentive of the will* [*Willkür*]. This capacity for simple respect for the moral law within us would thus be moral feeling, which in and through itself does not constitute an end of the natural predisposition except so far as it is the motivating force of the will [*Willkür*]. Since this is possible only when the free will [*Willkür*] incorporates such moral feeling into its maxim, the property of such a will [*Willkür*] is good character. The latter, like every character of the free will [*Willkür*], is something that can only be acquired; its possibility, however, demands the presence in our nature of a predisposition on which it is absolutely impossible to graft anything evil. We cannot rightly call the idea of the moral law, with the respect which is inseparable from it, *a predisposition* to *personality*; it is personality itself. . . . But the subjective ground for the adoption into our maxims of this respect as a motivating force seems to be an adjunct to our personality, and thus to deserve the name of a predisposition to its furtherance. (*Rel.* 22–3; 27)

There is nothing startlingly new here that we could not have inferred from the *Groundwork* or the *Critique of Practical Reason*. But if this predisposition to good is constitutive of our very nature as human beings, how are we to account for the fact that we do not always follow this predisposition; that we do not always do what we morally ought to do? Human beings are tempted to disregard the moral law, to adopt evil maxims – maxims that give priority to nonmoral incentives. It is this tendency or propensity (*Hang*) that Kant seeks to isolate with the introduction of the concept of radical evil. But what does Kant mean by a propensity (*Hang*)? He tells us that "by propensity (*propensio*) I understand the subjective ground of the possibility of an inclination (habitual craving, *concupiscentia*) so far as mankind in general is liable to it" (*Rel.* 23–4; 28). And how are we to distinguish a propensity (*Hang*) from a predisposition (*Anlage*)? "A propensity is distinguished from a predisposition by the fact that although it can indeed be innate, it *ought* not to be represented merely thus; for it can also be regarded as having been *acquired* (if it is good), or *brought* by man *upon himself* (if it is evil)" (*Rel.* 24; 28–9). We get a clearer idea of what Kant means by turning to his shocking footnote. He informs us that:

> A *propensity* (*Hang*) is really only the *predisposition* . . . to crave a delight which, when once experienced, arouses in the subject an *inclination* to it. Thus all savage peoples have a propensity for intoxicants; for though many of them are wholly ignorant of intoxication and in consequence have absolutely no craving for an intoxicant, let them but once sample it and there is aroused in them an almost inextinguishable craving for it. (*Rel.* 24; 28)[28]

"Radical evil" then, is not the name of some special type of evil (as Arendt maintains). And it certainly is not a form of evil that "we cannot conceive." On the contrary, we can clearly conceive it, and what it names is the propensity (*Hang*) not to do what duty requires, not to follow the moral law. Indeed, Kant's purpose in using the adjective *radikal* to qualify *Böse* is to indicate that this propensity is *rooted* in human nature, specifically in the corruption of the will (*Willkür*); he is appealing to the original, etymological meaning of *radikal*. There is no evidence that Kant means anything more than this.

Kant does distinguish different degrees of the "capacity for evil," but all three are related to the failure to adopt good maxims.

> First, there is the weakness of the human heart in the general observance of adopted maxims, or in other words, the *frailty* of human nature; second, the propensity for mixing unmoral with moral motivating causes (even when it is done with good intent and under maxims of the good), that is, *impurity*; third, the propensity to adopt evil maxims, that is, the *wickedness* of human nature, or of the human heart. (*Rel.* 24; 29)

We may think that "wickedness" names some horrendous form of evil. And Kant's rhetoric certainly makes it sound this· way.

> Third: the wickedness (*vitiositas, pravitas*) or, if you like, the *corruption* (*corruptio*) of the human heart is the propensity of the will [*Willkür*] to maxims which neglect the incentives springing from the moral law in favor of others which are not moral. It may also be called the *perversity* (*perversitas*) of the human heart, for it reverses the ethical order [of priority] among the incentives of a *free* will [*Willkür*]; and although conduct which is lawfully good (i.e., legal) may be found with it, yet the cast of mind is thereby corrupted at its root (so far as the moral disposition is concerned), and the man is hence designated as evil.
>
> It will be remarked that this propensity to evil is here ascribed (as regards conduct) to men in general, even to the best of them; this must be the case if it is to be proved that the propensity to evil in mankind is universal, or, what here comes to the same thing, that it is woven into human nature. (*Rel.* 25; 30)

Let us reflect carefully on Kant's characterization of the "third degree" of the capacity for evil with reference to the example of the sympathetic person that I discussed earlier. Suppose that such a person – even when it is pointed out to him – makes a conscious choice to continue to give priority to his feelings of sympathy for his fellow human beings as the *primary* incentive for his maxims (rather than "incentives springing from the moral law"). He trusts his heart more than his reason, even though his heart may occasionally lead him astray. And let us also grant, as Kant says we may, that the conduct springing from the incentive of sympathy is "lawfully good." He consistently acts in accord with duty, although not for the sake of duty. On the basis of Kant's classification of the degrees of evil, we would be compelled to judge such person as *wicked*. He presumably has a cast of mind that is corrupted at its root. Why? Because he gives priority to what Kant considers to be a nonmoral maxim when he ought to adopt a moral one. And even though, by hypothesis, his actions conform to the moral law, this is simply accidental, or contingent. But to judge such a person as the paradigm of *wickedness*, to put him in the same category as a mass murderer – at least, in respect to the degree of evil exhibited – is more than an awkward consequence of Kant's rigorism; it is morally perverse.

But we face still greater problems. Kant's analysis of radical evil as a propensity that is "woven into human nature" actually *obscures* (rather than clarifies) a cardinal point in his moral philosophy. The very concept of a propensity (*Hang*) is one that is parasitic upon our notion of causality. A propensity presumably has causal efficacy. Thus, in Kant's unfortunate example of a savage people who crave intoxicants, we think of such a propensity as having overwhelming causal power. Such a craving demands satisfaction unless it is resisted in the strongest possible manner. But the propensity to evil cannot be thought of in this way. It is not an active causal force "pushing" us, or tempting us, to be morally evil. There is no moral evil unless we *freely* adopt evil maxims. A *Willkür* that adopts such maxims is not causally determined by anything but itself; it is the spontaneous manifestation of our freedom. Few philosophers have been as insistent as Kant has been, in arguing that genuine freedom is unconditioned by any (natural) causal influences.[29]

It may be objected that the example of the craving for intoxicants is misleading, because it is a physical propensity, and Kant himself makes a sharp distinction between a physical (natural) propensity and a moral propensity.

> Every propensity is either physical, i.e., pertaining to the will [*Willkür*] of man as a natural being, or moral, i.e., pertaining to his will [*Willkür*] as a moral being. In the first sense there is no propensity to moral evil, for such a propensity must spring from freedom; and a physical propensity (grounded in sensuous impulses) towards any use of freedom whatsoever – whether for good or bad – is a contradiction. Hence a propensity to evil can inhere only in the moral capacity of the will [*Willkür*]. But nothing is morally evil (i.e., capable of being imputed) but that which is our own *act.* (*Rel.* 26; 31)

Kant realizes that the very idea of a moral propensity as "a subjective ground of the will [*Willkür*] which precedes all acts" is a problematic notion. If such a propensity results from the exercise of freedom, then this propensity must itself issue from an act of free will (*Willkür*). Although it may seem *ad hoc* and a bit contrived, Kant introduces *two* senses of "act" to resolve this problem. In the first sense, "act" refers to the exercise of freedom whereby the *Willkür* adopts the supreme maxim. (This is what Yovel calls a "global moral strategy.") The second sense refers to specific acts performed on the basis of this supreme maxim. But these distinctions do not alter the main point that I want to emphasize; on the contrary, they reinforce it. The alleged physical propensity for intoxicants is neither universal nor necessary; it is not a propensity of human beings as a species. It need not even result in the adoption of evil maxims. One can exercise one's free will (*Willkür*) to resist this temptation. If a propensity to moral evil "springs from freedom," one may begin to wonder whether there really is such a propensity. Why? Because if the propensity "springs from freedom," then its very existence depends upon "that exercise of freedom whereby the supreme maxim . . . is adopted by the will [*Willkür*]"

(*Rel.* 26; 31). But the *Willkür* is the capacity for choosing maxims freely. Choosing the supreme maxim, the subjective determining ground, is itself an act of the *Willkür*. But the *Willkür* is *not* conditioned or causally influenced by any propensity, physical or moral.

We can examine Kant's problem from a slightly different perspective. Kant makes two claims which, although not necessarily incompatible, nevertheless seem to undermine the very idea of a moral propensity to evil. The first is that this propensity is itself the result of an *act* understood as the exercise of freedom whereby the supreme maxim is adopted by the will (*Willkür*). The second is that we, as free moral agents, can always resist this alleged propensity (which we have adopted by the exercise of our freedom). But if both these claims are true, then it is difficult to understand what is left of the very idea of a "propensity to moral evil." It is extraordinarily paradoxical (if not incoherent) to claim that there is a propensity to moral evil that is universal and, "as it were, rooted in humanity itself," and yet that "we must, after all, ever hold man himself responsible for it" (*Rel.* 28; 33). Yet this is precisely what Kant does maintain. He unambiguously affirms that this is what we call "*radical* innate *evil* in human nature (yet none the less brought upon us by ourselves)" (*Rel.* 28; 33). He says that "We must not, however, look for an origin in time of a moral character [*Beschaffenheit*] for which we are held responsible; though to do so is inevitable if we wish to *explain* the contingent existence of this character" (*Rel.* 38; 46).

Readers might want to counter my reading of Kant by noting that when he introduces the idea of a propensity (*Hang*), he emphasizes that it is a *possibility*. He says, "By propensity (*propensio*) I understand the subjective ground of the possibility of an inclination . . . ." (*Unter einem Hange* (propensio) *verstehe ich den subjektiven Grund der Möglichkeit einer Neigung*) (*Rel.* 23; 28). Consequently, there is no incompatibility in ascribing such a propensity to human nature and affirming that human beings have the capacity of free choice (*Willkür*). But this is not the source of the difficulty that I find in Kant. Stressing possibility (*Möglichkeit*) does not distinguish a propensity from a predisposition. A predisposition (*Anlage*) is also "bound up with the possibility of human nature" (*Rel.* 23; 28). The main problem concerns the origin or source of this propensity to evil. Kant insists that we are the authors of this propensity; that it results from the exercise of *our* freedom; that it is "*brought* by man *upon himself*" (*Rel.* 24; 29). This is what is so difficult to accept: namely, that the propensity to evil is innate or inborn (*angeboren*), yet we are somehow responsible for it.

Sometimes, we can detect what appear to be opposing and contradictory claims within a single sentence. Consider one of the most famous (and frequently quoted passages) from the *Religion*: "This evil is *radical*,

(Self)
Spite

because it corrupts the ground of all maxims; it is, moreover, as a natural propensity, *inextirpable* by human powers, since extirpation could occur only through good maxims, and cannot take place when the ultimate subjective ground of all maxims is postulated as corrupt . . . . " (*Rel.* 32; 39). If the sentence had ended there, then a straightforward reading would lead us to think that evil is radical because the will (*Willkür*) is corrupt at its very source or origin. This is a very strong claim indeed, and can readily be assimilated to a secular version of the Christian doctrine of original sin. (This is the reading of radical evil that seems to have offended Goethe.) But consider how Kant completes the sentence: "yet at the same time it must be possible to *overcome* it, since it is found in man, a being whose actions are free" [*gleichwohl aber muss er zu überwiegen möglich sein, weil er in dem Menschen als frei handelndem Wesen angetroffen wird*] (*Rel.* 32; 39).

Suppose we ask, how is it possible to overcome this inextirpable natural propensity? The answer for Kant *must* be that this occurs by a free exercise of the will (*Willkür*). For this is the way in which "a being whose actions are free" manifests his freedom. But then, contrary to what has been affirmed in the first part of the sentence, it cannot be true that radical evil corrupts the ground of *all* maxims. If it did, there would be *no* possibility of adopting or willing a good maxim, and consequently no possibility of overcoming radical evil. The claim that Kant makes in the second part of the sentence is something he affirms over and over again in the *Religion*. Indeed, he makes an even more forceful claim. All human beings are radically evil – that is, possess the powerful propensity to become morally evil – but only some persons *do* become morally evil, and develop a morally evil character or disposition. But even such wicked persons can be reborn and become good. "A change of heart . . . must be possible because duty requires it" (*Rel.* 60; 70).

It may be thought that we can come to Kant's rescue by making a sharp distinction between human beings as a *species* and *individual* human beings. There is no doubt that when Kant affirms that man by nature is evil, he is referring to the human species. But even though he affirms that the species has a propensity to evil, he is not saying that this propensity determines the moral character of individual persons. Individuals may develop good or evil dispositions by virtue of the free choices they make. But this distinction between species and individuals does not really help to clarify the issue. On the contrary, it leads to greater difficulties. For if the propensity to evil "springs from freedom," and this propensity, and it is ascribable to the human species, then we would have to say that the human species *qua* species freely chooses this propensity. It is not clear that such a thesis is even intelligible.

Why does Kant allow himself to get entangled in such difficulties and paradoxes? It looks as if he wants to have his cake and eat it too! And in a way he does. Or, to switch metaphors, Kant is at war with himself. For, on the one hand, he never wants to compromise the basic claim of his moral philosophy: that human beings as finite rational agents are free, which means that they are *solely* and *completely* responsible for their moral choices and for the maxims they adopt. If we become morally good or evil, this is our own doing and a consequence of our own free will (*Willkür*). On the other hand, Kant also wants to affirm that all human beings have an innate propensity to moral evil. In order to have his cake and eat it too, he is then driven to claim that even though this propensity is woven into the fabric of human nature, it is a propensity that springs from our freedom, and one for which we are responsible. Later, I want to show that what at first seems at best an extremely strained and awkward position, and at worst a blatant contradiction, actually reveals one of the most enduring and attractive features of Kant's moral philosophy.

The more we focus on the details of Kant's analysis of radical evil, the more innocuous the concept seems to be (despite Kant's rhetoric about human wickedness).[30] After making the apparently dramatic claim that "man is evil by nature," Kant goes on to say, "Man is *evil*, can mean only, *he* is conscious of the moral law but has nevertheless adopted into his maxim the (occasional) deviation therefrom" (*Rel.* 27; 33). But do we need the *Religion* or any special concept of radical evil to know this? The *Groundwork* – indeed, the very project of Kant's moral philosophy – is based upon the idea that we do not always do what we ought to do; that we, as finite rational agents, are *not* holy wills, and consequently do not always follow the moral law. Presumably, the introduction of the concept of radical evil is intended to explain *why* (from a practical point of view) we deviate from following the moral law. We do not always follow the moral law *because*, as human beings, we have an innate propensity to evil. Our wills are corrupted at their root. But does this "because" really explain anything? Does it do any conceptual work? I do not think so. When stripped down to bare essentials, it simply reiterates the fact that human beings who are conscious of the moral law sometimes (freely) deviate from it. Furthermore, it is *always* within our power to resist this propensity, no matter how strong it is supposed to be. In short, radical evil – the alleged propensity to moral evil which is a universal characteristic of human beings – does not have *any* explanatory force (practical or theoretical) at all!

I have no doubt that Kant intended to make a much more forceful claim, that he thought he was showing something really fundamental about human beings when he asserted that man by nature is evil. My argument is that there is a disparity between what he *intends* and what he *says*. When we scrutinize what he actually says, when we see how he qualifies his key claims, it is difficult to avoid the conclusion that Kant himself eviscerates the notion of radical evil.

We have not yet come to the end of our difficulties with the concept of radical evil. According to Kant, radical evil is a *species* concept; it is universally applicable to all human beings woven into the very fabric of human nature. We all have an "evil heart." It is not, then, a contingent characteristic of *some* human beings, or even a contingent characteristic of *all* human beings. But what is the *justification* for making such a bold and controversial claim? If there is one lesson that we should have learned from the Critical Philosophy, it is that genuinely synthetic universal claims can never be justified by appeal to experience; their justification requires a "deduction" – a proof. Yet, when Kant reaches this crucial stage in his exposition, when we expect some sort of proof or justification of radical evil as a *universal* characteristic of human beings, *no* such proof is forthcoming. This is what Kant says: "That such a corrupt propensity must indeed be rooted in man need not be formally proved in view of the multitude of crying examples which experience *of the actions* of men puts before our eyes" (*Rel.* 28; 33–4). Kant follows this assertion with some empirical observations based upon (dubious) anthropological evidence; "melancholy" observations about "civilized peoples" and casual remarks about the nefarious international behavior of nation-states (*Rel.* 28–9; 34).[31] Henry Allison states the serious problem we confront here quite clearly, and even attempts to do what Kant himself failed to do: to provide an a priori deduction that will justify the claim that there is a universal propensity to moral evil.

> Kant insists not only that there is a propensity to evil but that it is "rooted in humanity itself" and, therefore, universal. What grounds, we may ask, does Kant offer for this apparently audacious claim?
>
> Kant's official answer to this obvious question is quite disappointing. . . . Instead of offering a "formal proof" of the universality of the propensity to evil, he simply asserts the necessity for such a proof is obviated by "the multitude of crying examples which experience *of the actions* of men put before our eyes." In short, he seems to treat it as an unproblematic empirical generalization. But clearly, even if for the sake of argument one accepts Kant's appeal to some rather selective anthropological evidence, the *most* that this evidence can show is that evil is widespread, not that there is a universal propensity to it. Moreover, since Kant insists that this propensity concerns only the ultimate subjective ground of one's maxims and is perfectly compatible with a virtuous empirical character, it is difficult to see what could conceivably falsify this claim. Consequently, it is also difficult to take seriously the suggestion that it is intended as an empirical generalization.[32]

Kant never gives – or even attempts to give – a *proof* of his controversial and bold claim that man is evil by nature.

It almost appears as if Kant is caught in what he has characterized (in the *Critique of Pure Reason*) as a "dialectical illusion." Such an illusion arises when we think we have genuine knowledge and can explain something, but actually do not, and cannot, have any legitimate knowledge. Starting from the fact that human beings sometimes adopt good maxims and sometimes adopt evil maxims, we seek to explain why they do not always follow the moral law. We presumably *explain* this failure by appealing to the doctrine of radical evil – the propensity towards moral evil that is rooted in our humanity. But it is an illusion to think that this enables us to explain or account for why we adopt evil maxims, why we sometimes succumb to this temptation. This alleged explanation turns out to be vacuous. For it does not explain anything about the individual free choices that we make, or even why we choose the ultimate subjective ground of our maxims. To ask *why* we freely choose to adopt good or evil maxims is to ask an *impossible* question. It is an impossible question because, ulti-mately, it is "inscrutable to us."

> When we say, then, Man is by nature good, or Man is by nature evil, this means only that there is in him an ultimate ground (inscrutable to us [*uns unerforschlichen*]) of the adoption of good maxims or of evil maxims (i.e., those contrary to law) and this he has, being a man; and hence he thereby expresses the character of his species. (*Rel.* 17; 20)

To drive home the point that the adoption of the ultimate subjective ground is inscrutable, Kant adds the following important footnote:

> That the ultimate subjective ground of the adoption of moral maxims is inscru-table is indeed already evident from this, that since this adoption is free, its ground (why, for example, I have chosen an evil and not a good maxim) must not be sought in any natural impulse, but always again in a maxim. Now since this maxim also must have its ground, and since apart from maxims no *determin-ing ground* of free choice [*Willkür*] can or ought to be adduced, we are referred back endlessly in the series of subjective determining grounds, without ever being able to reach the ultimate ground. (*Rel.* 17–18; 20)

It appears, then, that the concept of radical evil is a dialectical illusion because it seduces us into thinking that we can *explain* something that we cannot possibly explain – why we freely adopt the maxims (good or evil) that we actually do adopt – whether it be the choice of an ultimate subjective ground of maxims or the choice of specific maxims in concrete situations.

Diabolical evil

My aim in this chapter has been to understand what Kant means by radical evil. But, in the spirit of interrogation, I also want to explore how Kant's reflections about morality and radical evil help us to understand the forms of evil that have broken out in the twentieth century, including the evil and genocide evoked by the word "Auschwitz." John Silber (and many would agree with him) says that Kant is "the most important writer on ethics since Aristotle," and that he intended to "set forth doctrines that were not just theoretical in nature but were intended to guide everyday human conduct."[33] Despite Kant's language of "wickedness," "corruption," and "perversity," his analysis of evil and radical evil is disappointing. But some of Kant's reflections on duty – especially the absolute duty of a citizen to obey the sovereign power, and the duty of a soldier to obey orders of a superior – are more than disappointing; they are extremely disturbing.

Consider the case of Adolf Eichmann, who cited Kant (with reasonable accuracy) at his trial in Jerusalem in order to justify his conduct.[34] We certainly cannot blame Kant, the great champion of human dignity, for this perverse appropriation of the categorical imperative. Nevertheless, as Silber points out, "It may seem outrageous to find Kant's ethical doctrine, grounded as it is in the dignity of the moral person as an end-in-himself, used to exculpate a confessed accomplice to mass murder. But it should come as no surprise to Kant scholars, for Kant's views on the citizen's obligation to the sovereign strongly support Eichmann's position."[35] Kant's official doctrine is that the ban on resisting any supreme lawmaking is *absolute*. (Let us not forget that, for all the manipulation, lawlessness, and violence of the Nazis, "Hitler was made Chancellor in a constitutionally proper manner."[36]) I want to quote just three of the many passages that Eichmann might have cited from Kant to justify his acceptance of the *Führerprinzip*.

> Any resistance to the supreme lawmaking power, any incitement of dissatisfied subjects to action, any uprising that bursts into rebellion – that all is the worst, most punishable crime in a community. For it shatters the community's foundations. And this ban is *absolute*, so unconditional that even though that supreme power or its agent, the head of state, may have broken the original contract, even though in the subject's eyes he may have forfeited the right to legislate by empowering the government to rule tyrannically by sheer violence, even then the subject is allowed no resistance, no violent counteraction.

> There is no right of sedition (*seditio*), much less a right of revolution (*rebellio*), and least of all a right to lay hands on or take the life of the chief of state

when he is an individual person on the excuse that he has misused his authority. . . . It is the people's duty to endure even the most intolerable abuse of supreme authority.[37]

Thus it would be ruinous if an officer, receiving an order from his superiors, wanted while on duty to engage openly in subtle reasoning about its appropriateness or utility; he must obey.[38]

I certainly do not want to judge Kant by the way in which his statements have been misappropriated and distorted. Nor is it fair to criticize him for a failure to anticipate the systematic terror and violence practiced by the Nazis. I have no doubt that Kant, the great champion of universal human dignity, would have found ample grounds to condemn the Nazis. Nevertheless, the consistency, and even harshness, with which Kant opposes any active resistance to "the supreme lawmaking power," no matter how tyrannical it may become, should at least make us question his rigorism his insistence that this ban is *absolute* and *unconditional*.[39]

The Eichmann question concerns a soldier's duty to obey his superiors, but what about the supreme commander, Hitler himself? How does Kant's moral theory apply to the person who is ultimately responsible for giving the orders? Does Kant's understanding of evil and radical evil help us to judge the conduct of Hitler?[40] I cannot explore the complex historical debate concerning Hitler's intentions and motivations. I refer to Hitler primarily in order to raise some further questions about Kant's understanding of evil that I have not yet squarely addressed. To raise these questions, we need to return to some of the details of Kant's analysis of radical evil. Let us recall that in the *Religion*, Kant makes it perfectly clear that neither our sensuous nature nor our faculty of reason is the source of evil. The locus of evil is the will – or, more precisely, the corruption of the will (*Willkür*). In this respect, Kant stands in a tradition that goes back to St Augustine. We, and we alone, are responsible for the evil maxims that we freely adopt by an act of will (*Willkür*). In a famous passage, Kant categorically rejects the possibility of thinking of man as "a devilish being" (*einem teuflischen Wesen*).

In seeking, therefore, a ground of the morally evil in man [we find that] *sensuous nature* comprises too little, for when the incentives which can spring from freedom are taken away, man is reduced to merely *animal* being. On the other hand, a reason exempt from the moral law, a *malignant reason* as it were (a thoroughly evil will [*Wille*]) comprises too much, for thereby opposition to the law would itself be set up as an incentive (since in the absence of incentives the will [*Willkür*] cannot be determined), and thus the subject would be made a *devilish* being. Neither of these designations is applicable to man. (*Rel.* 30; 37)

But why can't human beings be devilish beings? And why is the idea of a "malignant reason" rejected? Why does Kant simply rule this out as impossible? The search for answers to these questions takes us to the very heart of Kant's moral philosophy, and to his understanding of radical evil. There are reasons why Kant rejects these possibilities. Before we can evaluate this rejection, we need to understand his reasons.

Kant is primarily concerned with man as a species, with the human race. If a malignant reason were *constitutive* of human nature, if man as a species were intrinsically devilish, then there would be no morality. The reason is clear. Morality presupposes freedom and choice. If one claims that malignant reason is *constitutive* of our human nature, there is no possibility that we could act otherwise. This means that a moral agent, by the exercise of his will, has the capacity to choose freely the maxims he adopts.

What about the possibility that *some* human beings are devilish beings? Once again, if this is interpreted to mean that some but not all human beings are intrinsically devilish, then the same considerations apply. For this would mean that some human beings are not really human – they do not have the capacity to choose between good and evil maxims. But suppose we consider the case of someone who is not innately (in the strong sense of innate) diabolical, but who *becomes* diabolical – who freely and consistently chooses to defy the moral law. Kant addresses this possibility when he writes:

> Man (even the most wicked) does not, under any maxim whatsoever, repudiate the moral law in the manner of a rebel (renouncing obedience to it). The law, rather, forces itself upon him irresistibly by virtue of his moral predisposition; and were no other incentive working in opposition, he would adopt the law into his supreme maxim as the sufficient determining ground of his will [*Willkür*]; that is, he would be morally good. (*Rel.* 31; 37)

But this passage is strikingly ambiguous; it is open to at least two very different interpretations, which must be carefully distinguished. In order to bring out this ambiguity, a review of the *Wille/ Willkür* distinction is in order. In the *Religion*, Kant emphasizes that the *Willkür* is that aspect of the faculty of volition by which we make free choices. Even when we recognize the moral law as the norm to which our maxims ought to conform, we nevertheless have the capacity to do (or not to do) what the moral law requires. We have the capacity to choose good or evil maxims. The *Wille* itself (in the narrow technical sense) is practical reason; it is the moral law, the supreme moral norm. The *Wille/ Willkür* distinction is introduced within a *unified* faculty of volition (sometimes also referred to as *Wille*). In short, there is no *Wille* without a *Willkür*, and there is no (human) *Willkür* without the *Wille*. *Wille* and *Willkür* are co-dependent, although we can distinguish their different functions. Allison crisply states the difference when he says: "Thus, it is *Wille* in the narrow sense that provides the norm and *Willkür* that chooses in light of this norm."[41] When Kant says that "the law . . . forces itself upon [man] irresistibly," he is making not a *causal* claim but a *normative* moral claim; he is asserting that we (finite moral agents) cannot help but recognize the objective moral law as the norm to which our maxims ought to conform. We cannot help but *acknowledge* the categorical imperative, regardless of whether we choose to obey it or not. This is the sense in which it is perfectly accurate to declare: "Man (even the most wicked) does not, under any maxim whatsoever, repudiate the moral law in the manner of a rebel (renouncing obedience to it)." To be a human being is to be a person who *recognizes* the authority of the moral law regardless of whether one chooses to do what it requires.[42]

We can now locate the crucial ambiguity in the above passage where Kant affirms the impossibility of man being a devilish being. Even if we accept his claim that human beings as a *species* are not devilish, and that no matter how wicked a person may be, he cannot avoid acknowledging the authority of the moral law, this does not address the issue of whether an *individual* can repudiate the moral law in the sense of freely choosing to defy it. I want to argue that this is not only possible, but also that, on Kant's own analysis of *Willkür*, it *must* be possible. It must be possible for an individual to *become* a devilish person. It must be possible for an individual to defy and repudiate the moral law in such a manner that he freely adopts a disposition (*Gesinnung*) in which he consistently refuses to do what the moral law requires. He consistently adopts evil maxims. This may be judged to be morally wicked and perverse, but nevertheless it is a perverse *possibility*.

To bring out the full significance of what I am claiming, I want to examine Silber's fundamental criticism of Kant's refusal to acknowledge the possibility of a human being becoming a "devilish being." Silber thinks that Kant's refusal to consider the possibility that individuals may consistently defy the moral law reveals a fundamental weakness in his moral philosophy. This is the primary reason why Silber claims that Kant's ethics is not adequate to account for Auschwitz.

Kant's ethics is inadequate to the understanding of Auschwitz because Kant denies the possibility of the deliberate rejection of the moral law. Not even a wicked man, Kant holds, can will evil for the sake of evil. His evil, according to Kant, consists merely in his willingness to ignore or subordinate the moral law when it interferes with his nonmoral but natural inclina-

tions. His evil is expressed in abandoning the conditions of free personal
fulfillment in favor of fulfillment as a creature of natural desire. . . . [Kant
denies] the possibility of a person knowingly doing evil for its own sake. By
insisting that freedom is a power whose fulfillment depends upon rationality
and that its irrational misuse is merely an impotence, Kant proposed a
theory that rules out the contravening evidence of human experience.[43]

Several commentators have sought to defend Kant against Silber's objection. Allen Wood, for example, addressing himself to an earlier version of
this criticism by Silber, says: "This, however, is a fallacy endemic to
philosophical criticism: the supposition that by pointing to 'facts' (which
no one disputes) one can give a philosophical justification of the manner
in which one has expressed the facts."[44] It is, of course, true that philosophical claims rarely are resolved by "pointing to 'facts'," and that the
crucial issue frequently turns out to be the *interpretation* of the alleged facts.
Nevertheless, Wood's dismissal of Silber's objection strikes me as a bit too
facile, for two reasons. In the first place, Kant himself – as we have seen
– supports his own thesis about the universality of radical evil by "pointing to 'facts'." Secondly, this is not quite what Silber means when he says,
"Kant's insistence to the contrary, man's free power to reject the law in
defiance is an ineradicable fact of human experience."[45] Silber is not
referring to empirical "facts" and "experience" in the restricted technical
sense in which these terms are used in the *Critique of Pure Reason*, where
they refer to the phenomenal realm. He is using them more broadly, in a
manner consistent with Kant's own usage when he speaks of "the *experience*
[*Erfahrung*] *of the actions* of men" in the *Religion* (*Rel.* 28; 34). Silber claims
that there are persons who deliberately and consistently reject the moral
law, even though they recognize what the moral law requires, and that
Kant does not adequately account for this possibility.[46]

Silber might have been more precise had he phrased his point in a
slightly different manner. An individual is judged to be evil if he chooses
a disposition (*Gesinnung*) – a supreme, overarching maxim – to adopt evil
maxims. We do not "observe" maxims directly; we infer their existence on
the basis of actions that human beings perform. Such an inference is
always fallible. We can never be absolutely certain when we ascribe a
maxim (even a supreme maxim) to someone. But, despite this fallibility,
we do judge persons to be evil (or good) on the basis of their actions. In
this sense, our *experience* of the actions of human beings is the basis for
making judgments about their evil character. So Silber might have said
that, on the basis of our moral experience, we judge some persons to be
devilish. And this is a possibility that Kant failed to consider.

We still haven't come to the heart of the matter – to what Silber is getting at in his criticism of Kant. For Silber is not arguing that human beings as a species are devilish, or that being devilish is somehow constitutive of our nature. And he is not even denying that human beings must acknowledge the authority of the moral law. On the contrary, his criticism depends on affirming this claim. Rather, he is underscoring something that Kant does not seem to consider: namely, that there are some persons (as well as characters in fiction) who, to use the Kantian terminology, incorporate into their maxims the primary incentive to *defy* the moral law.[47]

Although I agree with Silber that Kant does not explicitly deal with this possibility, ironically, his moral theory – as developed in the *Religion* – can effectively deal with it. In a very revealing footnote, Kant writes:

> For from the fact that a being has reason it by no means follows that this reason, by the mere representing of the fitness of its maxims to be laid down as universal laws, is thereby rendered capable of determining the will [*Willkür*] unconditionally, so as to be "practical" of itself; at least not so far as we can see. The most rational mortal being in the world might still stand in need of certain incentives, originating in objects of desire, to determine his choice [*Willkür*]. He might, indeed, bestow the most rational reflection on all that concerns not only the greatest sum of these incentives in him but also the means of attaining the end thereby determined, without ever suspecting the possibility of such a thing as the absolutely imperative moral law which proclaims that it is itself an incentive, and, indeed, the highest. Were it not given us from within, we should never by any ratiocination subtilize it into existence to win over our will [*Willkür*] to it; yet this law is the only law which informs us of the independence of our will [*Willkür*] from determination by all other incentives (of our freedom) and at the same time of the accountability of all our actions. (*Rel.* 21; 25)

Although Kant's phrasing is a bit turgid, his basic point is clear. Reason by itself may not be sufficient to motivate us to follow the moral law. We may recognize the fitness of our maxims as laid down by the universal law, but we may nevertheless, not yet be motivated to adopt these maxims and act accordingly. "The most rational mortal being in the world might still stand in need of certain incentives . . . to determine his choice." Of course, our respect for the law *may be* a sufficient incentive to act morally. But our *Willkür* may choose to defy the moral law. If recognition of the moral law can serve as an incentive to act morally, there can always be a counter-incentive. We can choose to be perverse, we can choose to be devilish, we can choose to defy the moral law. We may be told that such a choice is irrational, that we are refusing to recognize "the absolutely imperative moral law," that there is a performative contradiction whereby

we are both exercising and denying our freedom. But it does not follow
that we *cannot* do this! On the contrary, such a possibility is intrinsic to the
human *Willkür*. There are no *intrinsic* restraints on what the *Willkür* can
choose to do; we are "radically free."[48]

We can approach the issue of radical free choice [*Willkür*] from a slightly
different angle. Kant typically limits the incentives involved in the adoption of maxims to *two* kinds: the moral incentive to conform to the moral
law and nonmoral incentives that arise from our natural inclinations and
desires. At times, Kant even categorizes all nonmoral incentives under the
rubric of self-love, "which, when taken as the principle of all our maxims,
is the very source of evil" (*Rel.* 41; 49).[49] But why should we limit incentives to these two kinds? Why not recognize that there are other incentives
that are not easily assimilated to "self-love." It is difficult to see how the
incentives that motivate fanatics and terrorists who are willing to sacrifice
themselves for some cause or movement can be accounted for by self-love.
The horrors of the twentieth century (and not just this century) have
opened our eyes to the variety of types of incentives that motivate evil
actions.[50] Sometimes it seems as if Kant is operating with a highly abstract
formal principle. If an incentive is not a genuinely moral incentive – that
is, respect for the moral law – then it *must* (by stipulative fiat) be classified
as the incentive of self-love.[51] The difficulty here is rooted in Kant's limited moral psychology, in the narrow range of types of incentives that he
acknowledges.[52] If one is really to distinguish different types of evil, then
one must consider the full range of incentives that are involved in the
adoption of evil maxims and the performance of evil deeds. There are
major differences among those who may be misguided because they give
priority to their sympathetic feeling for their fellow human beings, those
(like Eichmann) whose primary incentive for performing their "duty" seems
to be advancing their own career, those who mock and defy the moral
law, and those who do evil for evil's sake. I am *not* suggesting that Kant is
unaware of these differences. There is plenty of evidence that he acknowledges them. But I am questioning whether he has provided the *conceptual*
resources to account and illuminate them. To claim that *all* evil maxims
are determined by the principle of self-love (no matter how broadly we
think of self-love) obscures more than it illuminates. *There is no free choice
(Willkür) unless there is the free choice to be morally evil, and even devilish.*

Unconditional moral responsibility

In concluding this chapter, I want to return to the question that motivated
this analysis originally: whether Kant's reflections on evil, especially radi-

cal evil, can help to guide our thinking about the evils we have witnessed in the twentieth century. The answer is a mixed one, for we need to distinguish the strengths and weaknesses of his reflections. Kant would not have agreed with Arendt that "radical evil" names a special type of evil that cannot be conceived. I have argued that Kant's concept of radical evil turns out to be little more than a way of designating the tendency (propensity) of human beings to disobey the moral law. There is an enormous disparity between Kant's rhetoric – his references to "wickedness," "perversity," and "corruption" – and the content of what he actually says. Against Kant's explicit rejection of the possibility that man is (or can become) devilish or diabolical, I have argued that his understanding of *Willkür* entails that *some* individuals can *become* devilish; and this conclusion is a *necessary* consequence of Kant's understanding of free choice (*Willkür*).

I have also claimed that Kant is at war with himself, and I want to spell this out in a bit more detail. When we understand *why* Kant gets entangled in these difficulties and double binds, we begin to appreciate both his importance and his relevance to the attempt to come to grips with the problem of evil. There is one cardinal principle that Kant refuses to compromise in any way. This is at once the source of his difficulties and also his profound insight into morality. Human beings are morally accountable and responsible for whatever they become, for the maxims that they adopt, even for their moral disposition. Kant never compromises on the principle that it is *always* within our power to choose between good and evil maxims, and that it is we (and we alone) who must bear the responsibility for these choices. There are no moral excuses such that we can say that we have been *compelled by natural causes* to choose or to will what is morally evil. This is why, no matter how much Kant insists that radical evil is a powerful propensity or tendency, that it is innate, that it is inextirpable, he never interprets this to mean that we are *causally* compelled to choose evil maxims and to do evil deeds. He absolutely insists that no matter how deeply rooted this propensity is within our human nature, it is not this propensity that is responsible for the evil that we do, but our free will (*Willkür*). This is why every time we think Kant is telling us that our will is fundamentally corrupt, that we are evil by nature, that this evil is woven into the very fabric of our humanity, he immediately qualifies what he says, reminding us that we, and we alone, are responsible for what we do. There is no escape from the radical freedom of our *Willkür*. And radical freedom means we must bear the complete moral responsibility for our choices, decisions, and actions.

We can now see why Kant is so relevant for coming to grips with the many faces of evil in the twentieth century. His uncompromising insistence that personal responsibility is inescapable goes against the grain of prevailing tendencies to find all sorts of excuses for our moral failures. Kant would sharply oppose the variety of "functional explanations" that seek to diminish the significance of individual responsibility, just as he would object to fashionable attempts to decenter or dissolve the moral agent such that it no longer even makes sense to speak about individual responsibility. Kant's understanding of freedom – not only the freedom manifested in self-legislation and obeying the moral law, but the more radical freedom of choice (*Willkür*) that this moral freedom presupposes – enables us to evaluate the actions of individuals in extreme situations.

Let us return to the opening epigraphs of this chapter where Hannah Arendt speaks of radical evil. One of the most troubling issues that arises in the attempt to comprehend totalitarianism and the phenomenon epitomized by Auschwitz is the assignment of responsibility – not only to the perpetrators – to those who gave orders and those who followed orders – but also to the so-called bystanders. We do not have to say that all those involved are responsible in the same way. There are crucial moral and legal differences to be made between, for example, a Hitler, a Heydrich, an Eichmann, and those bystanders who actively or passively supported the Nazis. Even the victims had to make drastic choices. Kant would never have endorsed a notion of collective responsibility that entailed saying that an entire people were *equally* responsible. But he would have insisted that insofar as individuals have the capacity of spontaneous free choice (*Willkür*), they are accountable and responsible moral agents.[53]

Finally, I want to consider again Kant's claim that the "ultimate subjective ground of the adoption of moral maxims" is *inscrutable*. I have already quoted the passage from the beginning of the first essay of the *Religion* where he asserts "that the ultimate subjective ground of the adoption of moral maxims is inscrutable." Kant not only begins his essay on radical evil with this claim, but he concludes the essay by reiterating that "the deeps of the heart (the subjective first ground of his maxims) are inscrutable to him" (*Rel.* 46; 56). Some commentators see this claim about inscrutability as a problem, or, more ungenerously, as a "cop-out." But I take it to be an indication of Kant's ultimate intellectual integrity and his profound understanding of our radical freedom. When confronted with the moral choices that human beings make, there is a great deal that we can know about why persons make the choices they do. Kant was acutely aware of how background, cultural conditions, and education can affect moral choices. But we still want to know ultimately why one person chooses good maxims and another chooses evil maxims. Or, to stick close to Kant's terminology, we want to know how we are to account for "the ultimate subjective ground of the adoption of moral maxims." For this ultimate subjective ground must itself be the result of an exercise of freedom. In the final analysis, we cannot explain why one person chooses to become good and another chooses to become evil. To imagine that we could explain this would be in effect to deny that our will (*Willkür*) is radically free. So, far from its being some sort of deficiency, it is Kant's way of acknowledging a profound moral truth about our radical free choice (*Willkür*). Human beings are responsible for the choices they make, but *ultimately*, we cannot explain why they make the moral choices they do; we cannot explain "the ultimate subjective ground of the adoption of moral maxims" – whether for good or for evil. Not only is this inscrutable; it *must* be inscrutable, because this is what it means to be a free and responsible person.

2

Hegel: The Healing of the Spirit?

The wounds of the Spirit heal, and leave no scars behind.

Phenomenology of Spirit

What happened, happened. But that it happened cannot be so easily accepted. I rebel: against my past, against history, and against a present that places the incomprehensible in the cold storage of history and thus falsifies it in a revolting way. Nothing has healed . . . .

Jean Améry, *At the Mind's Limits*

Hegel is the most systematically ambiguous philosopher in the history of philosophy. This is especially ironical because Hegel emphatically affirms that there is a single unified truth to be known, and that philosophy is the conceptual discipline by which the truth can be totally comprehended. Yet, even before his death, there were fierce debates among his disciples and critics about how he was to be understood. Unlike many other philosophers who have elicited divergent responses, the interpretations of Hegel have been violently contradictory. Nowhere is this more evident than in Hegel's conceptions of God and religion. Is Hegel a theist, a pantheist, or a thoroughgoing atheist? Is he a defender of the Christian faith, or one of its severest and most subversive critics? All these claims have been made for Hegel. This extreme divergence has been characteristic of the debates among left, center, and right Hegelians. These sharp disagreements, which started during Hegel's lifetime and raged in the decades immediately after his death, have persisted until the present.[1] Thus James Stirling, who wrote the first extensive study of Hegel in English, *The Secret of Hegel* (1865), declared that the secret of Hegel was to restore our faith, faith in God, faith in Christianity as the revealed religion. On the other hand, many commentators, beginning with Bruno Bauer and including Alexander Kojève and, most recently, Robert Solomon, have argued that Hegel is really an atheist. Robert Solomon, with Stirling in mind, announces that the real "secret" of Hegel is that he is "essentially an atheist."[2]

Conflicting and contradictory interpretations of Hegel are not restricted to his concepts of God, Christianity, and religion, however. They extend to every aspect of his philosophy. The question arises: What is it about Hegel's thought that invites and provokes such extreme contradictory interpretations? If we are to grasp what Hegel means by evil, and the significance of evil for his philosophy, then we must eventually confront this question. At this preliminary stage, I want to say that the source of these contradictory interpretations is not some superficial vagueness or obscurity of expression: contradictory tendencies are among the deepest features of Hegel's dialectical thinking, and go to the heart of his philosophy.

We find the most sustained discussion of evil in Hegel's *Lectures on the Philosophy of Religion*. Although the topics of religion, Christianity, and God were central to Hegel from his earliest writings, it was only during his Berlin period that he explicitly lectured on the philosophy of religion – a topic that was relatively new in Germany at the time. He gave four series of lectures at the University of Berlin (in 1821, 1824, 1827, and 1831). He never published these lectures; nor did he write a book based on them. It is only during the past few decades, due to the meticulous scholarship of his German and English editors, that we now have a reliable reconstruction of them.[3] These lectures were delivered during Hegel's mature years, long after he had published the *Phenomenology of Spirit* and the *Science of Logic*. His primary concern is religion as a form of *knowledge*, knowledge that concerns "the eternal truth." In the 1827 lectures, he begins by declaring that "[religion] is the loftiest object that can occupy human beings; it is the absolute object."

> It is the region of eternal truth and eternal virtue, the region where all the riddles of thought, all contradictions, and all the sorrows of the heart should show themselves to be resolved, and the region of the eternal peace through which the human being is truly human. . . . Everything that people value and esteem, everything on which they think to base their pride and glory, all of this finds its ultimate focal point in religion, in the thought and consciousness of God and in the feeling of God. God is the beginning and end of all things. God is the sacred center, which animates and inspires all things. Religion possesses its object within itself – and that object is God, for religion is the relation of human consciousness to God. (*L* 75–6)

The question immediately arises: What is the relation between this God-centered conception of religion and philosophy? Hegel is quite explicit.

> It must be said that the content of philosophy, its need and interest, is wholly in common with that of religion. The object of religion, like that of philosophy, is the eternal truth, God and nothing but God and the explication of God. Philosophy is only explicating *itself* when it explicates religion, and when it explicates itself it is explicating religion. For the *thinking* spirit is what penetrates this object, the truth; it is thinking that enjoys the truth and purifies the subjective consciousness. Thus religion and philosophy coincide in one. (*L* 78–9)

These are bold and controversial claims, especially when viewed against the background of traditional conceptions of the relation of religion to philosophy and the fierce discussion of this relationship by Enlightenment thinkers. If religion and philosophy "coincide in one," then there is no ultimate conflict between religion and philosophy, faith and knowledge. There is a single "eternal truth" that is known by both religion and philosophy. But then, what is the difference between religion and philosophy? It is only the *manner* of their concern with God. The medium of religion is what Hegel calls *Vorstellung* (frequently translated "representation"), whereas the medium of philosophy is *Begriff* (frequently translated "concept" or "notion") that is comprehended by speculative thinking (*Denken*). Religion, although not to be identified with philosophy, is a source of knowledge about God and the eternal truth.[4]

Here, then, at the very beginning of his lectures, we detect one of the sources of the deep ambiguity concerning Hegel's understanding of the relation of religion to philosophy. Religion and philosophy (along with art) are expressions of the Absolute Spirit. Consequently, the *object* of religion and philosophy – the "eternal truth" – is the same. Religion and philosophy differ not in the truth that they reveal, but only in "the peculiar character of their concern with God." But if this is so, and if, as Hegel frequently affirms, speculative thinking (*Denken*) is a superior form of knowledge to representation (*Vorstellung*), we can easily understand the temptation to declare that philosophy completely supersedes religion. There is nothing to be known by religion that cannot be known by philosophy. Hegel is sharply critical of the "prejudice" that he associates with Jacobi, "that the religious ceases to be religious when it is rendered comprehensible" (i. 254). Although Hegel affirms that philosophy supersedes religion, this does not mean that religion is dispensable. Speculative philosophy yields "the philosophical cognition of truth," but "nothing is further from its intention than to overthrow religion" (i. 251). "On the contrary, religion is precisely the true content but in the form of representation, and philosophy is not the first to offer the substantive truth. Humanity has not had to await philosophy in order to receive for the first time the consciousness or cognition of truth" (i. 251).

We can already understand why a Christian believer (or any believer in a transcendent God) might feel uneasy with this insistence that there is nothing that is known ultimately by religion – not even Revelation – that cannot be grasped conceptually by philosophy. We can also understand why some interpreters and critics of Hegel who want to argue that philosophy supersedes religion, can also argue (notwithstanding Hegel's claims to the contrary) that philosophy can dispense with religion altogether. Why do we need religion if we can rationally and philosophically comprehend the eternal truth that is the object of religion? In any apparent conflict between the cognitive claims of religion and philosophy, it will always be philosophy that decides what is true.

In the background here lies a controversial set of issues concerning religion, faith, and philosophy that had dominated German thought since the time of Kant. It is no exaggeration to say that Hegel always had Kant (and his legacy) in mind – not only in his lectures on religion, but in virtually everything he said and wrote. Hegel's relationship with Kant is extremely complex. From Hegel's perspective, his own philosophizing begins with Kant's insights and distinctions. Hegel asserts this on many occasions. But there is a dialectical irony in this reiterated insistence, because Hegel's "completion" of the Kantian project leads to conclusions that flatly contradict Kant's explicit claims and his stated intentions. Harold Bloom, in his reflections on poetry, has developed a provocative theory of the anxiety of influence and revisionism. According to Bloom, strong poets and thinkers are always battling with the giants who are their predecessors. This is how they assert their creativity and originality. "Revisionism . . . unfolds itself *only in fighting*. The spirit portrays itself as agonistic, as contesting for supremacy, with other spirits, with anteriority, and finally with every earlier version of itself."[5] This agonistic engagement is characteristic of Hegel's relationship with Kant, and shapes his understanding of evil. Hegel praises Kant and ruthlessly attacks him at the same time. At the core of Hegel's understanding of evil is a frontal attack on Kant's understanding of finitude (and infinitude) – the very quintessence of Kant's Critical Philosophy.

The agon between Hegel and Kant is clearly manifested in their differing understandings of the relationship between knowledge and faith and, consequently, in their differing conceptions of the relation between religion and philosophy. Kant thought that he had shown, once and for all, the impossibility of any theoretical or speculative knowledge of God. "I have therefore found it necessary to deny *knowledge*, in order to make room for *faith*."[6] Faith "transcends" the finite limitations of human knowledge. It is a dialectical illusion to think that, by theoretical reasoning, we can prove or disprove the existence of God, or achieve any theoretical knowledge of God's attributes. Dogmatism and its antithesis, militant atheism, share the same mistaken assumption. They both assume that we can achieve genuine knowledge of what we cannot possibly know. The only "access" to God is a practical one – God is one of the postulates of practical reason. Almost as soon as Kant had developed his understanding of faith and knowledge, he was attacked and criticized from a variety of perspectives. But few of Kant's contemporaries or immediate successors questioned his skeptical arguments about the very possibility of a speculative knowledge of God – at least, not until Hegel. Hegel characteristically argues that it is not a question of returning to a pre-critical standpoint, but of going forward "beyond" Kant. Starting with Kant's own premises, one must think them through to their ultimate conclusion. If we pursue the consequences of Kant's critical turn more rigorously than Kant himself did, we are led to a new affirmation of the actuality and, indeed, the necessity of a speculative philosophy of religion – that is, a philosophical comprehension of the eternal truth we call "God." Hegel defiantly asserts this against Kant, and against all those who think that speculative knowledge of God is impossible.

The finite and the infinite

In order to understand how Hegel seeks to justify his ambitious claims, and to set the context for his analysis of evil, we need to probe the most central distinction in his philosophy – that between the finite and the infinite. It is in his *Science of Logic* that he systematically explores the meaning of the finite and the infinite, and their dialectical relationship to each other. It is there that Hegel makes the all-important distinction between the "bad" or "spurious" infinite (*schlechte Unendliche*) and the "true" infinite (*wahrhafte Unendliche*).[7] In the Religion Lectures, he presupposes the results of the *Science of Logic*, and provides a more informal and accessible discussion of the finite and the infinite.

Hegel begins his discussion with a popular understanding of finitude. "When we talk of human being as finite, there are three forms to be considered in which finitude appears: first, the finitude of the *senses* generally, second, finitude in *reflection*, and third, the form of finitude as it is [found] in *spirit* and for *spirit*" (i. 289).

When we say, "human being is finite," this means that I as a human being am in relation with an other; there is present an other, a negative of myself with whom I have ties, and this bond with an other constitutes my finitude or a dependency on my part; we are mutually exclusive and behave as independent vis-à-vis one another. This constitutes an exclusion. As a being that has sense-awareness I am exclusive and excluded in this way; all living things are exclusive and excluded thus – they are singular. (i. 289)

In this initial characterization of finitude, Hegel stresses both dependence and exclusivity. Finitude presupposes a distinction between a singular being and its other – something that is literally beyond and outside me. Thus, as a natural creature, "I have many kinds of needs, many distinct types of relationship, manifold practical or theoretical relationships to what is outside me. All of these needs are limited in respect to their content; they are dependent or finite" (i. 289–90). For example, as a finite creature with needs and desires (such as hunger and thirst), I am dependent on something other than myself for their satisfaction. When they are satisfied, I experience "finite satisfactions"; but for as long as I am alive, there will always be new and other needs and desires to be satisfied. I do not think that there is anything esoteric or mysterious about this sense of finitude; it reflects a common, ordinary understanding of what it means to be a finite creature. Furthermore, Hegel is certainly not denying that, from a commonsense perspective, this is a perfectly proper way of speaking about human finitude.

The second form of finitude arises with reflection. We are not just natural creatures with appetites, needs, and desires. We are also reflective beings. For Hegel, "reflection" is a term of art that corresponds roughly to the cognitive and judgmental capacities that Kant associated with the understanding (*Verstand*).[8] "The standpoint of reflection, however, is the level at which the finite maintains itself, the level at which the antithesis of finitude and infinity is perennial; the very connecting of the two is the standpoint of reflection, and the two together make up the antithesis" (i. 291). Consequently, finitude – from the standpoint of reflection – presupposes an explicit antithetical distinction between the finite and the infinite. The infinite is that which is beyond and necessarily transcends the finite. Hegel illustrates what he means by appealing to the representation (*Vorstellung*) of God that is characteristic of religion. The Christian God is represented as an infinite being, a supreme being who infinitely transcends the finite beings that he creates.

God means here just the infinite, he is defined here only as that, as the other of the finite, as its beyond. To the extent that God is, I am not; to the extent that God touches me, the finite disappears. In this way God is

> defined by an antithesis that seems to be absolute. Inasmuch as the finite is defined simply as the other of the infinite, it is said that the finite cannot cognize or attain to the infinite, cannot grasp or conceive it. God is a beyond, we cannot lay hold of him. (i. 283)

Whether we are believers or not, we can recognize that this is a common way of distinguishing God from his creatures. Something like this basic antithetical distinction was fundamental for most (but not all) philosophers and theologians before Hegel. Moreover, this way of contrasting the finite and the infinite is absolutely central to Kant's philosophy. Hegel challenges this way of conceiving the relation of the finite and the infinite, and he makes a much more startling claim. When we think it through, we will realize that it is *self-contradictory*.

We can see why traditional Christian believers would be unsettled by Hegel's audaciousness. To question this antithesis is to question whether God infinitely transcends what he has created. But for Hegel, this traditional (and Kantian) way of understanding the relationship between what is finite and what is infinite is wholly inadequate. Bluntly stated – in the Hegelian idiom – it is *false*. This misguided understanding of the relation between the finite and the infinite has a much greater significance. Structurally, this is the way in which Kant conceives of all human knowledge and morality. We are finite human beings limited by both our sensibility and our understanding. We can, according to Kant, *think* more than we can *know*, but we cannot *know* the infinite, the unconditioned, the transcendent – that which is beyond all human finitude. If we fail to limit ourselves to what is within the bounds of knowledge and experience, we fall into the abyss of antinomies and contradictions. These antinomies and contradictions plunge reason into darkness, and require a thoroughgoing critique.

Hegel sees the same "logic" – the same reasoning – at work in the way in which Kant and his followers conceive of the categorical "ought." In the *Science of Logic*, in the very section in which he discusses the dialectical relation between the finite and the infinite, he introduces a remark about "the Ought" (*das Sollen*). It is clear that Hegel has Kant and his followers in mind when he writes that "the ought has recently played a great part in philosophy, especially in connection with morality and also in metaphysics generally, as the ultimate and absolute concept of the identity of the in-itself or self-relation, and of the *determinateness* or limit" (*SL* 133). Hegel explicitly relates this to transcendence and infinity when he adds: "In the ought the transcendence of finitude, that is infinity, begins. The ought is that which, in the further development, exhibits itself in accordance with the said impossibility as the progress to infinity" (*SL* 134). Hegel's agon

with Kant (and Fichte) becomes explicit when he speaks of it as a *prejudice.*
To claim that there are limitations of finitude that cannot be transcended
"is to be unaware that the very fact that something is determined as a
limitation implies that the limitation is already transcended" (*SL* 134).
This (Kantian) way of conceiving of the ought is only a *finite* transcending
of the ought. It is the bad or spurious infinite. "The philosophy of Kant
and Fichte sets up the ought as the highest point of the resolution of the
contradictions of Reason; but the truth is that the ought is only the standpoint which clings to finitude and thus to contradiction" (*SL* 136).

We can see where Hegel is leading us (or, as he would prefer to say,
where genuine thinking is necessarily leading us) when he writes: "We
must now ask whether the antithesis [between the finite and the infinite]
has truth, that is whether the two sides fall apart and subsist apart from
one another. In this regard it has already been said that if we posit the
finite as finite we have already passed beyond it" (i. 293). There is a
distinction to be drawn between the finite and the infinite, but it is not a
fixed ontological or epistemological dichotomy. Hegel's way of phrasing
this point is to say that we are confronted with a distinction that turns out
to be no distinction. When we represent the infinite as something that is
distinct from, the negative of, and excluded from the finite, we are really
representing it as something that is finite!

> If consciousness defines itself as finite in this way, and says in all humility,
> "I am the finite, and the infinite lies beyond," then this I makes in its
> humility the very same reflection that we have already made: that the
> infinite is only something evanescent, not something that has being in and
> for itself, but merely a thought posited by me. It is I who produce that
> beyond; the finite and the infinite are equally my product, and I stand
> above both of them, both disappear in me. I am lord and master of this
> definition: I bring it forth. They vanish in and through me. . . . I am the
> affirmation which at first I placed outside in a beyond; and the infinite first
> comes into being through me. I am the negation of negation, it is I in
> whom the antithesis disappears; I am the reflection that brings them both
> to naught. (i. 295)

Initially, we may feel that the reasoning here is a bit too facile; that there
is something like a sleight of hand. Stated in its starkest terms, Hegel
claims that there is something radically mistaken about conceiving of the
distinction between the finite and the infinite as a rigid ontological distinction. To think of the infinite as that which is beyond and outside the finite
is to conceive of it as the "bad," or "spurious," infinite – that is, to think
of it in a way that is dependent (parasitic) on finite concepts. (Remember
that when Hegel first describes the finite, he emphasizes its dependence

and exclusivity.) There is also something very characteristic in Hegel's dialectical style of thinking in this passage. What initially appears to be humility turns out (by the end of the passage) to be extreme arrogance. This is not simply a rhetorical trope; it is an indication of the dialectical logic of inversion.[9] When we properly comprehend (*begreifen*) the finite, we realize that it is only a moment in the true self-moving infinite totality, just as when we comprehend the true infinite, we realize that it is nothing but the totality of its finite moments that are always being sublated (*aufgehoben*). This means that implicit (*an sich*) in the finite is the true infinite. It is not "beyond" the finite – that is, something wholly other than the finite. We do not comprehend this truth as long as we restrict ourselves to the standpoint of natural or sensuous existence, or even to the level of understanding (*Verstand*). We must pass beyond these standpoints to the "higher standpoint" of spirit (*Geist*) and reason (*Vernunft*). "So far as the higher standpoint is concerned, it is the third standpoint or relationship – of the finite to the infinite in *reason*. The first was the *natural* relationship, the second that which obtains in *reflection*, the third, now, that which obtains in *reason*" (i. 301). This is a transition that is "properly dialectical."

From a human point of view, this means that I renounce my singularity and my subjectivity as a particular finite being. I come to realize that I am not exclusively a natural or a reflective being, but a *spiritual* being capable of universal thought (*Denken*). Hegel knows full well that from a natural, or even a reflective, human point of view, such a claim appears to be absurd or topsy-turvy. And he certainly realizes that to make such an assertion, without an attempt to demonstrate it, carries no rational conviction. In the introduction to his *Phenomenology of Spirit*, he says that "*One* bare assurance is worth just as much as another."[10] Hegel begins his *Phenomenology* with the standpoint of "natural consciousness." Taking its own claims and its own self-understanding with complete seriousness ineluctably leads to an inversion whereby we realize that we are *not* just sensuous and reflective beings, but quintessentially *spiritual* beings capable of universal thought (*Denken*). We find a similar dialectical movement in the Religion Lectures when Hegel says:

> I must be the particular subjectivity that has indeed been sublated [*aufgehoben*]; hence I must recognize something *objective*, which is actual being in and for itself, which does indeed count as true for me, which is recognized as the affirmative posited for me; something in which I am negated as this I, but in which at the same time I am contained as free and by which my freedom is maintained. This implies that I am determined and maintained as universal, and I only count for myself as universal generally. But this is now none other than the standpoint of *thinking reason* [*denkende Vernunft*] generally, and *religion itself* is this activity, it is thinking reason in its activity. *Philosophy*

is also thinking reason, the only difference being that in philosophy the activity that constitutes religion appears simultaneously in the form of *thought* [*Denken*], whereas religion, being thinking reason in naïve form, so to speak, abides rather in the mode of *representation* [*Vorstellung*]. (i. 302)

We must be careful not to misinterpret what Hegel is saying here. A common criticism and complaint about Hegel is that he *sacrifices* individuality and singularity (especially as it pertains to human beings) to abstract universality. There is no doubt that Hegel constantly uses the language of "sacrifice," "surrender," and "renunciation." But we must appreciate the dialectical force of this language. Hegel is a severe critic of all forms of abstract negation and abstract universality. He makes a crucial distinction between abstract negation and determinate negation.[11] The former entails a complete rejection of what is negated, whereas the latter preserves what is negated and brings forth its truth. It is the *activity*, or movement, of determinate negation that brings about the transition from the finite to the true infinite. Furthermore, this dialectical movement proceeds from abstract (false) universality to a fully concrete, determinate (true) universality that is fully differentiated.

We can state Hegel's main point in a non-Hegelian idiom. From a first-person point of view, I start with the conviction that I am nothing but a natural finite sensuous being. I insist upon this, and declare that everything else is "outside" me and different from what I am. What could be more obvious and certain? But the more rigorously I try to articulate and defend precisely what I mean, the more I come to realize that this initial certainty is false, and that I am more than this limited singular finite being. I come to realize that I am also a reflective being capable of understanding (*Verstand*). Indeed, if this were not the case, I could not even say what I mean when I assert that I am nothing but a finite sensuous being. But this reflective stance is still limited. I realize that I am a spiritual being capable of thinking and conceptually grasping the "eternal truth" – that there is a sense in which I am identical with spirit (*Geist*). (Of course, this dialectical movement is a long, difficult process involving many intermediate steps.) I am always resisting this movement. To be told that I am not just a natural creature, but also a spiritual being capable of pure thinking, strikes me as absurd. But the more stubbornly I resist, the more I experience the necessity of moving beyond my own singularity and particularity. The more I insist upon what initially seems so evident and certain, the more I realize its untruth. This is characterized as the movement from certainty (*Gewissheit*) to truth (*Wahrheit*). Yes, I do sacrifice myself as a singular being; I do renounce my finite individuality. But it is a sacrifice that does not lead to complete denial and emptiness. Rather, it is the very dialectical process by which I realize what I truly am. The real truth of finitude (including my own subjective finitude) is the true infinite.

Still, it does seem presumptuous to claim that there is an ultimate identity and unity between my finitude and the true finite. What Hegel means by this seemingly audacious claim becomes clearer when we grasp what he means by true infinity. His introduction of the concept of infinity in the *Phenomenology* can help to clarify this point. He says: "This simple infinity, or the absolute [Concept], may be called the simple essence of life, the soul of the world, the universal blood, whose omnipresence is neither disturbed nor interrupted by any difference, but rather is itself every difference, as also their supersession; it pulsates within itself but does not move, inwardly vibrates, yet is at rest . . . . The different moments of *self-sundering* and of becoming *self-identical* are therefore likewise only this movement of *self-supersession*" (*PS* 100–1). The model for what Hegel means by infinity is self-consciousness (*Selbstbewüsstein*), which he characterizes thus: "I distinguish myself from myself, and in doing so I am directly aware that what is distinguished from myself is not different [from me]. I, the selfsame being, repel myself from myself; but what is posited as distinct from me, or as unlike me, is immediately, in being so distinguished, not a distinction for me" (*PS* 102).

But how do these claims about the dialectical relationship between the finite and the true infinite bear on religion and on our conception of God? Hegel is quite explicit.

> The finite is therefore an essential moment of the infinite in the nature of God; and it may consequently be said that God is the very being who finitizes himself, who posits determinations within himself. God creates a world, that is he wills a world, he thinks a world, and determines himself – outside him[self] there is nothing to determine; that is he determines himself, he posits for himself an other over against himself so that there is God and there is the world – they are two. In this relationship God himself is held fast as the finite over against another finite, but the truth is that this world is only an appearance in which he possesses himself. Without the moment of finitude there is no life, no subjectivity, no living God. God creates, he is active: therein lies the distinguishing, and with distinction the moment of finitude is posited. The subsistence of the finite, however, must be sublated once more. On this view there are two kinds of infinity, the true infinite, and the merely bad infinite of the understanding. Thus the finite is a moment of the divine life. (i. 307–8)

This passage makes clear the equiprimordial nature – to use a Heideggerian expression – and the interdependence of the finite and the infinite. Far from denigrating the finite in the face of the infinite (God), Hegel is asserting just how essential the moment of finitude is. ("Without the moment of finitude there is no life, no subjectivity, no living God.") Hegel also acknowledges that there is a proper place for making a distinction between God and the world. There is a truth implicit in the conception of the infinite that sets it over against what is finite (created). But the most important point is that we must not reify this distinction into an ontological divide. We must recognize that the finite is a *moment* in the divine life, or eternal truth, just as we must recognize that the infinite itself is only an empty, bare abstraction unless it is understood as necessarily finitizing itself in its determinations. In short, we can "read" Hegel both forwards and backwards – from the perspective of the finite and from the perspective of the true infinite. From the perspective of the finite (especially my own finitude), I must necessarily come to the realization that the true infinite is implicit in what I am, and that when I fully actualize myself, I am identical with the true infinite. But we can also read it the other way around. The infinite itself is nothing other than the total manifestation of its finite moments, which are always superseding themselves. In classical terms, there is no ontological divide between transcendence and immanence.

This is an exquisite example of Hegel's systematic ambiguity. If we emphasize that God is nothing other than the totality of his finite manifestations, then we see the basis for interpreting Hegel as some sort of pantheist. If we stress that there is no distinction between God and the world, then we can see the basis for claiming that he is really an atheist, because there is no God who stands outside, and over against, the world. We can also see why some left Hegelians have claimed that spirit (*Geist*) is "really" just Hegel's way of referring to a fully realized humanity (*Menschlichkeit*). They have argued that if there is no ontological transcendence, that if "God" becomes completely immanent in the thought and deeds of human beings, then, in the final analysis, we can dispense with the signifier "God" altogether and restrict ourselves to referring to humanity. So too, if there is no ultimate difference between the truth that is revealed to us by faith and what we can learn by thinking (*Denken*) and reason (*Vernunft*), then all allegedly religious truth claims must be validated by reason. But if this is so, then, despite Hegel's occasional claims to the contrary, it is reason (*Vernunft*) and reason alone that properly becomes our final court of appeal. These contradictory readings cannot be resolved simply by appealing to appropriate texts, for the issue will always turn on how we read or interpret those texts. No doubt, Hegel would claim – and many of his commentators *have* claimed – these contradictory interpretations are one-sided. But I do not see that this settles the matter. The systematic ambiguity is intrinsic to Hegel's dialectical mode of thinking, which self-consciously seeks to encompass contradictory moments within a single totality.

When we come to the realization that the true infinite is already implicit in the finite, "we emancipate ourselves from the bogey of the antithesis between finite and infinite" – the bogey that is let loose when we are
told that "it is presumptuous for the finite to want to grasp the infinite"
(i. 309). When Hegel reaches this stage in his thinking, he does not restrain his biting polemic against those who claim that it is a sign of Christian humility to renounce a true *knowledge* of God.

> What a bogey! As if it were presumption to want to know the affirmative
> nature of God. We must decisively throw off this bogey through insight into
> what the real situation is regarding definitions of this kind, and regarding
> this antithesis of finitude and infinity.
>   The other form that runs counter to the affirmative knowledge of God is
> subjective untruth, which maintains the finite for itself, confessing its vanity,
> yet still retaining this acknowledged vanity and making it the absolute.
>   This vanity of self-preserving subjectivity, this I, we cast away from us
> when we sink ourselves in the content, in the matter at hand, and recognize
> ourselves in it, since we are then in earnest about this vanity; we renounce it
> in the cognition and recognition of the being that is in and for itself. (i. 310)

The relationship between the finite and the true infinite is dialectical.
Consequently, the finite is at once negated, affirmed, and sublated in the
true infinite. In the 1827 lectures Hegel gives a succinct statement of his
dialectical account.

> Genuine transition does not consist in change, in perennial alteration. Instead
> *the genuine other of the finite is the infinite*, and this is not bare negation of the finite
> but is affirmative, is being. That is the quite simple consideration involved
> here. This affirmative process is the process of our spirit; it brings itself about
> unconsciously within our spirit; but philosophy is having the consciousness of
> it. We bring the same thing to pass when we raise ourselves up to God. Thus
> the infinite itself is at first something finite or negative. The second [moment]
> is that it is something affirmative. There is a progression through different
> determinations, and it is by no means an external one but is rather necessity
> itself. This necessity is the deed of our spirit. (L 171)

Evil and finitude

It has been necessary to sketch the dialectic of the finite and the infinite
because this is the perspective from which Hegel characterizes evil. But
before turning to his discussion of evil, I want to pause and reflect on
how antithetical Hegel's conclusions are to the spirit and the letter of
Kant. Kant's Critical Philosophy presupposes and rests upon a sharp,

rigid distinction between the finite and the infinite. Most of Kant's philosophical distinctions – including understanding (*Verstand*) and reason
(*Vernunft*), phenomena and noumena, the conditioned and the unconditioned, knowledge and faith – can be related to the distinction between
the finite and the infinite. Kant's entire critical project can be viewed as a
meditation on what it means to be a limited, finite rational being who
must be distinguished from what is genuinely infinite and unconditioned.
But if Hegel is right, Kant never gets beyond the bad, or spurious, infinite.
His philosophy, as it stands, is not only radically incomplete, it is false,
and it leaves us with unresolved contradictions. Kant fails to see the ineluctable consequences of his own critical insights. He gets stuck in his
antinomies (despite his claims to resolve these antinomies), and fails to
realize that "*everything is inherently contradictory*" – that this law expresses the
truth (*SL* 439). This is the principle of all self-movement. "Something is
therefore alive only in so far as it contains contradiction within it, and
moreover is this power to hold and endure the contradiction within it" (*SL*
440). Kant fails to realize, or so Hegel claims, that "speculative thinking,"
the medium of genuine philosophy, "consists solely in the fact that thought
holds fast contradiction, and in it, its own self" (*SL* 440). If "revision," as
Harold Bloom defines it, consists in "fighting" and contesting the supremacy of one's spiritual predecessors, then Hegel's agon with Kant is an
exemplar of this contest.

But what, precisely, is the relation of evil to Hegel's distinction between
the spurious infinite and the true infinite? We gain an essential clue when
we turn to Hegel's discussion of "Determinate Religion" – the section of
his *Lectures on the Philosophy of Religion* where he discusses specific historical
religions. There he refers to "Oriental dualism." This is the dualism that
maintains that there are two fundamental oppositional principles, "the
realm of the good and that of evil." "The good is indeed the true and the
powerful, but it is in conflict with evil, so that evil stands over against it
and persists as an absolute principle. Evil ought surely to be overcome, to
be counterbalanced; but what ought to be is not. 'Ought' is a force that
cannot make itself effective, it is this weakness or impotence" (*L* 300–1).
But according to Hegel, such a dualism – one that lies at the heart of
many other, more pallid forms of dualism – is totally unacceptable. In
Hegelian terminology, this basic dualism is false and must be sublated.

> Religion and philosophy as a whole turn upon this dualism. This is the concern
> of religion and of philosophy – the distinction grasped in its complete universal-
> ity. In the mode of thought this antithesis attains the universality that is proper
> to it. Dualism is a form [of thought] even today; but when we speak of it today,
> it is in meager and delicate forms. Whenever we take the finite to be auto-
> nomous, so that the infinite and the finite stand opposed to one another, so

that the infinite has no part in the finite and the latter cannot cross over to the infinite, we have the same dualism as the antithesis of Ahriman and Ormazd, or that of Manichaeism – except that we lack the thought or the heart to represent these antitheses to ourselves [honestly]. *The finite, in the broadest sense maintaining itself as finite and autonomous, over against and thereby in conflict with the infinite or the universal, is what is evil.* (L 301, emphasis added)

This is a striking and extremely controversial claim. Consider its provocative consequences. The dualism of good and evil is not just one basic dualism among others. Hegel is suggesting that *all* philosophic dualisms are "meager" reflections of this fundamental antithesis of good and evil. He also makes the ambitious claim that religion and philosophy as a whole turn on this fundamental dualism. Evil is defined with reference to the antithesis of the finite and the spurious infinite. At this point, all sorts of questions arise. Why does Hegel characterize evil in this way? How does this description of evil relate to more traditional moral and religious understandings of evil? If this false opposition between the finite and the spurious infinite defines evil, does this mean that evil is sublated in the true infinite? What are the consequences of this conception of evil when we turn to the ordinary examples of evil that we encounter in our everyday lives? In order to answer these (and closely related questions), we must probe further into the meaning of evil.

Hegel's *Lectures on the Philosophy of Religion* is not limited to a discussion of the *concept* of religion, but seeks to bring out the truth (and falsity) of historical religions, culminating in what he calls the "consummate religion" (*vollendete Religion*) – that is, Christianity.[12] In the context of his discussion of Christianity, Hegel develops his distinctive (and highly selective) interpretation of the story of the Fall as it is told in Genesis. In his 1827 lectures, he introduces this discussion by first considering what he calls "natural humanity," taking up two antithetical views of the natural condition of human beings: "humanity is by nature good," and "humanity is by nature evil." Hegel's starting point is reminiscent of Kant's discussion of these antithetical claims in his *Religion*.

At this point we encounter two opposed definitions, both at once. The first is that *humanity is by nature good*. Its universal, substantial essence is good; far from being split within itself, its essence or concept is that it is by nature what is harmonious and at peace with itself. Opposed to this is the second characterization: *humanity is by nature evil* – that is, its natural, substantial aspect is evil. These are the antitheses that are present for us from the outset for external consideration: sometimes one view has been in vogue, and sometimes the other. It should be added, moreover, that this is not just the way that *we* view the situation; it is human beings [generally] who have this knowledge of themselves, of how they are constituted and what their definition is. (*L* 438)

As we might expect, it turns out that both these claims – when stated as abstract claims – turn out to be false. If "by nature," we intend to refer to human beings in their natural state before they become fully conscious of themselves, then humanity by nature is neither good nor evil. Hegel affirms that there is no good or evil without cognition or knowledge (*Erkenntnis*). It is only a spiritual being that is capable of such knowledge. We can say, however, that humanity is *implicitly* good. "It is [indeed] essential to say that humanity is good: human beings are implicitly spirit and rationality, created in and after the image of God [Gen. 1: 26–7]. God is good, and human beings as spirit are the mirror of God; they too, are *implicitly* good" (*L* 438). But to say that human beings are implicitly good is not to say that they are *actually* good. They are not yet good in and for themselves (*anundfürsichsein*); they are not yet what they ought to be. There is a lack, or deficiency, in this natural condition that needs to be overcome. But human beings do not immediately pass over into becoming good. A necessary stage in this development is one of cleavage (*Entzweiung*), or rupture. "It is correct that human beings are good by nature; but with that, one has only said something one-sided. It is this passing beyond the natural state of humanity, beyond its implicit being, that for the first time constitutes the cleavage within humanity; it is what posits the cleavage" (*L* 439).

We can now see the basis for saying that "Humanity is by nature evil." This means that insofar as humanity remains in a natural state, it is evil. "When humanity exists only according to nature [*nur nach der Natur ist*], it is evil" (*L* 440). There is an ambiguity in this formulation that needs to be clarified. We can refer to the natural condition of humanity *on the way* to becoming self-consciously spiritual. From this perspective, there is nothing intrinsically evil about this natural condition; on the contrary, it is implicitly good. But if human beings *will* to remain in this natural condition, then they are evil. Hegel makes this clear when he says, "the person who follows passions and instincts, and remains in the sphere of desire, the one whose law is that of natural immediacy, is the natural human being. At the same time, a human being in the natural state is one who wills, and since the content of the natural will is only instinct and inclination, this person is evil" (*L* 440). Although Hegel formulates his claim differently from Kant, he substantially agrees with Kant that there is nothing intrinsically evil about our natural passions and inclinations. Like Kant, Hegel also affirms that evil arises only with *willing*. In his *Lectures on the Philosophy of World History*, Hegel says:

This is the hallmark of the sublime and absolute destiny of man – that he knows what good and evil are, and that it is his will which chooses either one or the other. In short, he can be held responsible, for good as well as for evil, and not just for this or that particular circumstance and for everything around him and within him, but also for the good and evil which are inherent in his individual freedom.[13]

There is something fundamentally misleading in asking the question: "Is humanity good by nature or evil by nature?"

> It is false to ask whether humanity is only good by nature or only evil. That is a false way of posing the question. In the same way, it is superficial to say that humanity is both good and evil equally. Implicitly, according to its concept, human being is good; but this implicitness is a one-sidedness, and the one-sidedness is marked by the fact that the actual subject, the "this" is only a natural will. Thus both of them, both good and evil, are posited, but essentially in contradiction, in such a way that each of them presupposes the other. It is not that only one of them is [there], but instead we have both of them in this relation of being opposed to each other. (*L* 441–2)[14]

It is against this background that Hegel offers his interpretation of the biblical story of the Fall. Hegel emphasizes the *cognitive* dimension of religion; religion is fundamentally a form of knowledge (*Erkenntnis*) – although limited to representation (*Vorstellung*). Even when Hegel takes up the role of feeling (*Gefühl*) and devotion (*Andacht*), he is primarily concerned with their cognitive character.[15] "Human beings," Hegel tells us "become evil by cognizing, or as the Bible represents it, they have eaten of the tree of knowledge of good and evil [Gen. 3: 5–6]. Through this story cognition, intelligence, and theoretical capacity come into closer relationship with the will, and the nature of evil comes to more precise expression" (iii. 205).

> It is cognition that first posits the antithesis in which evil is to be found. Animals, stones, and plants are not evil: evil first occurs within the sphere of rupture or cleavage; it is the consciousness of being-for-myself in opposition to external nature, but also in opposition to the objective [reality] that is inwardly universal in the sense of the concept or of the rational will. It is through this separation that I exist for myself for the first time, and that is where the evil lies. Abstractly, being evil means singularizing myself in a way that cuts me off from the universal (which is the rational, the laws, the determinations of spirit). (iii. 206)

When Hegel says that "being evil means singularizing myself in a way that cuts me off from the universal," he is reiterating his point that evil arises in the opposition between myself as a finite being and the infinite that stands over and against me. But he adds something extremely important here. This singularizing of myself, this cleavage ("where evil lies") is a *necessary* stage in the development of the I, in its development from its natural state to becoming truly human, its spiritual condition. I become conscious of my being-for-myself in opposition to something that I take to be other than me.

The theme of diremption – self-diremption as internal cleavage – reverberates throughout Hegel's philosophy. It is already the dominant theme of the *Phenomenology of Spirit*, where Hegel speaks of the "highway of despair." Consequently, there is nothing accidental or merely contingent about this source of evil. "Inasmuch as it is spirit, humanity has to progress to this antithesis of being-for-self as such. . . . In this separation being-for-self is posited and evil has its seat; here is the source of all wrong, but also the point where reconciliation has its ultimate source. It is what produces the disease and is at the same time the source of health" (iii. 206). This means that the eruption of evil as cleavage and self-diremption is not only a necessary stage in the development of humanity; but in this self-diremption there is already an anticipation of reconciliation, the sublation of evil. Self-diremption not only gives rise to evil; it is necessary for the overcoming or sublation of evil. We must not think of this as merely a contingent historical movement; reconciliation is *always already* implicit in this self-diremption. This dialectical development parallels what we have already learned about the movement from the finite to the true infinite. The true infinite is already implicit in our finitude, but we must pass through the stage of cleavage (the spurious infinite) in order to realize true infinity. The eruption of evil and the ultimate reconciliation achieved do not simply "parallel" this dialectical movement; they are *this* dialectical movement.

We can see why Hegel's Religion Lectures – and indeed his entire system – can be read as a theodicy. If we take the essential impulse of theodicy (broadly understood) as the desire to give an account of evil whereby we can reconcile what appears to be evil with the reality of a (Christian) God, then this is precisely what Hegel is claiming to do. Even if one thinks that, properly deciphered, Hegel is really (as Kojève claims) an a-theist, we still have a theodicy, albeit a secular one, where evil is understood and justified as a necessary dialectical moment in the progressive development of humanity.

Adam's Fall

Let us turn to Hegel's interpretation of the Biblical story of the Fall. In his handwritten manuscript, which served as the basis for his lectures, Hegel points out some of the outstanding features of the story, as well as some of the apparent inconsistencies that appear in this "most excellent chain of consistency." (a) Adam is not prohibited from eating the fruit of any tree, but from the tree of the knowledge of good and evil. This, Hegel states, is the major point of the story, because "it is not a question of just any tree and ordinary fruit; [the allusion to] good and evil leads us at once into an entirely different region. These are absolute, substantial characteristics of spirit, not something like eating an apple" (iii. 105). (b) Although it is forbidden to eat of the tree of knowledge of good and evil, "yet this knowledge is what constitutes the nature of spirit – otherwise the man is a beast" (iii. 105). (c) The serpent promises that this knowledge will make Adam like God. This is the temptation of evil. But subsequently, what the serpent promises is said by God, "'Behold, Adam has become like one of us, knowing good and evil' (Gen. 3: 22). Here it is placed on the lips of God himself that precisely knowledge – the specific knowledge of good and evil in general, that is – constitutes the divine in humanity" (iii. 105). Hegel seizes upon what he takes to be contradictory (in "this most excellent chain of consistency"), because this is the way in which spirit develops and realizes itself. So he declares: "Just as the necessity of [our gaining this] knowledge is contradicted, so our knowledge itself appears to be contradicted by the fact [d] 'that punishment is incurred by this knowledge and is to take the form of physical necessity – {and of mortality, [which is] a necessary consequence of finitude.} {[e] And [yet mortality is] also not [to be viewed] as punishment: 'Lest he eat also of the tree of life . . . .' [cf. Gen. 3: 22]" (iii. 105).

This is a highly tendentious reading of the story of the Fall.[16] One might well criticize Hegel for imposing his own categories upon the story. But, consistent with his distinction between representation (*Vorstellung*), characteristic of the language of the Bible, and conceptual thinking, characteristic of speculative philosophy, Hegel declares that "it must be observed, quite generally that a deep speculative content cannot be portrayed in its true and proper form in images and mere representations, and hence it essentially cannot be portrayed in this mode without contradiction" (iii. 105). It is speculative thinking alone that comprehends the truth represented by the biblical story of the Fall.

> The deep insight of this story is that the eternal history of humanity, to be consciousness, is contained in it: (a) the original divine idea, the image [of God]; (b) the emergence of consciousness, knowledge of good and evil, {and at the same time responsibility;} (c) [the knowledge of good and evil emerges] as something that both ought not to be, i.e., it ought not to remain as knowledge, and also the means by which humanity is divine. Knowledge heals the wound that it itself is. (iii. 106)

Hegel's description of the Fall as the "eternal history of humanity" provides yet another perspective on evil and its sublation. We have seen how closely Hegel links knowledge (*Erkenntnis*), cleavage or rupture (*Entzweiung*), and evil (*Böse*). Peter Hodgson, the editor of the English edition of the *Lectures*, gives a lucid statement of their relationship.

> Cognitive knowledge (*Erkenntnis*) entails an act of judgment or primal division (*Ur-Teil*); it thus issues in separation, cleavage, rupture in two (*Ent-zwei-ung*) . . . . This cleavage or estrangement (*Entfremdung*) – the words are quite similar – is not, strictly speaking, in itself evil but rather is the inherent condition of finite spirit just because it is consciousness and cognizes, but finitely, that is, is unable finally to overcome the divisions posited by its acts of knowing. It is the *precondition* or *occasion* of evil, however, since evil entails the conscious or deliberate actualization of the state of separation, the choice to live in isolation from the depths of spirit, to cut oneself off from both the universal and the particular, to gratify immediate desires, to exist "according to nature" (*nach der Natur*). Yet self-rupture or self-estrangement gives rise not only to evil but also to the need for reconciliation, which may be seen when estrangement is associated with the anguish (*Schmerz*) of Jewish religion and the misery or unhappiness (*Unglück*) of Hellenistic-Roman culture. (*L* 65)

Hodgson adds a subtle, but an extremely important, point to our understanding of Hegel's account of evil. The cleavage (*Entzweiung*) of judgment is not in itself (intrinsically) evil. It is, rather, the *precondition* or occasion of evil, in the sense that, strictly speaking, evil results from the *conscious* or deliberate choice to remain in this state of separation, to insist on the rupture between the finite and the infinite, "to live in isolation from the depths of spirit."[17]

In the *Lectures*, Hegel tells us that self-rupture and self-estrangement give rise to evil and to the need for reconciliation. The self-estrangement takes two forms. "On the one hand, it is the antithesis of evil as such, the fact that it is humanity itself that is evil: this is the *antithesis vis-à-vis God*. On the other hand, it is the *antithesis vis-à-vis the world*, the fact that humanity exists in a state of rupture from the world: this is unhappiness or misery, the cleavage viewed from the other side" (*L* 447). The first form, Hegel calls anguish (*Schmerz*), and the second form, unhappiness (*Unglück*). In the background of this analysis of self-estrangement is the famous discussion of "Unhappy Consciousness" in the *Phenomenology of Spirit*. Unhappy consciousness is not simply the name of one stage (*Gestalt*) in the development of self-consciousness. It is a recurring motif in the *Phenomenology*, and indeed in all of Hegel's writings. Stephen Crites makes this point vividly when he writes:

It soon becomes apparent that the unhappy consciousness is not the afflic-
tion of some person in particular, or of an identifiable community, or
generation, or historical epoch. It is a universal crisis of self-conscious life
that occurs everywhere and always whenever spirit is being born. This
unhappiness is the travail of conscious life giving birth to spirit. It is suffered
not once but many times historically. In fact it is not so much a historical
phenomenon as the precondition of self-consciously historical life, appear-
ing in many different guises. Every person, every culture preserves at least
a dark memory of this unhappiness or a dark premonition of it on the
horizon, or both.[18]

In the *Lectures*, Hegel links this anguished experience of self-diremption
with evil.

> Human beings are inwardly conscious that in their innermost being they
> are a contradiction, and have therefore an infinite *anguish* concerning them-
> selves. Anguish is present only where there is opposition to what ought to
> be, to an affirmative. What is no longer in itself an affirmative also has no
> contradiction, no anguish. Anguish is precisely the element of negativity in
> the affirmative, meaning that within itself the affirmative is self-contradic-
> tory and wounded. This anguish is thus one moment of evil. Evil merely on
> its own account is an abstraction; it *is* only in antithesis to the good, and
> since it is present in the unity of the subject, the latter is split, and this
> cleavage is infinite anguish. If the consciousness of the good, the infinite
> demand of the good, is not likewise present in the subject itself, in its
> innermost being, then no anguish is present and evil itself is only an empty
> nothingness, for it *is* only in this antithesis. (*L* 447–8)

Good and evil are dialectically related; there is no good without evil and
no evil without good. Without the consciousness of the good, then "evil
itself is only an empty nothingness"; but without the consciousness of evil,
the good would also be an empty nothingness. Without the dialectical
opposition of good and evil, there would be no anguish. And without the
experience (*Erfahrung*) of this anguish, human beings would merely be
beasts. Spirit would never be born. Spirit may well heal all wounds without leaving any scars, but evil is a *necessary* stage in the realization of spirit.
Furthermore, this extreme infinite anguish presupposes not only a unity in
self-consciousness (otherwise self-diremption would be unintelligible), but
also a unity in God, and ultimately a unity – an identity – of self-consciousness and God. This is the true infinite.[19]

> Evil and anguish can be infinite only when the good or God is known as *one*
> God, as a pure, spiritual God. It is only when the good is this pure unity,
> only when we have faith in *one* God, and only in connection with such a

faith, that the negative can and must advance to this determination of evil and negation can advance to this universality. One side of this cleavage becomes apparent in this way, through the elevation of humanity to the pure, spiritual unity of God. This anguish and this consciousness are the condition of the absorption [*Vertiefung*] of humanity itself, and likewise into the negative movement of cleavage, of evil. This is an objective, inward absorption into evil; inward absorption of an affirmative kind is absorption into the pure unity of God. (*L* 448)

The necessity and justification of evil?

There is something at once majestic yet profoundly unsatisfying about Hegel's dialectical account of good and evil. Given the overall ambitions of his systematic philosophy, Hegel has provided an elegant account of the source and sublation of evil. Many traditional "solutions" to the problem of evil are compelled to deny the reality of evil as something positive because there seems to be no way to reconcile the existence of evil with the existence of an omnipotent, omniscient, and beneficent God. If we say that God is infinitely good – the very standard for what goodness is – then we must ultimately reject the ontological reality of evil. Classically, from St Augustine on, it has been claimed that God is not responsible for the evil that results from the misuse of our free will. God has given human beings this great gift of free will; it is as willing beings that we are created in the image of God. If human beings choose to misuse this free will, they must bear the responsibility for doing so. It is blasphemous to blame God for the sins of humans. But this "solution" has its own perplexities and aporias, especially when we also assert that God is omniscient and omnipotent. If God is our creator, and if he is truly omniscient, and consequently knows what human beings will do with their free will, can we really say that he is not responsible for creating a creature that commits evil deeds? I am not interested here in pursuing the various strategies that have been adopted to resolve such perplexities.[20] Rather, I want to emphasize that Hegel undercuts these traditional aporias because he conceives of humanity, God, and their relation to each other in a radically different manner. It is only when we think of the antithesis of good and evil as a fixed, rigid dichotomy that these aporias arise. But for Hegel, good and evil are dynamically and dialectically related. There is no good without evil, and there is no evil without good. This is just as true for finite human beings as it is for God who is infinite. We must not think of this opposition as some sort of disguised dualism. It is, rather, the rejection of all forms of dualism (including the dualism of humanity and God). Whether we focus on the development of finite human beings in their spiritual journey or on the becoming of an infinite God, the manifestation of evil is *necessary* for the concrete realization of an infinite *Geist* in which evil is sublated. The condition for evil in human beings is the self-diremption, or internal cleavage, whereby they make the transition from a natural condition to a fully human one. But we can also say that God as infinite Spirit only becomes manifest by self-diremption. The difference between God and human beings is that (*some*) human beings get stuck; they reify the distinction between the finite and the infinite; they willfully turn it into an unbridgeable chasm. They stubbornly refuse to move beyond this false dualism. "Finitude is the most stubborn category of the understanding" (*SL* 129). Hegel is certainly aware of the profound temptation to succumb to this reification of the finite and the spurious infinite. When he describes the journey undertaken in his *Phenomenology of Spirit* as the "highway of despair," he is acknowledging how, over and over again, human beings experience the pain and anguish of this self-diremption, and how they are tempted to reify it. This is why, in his classic commentary, Jean Hippolyte, begins his discussion of the section dealing with unhappy consciousness by declaring, "Unhappy consciousness is the fundamental theme of the *Phenomenology*."[21]

But in the depths of this despair and anguish, there is already present the promise of sublation and reconciliation. Even to speak of "promise" here can be misleading if we think of a promise as something that can be fulfilled only in the future.[22] The language "of dialectical movement" can mislead us if we think of this movement as a straightforward temporal sequence. The reconciliation involved in the sublation of evil is already presupposed in the anguish of self-diremption. Hegel is not "explaining away" evil. Good and evil are equiprimordial.

The failure to appreciate this essential feature of Hegel's dialectical thinking (which, unfortunately, is all too common) results in the grossest distortions and caricatures of Hegel. Ironically, Hegel even has an explanation for why there is such a great temptation to misread and caricature him. If we are stubbornly wedded to a notion of abstract negation as the only type of negation, and to a fixed rigid opposition between what is true and false, then we will think that the sublation of evil means the complete obliteration of evil. But sublation (*Aufhebung*) does not obliterate or eliminate what is sublated; what is sublated is always preserved, although in an altered form. In this sense, evil never is (or can be) completely obliterated.

I want to return to my opening remarks about the systematic ambiguity of Hegel's philosophy, for it has direct consequences for interpreting the dialectical relationship of good and evil. Hegel himself doesn't hesitate to characterize his philosophy as a theodicy. In his *Lectures on the Philosophy of World History*, he states:

[Our] investigation can be seen as a theodicy, a justification of the ways of God (such as Leibniz attempted in his own metaphysical manner, but using categories which were as yet abstract and indeterminate). It should enable us to comprehend all the ills of the world, including the existence of evil, so that thinking spirit may yet be reconciled with the negative aspects of existence; and it is in world history that we encounter the sum total of evil
. . . .

A reconciliation of the kind just described can only be achieved through a knowledge of the affirmative side of history, in which the negative is reduced to a subordinate position and transcended altogether. In other words, we must first of all know what the ultimate design of the world is, and secondly, we must see that this design has been realized and that evil has not been able to maintain a position of equality beside it.[23]

Despite this explicit reference to theodicy and God, it is not difficult to understand why the controversy between right, center, and left Hegelians broke out even before his death. Hegel's systematic ambiguity invites a humanistic, and even an atheistic, interpretation. It is Hegel who stresses the (ultimate) identity of humanity and God. It is Hegel who is always challenging any dichotomy between the finite and the infinite, between immanence and transcendence. It is Hegel who tells us that there is no ultimate conflict between faith and reason, and that religion and philosophy reveal the same eternal truth. But it is these claims that make many orthodox Christian believers wary of Hegel, because they take it as fundamental to their faith that God is transcendent and infinitely beyond all human finitude. We can well understand how Ludwig Feuerbach, who began as a committed disciple of Hegel, became one of his severest critics, and developed a humanistic, anthropological interpretation of the essence of Christianity. Even if one concludes that the "God-talk" in Hegel is dispensable, that the real "secret" of Hegel is his esoteric atheistic humanism, this does not significantly alter the dialectical account of good and evil. Instead of reading Hegel's narrative as the story of the self-realization of God through self-diremption whereby Absolute Spirit is fully realized, we would read this narrative as the progressive self-development of humanity (*Menschlichkeit*). But the same "logic" is at work on either of these readings. Evil turns out to be a necessary moment in this development – a development in which it is sublated (*aufgehoben*).

Thus far I have sought to probe the meaning of Hegel's dialectical account of good and evil, to defend him from common distortions and caricatures, and to highlight the originality and power of his doctrine. But I have also indicated that, despite its sweeping majesty, his account is profoundly unsatisfactory and raises numerous problems. I want to begin my critique with an observation regarding the texts of the *Lectures on the Philosophy of Religion*. Neither in Hegel's own handwritten manuscript, nor in any of the lecture notes by his students that are the basis for the reconstruction of the *Lectures*, do we find any sustained discussion of examples of evil. The closest we come is his account of the biblical story of the Fall. But here, as we have noted, Hegel highlights those aspects of the story that are shaped by, and support, his philosophy. Evil arises from the stubborn, willful reification of the abstract distinction between the finite and the spurious infinite. We can fill out some concrete details of what evil means by focusing on the ways in which self-centered individuals set themselves against anything that is universal, anything that transcends their immediate egoistic interests. In this respect, despite his polemic against Kant, Hegel's understanding of moral evil is not so very different from Kant's. It is the willful assertion of individual egoism (what Kant calls "self-love") in opposition to what is objectively universal. But the paucity of any discussion of the varieties and concrete manifestations of evil makes us pause. Hegel does not shy away from dealing with numerous concrete historical examples of different religions, so why does he not turn his attention to concrete historical forms of evil?

A defender of Hegel might retort that this is not a serious omission. Philosophy is not to be confused with empirical description. Philosophy is intended to provide the categories that are required to comprehend what is good and evil. In the *Lectures*, we are dealing with the concept of religion, its historical determinations, and its ultimate truth. But I find such a retort a bit too glib. After all, the point of a philosophical inquiry is to enable us to comprehend what there is, and such comprehension requires the ability to make essential discriminations. So it is always fair to ask – even on Hegelian grounds – whether a concept of good and evil enables us to sort out what we, phenomenologically, take to be good and evil. This does not mean that a philosophical account is restricted to making sense of what we commonly take to be evil. But, as Aristotle observed long ago, and Hegel reaffirms, the task of philosophy is to comprehend and explain phenomena – not to explain them away. Yet when we seriously attempt to grasp how Hegel's dialectical analysis of evil can help us to make sense of the evils that have occurred in the twentieth century – Auschwitz, the genocide in Rwanda, the many instances of humiliation, sadistic behavior, fanatical terrorist attacks, and the gratuitous infliction of human suffering that we witness daily – it seems strained and artificial to classify them as instances of the reification of the antithesis of the finite and the spurious infinite.

William Desmond sharply states the limits of dialectical thought.

Am I proposing the end or cessation of philosophical thinking? Does the matter [of evil] so stun and paralyse philosophy that no further thought is possible? Not at all. Though evil and forgiveness are others to dialectical thought that philosophy can never entirely encapsulate, the deepest point is this: about such recalcitrant others philosophy, in fact, can never stop thinking. The point is not to give up on thinking of these others, but dialectic will only take us so far. Dialectical philosophy comes to a limit that exceeds its thought. And we cannot but try to think that excess and that limit. A perplexity of thought arises that makes mind sleepless.[24]

The appeal to concrete examples rarely settles any philosophic issue, for the question can always be raised as to how we are to interpret these phenomena. Nevertheless, the gap between Hegel's sophisticated analysis of evil and our experience of evil in the world raises fundamental philosophic questions about the adequacy of his interpretation. Hegel's most serious deficiency becomes evident in what appears to be his greatest strength. I want to show this in what may seem to be an indirect manner, but one that will actually bring us to the heart of Hegel's philosophy.

Let us consider what Jean Hippolyte says about the relation of evil, sin, and forgiveness in his classic commentary on the *Phenomenology*. He cites the famous passage in the *Phenomenology* from which the first epigraph of this chapter is taken: "The wounds of spirit heal without leaving scars. The facts are not imperishable, but spirit absorbs them within itself, and the aspect of specificity that is present in facts, either as intention or as its [existing] negativity and its limit in the element of Dasein, disappears immediately."[25] In his commentary on this passage, Hippolyte writes:

> The whole long history of errors that human development presents and that the *Phenomenology* traces is indeed a fall, but we must learn that this fall is part of the absolute itself, that it is a moment of total truth. Absolute self cannot be expressed without this negativity: it is an absolute "yes" only through saying "no" to a "no," only by overcoming a necessary negation. Unity is only realizable by the continual conflict and by perpetual surpassing.[26]

Hippolyte also cites the perceptive remark of Josiah Royce in his *Lectures on Modern Idealism*: "The true life of spirit resides in this surpassing, not in the consciousness of sin which is always located within limits . . . nor in the consciousness of a beyond which is always transcendent, but rather in the consciousness of the forgiveness of sins, of a reconciliation through opposition."[27] These comments are made about the

Phenomenology, but they are equally applicable to the *Lectures on the Philosophy of Religion*. Hippolyte notes that the same basic idea is expressed in the *Lectures* in a sharper form.

> The determination that everyone remains what he is lies in the realm of finitude. He has done evil, therefore he is evil, evil is in him as his quality. But in morality and still more in religion, spirit is known to be free, as itself affirmative, so that this limit within man, which goes as far as evil, is a nothingness for the infinity of spirit. Spirit can manage things so that what has happened has not happened. Action does indeed remain in the memory, but spirit rids itself of it – the finite, evil in general, is negated.[28]

There is something deeply moving (and very Christian) about this passage. It is a glorious affirmation of ultimate reconciliation and Christian redemption. Furthermore, we can relate this yearning for unification and reconciliation to Hegel's own life experiences, and to what he felt was the most serious crisis of modernity. Jürgen Habermas tells us, "The motives for a philosophy of unification can be traced back to the crisis experiences of the young Hegel. They stand behind the conviction that reason must be brought forward as the reconciling power against the positive elements of an age torn asunder."[29] "By criticizing the philosophic oppositions – nature and spirit, sensibility and understanding, understanding and reason, theoretical and practical reason, judgment and imagination, I and non-I, finite and infinite, knowledge and faith – he wants to respond to the crisis of the diremption of life itself."[30]

Yet it is this very feature of Hegel's thinking that is so troubling and unacceptable. If Hegel had claimed that Spirit (*Geist*) heals itself, we might have taken him to mean that in the face of evil, it is always possible to respond and achieve some sort of overcoming of evil. But it is the much more extreme claim that Spirit heals itself and *does not leave any scars behind* that is unacceptable. For this entails that, in the final analysis, we can justify – indeed, we *must* justify – the existence of evil, including the evil epitomized by Auschwitz. (Later we will see that it is the absolute refusal to make this dialectical move that leads Levinas to claim that the problem of evil, "after Auschwitz," is a problem that arises after the "end of theodicy."[31]) Beginning with Hegel's contemporary, Schelling, moving through Nietzsche and Freud, and culminating with thinkers such as Arendt, Jonas, and Levinas, there is a sustained critique of this dialectical *reconciliation* of good and evil.[32]

Is it true that Spirit heals without leaving any scars? This question doesn't disappear even if we think, as some left Hegelians have suggested, that wherever Hegel speaks of "Spirit" (*Geist*), we should replace it with the term humanity (*Menschlichkeit*). For the same problem is posed in another register. Is it really true that in the progressive development of humanity all evils are (or can be) sublated? Hegel is always emphasizing ruptures, cleavages, and diremptions. He is fully aware of how violent and painful these can be in the life of an individual and the life of a people. But for all his insistence on these "ruptures," he is also always telling us that they are only "moments," or stages, in a grand dialectical process in which sublation is always operative. But is this true? Are there not violent ruptures and resistant cleavages that are so extreme, so radical, that they resist sublation? This is the objection that Auschwitz, as the exemplar of the most extreme, radical evil of the twentieth century, compels us to raise against Hegel. There is something hollow, something almost obscene, in thinking that Auschwitz can be interpreted as a necessary moment in the dialectical realization of Spirit or humanity. Here we really do come up against *limits* of dialectical thought. This evil positively *resists* any Hegelian comprehension and reconciliation. William Desmond makes this point when he says that "there is a *gap* between the reality of evil as lived and the concept of evil as thought. There is a *disproportion* between evil as either suffered or done and evil as said to illustrate the structure of rational necessity. Being and thought are not the same here – despite what father Parmenides said about the sameness of *noein* and *esti*, despite its reiteration by Plotinus and others, including Hegel. There is a nondialectical difference between being and understanding."[33]

The question I am raising goes to the very heart of Hegel's philosophy. It is not restricted to his understanding of the dialectic of good and evil – as if this could be separated and extracted from the rest of his philosophy. His understanding of the dialectical movement from the finite through the spurious infinite to the true infinite shapes Hegel's entire approach to the problem of evil. To grasp this movement, we must understand (and accept) Hegel's account of the difference between abstract negation and determinate negation, the identity of the finite and the true infinite, and the claim that the truth is the whole. So, to raise critical questions about the dialectic of good and evil is to raise critical questions about the most fundamental distinctions and themes in Hegel's philosophy.[34]

Hegel against Hegel

We can no longer accept Hegel's dialectical account of good and evil. The abysses, ruptures, and breaks we have experienced are too deep and too unbridgeable for us to believe in the type of sublation and reconciliation that is fundamental for Hegel. But I also think that we need to be wary of

a total rejection of Hegel. There is something extremely important that
we can appropriate from Hegel. Sometimes we have to think *with* a philosopher *against* himself, in order to bring forth what is still vital and
relevant. Read in one way, Hegel stands at the end of a tradition, a
tradition in which the fundamental impulse has been to give an account of
evil such that it can be reconciled with good, and which in religious terms
means reconciling evil with the existence of an all-beneficent God. Hegel
offers a strikingly original solution to the problem of evil. Yet he also
maintains that evil is transformed in the course of this dialectical development. Despite his originality, he still fits (as he himself affirms) within the
traditional project of theodicy. He is still concerned to justify the existence
of evil by showing how evil turns out to be a necessary dialectical moment
in the realization of the true infinite that is always already implicit in
human finitude.

But there is another way of reading or appropriating Hegel. We must
recognize that for Hegel evil is not simply, or exclusively, a religious issue.
Evil manifests itself in morality, ethics, and politics. We experience the
diremptions, ruptures, and cleavages that comprise evil in all aspects of
human life. The existence of concrete evils always presents us with a
challenge. Hegel refuses to ontologize or to reify these cleavages. He
refuses to endorse any suggestion that evil is so fundamental and so ineradicable that there is no possibility of overcoming it. We can read
Hegel, as so many have read him, as setting us the task (*Aufgabe*) of confronting the evil we encounter and seeking to overcome it in ways that are
not merely abstract, but concrete, in the ethical and political institutions
that we develop. Hegel himself never suggests that evil can be completely
eradicated. It is always bursting forth in new guises and new forms. It is
utopian (in the pejorative sense) to think that we can ever reach a stage of
history in which it would even make sense to speak of the elimination of
all evils; but it certainly does make good Hegelian sense to refuse to accept
evil as it presents itself, to reify it in such a way that we stand impotent
before it. I fully realize that to speak of this *Aufgabe* of confronting evil is to
speak in a manner that is not always consonant with Hegel's explicit
statements.[35] This is what I mean when I say that we must think with
Hegel against Hegel. He himself is always emphasizing the struggle in
human encounters with evil, the struggle that is the deepest characteristic
of our historical situatedness.

If we read Hegel against the grain, then it makes good sense to speak of
the task of overcoming concrete evils, even though we realize that there
can be no finality to this task. This is not simply a matter of an abstract
"ought," but requires the concrete transformation of social and political
institutions. Hegel, who characterizes our spiritual path as a "highway of

despair," counsels against the despair that results from standing frozen and impotent before evil, from failure to struggle to overcome it in its many guises.

In another context, I have argued that we should displace Hegel's grand metaphor of *Aufhebung* – his master concept for reconciling ruptures and diremptions – with the metaphors of constellation and force field as Walter Benjamin and Theodor Adorno use them.[36] These alternatives challenge the very idea of a culminating *Aufhebung* that valorizes unity, harmony, integration, wholeness, and totality. They call into question the powerful underlying current of progressive teleology and divine providence that informs and shapes Hegel's philosophy. These alternatives suggest that we need to recognize that there are ruptures and evils that cannot be overcome, that cannot be reconciled (and to which we cannot reconcile ourselves). We must resist what Adorno so incisively characterized as extorted reconciliation. There are wounds that leave *permanent* scars. There are evils that cannot be sublated. We can at once recognize the ways in which evils burst forth in ever-new ways, and at the same time struggle to fight these evils and overcome them. Whether we speak the language of Spirit (*Geist*) or that of humanity (*Menschlichkeit*), this is the task (*Aufgabe*) that most truly defines our spiritual journey – that is, the achievement of our true humanity.

3

Schelling: The Metaphysics of Evil

Where there is no battle there is no life.

Of Human Freedom

In pursuing my inquiry into Kant's concept of radical evil, I noted a deep (unresolved) tension in Kant's moral philosophy, especially in regard to his understanding of the role of freedom in the adoption of evil maxims. According to Kant, we are truly and genuinely free when we follow the moral law, when we do what the categorical imperative requires, when we adopt good maxims (maxims in accord with the objective moral law), and act accordingly. Although we cannot achieve theoretical knowledge of freedom, we can and *must* postulate human freedom. Freedom as spontaneity is a type of "nontemporal" causality, but it is not to be identified with natural (temporal) causality. This is Kant's official position, and the primary legacy of his moral philosophy. But this is not (and cannot be) the whole story. If freedom consisted exclusively in giving the moral law to ourselves, we would not be able to account for the possibility (and actuality) that we do not always do what we ought to do. With his characteristic intellectual integrity, Kant seeks to meet this problem squarely when he introduces the *Wille/Willkür* distinction. At least two different primary senses of freedom must be distinguished: first, the freedom achieved when we give the moral law to ourselves, when we do what the norm of *Wille* requires; and secondly, the freedom to choose (*Willkür*) to follow – or not to follow – what the moral law requires. These two aspects of the faculty of volition are interdependent; they presuppose each other. There would be no morality – indeed, no possibility of morality – without the capacity to choose between good and evil maxims. But neither would there be any morality if our choices were simply arbitrary, if we failed to recognize that there is a universal norm that we ought to follow. Although the difference between good and evil maxims depends on whether we give priority to moral or nonmoral incentives in our maxims, we are free – radically free – in choosing which maxims to adopt. This does not mean that we are indifferent. Respect for the moral law is a *sufficient* rational incentive to adopt good maxims. We can recognize the normative power of what the *Wille* requires, and we can freely choose (*Willkür*) to follow the moral law.

The introduction of the concept of radical evil is intended to help explain why we do not always do what we ought to do. Man is evil by nature. This is what Kant calls an "evil heart," an innate propensity (*Hang*) in the human species to adopt evil maxims. We are responsible for this propensity. The propensity to evil, understood as "a subjective determining ground of the [*Willkür*]," is an "exercise of freedom" (*Rel.* 26). But we can resist this propensity, even though it is woven into the fabric of human nature. If we press Kant, and ask why it is that some persons consistently choose good maxims and others choose evil maxims, why it is that some persons become morally good and others evil, we are told that this is (ultimately) "inscrutable." As rational moral agents, we are capable of acting on principle; but the more that Kant stresses our unconditioned ability to choose between good and evil maxims, the more inscrutable it becomes as to why some persons become good, and others evil.

Among Kant's immediate successors, the philosopher who grasped most deeply the movement of Kant's thought was Schelling.[1] It was he who declared that "the real and vital conception of freedom is that it is a possibility of good and evil" (*HF* 26; 25), and who insisted that in order to understand the essence of human freedom (*das Wesen der menschlichen Freiheit*), we must squarely confront the "problem of evil." Schelling's 1809 treatise on freedom is especially thought provoking, because he affirms that we must acknowledge "the reality of evil" (*die Realität des Bösen*) (*HF* 26; 25). He departs from the dominant Western philosophical and theological tradition that denies the reality of evil, claiming that evil lacks positive ontological status, and conceiving of evil as a privation of being or goodness. This is a tendency that can be traced back to Plato and that reached its culmination in Leibniz. But the traces of this tradition can still be found in Kant and Hegel. Schelling not only refuses to follow this tradition, he mocks it, and specifies the difficulty that must be confronted in a most striking way.

> This is the point of profoundest difficulty in the whole doctrine of freedom, which has always been felt and which applies not only to this or that

system, but more or less, to all. To be sure it applies most strikingly to the concept of immanence, for either real evil is admitted, in which case it is unavoidable to include evil itself in infinite Substance or in the Primal Will, and thus totally disrupt the conception of an all-perfect Being: or the reality of evil must in some way or other be denied, in which case the real conception of freedom disappears at the same time. (*HF* 26; 25)[2]

Heidegger is helpful in distinguishing the several concepts of freedom that arise in the course of Schelling's *Untersuchungen*. The first five closely parallel Kant: "1) freedom as capability of self-beginning: 2) freedom as not being bound to anything, freedom *from* (negative freedom); 3) freedom as binding oneself to, *libertas determinationis*, freedom *for* (positive freedom); 4) freedom as control over the senses (inappropriate freedom); 5) freedom as self-determination in terms of one's own essential law (appropriate freedom), formal concept of freedom. *This includes all the previous determinations*" (*ST* 88; 104). It is in the sixth and seventh concepts of freedom (especially as interpreted by Schelling) that we find his distinctive contribution and movement beyond Kant: 6) "Man's freedom is the capability of good and evil" (*ST* 97; 117); and finally 7) "if freedom as the capability of evil must have a root independent of God, and if God, on the other hand, is to remain the one and sole root of beings, then this ground of evil independent of God can only be in God. There must be in God something which God himself 'is' not. God must be conceived more primordially" (*ST* 103; 124). This final conception is both perplexing and obscure. My inquiry is oriented towards explicating what it means.

Real evil and concrete freedom are inextricably linked. If we deny the reality of evil, then we are compelled to deny the reality of freedom. Schelling amplifies the Kantian thesis that freedom is the most fundamental principle of all philosophy. But freedom entails the reality of evil. Thus we can characterize Schelling's treatise on human freedom as at the same time "a metaphysics of evil" (*ST* 98; 118). As Heidegger phrases it, evil is "a way of man's *being*-free" (*eine Weise des Frei-sein des Menschen*) (*ST* 106; 128). We seem to be driven to a conclusion that is unacceptable for Christian believers, of ascribing the reality of evil to "infinite Substance" – that is, to God. This is the conclusion that virtually all theodicies – from St. Augustine to Leibniz – have sought to avoid. And this is a primary reason why evil has been taken to be "unreal."[3]

Before pursuing Schelling's highly original way of confronting this problem, we must briefly address the complex personal and philosophical relationship between Schelling and Hegel. The bare facts are relatively clear. In their youth, Schelling and Hegel were close personal friends and intellectual companions. Schelling was five years younger than Hegel. At the age of 15 he enrolled at the University of Tübingen where he shared living quarters with Hegel and Hölderlin. In 1798, at the age of 23, Schelling was called to Jena to become a professor, and in 1801, with Schelling's strong support, Hegel became a *Privatdozent* at Jena. During this early period, Schelling and Hegel edited a philosophical journal together. Cordial relations between Schelling and Hegel lasted until the publication in 1807 of Hegel's *Phenomenology of Spirit*, in which he obliquely but sharply criticized Schelling's conception of the Absolute. Later, especially as the fame of Hegel overshadowed him, Schelling attacked Hegel, accusing Hegel of stealing his ideas. The final irony came when, ten years after Hegel's death in 1831, Schelling was appointed to Hegel's chair at the University of Berlin. During this last phase of his philosophical career, (when Kierkegaard and some of the young Hegelians attended his lectures), Schelling criticized Hegel's "negative philosophy," arguing that it should be superseded by his own "positive philosophy."

Subsequent history has treated Schelling badly. In part, this is because Schelling seemed to keep changing his philosophical positions. Schelling scholars have endlessly disputed "how many" Schellings there are, or how many "stages of development" he passed through.[4] Furthermore, some of his wild, speculative ideas about theosophy and *Naturphilosophie* no longer seem worthy of serious philosophical interest. Schelling has been understood primarily as a transitional figure in the development of German Idealism, who was surpassed by Hegel. This is how Hegel viewed Schelling, and it is still the prevailing orthodoxy. But there are signs that this negative evaluation is beginning to change. In his 1936 lecture course, Heidegger does not hesitate to single out the philosophical importance of Schelling's treatise. He says, "Schelling is the truly creative and boldest thinker of this whole age of German philosophy. He is that to *such* an extent that he drives German Idealism from within right past its own fundamental position" (*ST* 4; 4). Several scholars of German Idealism, including Dieter Henrich and Manfred Frank, have argued that Schelling is an original thinker whose insights anticipated issues that are at the core of recent debates about poststructuralism and postmodernity. There are even indications that this new appreciation of Schelling is having a much wider international intellectual influence.[5] The rediscovery of this "new" Schelling is directly relevant to my own criticisms of Hegel's account of good and evil. I have argued that Hegel's account of evil is based upon his understanding of the dialectical passage from finitude through the spurious infinite to the true infinite whereby a sublation of evil is achieved. Insofar as we question this dialectical movement, insofar as we criticize Hegel's understanding of determinate negation and the concept of sublation (*Aufhebung*), we are calling into question his understanding of evil. These are the very issues that stand at the center of Schelling's late critique of Hegel's "negative philosophy."[6]

Although it is fascinating to follow the twists and turns of the debates about the relations of Schelling and Hegel, I want to limit myself to an examination of Schelling's 1809 treatise, in order to bring out the originality and significance of his confrontation with the problem of evil. To anticipate my major thesis, I see Schelling not as a transitional figure en route to Hegel, but rather as a transitional figure in *transforming* our understanding of the problem of evil. From a backward-looking perspective, he brings a certain tradition of theodicy to a close. This is the tradition that is primarily concerned with "justifying" evil, and with showing how the existence of evil can be reconciled with a religious faith in the existence of God. But from a forward-looking perspective, Schelling breaks with this tradition, and clears the way for new types of psychological questions concerning evil – questions that are central for Nietzsche and Freud.

Real evil

Let us return to Schelling's critique of the attempts to explain away "real evil." With polemical flair and finesse, Schelling runs through these attempts to reconcile the existence of the Christian God with evil – attempts that seek to show that evil is unreal, a privation of good, or somehow a moment or aspect of a larger good. He is critical of all "attenuated conceptions of God as *actus purissimus* and similar notions which earlier philosophy set forth" (*HF* 30; 28). He exposes the fallacy of thinking that we can assert that the source of evil is not to be found in God. To claim, as St Augustine did, that although God gave humans the gift of free will, God is not responsible for the misuse that humans make of this gift is a "dodge"; for it fails to acknowledge that genuine "freedom is a power for evil" (*HF* 28; 27). But Schelling is also critical of Manichaeism, and indeed of any metaphysical, dualistic conception of two equal primordial forces of good and evil. "One may be tempted to throw oneself into the arms of dualism. However, if this system is really thought of as a doctrine of two absolutely different and mutually independent principles, it is only a system of self-destruction and the despair of reason" (*HF* 28; 27). Schelling is in agreement with those Christian theologians and philosophers from St Augustine to Hegel who have not only rejected Manichaeism, but have recoiled from it in horror. Furthermore, Schelling affirms that

> even if one wished to eliminate every connection between the world's creatures and God, and not merely to deny their identity, and if one wished to

regard their present existence and thus the existence of the world as a withdrawal from God, the difficulty would only be pushed back a point but would not be eliminated. *For in order to have flowed forth from God, things must already have been in God in some way or other.* (*HF* 28–9; 27, emphasis added)

It may seem that Schelling is driving himself (and us) into an impossible bind. He tells us that human beings are free, and that freedom is the "possibility of good and evil." Furthermore, evil is real, and cannot be explained away as a deficiency or a privation. In seeking the origin of evil, we cannot appeal to a metaphysical dualism of good and evil. It looks as if we are being ineluctably driven to the conclusion that the source of evil lies in the source of all being, God. But if God is truly all-benevolent, the very standard and source of goodness, then to affirm that he is the source of evil (without any further qualification) is a blasphemous contradiction. How can a benevolent and loving God be the *origin* of the reality of evil? How, then, are we to account for the origin of evil and human freedom? This is the fundamental problem that Schelling addresses in his treatise on freedom. Heidegger gives a succinct statement of the difficulty that Schelling confronts. "But if freedom as the capability of evil must have a root independent of God, and if God, on the other hand, is to remain the one and sole root of beings, then the ground of evil independent of God can only be in God. There must be in God something which God himself 'is' not. God must be conceived more primordially" (*ST* 103; 124). Let us follow the movement of Schelling's thinking in grappling with this problem. Because Schelling affirms that freedom stands at the center of any systematic conception of philosophy, I will have to follow a number of byways in reconstructing the pathway of his questioning. What I want to show is just how insightful Schelling is, and how he takes us beyond both Kant and Hegel.

Two cautionary remarks are in order, to orient our inquiry. The title of Schelling's treatise speaks of "the essence of human freedom" (*das Wesen der menschlichen Freiheit*). But Schelling does not focus his attention exclusively on *human* freedom. First he seeks to understand freedom in a more general sense, and to find out how it is related to the rest of being (including God). It is only in this larger metaphysical context that we can understand what is distinctive about human freedom. The second cautionary remark concerns the language of German idealism (and Schelling's appropriation of, and attempt to move beyond, it). The vocabulary of Idealism – "Absolute," "Ground," "Spirit," etc. – is not only remote from us; but we have become profoundly suspicious of it. Furthermore, the very idea of a *Naturphilosophie*, a philosophy of nature that is not identified with what we now take to be the proper domain of philosophy of the natural sciences, may strike us as an outdated "romantic" notion which is better discarded than taken seriously. Consequently, it is all too easy to dismiss Schelling's thinking as obscure, dated, fantastic, and irrelevant for contemporary "serious" philosophical inquiry. Without discounting the very real difficulties to be encountered in his thought and language, I nevertheless think that such a dismissive attitude is a serious mistake; for there is much to be learned from Schelling for our own reflections on freedom, responsibility, and evil. In approaching him, a hermeneutical generosity and sensitivity are required, in order to understand what he is saying and why. We must be willing (at least initially) to bracket or suspend judgment about the validity of his claims.

Thus far, we have only a vague, and abstract idea of what Schelling means by evil and freedom. It is not even clear what he means by the "reality" of evil. Just when we might expect him to meet the challenge of the "profoundest difficulty in the whole doctrine of freedom," he pursues what appears to be an irrelevant digression. He tells us that an adequate treatment of freedom and evil must be based on "the fundamental principles of a genuine philosophy of nature" (*HF* 31; 29). In a remark that is at once cryptic and extremely abstract, Schelling declares: "The Philosophy of Nature of our time first established the distinction in science between Being insofar as it exists, and Being insofar as it is the mere {ground} of existence" (*HF* 31; 29–30). Why does Schelling introduce "the Philosophy of Nature" at this point in his treatise, and what does this obscure statement mean?

In his preface, Schelling refers to the distinction between nature and spirit that plays such a prominent role in German Idealism, one that can be traced back to Kant's dichotomy between the phenomenal realm of nature and the noumenal realm of freedom.[7] Like many of Kant's immediate successors, Schelling was profoundly dissatisfied with this dichotomy, and sought to overcome it. Indeed, he declares, that "the whole of modern European philosophy since its inception (through Descartes) has this common deficiency – that nature does not exist for it and that it lacks a living basis" (*HF* 30; 28–9). Schelling argues that Kant (especially the Kant of the *Critique of Pure Reason*) advanced a totally inadequate conception of nature as a dead mechanical system, one devoid of any principle of life or spirit. As with other German Idealists (including Hegel), the fundamental drive in Schelling's thinking is the attempt to overcome dualisms – whether ontological, metaphysical, or epistemological. He argues for a much richer, more vital, organic conception of nature – one that takes its departure from some of Kant's claims in the *Critique of Judgment*. Schelling seeks to develop a *differentiated* monism in which there is no ultimate divide between nature and spirit. This differentiated monism can also be characterized as an enriched nonreductive naturalism, or a concretely embodied idealism.[8] Schelling calls this higher system, this higher unity, a "higher realism" (*höherer Realismus*). This is one reason why he begins his treatise with a discussion of pantheism. During the late eighteenth century and early nineteenth century, a fierce controversy raged in Germany about pantheism, about what it meant and entailed, and about who was and who was not a pantheist. Virtually every philosopher of the time felt he had to take a stand on the relevant issues. Schelling wants to show that there is a way of interpreting pantheism (the correct way), which is not only compatible with freedom, but *requires* freedom. In short, pantheism – correctly understood – is a systematic philosophy that does justice to nature and freedom, substance and subject.[9]

Ground and existence

But how does this excursus into Schelling's *Naturphilosophie*, his "higher realism," help us to understand the cryptic remark quoted above in which he distinguishes ground and existence? We must keep in mind that, although Schelling wants to avoid any suggestion of an ontological or metaphysical dualism, he nonetheless claims that we must make important distinctions (which are not to be reified). Ground (*Grund*) and existence (*Existenz*) are primary, and essential distinctions in Being (*Wesen*).[10] The philosophy of nature has established the importance and universality of this distinction. Schelling applies this distinction to the being of God. "As there is nothing before or outside of God he must contain within himself the ground of his existence . . . . This ground of his existence, which God contains [within himself], is not God viewed as absolute, that is insofar as he exists" (*HF* 32; 30). So how are we to understand this distinction between ground and existence? We gain our first significant clue (and also see why Schelling has introduced the discussion of *Naturphilosophie*) when Schelling offers the following analogy to elucidate the relation of ground and existence.

> By analogy, this relationship can be explicated through reference to the relation of gravitation and light in nature. Gravitation precedes light as its eternally dark basis, which is itself not *actual* and flees into the night when light (which truly exists) appears. Even light does not completely break the seal by which gravity is held . . . . With regard to the precedence [of gravity over light], moreover, this is to be thought of neither as precedence in time nor as priority of essence. In the cycle whence all things comes, it is no contradiction to say that which gives birth to the one is, in its turn, produced by it. There is here no first and no last, since everything mutually

implies everything else, nothing being the 'other' and yet no being without the other. God contains himself in an inner {ground} of his existence, which to this extent, precedes him as to his existence, but similarly God is prior to the {ground} as this {ground}, as such, could not be if God did not exist in actuality. (*HF* 32–3; 31)

We can appreciate the point of this analogy without endorsing Schelling's "dynamic physics." Although there is no gravity without light, and no light without gravity, we can nevertheless draw a distinction between them. Furthermore, the distinction between gravity and light is not a "mere" conceptual distinction. Gravity is taken to be the "eternally dark basis" that is the ground of actually existing light. So, with respect to God, we can distinguish the ground of his being from his actual existence (even though we acknowledge their essential *unity* in God). The analogy sketched here between gravity and light is a first preliminary step in clarifying the meaning and relationship of ground and existence. Schelling himself is aware of this. Indeed, his method of explication is to proceed by providing other analogies and metaphors in order to specify his meaning.[11]

If we want to bring this Being (God) "nearer to us from a human standpoint, we may say":

It is the longing which the eternal One feels to give birth to itself. This is not the One itself, but is co-eternal with it. This longing seeks to give birth to God, i.e. the unfathomable unity, but to this extent it has not yet the unity of its own self. Therefore, regarded in itself, it is also will: but a will within which there is no understanding, and thus not an independent and complete will, since understanding is actually the will in willing . . . . We are speaking of the essence of longing regarded in and for itself, which we must view clearly although it was long ago submerged by the higher principle which had risen from it, and although we cannot grasp it perceptively but only spiritually, i.e. with our thoughts. (*HF* 34; 32)[12]

What initially sounds so strange and fantastic becomes more intelligible and vivid when we realize that Schelling is isolating an ontological "double principle" that he takes to be standing at the very heart of all beings, including God, human beings, and the whole of nature. There are affinities between Schelling's double principle and Nietzsche's double principle of the Dionysian and the Apollonian. This becomes even clearer when Schelling writes that "the world as we now behold it, is all rule, order and form: but the unruly [*das Regellos*] lies ever in the depths as though it might again break through, and order and form nowhere appear to have been original, but it seems as though what had initially been unruly had been brought to order" (*HF* 34; 32). In beings other than God, the principle of light, order, and form never completely masters or subdues what is unruly.

We can detect affinities not only with Nietzsche, but also with Freud. It is out of this "primal longing," this unconscious source of longing, that consciousness and rationality emerge. "Man is formed in his mother's womb; and only out of the darkness of unreason (out of feeling, out of longing, the sublime mother of understanding) grow clear thoughts (*HF* 35; 33). We can also turn back to classical sources for Schelling's "double principle." He explicitly cites Plato when describing this primal longing. "This primal longing moves in anticipation like a surging, billowing sea, similar to the 'matter' of Plato, following some dark, uncertain law, incapable in itself of forming anything that can endure" (*HF* 35; 33).

Returning to the application of this double principle to God, Schelling writes: "Out of this which is unreasonable, reason [*Verstand*] in the true sense is born. Without this preceding gloom, creation would have no reality; darkness is its necessary heritage. Only God – the Existent himself – dwells in pure light; for he alone is self-born" (*HF* 34; 32). God, then, is a unity of ground and existence; he is alone the being who is self-born. Near the end of his inquiry, Schelling explicitly raises the question concerning the justification for introducing this crucial distinction.

> Here at last we reach the highest point of the whole inquiry. The question has long been heard: What is to be gained by that initial distinction between being insofar as it is {ground}, and being insofar as it exists? For either there is no common ground for the two – in which case we must declare ourselves in favor of absolute dualism; or there is such common ground – and in that case, in the last analysis, the two coincide again. In that case we have one being in all opposites, an absolute identity of light and darkness, good and evil, and all the inconsistent consequences which must befall any intellectualistic system and which this system too, has indeed been accused for quite some time. (*HF* 87; 77–8)

Schelling's subtlety is exemplified in his delicate systematic balance. In his "higher realism" Schelling seeks to avoid two extremes: absolute dualism and an undifferentiated homogeneous monism. His *via media* is important for understanding human freedom as the power of good and evil. He wants to avoid the consequence that there is an absolute duality of good and evil (that is how he understands Manichaeism), as well as those pseudo-solutions that reconcile good and evil by denying the reality of evil. Schelling recognizes that the intelligibility of his system demands that "there must be a being *before* all {ground} and before all existence, that is before any duality at all." He calls this the "primal ground," or the "groundless" (*Ungrund*). "As it precedes all antitheses these cannot be distinguishable in it or be present in any way at all" (*HF* 87; 77–8). This is what he calls "indifference" (*Indifferenz*). "Indifference is not a product of antitheses, nor are they implicitly contained in it, but it is a unique being, apart from all antitheses, in which all distinctions break up. It is naught else than just their non-being and therefore has no predicates except lack of predicates, without its being naught or a non-entity" (*HF* 87; 78). "Thus out of this neither-nor, or out of indifference, duality immediately breaks forth (which is something quite different from opposition . . .) and *without* indifference, that is, *without* the groundless, there would be no twofoldness of the principles" (*HF* 88; 78).[13]

The being of God is indissoluble. Consequently, in God there is a unity of ground and existence. Nevertheless, we can still say that the ground of God's existence "precedes" his actual existence. Heidegger elucidates this difficult point.

> God *as the existing one* is the *absolute* God, or God as he himself – in brief: God-himself. God considered as the ground of his existence "is" not yet God truly as he *himself*. But still, God "is" his ground. It is true that the ground is something distinguished from God, but yet not "outside of" God. The ground in God is that in God which God himself "is" not truly himself, but is rather ground *for* his selfhood. (*ST* 109–10; 131)

At this point a reader – even a sympathetic reader – may want to give up in despair. The distinction that Schelling introduces between ground and existence may seem to be a tortured one. One may feel that Schelling's balancing act and Heidegger's commentary are good examples of why Carnap and the other logical positivists turned their backs on this sort of metaphysical speculation, and declared it to be not simply false, but meaningless. Yet, with a little imagination, I believe we can grasp Schelling's main point (even if we want to question its validity). Although Schelling affirms that God – as the Absolute – is a unity, this does not mean that we cannot distinguish different aspects of God's being. After all, this has always been true of the theological tradition – especially the Christian theological tradition – which also distinguishes God's attributes and asserts the absolute unity of his being. Even atheists have no difficulty distinguishing different attributes or aspects of the alleged God whose existence they deny. In God, his ground – the principle of darkness – is transformed by his existence – the principle of light – in his actual existence. We can even relate this distinction to God's self-revelation. As "mere" ground, God has "not yet" revealed himself. But when God does reveal himself, then and only then does God exist in his full actuality.[14] We can go one step further and grasp the co-dependent relationship between God and human beings. God *requires* human beings for his own self-revelation. Heidegger explicates what Schelling means:

> Thus, there must be something which, although it originates from the inmost center of the God and is Spirit in its way, yet still remains separated from him in everything and is something individual. But this being is man. Man must be in order for the God to be revealed. What is a God without man? The absolute form of absolute monotony. What is man without God? Pure madness in the form of the harmless. Man must be in order for the God to "exist." Fundamentally and generally expressed, this means that certain conditions commensurate with the nature of Being and the nature of God must be fulfilled to make God possible as the existing Spirit, that is, to make man possible. But then this means that the conditions of the possibility of the revelation of the existing God are at the same time the conditions of the possibility of the faculty of good and evil, that is, of that freedom in which and as which man has his being. To demonstrate the possibility of evil means to show how man must be, and what it means that man is. After all this it becomes clear that the ground of evil is nothing less than the ground of being human. (*ST* 119; 143)[15]

Schelling departs from the philosophical and theological tradition whereby God is thought to be completely self-sufficient. On the contrary, God needs his creatures (specifically human beings) in order to reveal himself, and in order to actually exist. Self-revelation is not an accidental, but rather an essential, characteristic of God. This way of conceiving of the relation between God and created human beings has direct consequences for Schelling's understanding of freedom. On the basis of what we have explicated thus far, it might seem that Schelling's system is "God-centered." Although this is correct, it is nevertheless misleading unless it is properly qualified. We can invert the relation of God and human beings. For human beings stand at the center of God's creation and revelation. Not only are human beings required for God's self-revelation, they bear a special burden of responsibility. It is *only* with human beings that freedom becomes the power of good and evil. "If in a man the dark principle of selfhood and self-will is completely penetrated by light and is one with it, then God, as eternal love or as really existent, is the nexus of the forces in him. But if the two principles are at strife, then another spirit occupies the place where God should be" (*HF* 68; 61). This is the evil spirit that can act only in and through human beings. Žižek forcefully underscores the sense in which Schelling's "God-centered" system is also anthropocentric. "Schelling is radically 'anthropocentric': the whole of nature, the universe as such, was created in order to serve as the setting of man's ethical struggle, for the battle between Good and Evil."[16] Human beings need

God, but it is just as true to say that God needs human beings, who bear a special responsibility.[17] We can now anticipate how Schelling's reflections on the unity of ground and existence, the unity of the principles of darkness and light, enable us to grasp the reality of evil that is intrinsic to human freedom. In human beings, the unity that is found in God is broken; the dark, unruly principle that is the ground of being overwhelms the principle of light.

Self-will and the principle of darkness

In order to clarify the origin of evil in humanity, we need to continue the narrative of God's creation and revelation. "The process of creation consists only in an inner transmutation, or revelation in light of what was originally the principle of darkness" (*HF* 38; 35). But how is this "principle of darkness" manifested in human beings? "The principle of darkness, insofar as it was drawn from the depths and is dark, is the *self-will* of creatures, but *self-will*, insofar as it has not yet risen to complete unity with light, as the principle of understanding cannot grasp it and is a craving or desire, that is *blind will* (*HF* 38; 35, emphasis added). Schelling's "self-will" is much darker and much more unruly than Kant's "self-love." This perverted self-will is the source of evil in human beings – a self-will that stands "opposed to reason as universal will." "This elevation of the most abysmal center into light, occurs in no creatures visible to us except man. In man there exists the whole power of the principle of darkness and, in him too, the whole force of light" (*HF* 38; 35).

We have reached the crucial stage in the narrative of the origin of evil in human beings. It is only human beings (of all the beings created by God) who can *separate* and *reverse* what is indissoluble in God – the principles of ground and existence. "If, now, the identity of both principles [darkness and light] were just as indissoluble in man as in God, then there would be no difference – that is, God as spirit would not be revealed. Therefore that unity which is indissoluble in God must be dissolvable in man – and this constitutes the possibility of good and evil" (*HF* 39; 36). In human beings, and in human beings *alone*, there is a clash, a conflict of two wills – the will to good and the will to evil. "And just as there is an ardor for good, there is an enthusiasm for evil" (*HF* 48; 44). This is what is distinctive about human beings, and this is the essence of human freedom.[18] Evil as such can arise only in created beings, specifically human beings, although it can be traced back to the ground of God's being. Strictly speaking, there is no duality of principle in God – only a *potential* duality that is manifested in God's creatures. Ground and existence, dark-

ness and light, become *principles* only when they are independent and
separable. It is only human beings who "can deliberately cut the eternal
nexus of forces." Schelling makes this point emphatically by endorsing
Franz Baader's claim that "it would be desirable if the rottenness in man
could only go as far as animality, but unfortunately man can only stand
above or beneath animals" (*HF* 49; 45).

To bring out the complexity and subtlety of Schelling's understanding
of the human condition, I want to consider again what initially seems to
be an obscure and perplexing claim: "That principle which rises up from
the depths of nature and by which man is divided from God, is the
selfhood in him; but by reason of its unity with the ideal principle, this
becomes spirit" (*HF* 39; 37). Human beings are natural beings, but they
are not merely natural beings. It is more accurate to say – in accordance
with Schelling's version of naturalism – that human beings are natural
beings who also manifest a spiritual dimension. Evil is not simply a reversal of the two independent principles of darkness and light. Rather, it
is the conscious (*spiritual*) elevation of the principle of darkness over the
principle of light. As Heidegger says, "Evil attains its true essential reality
only in Spirit, in the Spirit of the creature which as selfhood can place
itself furthest away from God and against God and can claim the whole of
being for itself" (*ST* 177; 214–15).[19] And Žižek says: "This 'egoistic' perversion of Spirit which is inherent to the very notion of actually existing
Spirit forms the core of Schelling's conception of Evil, at which he arrived
by the radicalization of Kant's notion of 'radical evil' in *Religion within the
Limits of Reason Alone*."[20] "When man emerges as self-consciousness, he
posits himself as a self-centered being, as a subject who reduces all other
entities to a medium of his self-assertion, to mere objects to be appropriated and exploited."[21]

Before proceeding, let us pause, in order to reflect on Schelling's distinctive understanding of evil. Schelling can affirm what has always seemed
unacceptable for Christian theodicies. God "is" the origin of the reality of
evil. But he is the origin in a very special sense. It is the ground of God's
being, the potentially independent principle of darkness, that *becomes* the
origin of evil in human beings. This occurs when human beings, as conscious spiritual beings, elevate this dark principle by a free act of self-will,
and violently reverse what is unified and indissoluble in God. Consequently, what is not *intrinsically* evil in God becomes the source of evil in
human beings. This is why I suggested earlier that, despite Schelling's
polemical attack on traditional theodicies that seek to deny the reality of
evil, he does not escape the specter of theodicy. For he also affirms that
"the first cause of all can never be evil in itself" (*HF* 51; 47).

We can now indicate some of the ways in which Schelling highlights features of evil that were either neglected or not sufficiently emphasized by Kant or Hegel. Schelling is far more radical than Kant in his conception of radical evil. For Schelling can make sense of the depth and the power of this active propensity to evil.

> There is, therefore, *universal* evil, even if it is not active from the beginning but it is only aroused in God's revelation through the reaction of {ground}, and indeed never reaches realization, but is nonetheless constantly striving towards it. Only after recognizing evil in its universal character is it possible to comprehend good and evil in man too. (*HF* 58; 52)

We can also appreciate how Schelling's *Naturphilosophie* is relevant for his description of evil in human nature. Despite the attempt by Kant to bridge the gap between natural causality and freedom, Kant never goes so far as to maintain that there is continuity between nature and freedom. He does not explain clearly how the alleged propensity to evil can have a powerful *causal* influence upon us. But there is no such gap in Schelling; there is no gap between nature and spirit, or between causal necessity and freedom. Recall that in the preface to his treatise, Schelling declares that "the root of this old contrast [between nature and spirit] has been dislodged," and "the implanting of a sounder insight may confidently be entrusted to the general progress towards better understanding" (*HF* 3; 4). Schelling portrays a much more ominous sense of the power of evil – a power that is never completely mastered and can always break out with ever-renewed vigor.

Although Schelling's *Untersuchungen* was published long before he elaborated his explicit critique of Hegel, we can detect the source of his objections to Hegel. The principle of darkness can never be completely mastered, never be completely sublated (*aufgehoben*). Schelling rejects the idea that "the wounds of the Spirit heal, and leave no scars behind." Against Hegel, he insists that it is precisely because man is a self-conscious *spiritual* being that evil exists; evil becomes real when man as a self-willed spiritual being *reverses* the principles of ground and existence. Only a spiritual being can accomplish this. Schelling is frequently at his most illuminating in his use of metaphors and analogies. We get a vivid sense of the power of evil when he describes a person who experiences the lure of evil as like someone "who is seized by dizziness on a high and precipitous summit [and who] seems to hear a mysterious voice calling to him to plunge down, or as in the ancient tale, the irresistible song of the sirens sounded out of the deep to draw the passing mariner down into the whirlpool" (*HF* 59; 53).

A perverted self-will can act on an evil principle even when it goes *against* natural inclinations. Žižek effectively brings out this point when he writes, that "evil does not reside in finitude as such, in its deficiency with regard to an infinite God – it can emerge only in a finite creature which again rejoins the Infinite – that is, when the unity of the Finite and the Infinite is re-established in man *qua* finite but free being. The problem of Evil could then be restated as follows: how is the *false* unity of Ground and Existence possible?"[22] Evil turns out to be *"not particularity as such but its erroneous, 'perverted' unity with the Universal: not 'egotism' as such, but egotism in the guise of its opposite."* To illustrate this, Žižek gives the following example:

> When a political agent (Party, etc.) claims to represent the universal interest of the State or Nation – in contrast to its opponents who, of course, are accused of pursuing only their narrow power-seeking goals – it thereby structures the discursive space so that every attack upon it – on this particular political subject – is *eo ipso* an attack on the Nation itself. 'Evil' in its most elementary form is such a 'short circuit' between the Particular and the Universal, such a presumption to believe that my words and deeds are directly words and deeds of the big Other (Nation, Culture, State, God), a presumption which 'inverts' the proper relationship between the Particular and the Universal: when I proclaim myself the immediate 'functionary of Humanity' (or Nation or Culture), I thereby effectively accomplish the exact opposite of what I claim to be doing – that is, I degrade the Universal dimension to which I refer (Humanity, Nation, State) to my own particularity, since it is my own particular point of view which decides on the content of Humanity. I am therefore caught in the infernal cycle of 'the purer you are, the dirtier you are': the more I refer to the Universal in order to legitimate my acts, the more I effectively abase it to a means of my own self-assertion.[23]

According to Schelling, there is a dangerous illusion of omnipotence that arises from this extreme "exaltation of self-will" – one that revolts against the divine nexus of ground and existence in God, and seeks to rival God.

> But that evil is this very exaltation of self-will is made clear from the following. Will, which deserts its supernatural status in order to make itself as {universal} will, also particular and creature will, at one and the same time, strives to reverse the relation of principles, to exalt the {ground} above the cause, and to use that spirit which it received only for the center, outside the center and against the creature, which leads to disorganization within and outside itself. Man's will may be regarded as a nexus of living forces; as long as it abides in its unity within the universal will these forces remain in their divine measure and balance. But hardly does self-will move from the center which is its station, than the nexus of forces is also dissolved; in its place a merely particular will rules which can no longer unite the forces among themselves as before, but must therefore strive to form or compose a special and peculiar life out of the now separate forces, an insurgent host of desires and passions – since every individual force is also an obsession and passion. (*HF* 41; 37–8)

Evil becomes real when human beings freely choose to reverse the principles of ground and existence, darkness and light, and thereby *unify* these principles in a false and perverted way. This is a delusion of omnipotence, because human beings seek to rival God, instead of trying to reproduce in themselves "divine measure and balance."

I want to approach Schelling from a different perspective, in order to show how insightful he is about the character of evil. Earlier, I argued that Schelling's *Naturphilosophie* is relevant to his analysis of evil, because it enables us to make sense of the causal efficacy of the propensity to evil. Schelling seeks to overcome the split between nature and spirit, the divide between causal necessity and freedom that Kant never quite resolved. Regardless of Kant's intentions, his characterization of nature, especially in the *Critique of Pure Reason*, has contributed to the technological denigration of nature that is so prevalent in the modern age. Nature in itself lacks any intrinsic moral worth or dignity, because moral worth and dignity are attributable only to free rational agents, beings who are ends-in-themselves.

Vittorio Hösle shows how Schelling's conception of nature is extremely fertile for dealing with philosophical issues pertaining to ecology and the environment. Schelling is a sharp critic of a technological or instrumental conception of nature. The system of nature encompasses freedom; consequently everything in nature possesses intrinsic dignity. Nevertheless, human beings pose a serious threat to the rest of nature because their natural animal egotism can be elevated and "spiritualized" into a principle for exploiting nature.[24] Žižek, building on Hösle's discussion, shows how this denigration and exploitation of nature by human beings is directly related to evil. "Good and Evil are modes of the *unity* of Ground and Existence." He underscores this point in order to forestall the misleading inference that Schelling is surreptitiously introducing a new form of ontological dualism when he distinguishes between ground and existence.

> Schelling's thesis here is much more subtle: both Good and Evil are modes of the *unity* of Ground and Existence; *in the case of Evil, this unity is false, inverted* – how? Suffice it to recall today's ecological crisis: its possibility is opened by man's split nature – by the fact that man is simultaneously a living organism (and, as such, part of nature) and a spiritual entity (and, as such, elevated above nature). If man were only one of the two, the crisis could not occur: as part of nature, man would be an organism living in symbiosis with his environment, a predator exploiting other animals and plants yet, for that very reason, included in nature's circuit and unable to pose a fundamental threat to it; as a spiritual being, man would entertain towards nature a relationship of contemplative comprehension with no need to intervene actively in it for the purpose of material exploitation.

What renders man's existence so explosive is *the combination of the two features*: in man's striving to dominate nature, to put it to work for his purposes, 'normal' animal egotism – the attitude of a natural-living organism engaged in the struggle for survival in a hostile environment – is 'self-illuminated', posited as such, raised to the power of Spirit, and thereby exacerbated, universalized into a propensity for absolute domination which no longer serves the end of survival but turns into an end-in-itself. This is the true 'perversion' of Evil: in it, 'normal' animal egotism is 'spiritualized', it expresses itself in the medium of Word – we are no longer dealing with an obscure drive but with a Will which, finally, 'found itself.'[25]

There is something chilling and frightening about this transformation of animal egotism into a *spiritualized* will – this absolute domination – because it is only a "small step" from this spiritualized will to "the triumph of the will" that justifies the genocidal extermination of "subhuman races."

The moral psychology of evil

These reflections of Schelling enable us to better understand the sense in which his system as, at once, anthropomorphic (indeed, anthropocentric) and radically anti-anthropomorphic. When a philosopher's thinking is declared to be anthropomorphic or anthropocentric, this is frequently intended as a negative criticism. I think that Heidegger's warning is perfectly appropriate when he poses the question: "Does it not rather follow primarily that *before* everything the question must be asked who is man?" (*ST* 163; 197).[26] Human beings are not only required for God's self-revelation; they bear a special place and responsibility in Schelling's system. The battle between good and evil takes place only in human beings. Like Kant, Schelling affirms that, in the final analysis, it is inscrutable why some human beings choose to do evil and others choose to do good. "[E]vil ever remains man's own choice; the {ground} cannot cause evil as such, and every creature falls through its own guilt. But just how the decision for good or evil comes to pass in the individual man, that is still wrapped in total darkness" (*HF* 59; 53–4). We must keep in mind that, despite the title of his treatise (which speaks of "the essence of human freedom"), Schelling explores a much broader, metaphysical conception of freedom. He is primarily concerned with placing human freedom within a more comprehensive cosmological and metaphysical system. The universal distinction between ground and existence is applicable to all beings. Heidegger is right when he characterizes Schelling's treatise as a "metaphysics of evil" (*ST* 104; 125). But there is still another sense in which

Schelling's systematic approach is anti-anthropocentric and anti-anthropomorphic. The intent of his total system is to oppose, in the strongest
possible way, the anthropocentric "spiritual" elevation of a narcissistic
self-will that seeks to dominate the rest of nature.

In concluding, I want to review some of the main stages in Schelling's
thinking, and to anticipate what is yet to come. Schelling begins his
treatise with an examination of the various interpretations of pantheism.
He does this in order to show that there is a way of understanding
pantheism that is compatible with freedom. Pantheism does not entail
fatalism. There is no inherent contradiction between the philosophical
demand for system and freedom. There is a system of freedom. Schelling
then focuses on the inextricable linkage between freedom and evil. There
is no human freedom without evil. Freedom is the power of good *and*
evil. All attempts to deny the reality of evil are unsatisfactory evasions.
To deny the reality of evil is to deny the reality of freedom. And freedom is the most fundamental principle of any adequate system of philosophy. But then the question arises as to how we are to account for the
possibility and origin of evil without asserting that God is intrinsically
evil or that there is a metaphysical dualism of good and evil. To provide
this account, Schelling introduces the distinction between ground and
existence – a distinction derived from the philosophy of nature
(*Naturphilosophie*) which is applicable to all beings, including God. When
we apply this distinction to God, we learn that in God there is an
essential, harmonious unity of ground and existence, of darkness and
light, even though we can also say that in God the ground of his existence precedes his *actual* existence. This ground is identified with God's
longing to reveal himself in and through his creation. From a human
point of view, the ground in God that precedes his actual existence is
"the longing which the eternal One feels to give birth to itself . . . .
Following the eternal act of self-revelation, the world as we now behold
it, is all rule, order and form; but the unruly lies ever in the depths as
though it might again break through" (*HF* 34; 31–2). In human beings
the two *potential* principles of darkness and light (which exist in God as a
indissoluble unity) can be separated, and their unity can be inverted and
perverted. Human beings *can* emulate the true unity and harmony that
are found in God. But they *can* also elevate the principle of darkness
over the principle of light into a false unity. They thereby revolt violently against the divine order. Good and evil are both ways of being
free. Evil is the assertion of one's particular, idiosyncratic, narcissistic
will over universal will – or, more accurately, it involves deceiving oneself into believing that one's particular will is identical with the universal
will. Evil involves the delusion that one is omnipotent – a rival to God.

Schelling gives a much more concrete and compelling account of the temptation, power, and causal efficacy of the propensity to evil than we find in either Kant or Hegel. Radical evil – evil that goes to the root – is grounded in the cosmological principle of darkness that is unruly, unconscious, chaotic, and always threatening, a principle that humans can never completely master or subdue. The great drama of human life is the strife between good and evil. But human beings can freely choose to resist this temptation to evil. In this respect, Schelling is in basic agreement with Kant. Human beings are solely responsible for their deeds, whether they are good or evil. "Man's being is essentially *his own deed*" (*HF* 63; 57). Schelling also agrees with Kant that, in the final analysis, we cannot answer the question of why an individual person chooses good or evil. It is inscrutable. This is not a criticism of Schelling (or Kant), but rather an honest statement of what radical unconstrained will (*Willkür*) involves. Furthermore, Schelling emphasizes that to be fully human we must engage in the battle between good and evil with passion and intensity. "Activated selfhood is necessary for life's intensity; without it there would be complete death, goodness slumbering; for where there is no battle there is no life" (*HF* 80; 71). We can discern the traces of German Romanticism, as well as Schelling's anticipation of Nietzsche and Freud, when he declares:

> Whoever has no material or force of evil in himself is also impotent for good . . . .The passions against which our negative morality is at war are forces each of which has a common root with its corresponding virtue. The soul of all hatred is love and in the most violent anger there is seen nothing but the quietude which was attacked and aroused in the innermost center. (*HF* 81; 72)

Although Schelling exhibits a profound awareness of the power of human passions and emotions, including the dark passions, he is certainly no irrationalist. He calls for a delicate balance in the human personality.

> Only in personality is there life; and all personality rests on a dark foundation which must, to be sure, also be the foundation of knowledge. But only reason can bring forth what is contained in these depths, hidden and merely potential, and elevate it to actuality . . . . As in life we actually trust only vigorous reason, and miss all true tenderness in those especially who always expose their feelings to our gaze, so too, where we are considering truth and knowledge, selfhood which has merely reached the point of feelings cannot win our confidence. The emotions are glorious when they stay in the depths, but not when they come forth into the day and wish to become of the essence and to rule. (*HF* 95–6; 85)

Schelling is a philosopher who has been damned, and occasionally honored, but rarely studied carefully for his philosophical insights. In the Anglo-American philosophical world of the twentieth century, he has been almost completely ignored.[27] He is one of those thinkers whose insights, projects, and proposals often outstrip his attempts to provide detailed analyses and careful step-by-step argumentation. But I have tried to show how insightful Schelling is about the reality and power of evil – even if we remain skeptical about his theological claims. He is one of the very few modern thinkers who have refused to "explain away" evil as a privation, or to argue that evil can be sublated (*aufgehoben*) into a higher unity. We can never escape from this reality, or from the ways in which evil can burst forth in new guises. Schelling's conception of evil as a "spiritualized" assertion of a perverted self-will that glorifies itself, has delusions of omnipotence, and takes itself to be the expression of universal will is especially relevant for an understanding of twentieth-century totalitarianism and terrorism. Even in a post-totalitarian world, we witness the temptation of those who think that they can impose their particular self-will on others by claiming universality for it.

At the beginning of my discussion of Schelling, I suggested that we can view him from a double perspective. Like Kant and Hegel, he is still haunted by the specter of theodicy. He is also concerned to show that we can reconcile the reality of evil with a God who is just and good. When we understand how ground and existence are harmoniously unified in God, but perversely reversed in human beings, we realize that God is not intrinsically evil. We can ascribe to God only the dark ground that *becomes* the source of evil in human beings. Read in this way, Schelling can be interpreted as a thinker who brings a certain tradition of theodicy to an end.

But we can also read Schelling from a forward-looking perspective, anticipating what comes after him. Schelling's originality consists in clearing a space for a richer, more complex, and more robust moral psychology – an opening that becomes the starting place for the probings of Nietzsche and Freud. He has profound insight into the violent battle that takes place in the soul of human beings. He grasps the power of the unruly, dark, unconscious forces that shape human life. He understands our human precariousness and contingency whereby we never completely master these unconscious forces. He is skeptical of any philosophical or rationalistic ideal that deludes itself into thinking that we can achieve complete transparency, equilibrium, and control over our unruly passions. He recognizes the frailty of human reason with its demand for form and well-ordered rule. We can never be complete masters of our destiny, but we are not completely impotent in the face of evil. The human condition is one in which there is a constant struggle between good and evil. Schelling does more than anticipate what is developed with much greater finesse by Nietzsche and Freud; he opens a clearing for new ways of questioning evil.

Intermezzo

Before proceeding to part II, I want to pause and briefly review what we have learned thus far. I began this study with Kant, because it was he who coined the powerfully evocative expression "radical evil." With him, the traditional "problem of evil," conceived as a problem of theodicy, began to lose its grip on modern consciousness. We have seen that it was never completely abandoned by Kant, Hegel or Schelling. Nevertheless, they were primarily concerned with giving a philosophical account of evil, rather than with showing how evil can be reconciled with a belief in a benevolent God. There are similarities, as well as striking differences, among these three thinkers. In different ways, each stresses the role of the *will* in accounting for the evil deeds of human beings, even though they differ in their understanding of the nature of will. Our natural inclinations, passions, and desires are not evil in themselves. The body and our sensuous nature are not the source of evil. We cannot account for evil by appealing to a corrupt human reason. Evil is to be explained with reference to a perverse will, to the responses and decisions that we freely choose. One consequence of this line of thinking is to emphasize human responsibility and accountability for the existence of moral evil.

I have argued that Kant's moral philosophy presupposes a distinction between (at least) two fundamental senses of freedom: freedom as self-legislation whereby we, as practical rational agents, give the moral law to ourselves and adopt moral maxims; and freedom as *Willkür*, the radical ability to choose to adopt and follow good *or* evil maxims. I have criticized Kant's conception of radical evil as a universal propensity (*Hang*) rooted or grounded in human nature. My criticism of Kant is not an objection to the idea of such a propensity, but rather to the specific way in which he develops and argues for this idea. Despite Kant's explicit intentions, and his dramatic rhetoric about wickedness, his conception of radical evil turns out to be very dubious (and confused). But this is not what is most important or relevant about Kant's reflections on evil. I have sought to understand *why* Kant is at war with himself, why he so drastically qualifies what he categorically asserts when he tells us that man is by nature evil, and yet that this propensity issues from our freedom. Kant never compromises or weakens his fundamental thesis that we, and we alone, are responsible for the evil we do. No matter how much the propensity to evil may lure us, no matter how corrupt we may become, it is *always* within our power to resist evil and to adopt good maxims. Finally, I admire Kant for insisting that the perversion of the will (*Willkür*) "whereby it makes lower incentives supreme among its maxims, that is, of the propensity to evil, remains inscrutable to us" (*Rel.* 38; 46). It is inscrutable because we are radically free. We can try to explain why an individual chooses a good or an evil maxim, but *ultimately* we cannot give a complete explanation for this choice; that is, we cannot specify necessary and sufficient conditions that explain our free choices. We will see, especially in part III, how the very meaning of responsibility has become a major theme in the discourse concerning evil today.

Hegel builds upon Kant and is a severe critic of him. There is a systematic ambiguity at the heart of Hegel's philosophy. But there is no ambiguity in Hegel's rejection of what he takes to be the very foundation of Kant's philosophy (including his moral philosophy). Baldly stated, Hegel claims that Kant's entire philosophy rests upon a *false* opposition between the finite and what Hegel calls the spurious infinite (*schlechte Unendliche*). Kant's failure consists in failing to acknowledge that we must *necessarily* pass beyond this false antithesis to the true infinite in which finitude is sublated (*aufgehoben*). Evil is the consequence of a *willful*, "stubborn finitude" that perversely refuses to move beyond this false antithesis. For all the systematic appeal of Hegel's conception of determinate negation and his understanding of dialectical movement, there is something profoundly unsatisfying and misguided about the Hegelian claim that the wounds of the Spirit heal and *leave no scars behind*. When Spirit moves beyond the false antithesis of the finite and the spurious infinite, then evil itself (although not obliterated) is nevertheless transformed. Reconciliation and redemption are not only possible but *necessary*, because they are always already implicit (*an sich*) in the manifestation of evil. In light of our twentieth-century experiences of the vicissitudes of evil, which defy total comprehension, we can no longer accept Hegel's narrative. We have witnessed the limits of dialectical thought. There are abysses and breaks so deep in the eruption of ever-new forms of evil that it is almost obscene to speak of their "spiritual" transformation and sublation.

Ironically, for all Hegel's originality, his solution to the "problem of evil" is very traditional. He explicitly characterizes his philosophy as a theodicy whereby we come to see evil as a necessary stage in the becoming of Absolute Spirit. Yet, I have also argued that we can think *with* Hegel *against* Hegel. We can interpret Hegel as presenting some of the strongest arguments against the temptation to reify evil, to take it as something ontological or existentially fixed. When we stress the historical and political dimensions of his philosophy, then it becomes evident that the stubborn persistence of evil presents us with a challenge, or task (*Aufgabe*). There is a *rational* demand to confront evil and to seek to eliminate it. With equal passion, Hegel opposes the sentimental belief that man is intrinsically good as well as the doctrine that man is intrinsically evil. It is not surprising that Hegel has inspired many later thinkers (beginning with Marx) who refuse to accept the existence of evil as some sort of fundamental ontological given.

I have discussed Schelling after examining Hegel because I want to break with, and oppose, the entrenched tradition that interprets Schelling's philosophy as a transition to Hegel. Such an interpretation obscures and distorts his highly original contribution to the discourse of evil. At first glance, Schelling's monograph on human freedom – steeped in the language of pantheism, *Naturphilosophie*, and German Idealism – seems quite remote from us. But if we approach Schelling with hermeneutical sensitivity, we appreciate how insightful he is about evil, and how he prepares the way for new questions about it. He refuses to deny the reality of evil, and sees it as intrinsic to human freedom. He has a vivid sense of the battle between good and evil that takes place within us. He gives a more robust account of radical evil, of the power and causal efficacy of the propensity of evil. He grasps the *unconscious* dimension of this propensity, and challenges the idea that human beings can achieve complete mastery over the dark forces that are constitutive of our very being. But Schelling does not glorify this evil propensity, and he is certainly not an irrationalist. He grasps the extent to which human beings can fall prey to believing they are omnipotent, to believing that they can rival God and carry out their projects of total domination over nature and other human beings. What I find most important about Schelling is the manner in which he prepares the way for probing the moral psychology of evil. To pursue this moral psychology, we must turn to Nietzsche and Freud.

Part II

The Moral Psychology of Evil

4

Nietzsche: Beyond Good and Evil?

Nothing burns one up faster than the affects of *ressentiment*. Anger, pathological vulnerability, impotent lust for revenge, thirst for revenge, poison-mixing in any sense – no reaction could be more disadvantageous for the exhausted . . . . *Ressentiment* is what is forbidden *par excellence* for the sick – it is their specific evil – unfortunately also their most natural inclination.

Ecce Homo

What can we learn about evil from Nietzsche's critique of morality? The question is simple and direct, but the answer is complex and will require the exploration of many byways in his thinking. First we must grasp what Nietzsche means by a "critique of morality," and how it is related to his understanding of genealogy. Second, Nietzsche's critique of morality requires a close examination of the values of good and evil, and of how this value orientation emerges in reaction to the dichotomy of good and bad. Finally, we must comprehend what Nietzsche means when he speaks of "Beyond Good and Evil."

On the Genealogy of Morals is subtitled "A Polemic" (*Eine Streitschrift*), followed by these words: "A Sequel to My Last Book, Beyond Good and Evil, Which it is Meant to Supplement and Clarify."[1] The *Genealogy* can be read as an exegesis and commentary on the very phrase "Beyond Good and Evil." In the preface of the *Genealogy*, Nietzsche explains what he means by exegesis, and what such an exegesis requires.

An aphorism, properly stamped and molded, has not been "deciphered" when it has simply been read; rather, one has then to begin its *exegesis*, for which is required an art of exegesis. I have offered in the third essay of the present book an example of what I regard as "exegesis" in such a case – an aphorism is prefixed to this essay, the essay itself is a commentary on it. To be sure, one thing is necessary above all if one is to practice reading as an *art* in this way, something that has been unlearned most thoroughly nowadays – and therefore it will be some time before my writings are "readable" – something for which one has almost to be a cow and in any case *not* a "modern man": *rumination*. (*G* 23; 267–8)

The hypothesis that I want to explore and defend in this chapter is that the *Genealogy* should be read as a rumination on the meaning of the phrase "Beyond Good and Evil." Perhaps because this expression has become so familiar to us, it has lost its shock value. Much of the commentary on the *Genealogy* has been concerned with the sharp oppositions that Nietzsche introduces in his first essay: "Good and Evil," "Good and Bad." But Nietzsche not only probes the meaning and genealogy of these oppositions; he also deals with the *strife* between them. I hope to show that when we take this strife seriously, we will achieve a deeper and subtler understanding of what Nietzsche means by evil – the evil that threatens modern man. We will see how evil is epitomized by *ressentiment*.

But what about the seemingly innocent term "beyond" (*Jenseits*). Nietzsche drops hints about its meaning when he raises a series of questions at the end of the first essay.

> Was that the end of it? Had the greatest of all conflicts of ideals placed *ad acta* for all time? Or only adjourned, indefinitely adjourned?
>
> Must the ancient fire not some day flare up much more terribly, after much longer preparation? More: must one not desire it with all one's might? even will it? even promote it?
>
> Whoever begins at this point, like my readers, to reflect and pursue his train of thought will not soon come to the end of it – reason enough for me to come to an end, assuming it has long since been abundantly clear what my *aim* is, what the aim of that dangerous slogan is that is inscribed at the head of my last book *Beyond Good and Evil*. – At least this does *not* mean "Beyond Good and Bad." (*G* 55; 302)

What is Nietzsche's aim? What is the aim of that dangerous slogan "Beyond Good and Evil"? These questions are even more perplexing when we consider what Nietzsche has to say about "beyond" in *Ecce Homo*.[2] There he explicitly mocks the very idea of "beyond." In the section "Why I am So Clever," he emphatically states " 'God,' 'immortality of the soul,' 'redemption,' 'beyond' – without exception, concepts to which I never devote any attention, or time; not even as a child" (*EH* 236). And again, "What mankind has so far considered seriously have not even been realities but mere imaginings – more strictly speaking, *lies* prompted by the bad instincts of sick natures that were harmful in the most profound sense – all these concepts, 'God,' 'soul,' 'virtue,' 'sin,' 'beyond,' 'truth,' 'eternal life' " (*EH* 256).

If we are to give an exegesis of "beyond" as it appears in "Beyond Good and Evil," then our first task is to examine the contrasts of "Good and Bad" and "Good and Evil." The outlines of Nietzsche's narrative have been repeated so frequently that it is all too easy to miss the point of what he is saying and why. Nevertheless, before elucidating the subtleties and perplexities of this narrative, I want to begin with a straightforward account of Nietzsche's claims.

Good and bad versus good and evil

By contrast with the misguided moral genealogy of the English psychologists who have sought to account for the origin of moral distinctions by an appeal to their utility, Nietzsche claims that the origin of good (in the good/bad contrast) arises with the "noble, powerful, high-stationed and high-minded, who felt and established themselves and their actions as good, that is of the first rank, in contradistinction to all the low, low-minded, common and plebeian. It was out of this *pathos of distance* that they first seized the right to create values and to coin names for values (*G* 26; 273). These aristocratic nobles used the expression "good" to refer to themselves and their distinctive activities. They first seized the right to create values. "Bad" was the term used to refer to those who lacked these noble characteristics; and to what was other than, and lower than, the good. The modern concepts of "utility," "egoistic," or "unegoistic" had nothing to do with this good/bad contrast. It is anachronistic – or, as Nietzsche says, "unhistorical" – to read these categories back into the aristocratic contrast of the noble and the plebeian. On the contrary, Nietzsche writes:

> The signpost to the *right* road was for me the question: what was the real etymological significance of the designations for "good" coined in the various languages? I have found they all led back to the *same conceptual transformation* – that everywhere "noble," "aristocratic" in the social sense, is the basic concept from which "good" in the sense of "with aristocratic soul," "noble," "with a soul of high order," with "a privileged soul" necessarily developed: a development which always runs parallel with that other in which "common," "plebeian," "low" are finally transformed into the concept "bad." (*G* 27–8; 275)

These aristocratic men call themselves truthful, courageous, powerful, and noble. They are the pure, who distinguish themselves from the impure and the unclean. Nietzsche warns his readers not to interpret these epithets as being merely symbolic. "The 'pure one' is from the beginning merely a man who washes himself, who forbids himself certain foods that produce skin ailments, who does not sleep with dirty women of the lower strata, who has an aversion to blood – no more, hardly more!" (*G* 32; 279)

If this state of affairs had perpetuated itself, then presumably the contrasting values of good/evil would never have arisen. This later contrast is created in *reaction* to the good/bad opposition. As Nietzsche's narrative unfolds, we discover that another class of individuals arises: the priestly aristocrats. Unlike the healthy nobility, there is "something *unhealthy* in such priestly aristocracies and in the habits ruling in them which turn them away from action and alternate between brooding and emotional explosions, habits which seem to have as their invariable consequence that intestinal morbidity and neurasthenia which has afflicted priests at all times" (*G* 32; 279). (Throughout the *Genealogy*, Nietzsche emphasizes the somatic and physiological grounding of psychological dispositions and ethical evaluations.)

But how did the priestly mode of evaluation branch off from the knightly, aristocratic mode, and develop into its opposite? Nietzsche explains this in a variety of ways. A fierce, jealous opposition develops between the priestly class and the warrior class. The priestly class is no match for the aristocratic nobles when it comes to war. The priests are physically and psychologically impotent.

> As is well known, the priests are the *most evil enemies [die bösesten Feinde]* – but why? Because they are the most impotent. It is because of their impotence that in them hatred grows to monstrous and uncanny proportions, to the most spiritual and poisonous kind of hatred. The truly great haters in world history have always been priests; likewise the most ingenious [*Geistreich*] haters: other kinds of spirit hardly come into consideration when compared with the spirit of priestly vengefulness. Human history would be altogether too stupid a thing without the spirit that the impotent have introduced into it. (*G* 33; 280–1)

What does Nietzsche mean by the seemingly perverse claim that human history would be too stupid a thing (*dumme Sache*) without the spirit that the impotent have introduced into it? (We shall see how this and other similar remarks are vital for my exegesis.) At this preliminary stage, I simply want to note that this is the place where Nietzsche first introduces his reference to the Jews as the priestly people *par excellence*. They are the prime example of the "creativity" of the great haters – haters who create a new value system.[3]

All that has been done on earth against "the noble," "the powerful," "the masters," "the rulers," fades into nothing compared with what the *Jews* have done against them; the Jews, that priestly people, who in opposing their enemies and conquerors were ultimately satisfied with nothing less than a radical revaluation of their enemies' values, that is to say, an act of the *most spiritual revenge*. For this alone was appropriate to a priestly people, the people embodying the most deeply repressed priestly vengefulness. It was the Jews who, with awe-inspiring consistency, dared to invert the aristocratic value-equation (good = noble = powerful = beautiful = happy = beloved of God) and to hang on to this inversion with their teeth, the teeth of the most abysmal hatred (the hatred of impotence), saying "the wretched alone are good; the poor, impotent, lowly alone are good; the suffering, deprived, sick, ugly alone are pious, alone are blessed by God, blessedness is for them alone – and you, the powerful and noble are on the contrary the evil, the cruel, the lustful, the insatiable, the godless to all eternity; and you shall be in all eternity the unblessed, accursed, and damned! (*G* 33–4; 281)

This passage (which concludes with a parody of the New Testament) makes it clear that the primary target of Nietzsche's polemic is not exclusively the Jews, but the Judeo-Christian tradition. "One knows *who* inherited this Jewish revaluation" (*G* 34; 281). The conclusion of this section, which refers to section 195 of *Beyond Good and Evil*, makes this explicit.

The Jews – a people "born for slavery," as Tacitus and the whole ancient world say; "the chosen people among the peoples," as they themselves say and believe – the Jews have brought off that miraculous feat of an inversion of values, thanks to which life on earth has acquired a novel and dangerous attraction for a couple of millennia: their prophets have fused "rich," "godless," "evil," "violent," and "sensual," into one and were the first to use the word "world" as an opprobrium. This inversion of values (which includes using the word "poor" as synonymous with "holy" and "friend") constitutes the significance of the Jewish people: they mark the beginning of the slave rebellion in morals. (*BGE* 108; 118–19)

In sum, a great inversion has taken place in the course of history. The "original" values of good and bad have been reversed. The great "creative" act of the priestly haters has been to turn the tables on the aristocratic nobles – to condemn them and their actions as evil, and to claim that the vengeful haters, the impotent, and the weak are the truly good. "Israel, with its vengefulness and revaluation of all values, has hitherto triumphed again and again over all other values, over all *nobler* ideals" (*G* 35; 283). Nietzsche concludes his narrative of the triumph of good and evil over good and bad in a hyperbolic fashion.

The symbol of this struggle, inscribed in letters across all human history, is "Rome against Judea, Judea against Rome" – there has hitherto been no greater event that *this* struggle, *this* question, *this* deadly contradiction
. . . .

Which of them has won *for the present*, Rome or Judea? But there is no doubt: consider to whom one bows down in Rome itself today, as if they were the epitome of all the highest values – and not only in Rome but over almost half the earth, everywhere that man has become tame or desires to become tame: *three Jews*, as is known, *one Jewess* (Jesus of Nazareth, the fisherman Peter, the rug weaver Paul, and the mother of the aforementioned Jesus, named Mary). This is very remarkable: Rome has been defeated beyond all doubt. (*G* 52–3; 300–1)

To complete this preliminary sketch of the battle between the two sets of values (good/bad versus good/evil), I want to note the introduction of what will turn out to be the most important concept in the *Genealogy*, and the most important concept for understanding what Nietzsche means by evil – *ressentiment*.[4] Nietzsche begins section ten as follows:

The slave revolt in morality begins when *ressentiment* itself becomes creative and gives birth to values: the *ressentiment* of natures that are denied the true reaction, that of deeds, and compensate themselves with an imaginary revenge. While every noble morality develops from a triumphant affirmation of itself, slave morality from the outset says No to what is "outside," what is "different," what is "not itself", and *this* No is its creative deed. This inversion of the value-positing eye – this *need to* direct one's view outward instead of back to oneself – is of the essence of *ressentiment*: in order to exist, slave morality always first needs a hostile external world; it needs physiologically speaking, external stimuli in order to act at all – its action is fundamentally reaction. (*G* 36–7; 284–5)

Nietzsche's irony not withstanding, let us note that he characterizes this revolt as "creative." Later, when we examine what Nietzsche means by a transvaluation of values, we should not forget that the one "historical" example that he gives of such a transvaluation is the slave revolt.

I have stayed close to Nietzsche's own words in presenting his account of the origins of the good/bad and the good/evil distinctions, and of the struggle that takes place between these competing value orientations. But there is one major respect in which this sketch is misleading and can result in a serious misinterpretation of Nietzsche's aims. It looks as if we are confronted with a set of stark oppositions, where the good/bad distinction is taken to be entirely positive, and the good/evil distinction is entirely negative. We might think that Nietzsche is indicating that the slave revolt, the triumph of Judea over Rome, is an unmitigated disaster. But such an interpretation would be deeply flawed; for it would fail to take into account the fact that Nietzsche is a supreme dialectician and a dialectical ironist. To bring out the significance of Nietzsche's depiction of the battle of good/bad versus good/evil, we need to step back and ruminate. What is Nietzsche doing in the *Genealogy*? Indeed, what does he even mean by "genealogy"? What is its aim, and how does he accomplish this aim? To answer these questions, we must return to the beginning – not just to the beginning of the opening essay, but to Nietzsche's provocative, compact preface.

The dialectical ironist

Nietzsche begins the preface by declaring: "We are unknown to ourselves, we men of knowledge – and with good reason. We have never sought ourselves – how could it happen that we should ever *find* ourselves?" (*G* 15; 259). This claim by itself is not particularly striking. Many philosophers, beginning with Socrates, have claimed that we are ignorant of ourselves. But Nietzsche makes a much more radical and paradoxical claim. "So we are necessarily strangers [*notwendig fremd*] to ourselves, we do not comprehend ourselves, we *have* to misunderstand ourselves, for us the law 'Each is furthest from himself' applies to all eternity – we are not 'men of knowledge' with respect to ourselves" (*G* 15; 259). Nietzsche is the first major thinker (but not the last) to state categorically that we are *necessarily* strangers to ourselves, that we not only do, but *must* misunderstand ourselves. Why is this so? Nietzsche does not answer this question explicitly in the preface (although we shall see that when the preface is reread in light of what follows, the answer is already implicit in it). He proceeds to raise a new type of question. He does not simply ask about the conditions under which human beings devised the value judgments good and evil; he wants to inquire into the *value* of this distinction.

> Fortunately I learned early to separate theological prejudice from moral prejudice and ceased to look for the origin of evil *behind* the world. A certain amount of historical and philological schooling, together with an inborn fastidiousness of taste in respect to psychological questions in general, soon transformed my problem into another one: under what conditions did man devise these value judgments good and evil? *and what value do they themselves possess?* Have they hitherto hindered or furthered human prosperity? Are they a sign of distress, of impoverishment, of the degeneration of life? Or is there revealed in them, on the contrary, the plenitude, force and will of life, its courage, certainty, future? (*G* 17; 261–2)[5]

What Nietzsche calls for – what is needed – is a critique of morality, a critique in which the *value* of the values of good and evil are called into question, a critique that reveals the conditions and the circumstances in which they have arisen and evolved. But if we pause to ruminate, then we see that this new demand is extremely paradoxical. The perplexities it engenders stand at the center of some of the most heated and controversial debates among Nietzsche interpreters. What does Nietzsche mean by a critique of moral values? The very semantics of critique seems to demand some standard, some criterion, some basic norm, from which we can conduct such a critique. But then – especially for philosophers – the question immediately arises about the status of this presupposed standard or norm for conducting a critique. The philosopher wants to know whether the standard can be *justified*. And by justification, he means, are there reasons – good reasons – for adopting such a standard? He suspects that if good reasons are not forthcoming, the critique is arbitrary and thus invalid. This line of thinking, especially for philosophers, seems so reasonable and self-evident that it is difficult to even imagine an alternative. Yet Nietzsche not only eschews the search for such a grounding of his critique of morals, he mocks the search for a rational foundation of morality. In *Beyond Good and Evil*, he writes:

> With a stiff seriousness that inspires laughter, all our philosophers demanded something far more exalted, presumptuous, and solemn from themselves as soon as they approached the study of morality: they wanted to supply a *rational foundation* for morality [*die Begründung der Moral*] – and every philosopher so far has believed that he has provided such a foundation. (*BGE* 9; 107)

It is at this point that many critics of Nietzsche are ready to pounce – to claim that he is caught in a self-referential paradox, or a performative contradiction – and to say that, willy-nilly, he is trapped in a self-defeating relativism. But Nietzsche is well aware that these are just the sorts of objections that will be raised against him. And, as I want to show, he seeks to blunt the sting of these obvious objections by questioning and challenging the very standpoint from which they are raised. I do not think, therefore, that any of these criticisms hit their target. To support my case, I want to raise a number of relevant questions.

What is Nietzsche doing in his Genealogy? I have already given a general answer. He is engaged in a critique of morality – a critique directed to exposing our distinction between good and evil, our moral prejudices. Why these? Because they are the primary values that prevail in modernity – specifically in modern Europe. Now although this seems relatively straightforward, it has an important consequence. Nietzsche is not interested primarily in what we might take to be an "objective" or "neutral" account of the history of morality. He is deliberately using "historical" material for a specific polemical purpose – to expose what he takes to be the "dishonest lie" that stands at the heart of this morality, *our* morality. If we were to (mis)read his first essay as purporting to provide a fair and accurate historical account of the genesis of the values good/bad and good/evil, then we would certainly judge it to be a miserable failure. Nietzsche gives the scantiest evidence to justify his ambitious generalizations. His story of the origins seems much more like a fiction or a myth that he has created. He might even affirm that his account of the slave revolt is itself a "noble lie." But the purpose of this "noble lie" – this fiction – is to compel us to question our morality, to raise just the sorts of questions about our "moral prejudices" that have not been asked, and indeed have been suppressed and repressed. Nietzsche's polemic is intended to show that what we assume to be universal morality is historically contingent, and is itself a reactive, negative morality motivated by *ressentiment*. If this is what Nietzsche is doing, if his aim is self-consciously and deliberately polemical, if he is freely using historical material to invent a noble lie, then we must probe what he means by genealogy, and how it contributes to this task.

What is genealogy? An adequate answer to this question would require a careful analysis of Nietzsche's famous essay "On the Uses and Disadvantages of History for Life."[6] In this essay, which is a meditation on the value of history, Nietzsche outlines his three, famous kinds of history: monumental, antiquarian, and critical. Monumental history is governed by the ethical impulse to counter what is base and petty. Antiquarian history (at its best) teaches veneration of a people's or a nation's past. And critical history mercilessly exposes past contingencies, both the violence and the weaknesses exhibited in the past.[7] All three forms can be used and abused. They can promote higher, life-enhancing activities, or they can paralyze creative action and thereby contribute to a degeneration of human life.

"The genuine historian" (*der echte Historiker*) is the rare person who knows how to blend and use the several kinds of history in order to promote a higher form of life. The value of this genuine history "will be seen to consist in its taking a familiar, perhaps commonplace theme, an everyday melody, and composing inspired variations on it, enhancing it, elevating it, elevating it to a comprehensive symbol, and thus disclosing in the original theme a whole world of profundity, power, and beauty" (UD 93). Peter Berkowitz gives a succinct description of this artistic task of the genuine historian.

The genuine historian is both a knower and a creator whose comprehensive making of art is based on his universal knowledge. He "must possess the power to remint [*umzuprägen*] the universally known into something never heard of before, and to express the universal so simply and profoundly that the simplicity is lost in the profundity and the profundity in the simplicity" (UD 6, p. 94). Rich with great and exalted experiences, "great historians" recover, correctly interpret and beautifully express through their histories "the great and exalted things of the past" (UD 6, p. 94.)[8]

The genuine historian creatively reshapes the past in order to serve the needs of the present and to give direction to the future. Genealogy is the *art* performed by the genuine historian who knows how to blend monumental, critical, and antiquarian history in an imaginative manner for the purpose of furthering higher forms of life. This is the art that Nietzsche performs in his *Genealogy*. Insofar as he evokes images of a past nobility and glory, he is engaged in monumental history; insofar as he employs his knowledge of philology to probe the etymological meanings of the value terms good/bad, noble/base, he draws upon antiquarian history; and insofar as he lays bare the violence, cruelty, and impotence involved in the slave revolt, he is making use of critical history. Such a genealogy comes "close to free poetic invention" (UD 70). Consequently, to claim that Nietzsche's narrative of the origins of the values good/bad and good/evil is a fiction is not to criticize him; it is rather to restate his intention and aim. Furthermore, it is crucial to appreciate the temporality of his genealogy. It is not really about the past, but is primarily concerned with the present and with future possibilities. (The subtitle of *Beyond Good and Evil* is "Prelude to a Philosophy of the Future" (*Vorspiel einer Philosophie der Zukunft*).) The critique of our present morality is performed with an eye to discerning the possibilities immanent within it for overcoming (*überwindung*) it. Yet the specter of "justification" haunts us. Even if one concedes that Nietzsche's narrative is a "poetic fiction," an artistic, imaginative blending of different types of "history" for the purpose of critiquing the present and opening up future possibilities, we still want to know how we are to judge it, how we are to determine its critical effectiveness. So we are led back to the question, How does Nietzsche "justify" his critique of our present morality?

To answer this question, we need to return to our straightforward account of Nietzsche's narrative of the origin of the good/evil contrast as a reaction to the aristocratic good/bad distinction. At first glance, the contrast between these two sets of valuation is so antithetical that we may think that Nietzsche is unequivocally praising the knightly aristocratic valuation scheme, and unconditionally condemning the reactive good/evil morality. But when we take a closer look, we see that his evaluation is more complex and dialectical. When he first introduces his notion of the priestly aristocracy, he tells us, "it is only fair to add that it was on the soil of this *essentially dangerous* form of existence, the priestly form, that man first became *an interesting animal*, that only here did the human soul in a higher sense acquire *depth* and become *evil* – and these are the two basic respects in which man has hitherto been superior to other beasts!" (*G* 33; 280). The italicized words here are Nietzsche's, and in his rhetorical lexicon, all of them are positively valued. They enhance life. Or again, in a passage cited previously, "human history would be altogether too stupid a thing without the spirit that the impotent introduced into it" (*G* 33; 281). When he characterizes the hatred of the Jews who began the slave revolt, he describes it as "the profoundest and sublimest kind of hatred, capable of creating ideas and reversing values, the like of which has never existed on earth before" (*G* 34; 282).

Nietzsche is not simply praising the value of his noble aristocrats and condemning the values of the reactive priests. And he certainly is not advocating any sort of nostalgic return to a mythic history of pure nobles. His genealogy is *dialectical* – dialectical in a very precise sense. Nietzsche's dialectical mode of thinking is sharply contrasted with the "prejudice" of metaphysicians. "The fundamental faith of the metaphysicians is *the faith in opposite values*" (*BGE* 10; 10).[9] His critique of the morality of good and evil seeks to expose both its *dangers* and its *creative* possibilities. In all three essays, Nietzsche artfully brings his readers to the point where they glimpse the possibility of a higher, more creative, life-affirming ethic that may *yet* still arise (at least for a few superior individuals) out of the ashes of its opposite – the slave morality that up to now has triumphed and prevailed.[10] We can also grasp the precise import of Nietzsche's "beyond." This beyond is an overcoming (*überwindung*) of the morality of good and evil – an overcoming that is possible only by *experiencing* the morality of good and evil in its full power, intensity, and danger, and passing through and beyond it. This beyond, then – to speak oxymoronically – is an *immanent* beyond, not a transcendent one. When Nietzsche tells us in *Ecce Homo* that he never devoted any attention or time to the concept of a beyond, he is referring to a transcendent beyond. But the very aim of Nietzsche's *Genealogy* is to open the possibility of a higher, life-affirming ethic that can grow out of the soil of the morality of good and evil.

What is the basis for placing a higher evaluation on what Nietzsche describes as life affirming? The question of "justification" comes back to haunt us. Implicitly or explicitly, Nietzsche is always evaluating the competing schemes that he describes. His language secretes *his* value biases. Is Nietzsche not caught up in a performative contradiction when he undermines the rational basis for any critique of morality, including his own, as so many of his critics have charged? I do not think that Nietzsche falls into this trap – a trap that philosophers are all too ready to set for him. Rather, he urges us to set aside the question of "justification" – to reject what initially appears so eminently reasonable. To show this, I want to appropriate and modify some distinctions introduced by Richard Rorty in his characterization of "the ironist."[11]

To explain what he means by an "ironist," Rorty introduces the idea of a "final vocabulary." A final vocabulary consists of "the words in which we formulate praise of our friends and contempt for our enemies, our long-term projects, our deepest self-doubts and highest hopes." Such a vocabulary is not final because it rests upon a solid rational foundation, but in the sense that "if doubt is cast on the worth of these words, their user has no noncircular argumentative recourse" whereby to defend them. Rorty distinguishes two aspects of this final vocabulary. It is made up of "thin, flexible, and ubiquitous terms such as 'true,' 'good,' 'right,' and 'beautiful.'" But much more important are the "thicker, more rigid, more parochial terms."[12] If we apply this distinction to Nietzsche, then his thicker terms include "healthy," "life-enhancing," and "life-affirming." Rorty then specifies three conditions for the ironist. Although Nietzsche would probably reject the first two, he would accept the third (when properly interpreted).[13] Insofar as the ironist philosophizes, she "does not think that her vocabulary is closer to reality than others, that it is in touch with a power not herself." Ironists see "the choice between vocabularies as made neither within a neutral and universal metavocabulary nor by an attempt to fight one's way past appearances to the real, but simply by playing off the new against the old."[14] If this third condition has a distinctive Nietzschean ring, it is because Rorty derived it from Nietzsche.

The opposite of irony is common sense – that is, accepting common beliefs without any genuine critical reflection, as if they are simply self-evident. This is the way in which proponents of the slave morality of good and evil judge their own morality. They think that their value scheme is universal. It is what any reasonable person (that is, good Christian) believes. Nietzsche's critique of morality is directed to exposing the self-deceptive illusion that the morality of good and evil is *the* universal, *the* only genuine morality. He also wants to show that the good/evil morality, which appears so reasonable, is founded on *ressentiment*.

But what happens when common sense is seriously challenged. According to Rorty, the first line of defense is to "go Socratic." "The question 'What is x?' is now asked in such a way that it cannot be answered simply by producing paradigm cases of x-hood. So one may demand a definition, an essence."[15] The philosopher who thinks it is possible to find a rational grounding for his final vocabulary is what Rorty labels the "metaphysician."

The metaphysician is someone who takes the question "What is the intrinsic nature (e.g. of justice, science, knowledge, Being, faith, morality, philosophy)?" at face value. He assumes that the presence of a term in his own vocabulary ensures that it refers to something which *has* a real essence. The metaphysician is still attached to common sense, in that he does not question the platitudes which encapsulate the use of a given final vocabulary, and in particular the platitude which says there is a single permanent reality to be found behind the many temporary appearances.[16]

This description of the metaphysician comes close to Nietzsche's characterization of the philosopher in the third essay of the *Genealogy*, where he shows how the philosopher exemplifies the ascetic ideal. But even if it is conceded that the metaphysician or the philosopher deludes himself by thinking he can ground his final vocabulary with good solid reasons, how does the ironist "justify" his final vocabulary? The point is that he *doesn't* – and he doesn't even pretend to. He laughs at those who think they can pull off this trick. Searching for such grounding is seeking metaphysical comfort. But what is the alternative? Nietzsche may detest the type of value relativism whereby all values are leveled out and become bland; but how does he avoid this consequence? The metaphysician/philosopher will certainly retort that anyone who does not justify his basic convictions with good solid reasons, and who does not think that this is even *possible*, is a relativist. Rorty himself makes this point.

The metaphysician responds to this sort of talk by calling it "relativistic" and insisting that what matters is not what language is being used but what is true. Metaphysicians think that human beings by nature desire to know. They think this because the vocabulary they have inherited, their common sense, provides them with a picture of knowledge as a relation between human beings and "reality," and the idea that we have a need and a duty to enter into this relation. It also tells us that "reality," if properly asked, will help us determine what our final vocabulary should be. So metaphysicians believe that there are, out there in the world, real essences which it is our duty to discover and which are disposed to assist in their own discovery.[17]

Given the content and tone of what Rorty says about the metaphysician/philosopher, Nietzsche might well consider him to be a true disciple!

But what recourse does the ironist have if he is challenged about the status of his final vocabulary? What recourse does Nietzsche have if we start asking what is the basis for praising life-affirming values and condemning life-degenerating values? Rorty labels the alternative "redescription." Redescription covers a variety of rhetorical, poetic, and metaphoric devices – including story telling, vivid examples, inventive fictions, and myths – all

The Moral Psychology of Evil

of which are used to make a specific vocabulary, a way of viewing the world as attractive and as persuasive as possible. The type of ironist that Rorty favors is, appropriating Harold Bloom's expression, "the strong poet" – someone who has the imaginative creative ability to break through entrenched, deadening ways of "normal" description in order to invent startling new creative forms of perceiving, feeling, and evaluating.[18] Nietzsche does not justify his critique of morality by an appealing to rational grounds or metaphysical foundations; he "justifies" it by imaginative redescription, by opening up new possibilities – possibilities that only strong poets are capable of creating. I place "justifies" in scare quotes deliberately, because by the standards of the metaphysician/philosopher this is *no* justification at all. It is too relativistic. But the very plausibility of this standard objection presupposes that it is possible to ground one's final vocabulary, by giving a noncircular argument that will justify it. This is what Nietzsche and Rorty are challenging. This is the self-deceptive illusion of the metaphysician. He thinks that there really is something "better," "firmer," "more solid" than redescription. But there isn't – or so Nietzsche and Rorty claim.

We can interpret Nietzsche as engaged in a two-stage strategy (although these stages are frequently blended together). The first stage involves questioning traditional philosophical understandings of grounding, rational argumentation, and seeking solid foundations. He ridicules and "laughs" at the suggestion that this is even possible. He is certainly wily and sophisticated enough to recognize that this is just as true for his own striking claims about "knowledge," "reality," and "morality." He wants to expose the self-deceptive *prejudice* about rational foundations that lies at the heart of philosophy. This aspect of his strategy is directed towards eliminating this fiction. But Nietzsche is even more radical. The second stage is to challenge the implicit either/or that plays such a significant role in the thinking of the metaphysician/philosopher. For the metaphysician is convinced that there are only two alternatives: either "serious" rational grounding or self-defeating relativism. This is the most disastrous prejudice of all – and it keeps philosophy in constant oscillation.[19] This way of thinking needs to be abandoned, and replaced by the frank recognition that there is nothing more fundamental than imaginative and poetic redescription. Or, to use Nietzsche's own vocabulary, one needs to invent and experiment with multiple styles and perspectives, in order to show which fictions are creative and life-enhancing, and which are destructive and dangerously self-deceptive. The proper question to ask about Nietzsche's critique of morality is *not* whether it rests on a secure "rational foundation," but rather, whether, in its graphic details, it enables us to expose what has been hidden and encrusted in moral platitudes – that is, whether it enables us to *know and see differently*.

Interpreting Nietzsche in this way helps to situate what have been called his "perspectivism" and his "stylistic pluralism."[20] Recently, there has been a great deal of discussion (pro and con) of Nietzsche's "perspectivism." There is something excessive and off-center about this debate, because it tends to suggest that Nietzsche was primarily interested in making a contribution to the epistemological issues that obsess so many contemporary philosophers. One of Nietzsche's clearest most forceful statements about perspective appears in the *Genealogy*. Because it is so relevant for understanding Nietzsche's critique of morality and his reflections on evil, I want to quote it at length.

> But precisely because we seek knowledge, let us not be ungrateful to such resolute reversals of accustomed perspectives and valuations with which the spirit has, with apparent mischievousness and futility, raged against itself for so long: to see differently in this way for once, to *want* to see differently, is no small discipline and preparation of the intellect for its future "objectivity" – the latter understood not as "contemplation without interest" (which is a nonsensical absurdity), but as the ability *to control* one's Pro and Con and to dispose of them, so that one knows how to employ a *variety* of perspectives and affective interpretations in the service of knowledge.
>
> Henceforth, my dear philosophers, let us be on guard against the dangerous old conceptual fiction that posited a "pure, will-less, painless, timeless knowing subject"; let us guard against the snares of such contradictory concepts as "pure reason," "absolute spirituality," "knowledge in itself": these always demand that we should think of an eye that is completely unthinkable, an eye turned in no particular direction, in which the active and interpreting forces, through which alone seeing becomes seeing *something*, are supposed to be lacking; these always demand of the eye an absurdity and nonsense. There is *only* a perspective seeing, *only* a perspective "knowing"; and the *more* affects we allow to speak about one thing, the *more* eyes, different eyes, we can use to observe one thing, the more complete will our "concept" of this thing, our "objectivity," be. But to eliminate the will altogether, to suspend each and every affect, supposing we were capable of this – what would that mean but to *castrate* the intellect? (*G* 119; 382–3)

There are several points in this rich passage that I want to emphasize. Consider the way in which it begins, "But precisely because we seek knowledge." Nietzsche is certainly not denying the possibility of knowledge; he is categorically affirming it. Furthermore, he makes a number of claims that he takes to be *true*. He is denying the possibility of a "timeless knowing subject" and "pure reason." He is challenging the very possibility of "transcendental" knowledge. We would make a mockery of Nietzsche's strong claims if we failed to take seriously what he affirms. Indeed,

Nietzsche's claims about perspective ("There is *only* perspective seeing, *only* perspective 'knowing'") are themselves dependent on the truth of his assertions. So too when he says, "the *more* eyes, different eyes, we can use to observe one thing, the more complete will our 'concept' of this thing, our 'objectivity' be," he is not calling into question the idea of "objectivity," but calling attention to a more *adequate* notion of what "objectivity" means. Nietzsche's stinging critiques are directed toward what he takes to be *false*, misleading, and harmful conceptions of knowledge, truth, and objectivity. He is certainly not advocating a form of "relativism" such that we lose all sense of hierarchy, value and judgment.[21]

I have used Rorty's expression "redescription" to characterize Nietzsche's critique of morality; but the term is perhaps too bland to capture the richness, vividness, and power of Nietzsche's language. It is more illuminating to compare Nietzsche with another poet/philosopher, one about whom Nietzsche was ambivalent, the Platonic Socrates. There is a consistent strand in Nietzsche's relentless criticism of Socrates. He portrays Socrates as initiating the type of philosophical inquiry that is always searching for essences and for rational justification, one that seeks to supplant the old gods of the Greeks with the new god of *logos*. This is the Platonic Socrates who is at war with Homer, the tragedians, and the poets. But there is *another*, subversive reading of the Platonic dialogues. Just at the points where we expect Socrates to provide some definitive "rational account," we are offered myths, allegories, similes, and metaphors. (Consider the central books of the *Republic*, or the role that myth plays in the *Phaedrus*.) These myths and fictions have far more persuasive power than the inconclusive arguments offered by Socrates. Despite the seductive charm of these poetic devices, the Platonic Socrates is constantly telling us that they are only approximations, second best to what can be grasped ultimately by a rational account. It seems that *mythos* is to be subordinated to a "higher" *logos*. This is the Socrates whom Nietzsche criticizes so relentlessly. But in Nietzsche's own heroic contest, in his *agon* with the Platonic Socrates, he seeks to effect a dramatic reversal – to show that *mythos* cunningly triumphs over *logos*. We remember the power, fertility, and suggestiveness of Socrates' stories and myths long after we have forgotten his limp, unpersuasive arguments. It is the ironic, playful, subversive Socrates that Nietzsche admires. And in this spirit, Nietzsche's own distinctive creative use of *mythos* is used to "justify" his critique of morality. Nietzsche is a dialectical ironist because he eschews the metaphysician's fundamental faith – the faith in opposite values. On the contrary, he seeks to show how something originates out of its opposite. His critique of morality is intended to show how a "higher ethic" may arise out of its opposite – the good/evil morality. It is this dialectical transition, this movement *beyond* good and evil, that we must now explore in greater detail.

Evil and ressentiment

Let us return to the account that I gave of the origin of good/evil in reaction to the good/bad ethic. Initially we might think that "evil" is simply the expression invented by the priestly class to name and condemn everything that the aristocratic nobles take to be good. But the matter is not quite so straightforward. I have already quoted the passage in which Nietzsche first introduces his discussion of the priestly class: "As is well known, the priests are the *most evil enemies* – but why? Because they are the most impotent. It is because of their impotence that in them hatred grows to monstrous and uncanny proportions, to the most spiritual and poisonous kind of hatred" (*G* 33; 280). Whereas "evil" in the mouths of the priests is used to designate what the aristocrat nobles take to be good. It is the priests who are "*the most evil enemies*" from Nietzsche's perspective. What Nietzsche – or, more accurately, the narrator of the *Genealogy* – means by "evil" (when he calls the priests evil) is quite different from what the priests mean when they damn the aristocratic nobles as evil. What, then, is the characteristic of the priestly class that Nietzsche calls evil? His references to "impotence" and the growth of "hatred" anticipate his discussion of *ressentiment*, Nietzsche's treatment of *ressentiment* is dialectical. It is a poisonous danger, yet becomes "creative and gives birth to values." The power of *ressentiment* cannot be underestimated, for it is by virtue of this power that the impotent triumph over the noble aristocracy.

> While the noble man lives in trust and openness with himself . . . , the man of *ressentiment* is neither upright nor naïve nor honest and straightforward with himself. His soul *squints*; his spirit loves hiding places, secret paths and back doors, everything covert entices him as *his* world, *his* security *his* refreshment; he understands how to keep silent, how not to forget, how to wait, how to be provisionally self-deprecating and humble. A race of such men of *ressentiment* is bound to become eventually *cleverer* than any noble race. (*G* 38; 286)[22]

Although Nietzsche identifies the "men of *ressentiment*" primarily with the priests who instigate the slave revolt, he acknowledges that it is a more general psychological phenomenon. Even the nobles may temporarily experience *ressentiment*. "*Ressentiment* itself, if it should appear in the noble man, consummates and exhausts itself in immediate reaction, and therefore does not poison: on the other hand, it fails to appear at all on countless occasions on which it inevitably appears in the weak and impotent" (*G* 39; 287).

Nietzsche explores the psychological dynamics of *ressentiment* in his second essay, " 'Guilt,' 'Bad Conscience,' and the Like." He begins this essay with an inquiry into what is required "to breed an animal *with the right to make promises*" (*G* 57; 307). This "presupposes as a preparatory task that one first *makes* men to a certain degree necessary, uniform, like among like, regular, and consequently calculable" (*G* 58–9; 309). It is only after man has been forcibly *made* into an animal who is responsible that the consciousness of guilt becomes possible. This consciousness is an internalization of what was once an external contractual relationship between creditor and debtor. According to this genealogical account, it was in the sphere of legal obligations "that the moral conceptual world of 'guilt,' 'conscience,' 'duty,' 'sacredness of duty' had its origin" (*G* 65; 316). The development sketched here is from the external (legal) obligations to their *internalization* in the form of moral conscience. This is a movement from legal debts (*Schülden*) to moral guilt (*Schüld*). The most striking feature of Nietzsche's analysis of *ressentiment* (one that clearly anticipates Freud) is this internalization (*Verinnerlichung*) hypothesis.

> All instincts that do not discharge themselves outwardly *turn inward* – this is what I call the *internalization* of man: thus it was that man first developed what was later called his "soul." The entire inner world, originally as thin as if it were stretched between two membranes, expanded and extended itself, acquired depth, breadth, and height, in the same measure as outward discharge was *inhibited*. Those fearful bulwarks with which the political organization protected itself against the old instincts of freedom – punishments belong among these bulwarks – brought about that all those instincts of wild, free, prowling man turned backward *against man himself*. Hostility, cruelty, joy in persecuting, in attacking, in change, in destruction – all this turned against the possessors of such instincts: *That* is the origin of the "bad conscience." (*G* 84–5; 338–9)[23]

The dialectical character of Nietzsche's thinking is vividly illustrated in the way in which he analyzes "bad conscience." He is scathing in his characterization of bad conscience, but at the same time indicates the *constructive* role that it plays in man's development.

> The man, who from lack of external enemies and resistances and forcibly confined to the oppressive narrowness and punctiliousness of custom, impatiently lacerated, persecuted, gnawed at, assaulted, and maltreated himself; this animal that rubbed itself raw against the bars of its cage as one tried to "tame" it; this deprived creature, racked with homesickness for the wild,

who had to turn himself into an adventure, a torture chamber, an uncertain and dangerous wilderness – this fool, this yearning and desperate prisoner became the inventor of the "bad conscience." But thus began the gravest and uncanniest illness, from which humanity has not yet recovered, man's suffering *of man, of himself* – the result of a forcible sundering from his animal past, as it were a leap and plunge into new surroundings and conditions of existence, a declaration of war against the old instincts upon which his strength, joy, and terribleness had rested hitherto. (*G* 85; 339)

Now it certainly looks as if Nietzsche is portraying man, the inventor of "bad conscience," as if he were terminally ill, caught up in a never ending spiral of self-hate, self-laceration, and self-torture. But Nietzsche's use of such active verbal forms, "lacerated," "persecuted," "forcible sundering," should warn us that there is something more going on here than unconditional condemnation. And in the very next paragraph, Nietzsche makes this explicit:

Let us add at once that, on the other hand, the existence on earth of an animal soul turned against itself, taking sides against itself, was something so new, profound, unheard of, enigmatic, contradictory, *and pregnant with a future* that the aspect of the earth was essentially altered. Indeed, divine spectators were needed to do justice to the spectacle that thus began and the end of which is not yet in sight – a spectacle too subtle, too marvelous, too paradoxical to be played senselessly unobserved on some ludicrous planet! From now on, man is *included* among the most unexpected and exciting lucky throws in the dice game of Heraclitus' "great child," be he called Zeus or chance, he gives rise to an interest, a tension, a hope, almost a certainty, as if with him something were announcing and preparing itself, as if man were not a goal but only a way, an episode, a bridge, a great promise. (*G* 85; 339–40)

If we are caught in the metaphysician's trap of "faith in opposite values," then the above claims may seem thoroughly baffling. But the dialectical thinking of Nietzsche makes it clear that *ressentiment* and "bad conscience" are *double-edged*. If *ressentiment* is left to fester, it becomes a dangerous poison, and leads to a type of nihilism that undermines *all* valuation. But the illness that Nietzsche describes is *"pregnant with a future."* Bad conscience is an illness, "but an illness as pregnancy is an illness" (*G* 88; 343). Within the interstices of this illness is also a "great promise," a hope, a bridge, "as if something were announcing and preparing itself." Nietzsche does not yet tell us what this is, but it is becoming increasingly evident that it is *beyond* good and evil, a self-overcoming of *ressentiment*.

It is at this point that the aesthetic coherence and the ironical dialectical power of the *Genealogy* become fully manifest. If we go back to the preface (and read it again), we see that Nietzsche has already indicated the direction of his thinking – where he is leading his discerning reader. The morality of good and evil is the supreme danger (*Gefahr*). If left unchecked, it ineluctably leads to the most sinister symptom of European culture – the type of nihilism exhibited by the triumph of the "last man" as he is portrayed in *Zarathustra*. This is what Nietzsche most abhors and fears, and this is what, if left unopposed, is the most likely consequence of the modernity characteristic of "European culture." The most fundamental battle at the heart of the *Genealogy* is not between the good/bad ethic

and the good/evil morality. *It is Nietzsche's strenuous war against the nihilism of the "last man."* Morality is double-edged, which is why it must be approached dialectically. Insofar as morality expresses a *will* – even if the will turns out to be a will to nothingness – it is an illness that is also a pregnancy, a promise, and a hope. Specifically, it is the promise of overcoming nihilism. This is the theme announced in the preface, and this is what Nietzsche explicitly affirms in the last section of his final essay. But he has already anticipated this grand finale in the second essay.

> We modern men are the heirs of the conscience-vivisection and self-torture of millennia: this is what we have practiced longest, it is our distinctive art perhaps, and in any case our subtlety in which we have acquired a refined taste. Man has all too long had an "evil eye" for his natural inclinations, so that they have finally become inseparable from his "bad conscience." An attempt at the reverse would *in itself* be possible – but who is strong enough for it – that is, to wed the bad conscience to all the *unnatural* inclinations, all those aspirations to the beyond, to that which runs counter to sense, instinct, nature, animal, in short all ideals hitherto, which are one and all hostile to life and ideals that slander the world. To whom should one turn today with *such* hopes and demands? (*G* 95, 351)

Nietzsche is fully aware that this diatribe against modern man is shocking and offensive. But this hyperbolic critique is required in order to clear the way for the possibility of erecting a new ideal. "But have you ever asked yourselves sufficiently how much the erection of *every* ideal on earth has cost?" (*G* 95; 351). But there still remains a final question: Is a new ideal really possible? Is it really possible to overcome the pervasive entrenched morality of good and evil, to envision what is *beyond* good and evil? In a passage that mimics and maliciously parodies that other source of "good news," the *New Testament*, Nietzsche declares:

> Is this even possible today – But some day, in a stronger age than this decaying, self-doubting present, he must yet come to us, the *redeeming* man of great love and contempt, the creative spirit whose compelling strength

will not let him rest in any aloofness or any beyond, whose isolation is misunderstood by the people as if it were flight *from* reality – while it is only his absorption, immersion, penetration *into* reality, so that, when he one day emerges again in the light, he may bring home the *redemption* of this reality: its redemption from the curse that the hitherto reigning ideal has laid upon it. This man of the future, who will redeem us not only from the hitherto reigning ideal but also from that which was bound to grow out of it, the great nausea, the will to nothingness, nihilism; this bell-stroke of noon and of the great decision that liberates the will again and restores its goal to the earth and nothingness – *he must come one day.* (G 96; 352)

Beyond good and evil

The *Genealogy* should be read as an exegesis and rumination on the meaning of that "dangerous slogan" – "Beyond Good and Evil." Each of the essays in the *Genealogy* contributes to the dialectical critique of morality. With each succeeding essay, our understanding of this slogan becomes more profound. The three essays are experiments in the art of perspectival knowing, the art of seeing differently. Each essay deepens Nietzsche's "hermeneutics of suspicion," the unmasking that enables us to discern and criticize what underlies our morality.[24] The first essay provides the initial account of the origin of the morality of good and evil. The second essay probes the psychological conditions and dynamics of this morality, focusing on the role of *ressentiment* and the formation of bad conscience. The third essay examines the meaning of ascetic ideals, the ideals professed and exemplified by the proponents of the morality of good and evil. This third essay is a portrait gallery of the character types governed by ascetic ideals, but its main targets are those philosophers and scholars who think (that is, who delude themselves) that they are superior to the religious priests. They too exhibit the illness that arises from *ressentiment*, but in a secular form. But does this ascetic ideal serve any *function*? Is there any *purpose* achieved by this extreme self-laceration?

It must be a necessity of the first order that again and again promotes the growth and prosperity of this *life-inimical* species – it must indeed be in the *interest of life itself* that such a self-contradictory type does not die out. For an ascetic life is a self-contradiction: here rules a *ressentiment* without equal, that of an insatiable instinct and power-will that wants to become master not over something in life but over life itself, over its most profound, powerful, and basic conditions; here an attempt is made to employ force to block up the wells of force; here physiological well-being itself is viewed askance, and especially the outward expression of this well-being, beauty, and joy; while pleasure is felt and *sought* in ill-constitutedness, decay, pain, mischance,

ugliness, voluntary deprivation, self-mortification, self-flagellation, self-sac-
rifice. All this is in the highest degree paradoxical: we stand before a dis-
cord that *wants* to be discordant, that *enjoys* itself in this suffering and even
grows more self-confident and triumphant the more its own presupposition,
its physiological capacity for life, *decreases.* (*G* 117–18, 381)

This paradoxical, self-contradictory, self-lacerating phenomenon is not
the worst; it is still a perverse form of *strength.* The ultimate degradation
arises when this perverse form of will, a will turned against itself, dissipates
– the calamity of a nihilism in which there is no longer fear, but only
nausea and pity.[25] "What is most to be feared, what has a more calami-
tous effect than any other calamity, is that man should inspire not profound fear but profound *nausea, also* not great fear but great *pity.* Suppose
these two were one day to unite, they would inevitably beget one of the
uncanniest monsters: the 'last will' of man, his will to nothingness, nihilism" (*G* 122; 386). Nietzsche sounds his warning: this meaningless nihilism
would not only be the greatest calamity, it *is* the most likely fate of European culture. Nietzsche's hyperbolical contrast between the healthy affirmation of life and the self-contradictory laceration of ascetic priests who
minister to the sick herd reaches an almost deafening crescendo in his
third essay.

I have already indicated Nietzsche's finale. The last section of his third
essay is not only a direct answer to the question, "What is the meaning of
ascetic ideals?" but also the grand finale to the three acts, or movements,
of the *Genealogy* – a concluding crescendo that integrates the motifs of the
first two essays, and brings us back to his preface/overture. I now want to
show this in detail by citing this finale in its entirety, and commenting on
it paragraph by paragraph.[26]

> Apart from the ascetic ideal, man, the human *animal,* had no meaning so
> far. His existence on earth contained no goal: "why man at all?" was a
> question without an answer, the *will* for man and earth was lacking; behind
> every great human destiny there sounded as a refrain a yet greater "in
> vain!" *This* is precisely what the ascetic ideal means: that something was
> *lacking,* that man was surrounded by a fearful *void –* he did not know how to
> justify, to account for, to affirm himself, he *suffered* from the problem of his
> meaning. He also suffered otherwise, he was in the main a sickly animal;
> but his problem was *not* suffering itself, but that there was no answer to the
> crying question, "*why* do I suffer?" (*G* 162; 429)

We can finally grasp the meaning of the ascetic ideal – that is, its hidden,
latent meaning. Nietzsche's exegesis, his experiment in the hermeneutics of
suspicion, has brought forth what has thus far been concealed. Ascetic

ideals have served the function of giving *meaning* to human suffering; they have provided man with a goal in the face of "a fearful *void*," something he desperately needs in order to endure suffering. For it is not suffering that man finds unbearable, but *meaningless* suffering. Ascetic ideals are reactive "inventions" that serve to "justify" suffering. What is striking about this opening paragraph – and indeed the entire final section – is that there is no mention of the aristocratic nobles and their good/bad ethic. Nietzsche is not advocating a nostalgic return to some golden era. That would distort the directional temporality – the pointing to the future – that is evident on almost every page of the *Genealogy*. Nietzsche's primary objective, his primary aim, is a critique of *present* morality for the sake of moving beyond it – opening us to new *future* possibilities.

> Man the bravest of animals the one most accustomed to suffering, does *not* repudiate suffering as such; he *desires* it, he even seeks it out, provided he is shown *a meaning* for it, a *purpose* of suffering. The meaninglessness of suffering, *not* suffering itself, was the curse that lay over mankind so far – *and the ascetic ideal offered man meaning!* It was the only meaning offered so far; any meaning is better than none at all; the ascetic ideal was in every sense the *"faute de mieux" par excellence* so far. In it, suffering was *interpreted*; the tremendous void seemed to have been filled; the door was closed to any kind of suicidal nihilism. This interpretation – there is no doubt of it – brought fresh suffering with it, deeper, more inward, more poisonous, more life-destructive suffering: it placed all suffering under the perspective of *guilt*. (*G* 162; 429)

This paragraph shows why it is so important to approach Nietzsche as a dialectical thinker, and why he is not one of those metaphysicians who has a "faith in opposite values." Nietzsche ironically brings forth the *positive* contribution of what he is criticizing. This passage brings out the double significance of Nietzsche's frequent references to danger (*Gefahr*) – danger as both *threat* and *opportunity*. We will not understand our present morality, a morality based on *ressentiment*, unless we see how it became a "creative" force – how it saved man from "suicidal nihilism." Man can endure suffering as long as he can give meaning to, and interpret, this suffering – even if this interpretation is a self-destructive one. This is what the priestly class accomplished; this is what *their* transvaluation of values achieved. Up to now, the invention of a severe judge, the Judeo-Christian God, the basis of the religious ascetic ideal has been the *only* viable interpretive scheme that has been available to man. It has saved man from suicidal nihilism.

The claim that man is the "bravest of animals" may seem to be in conflict with Nietzsche's many references to the nausea he feels at the

sight of man. But there is no real contradiction here. Nietzsche is con-
temptuous of the domesticated animal that man has become, and he
warns against the triumph of the "last man." But, at the same time, he is
projecting a future possibility – an ideal of what man (at least, a few rare
free spirits) may yet become – the "redeemers" of a degenerate humanity.

> But all this notwithstanding – man was *saved* thereby, he possessed a mean-
> ing, he was henceforth no longer like a leaf in the wind, a plaything of
> nonsense – the "sense-less" – he could now *will* something; no matter at
> first to what end, why, with what he willed: *the will itself was saved* (*G* 162;
> 429)

Ironically, this is what the priests have always claimed – that they (and
their God) have *saved* man. Nietzsche does not dispute this. They are
right, absolutely right! Indeed, their great positive contribution has been
to save the *will* – without which there would be no possibility of overcoming the morality of good and evil. But now we must reveal the hidden *aim*
of saving this will.

> We can no longer conceal from ourselves *what* is expressed by all that
> willing which has taken its direction from the ascetic ideal: this hatred of
> the human, and even more of the animal, and more still of the material,
> this horror of the senses, of reason itself, this fear of happiness and beauty,
> this longing to get away from all appearance, change, becoming death,
> wishing, from longing itself – all this means – let us dare to grasp it – *a will*
> *to nothingness*, an aversion to life, a rebellion against the most fundamental
> presupposition of life; but it is and remains a *will* ... and to repeat in
> conclusion what I said in the beginning: man would rather will *nothingness*
> than *not* will (*Lieber will noch der Mensch* das Nichts *wollen, als nicht wollen.* (*G*
> 162–3; 430)

Nietzsche succinctly expresses his grand dialectical inversion in these final
words of his concluding essay. I want to underscore the strong cognitive
claims of these final remarks. Recall the opening lines of his preface. "We
are unknown to ourselves, we men of knowledge – and with good reason.
We have never sought ourselves" (*G* 15; 259). The *Genealogy* is an experiment in perspectival *knowing* directed towards knowing who we are. We
are creatures shaped by a self-lacerating, self contradictory morality based
upon a poisonous *ressentiment*. When Nietzsche affirms that the will that
has been saved is a will to nothingness, he sums up his critique of morality. We now have an answer to the question raised in the preface: what is
the value of our morality of good and evil? But we have discovered that
the answer is double-edged. The value of morality is that it has saved the

will, but the will that has been saved is "a will to nothingness, an aversion [*Widerwillen*] to life, a rebellion against the most fundamental presuppositions of life."

Note, however, that Nietzsche immediately adds, "but it is and remains a *will*" (*G* 163; 430). This is the most consequential "but" in the entire *Genealogy*, because without such a will, we would have already succumbed to "suicidal nihilism." All would be lost! Without this saving of the will, there would be no possibility at all of passing *beyond* good and evil, no hope at all for humanity. Nietzsche does *not* affirm that this possibility will be realized. There is no grand dialectical synthesis, no Hegelian *Aufhebung*, in his ironic dialectic. He leaves us with only a *possibility*, but one accompanied by a deepened knowledge of what the transvaluation of values, the movement beyond good and evil, requires. He repeats what he said at the beginning: that "man would rather will nothingness than not will." We also heard it at the beginning of the final movement, the beginning of the third essay: "That the ascetic ideal has meant so many things to man, however, is an expression of the basic fact of the human will, its *horror vacui: it needs a goal* – and it will rather will *nothingness* than *not* will" (*G* 97; 357). But we *first* heard this motif in the preface.

> It was precisely here that I saw the *great* danger to mankind, its sublimest enticement and seduction – and to what? to nothingness? it was precisely here that I saw the beginning of the end, the dead stop, a retrospective weariness, the will turning *against* life, the tender and sorrowful signs of the ultimate illness: I understood the ever spreading morality of pity that had seized even on philosophers and made them ill, as the most sinister symptom of a European culture that had itself become sinister, perhaps as its bypass to a new Buddhism? To a Buddhism for Europeans? To – *nihilism*? (*G* 19; 264)

What we learn from Nietzsche about evil

I want to return to the question that initiated my inquiry: what can we learn about evil from Nietzsche's critique of morality? Consider once again the meaning of "Beyond Good and Evil." It is, of course obvious (because Nietzsche explicitly tells us) that "this does *not* mean 'Beyond Good and Bad'" (*G* 55; 302). Yet there is a sense in which "Beyond Good and Evil" *is* "Beyond Good and Bad." The value polarity good/evil emerges in reaction to, and consequently presupposes, a good/bad ethic. So passing beyond good and evil entails passing beyond a naïve form of the aristocratic noble ethic. The "beyond" in "Beyond Good and Evil" is not a *transcendent* beyond, but an *immanent* one, a beyond achievable only by a few extraordinarily gifted and healthy individuals. The transcendent beyond is an invention of ascetic priests that is used to justify human suffering (and thereby also to increase it) – an "invention" that serves the purpose of blocking the path to suicidal nihilism. Nietzsche's "beyond" is a beyond that can be achieved only by dialectically passing through and beyond the morality of good and evil; honestly confronting the knowledge that the will that has been saved is a self-contradictory will, a will to nothingness; and finally transforming this will into a creative, life-affirming will. The slave revolt – the only "historical" example of the transvaluation of values that Nietzsche has examined in detail – shows the fire, strength, and violence required to create a new transvaluation of values.

At this point, we must face a problem that confronts every interpreter of Nietzsche, sometimes with disastrous results. How are we to interpret the substantive content of this beyond? Is it intended as a prophecy about the future? A promise of the coming of the overman (*Übermensch*)? A telos for which we should strive? A myth or noble lie invented to encourage us to engage in individual projects of self-creation and self-overcoming? A justification for a master race? A sign that Nietzsche has not escaped from metaphysics, but is the last metaphysician? (These do not exhaust the possibilities; nor is this a set of exclusive alternatives.) Unfortunately, with a certain amount of judicious (or malicious) selectivity, one can find textual evidence in Nietzsche's corpus to support or falsify any of these proposed interpretations. One must also give some account of how these alternative interpretations of the movement beyond good and evil are compatible with the doctrine of eternal return. In the context of my inquiry, I want to insist upon only two points that any adequate interpretation of Nietzsche must take into account.

First, Nietzsche understands the movement beyond good and evil as only a *possibility* – and indeed, not even the most likely possibility. What is far more likely is the complete dissipation of the will – the triumph of the "last man." In this respect, Nietzsche is the godfather of all those prophets of doom who lament that everything is going downhill, becoming bland, routinized, and meaningless. It is because Nietzsche sees this as the most likely outcome of our modern morality that his polemic is so strident and hyperbolic. But, unlike other prophets of doom, Nietzsche refuses to claim that this destiny is *inevitable* or *necessary*. Nietzsche's ironic dialectic eschews any suggestion of a necessary development. There are only *contingent* possibilities.

Secondly, although I have underscored the future-oriented temporality of the *Genealogy*, this emphasis on future possibilities must not be misinterpreted. It is not a prediction or a prophecy about the future, rather, it is a rhetorical trope used by Nietzsche in his polemic and critique of our *present* morality of good and evil. It is intended to make his critique of the present as sharp, as vivid, and as devastating as possible. Nietzsche shocks us into the realization that a dangerous, poisonous *ressentiment* underlies and pervades modern morality. (This is also the basis of his critique of democracy.) Just as Nietzsche creatively invents a fiction of an age of noble aristocrats to heighten our awareness of the character of our good/ evil morality, so he imaginatively projects an idealized future possibility to enable us to discern the "suicidal nihilism" that lies at the heart of our present morality. In short, Nietzsche uses his construction of the past and the future for the purposes of his critique of the *present*.

In answer to the question of what we can learn about evil from his critique of morality, it is not primarily to be found in the description of what evil means for the priestly class and the slave revolt. If we take Nietzsche's claims for "perspectival knowing" seriously, this conception of evil arises within and from the perspective of the great haters – the ascetic priests. But what is evil from Nietzsche's perspective, from the perspective of Nietzsche's final vocabulary, with its polarity between what is life-affirming and what is life-denying? Or, to be even more precise, how does evil look from the perspective of the dialectical narrator of the *Genealogy?* Evil from this perspective is not be confused with its meaning as used by the priests. When the narrator of the Genealogy declares that the priests are the most evil enemies because of their impotence, he is asserting that evil is the violent manifestation of *ressentiment* – the most pervasive and dangerous feature of our modern morality. Even here we must be sensitive to Nietzsche as a dialectical ironist. *Ressentiment* as expressed in the ascetic ideals of the religious and secular priests serves the function of preserving the will, and thereby blocking the way to suicidal nihilism. But this very *ressentiment* – if left unchecked – is ultimately a vicious, self-destructive force.

In his second essay, Nietzsche declares that if psychologists "would like to study *ressentiment* close up for once" (*G* 73; 325), then they should turn to where this plant blooms today, in anti-Semites. This passage is by no means an aberration in Nietzsche's writings (even though it has been ignored or deliberately suppressed by those who want to use him to "justify" *their* anti-Semitism). Nietzsche uses his most barbed rhetorical weapons to condemn this vicious form of *ressentiment*. Consider his devastating portrait of anti-Semites as men of *ressentiment*.

> This hoarse, indignant barking of sick dogs, this rabid mendaciousness and rage of "noble" Pharisees, penetrates even the hallowed halls of science (I again remind readers who have ears for such things of that Berlin apostle of revenge, Eugen Dühring, who employs moral mumbo-jumbo more inde-

cently and repulsively than anyone else in Germany today: Dühring, the foremost moral bigmouth today – unexcelled among his own ilk, the anti-Semites.)

They are all men of *ressentiment*, physiologically unfortunate and worm-eaten, a whole tremulous realm of subterranean revenge, inexhaustible and insatiable in outbursts against the fortunate and happy [*die Glücklichen*] and in masquerades of revenge and pretexts for revenge: when would they achieve the ultimate, subtlest, sublimest triumph of revenge? (*G* 123–4; 388)

Or again:

I also do not like these latest speculators in idealism, the anti-Semites, who today roll their eyes in a Christian-Aryan-bourgeois manner and exhaust one's patience by trying to rouse up all the horned-beast elements in the people by a brazen abuse of the cheapest of all agitator's tricks, moral attitudizing. (*G* 158; 425)[27]

It is a bitter irony, in light of the anti-Semitic distortion of his texts by his sister, Elizabeth Förster-Nietzsche, and the use the Nazis made of him, that Nietzsche should single out the anti-Semite as the *exemplar* of the most vicious form of *ressentiment*. Nietzsche has a profound understanding of the psychological dynamics of *ressentiment*, how it is internalized, grows, festers, and explodes in vicious and destructive ways. It is the basic concept of his moral psychology. It is, of course, true that Nietzsche says that if *ressentiment* should appear in the noble aristocrat, it consummates and exhausts itself in its immediate reaction, and "therefore does not poison" (*G* 39; 287); and Nietzsche also suggests that those individuals who are beyond good and evil will no longer suffer from the poisonous effects of *ressentiment*. But these possibilities are far less persuasive than Nietzsche's account of the *ever-present* danger of venomous outbursts of this form of evil. Nietzsche is not solely concerned with *ressentiment* in the individual psyche. It has social, political, and cultural manifestations. He is deeply suspicious of so-called modernization processes in society and politics, and all talk of progressive developments. Furthermore, he is insightful about the explosive dangers of modern nationalisms. He has an acute sense of the dark underside of these processes – where *ressentiment* festers, and then bursts forth in an orgy of vicious destruction.

In my discussion of Schelling, I indicated that he was aware of the psychological power of evil, how it is always latent, and always poses a threat. Schelling opened a pathway that was pursued by Nietzsche. This is not to suggest that Schelling influenced Nietzsche directly. Nietzsche force-fully asked new sorts of questions about evil, and transformed the dis-course of evil by probing its moral psychological complexities more deeply than any previous thinker. Twentieth-century thinkers have returned over and over again to Nietzsche, because of his insight into the psychological dynamics of *ressentiment*, the ways in which it is related to envy, jealousy, and hatred; the multifarious individual, social, political, and cultural forms it can take; its poisonous festering, and its *ever-present* dangerous consequences. We may not be fully convinced by Nietzsche's vivid "redescriptions." We may criticize him for his exaggerations and rhetorical excesses. We may question his fictional histories. We may question the myths and masks he creates. We may think that there is something excessive in the way in which Nietzsche views *ressentiment* as the *sole* basis and key for understanding Judeo-Christian morality, and for his relentless criticism of modern European culture. But if we read Nietzsche as graphically portraying the psychological dynamics and dangers of *ressentiment*; if we read him as posing hard questions, as warning us about the dark side of modern morality and modern socialization processes, then I think we must conclude that he has made a major contribution to the ongoing discourse of evil.[28]

5

Freud: Ineradicable Evil and Ambivalence

In reality, there is no such thing as "eradicating" evil.
Freud, "Thoughts for the Times on War and Death"

If we pursue Kant's analysis with rigor, and ask why – in the final analysis – some persons choose to adopt good maxims and some evil maxims, we are told that the answer is "inscrutable" [*unerforschlich*]. Recognition of the objective moral law can provide a sufficient incentive for motivating us to adopt good maxims. But if we are genuinely free, if we have the capacity to choose between good and evil, then there can be no ultimate causal constraints on the *Willkür*. Yirmiyahu Yovel speaks of this as "the 'black hole' of choice."

> The "black hole" of choice persists in Kant's theory of the will. Kant stresses this himself when speaking of the "inscrutable" origin of freedom, and of the choice of good or evil. He did not consider this a failure, however, for it was his deliberate intention . . . . [Kant] deliberately let the power of choice maintain its residual irrationality, the price, we might say, of freedom and individual personality. In this respect, he was unable and unwilling to fully rationalize the will.[1]

I agree that this is not a failure; indeed, I have argued that this understanding of free choice (*Willkür*) is a necessary consequence of Kant's understanding of freedom, morality, and responsibility. To be free means to have the capacity to choose between good and evil maxims. But even if we grant Kant's main point, there is another sense in which we can ask why human beings make the choices they make. Can we gain a deeper understanding of human nature, and in particular the human psyche, that will enable us to understand why human beings make the choices they do? There is nothing in Kant's moral philosophy that rules out the possibility of such an investigation, as long as we are clear about its limits. It may seem, especially if we restrict our understanding of Kant's moral philosophy to the *Groundwork* and the *Critique of Practical Reason*, that the study of nature (including human nature) cannot teach us anything about freedom and morality. But such an inference would be unwarranted. We have seen how, in the *Religion*, Kant introduces a concept of human nature that softens the dichotomy between nature and freedom without denying the distinction. When Kant declares that man is evil by nature, he is not using "nature" in the same sense as in the *Critique of Pure Reason*. Strictly speaking, moral predicates (good or evil, right or wrong) do not apply to nature in the restricted sense – nature as phenomenal. Furthermore, the very introduction of radical evil as a propensity (*Hang*) is intended to indicate how we are affected by this characteristic of our human nature. We have also seen how Hegel, Schelling, and Nietzsche (although in very different ways) call into question any sharp dichotomy between nature and freedom. Nevertheless, they do not think that the continuity between nature and freedom diminishes our capacity to choose freely. Indeed, in all three, we discern the beginnings of a more complex and ambivalent understanding of human nature – one that moves beyond Kant's stark opposition of self-love and rational will. Even Hegel, who places so much emphasis on the ultimate triumph of reason (*Vernunft*), has a subtle understanding of the forces of irrationality. The *Phenomenology* is a "highway of despair." Over and over again we undergo the experience of pain, frustration, and despair because just when we think we have achieved a true rational comprehension of who and what we are, we discover that we are mistaken and self-deceived. This is the very character of our experience (*Erfahrung*), and is integral to our formation (*Bildung*). Schelling and Nietzsche press this point to its extreme. Recall that Nietzsche begins his *Genealogy* by declaring that we are not only unknown to ourselves, but we *must* misunderstand ourselves. Schelling and Nietzsche open up the terrain by questioning the psychological complexities of human beings, and the way in which evil erupts in human beings.

Freud is certainly not a traditional moral philosopher. He is not concerned with analyzing the meanings "good and evil," or "right and wrong." Nor does he deal with justification of moral judgments. The philosophical (and theological or anti-theological) issues that are so central for Kant, Hegel, Schelling, and Nietzsche are not Freud's primary concern. Freud's skepticism regarding philosophy and traditional accounts of morality is well known, although he certainly thinks that philosophers have sometimes had important insights into the human psyche. Yet, the picture of the dynamics of the human psyche that emerges from Freud's investigations has fundamentally altered our understanding of why we make the choices and decisions we do, how moral conscience arises and develops, what role reason does and does not play in making choices, and the ineradicability of evil. Freud does have, as Philip Rieff has so eloquently demonstrated, "the mind of a moralist." He advocates (and practices) a demanding "ethic of honesty" – that bears a close resemblance to the ethic preached by that other great immoralist, Nietzsche.[2]

In this chapter I want to show that, despite Freud's skepticism about philosophy (including moral philosophy), he illuminates questions concerning evil that have not been adequately addressed by moral philosophers. Pursuing a theme that was already anticipated by Nietzsche, Freud enables us to understand better the powerful eruptions of evil in civilized societies; the constant threats that it poses; and the reason why evil is ineradicable.

I want to begin the investigation of Freud's moral psychology by turning to one of his most controversial and provocative books, *Totem and Taboo*, a book that continued to have special significance for Freud until the end of his life.[3] In a letter to Sandor Ferenczi (May 4, 1913), he declared: "I am now writing about the totem with the feeling that it is my greatest, best, and perhaps my last good thing. Inner certainties tell me that I am right." A few days later, he wrote again: "I haven't written anything with so much conviction since The Interpretation of Dreams."[4] Despite Freud's own doubts about the scientific status of his speculative hypotheses, and despite the sharp, severe criticism he received concerning his use of anthropological and ethnological evidence, Freud repeatedly returned to the hypotheses that he advanced in the book.[5] In *Group Psychology* (1921), he again takes up the theme of the primal horde and the patricide of the band of brothers. In his 1922 paper "A Seventeenth-Century Demonological Neurosis," he explains how the Devil becomes a substitute for the loved father by referring back to the ambivalence experienced by the brothers when they murder the primal father. He writes, "It does not need much analytic perspicacity to guess that God and the Devil were originally identical – were a single figure which was later split into two figures with opposite attributes . . . . Thus the father, it seems, is the individual prototype of both God and the Devil. But we should expect religions to bear ineffaceable marks of the fact that the primitive primal father was a being of unlimited evil – a being less like God than the Devil" (*SE* XIX, 86). The most significant return to *Totem and Taboo* is to be found in the last book that Freud published, *Moses and Monotheism* (1939). He explicitly says that it represents a continuation of the themes he set forth "twenty-five years ago in *Totem and Taboo*" (*SE* XXIII, 53). Once again he repeats the story of the murder of the primal father by the band of brothers, and he claims that the murder of Moses in the desert is a repetition of this "original murder." Moreover, he defends his construction against the "violent reproaches" of his critics.[6]

The ambivalence of the band of brothers

Totem and Taboo consists of four essays, but it is best known for the final essay, "The Return of Totemism in Childhood," in which Freud, in his search for a psychoanalytic account of the origin of totemism, tells the story of how the despotic father of the primal horde appropriates all the females for himself and exiles the younger males, including his own sons. The brothers have powerful, ambivalent feelings toward their tyrannical father; he is at once loved and honored, but also feared and hated. The brothers rise up, murder their father, and then in a totem meal devour him. Here is Freud's account.

> One day the brothers who had been driven out came together, killed and devoured their father and so made an end of the patriarchal horde. United, they had the courage to do so and succeeded in doing what would have been impossible for them individually . . . . Cannibal savages as they were, it goes without saying that they devoured their victim as well as killing him. The violent primal father had doubtless been the feared and envied model of each of the company of brothers: and in the act of devouring him they accomplished their identification with him, and each of them acquired a portion of his strength. The totem meal, which is perhaps mankind's earliest festival, would thus be a repetition and commemoration of this memorable and criminal deed, which was the beginning of so many things – of social organization, of moral restrictions, and of religion. (*SE* XIII, 141–2)[7]

The final sentence indicates why this narrative – this "scientific myth" – is so important for Freud. *Totem and Taboo* was one of Freud's first systematic attempts to apply the findings of psychoanalysis to the origins of social organization, morality, politics, and religion. We find here Freud's account of the origin of the moral imperative, "Thou shalt not murder" – a command that, paradoxically, is based upon the primal violent murder of the father.[8] After this murder, the brothers band together in solidarity to guarantee the security of their lives.

> In thus guaranteeing one another's lives, the brothers were declaring that no one of them must be treated by another as their father was treated by

them all jointly. They were precluding the possibility of a repetition of their father's fate. To the religiously-based prohibition against killing the totem was now added the socially based prohibition against fratricide. It was not until long afterwards that the prohibition ceased to be limited to members of the clan and assumed the simple form: 'Thou shalt do no murder.' The patriarchal horde was replaced in the first instance by the fraternal clan, whose existence was assured by the blood tie. Society was now based on complicity in the common crime; religion was based on the sense of guilt and remorse attaching to it; while morality was based partly on the exigencies of this society and partly on the penance demanded by the sense of guilt. (*SE* XIII, 146)[9]

But how does the story of the primal horde bear on the question of evil? To anticipate, Freud uses this story to show the deep ambivalence that marks the human psyche – an ambivalence in which murderous impulses are internalized and repressed, but are never completely eradicated. In order to see how this unfolds, and how the myth of the primal horde is used to explain the origin of social organization, religion, and morality, we need to probe some of the key claims that Freud makes about taboo and totemism – themes that he explores in the first three essays.

Freud appeals to the psychoanalytic understanding of obsessional neurotics and children (our primitives) in order to aid our understanding of the anthropological phenomena of totemism, exogamy, and taboo.[10] Drawing upon J. G. Frazer's *Totemism and Exogamy* (1910) and Andrew Lang's *The Secret of the Totem* (1905), Freud focuses on the close connection between totemism and exogamy. In primitive societies (Freud's example is the Australian Aborigines) the entire social organization seems designed to avoid incestuous sexual relationships. Freud rejects the claim that there is a natural aversion to incest. On the contrary, it is the natural *temptation* to incestuous relations that is the key to understanding the role that taboos play in preventing incest. We learn from psychoanalysis that "a boy's earliest choice of objects for his love is incestuous and that those objects are forbidden ones – his mother and his sister." As a child develops, he is liberated from incestuous attractions, but in neurotics these "incestuous fixations of libido continue to play (or begin once more to play) the principal part in his unconscious mental life" (*SE* XIII, 17). Actually, one is never *completely* liberated from incestuous attraction; it is repressed and becomes unconscious. Freud concludes his first essay, "The Horror of Incest," by telling us: "It is therefore of no small importance that we are able to show that these same incestuous wishes, which are later destined to become unconscious, are still regarded by savage peoples as immediate perils against which the most severe measures of defence must be enforced" (*SE* XIII, 17).[11]

But how does this horror of incest and its strict prohibition shed any light on the phenomenon of totemism? To understand this, we have to consider the meaning and function of taboo.

> The meaning of 'taboo', as we see it, diverges in two contrary directions. To us it means, on the one hand, 'sacred', 'consecrated', and on the other hand 'uncanny' [*unheimlich*], 'dangerous', 'forbidden', 'unclean'. The converse of 'taboo' in Polynesian is 'noa', which means 'common' or 'generally accessible'. Thus 'taboo' has about it a sense of something unapproachable, and is principally expressed in prohibitions and restrictions. (*SE* XIII, 18)

Taboos are more primitive phenomena than religious and moral prohibitions, for they appear to "have no grounds and are of unknown origin" (*SE* XIII, 18), yet the *traces* of these primitive taboos enable us to account for the psychic power of more developed religious and moral prohibitions.[12] Freud's major point is that with the persistence of taboos, there is also the persistence of the original desires to do what is prohibited. In this respect, taboos are similar to obsessional neurotic prohibitions. It is this persistence of taboos *together* with the persistence of the original prohibited desires that accounts for the ambivalent attitude towards taboos. "In their unconscious there is nothing they would like more than to violate them, but they are afraid to do so; they are afraid precisely because they would like to, and the fear is stronger than the desire. The desire is unconscious, however, in every individual member of the tribe just as it is in neurotics" (*SE* XIII, 31).

We can discern the logic of Freud's psychoanalytic account of the origin of taboos, especially the taboo against incest – a taboo that is based on the Oedipus complex – "the nuclear complex of the neuroses" (*SE* XIII, 129). Contrary to the belief that the horror of incest is some sort of natural instinct, Freud claims that the incestuous desire by the male child for his mother is what is psychologically primitive. This desire does not completely disappear; it is repressed and becomes unconscious. Consequently, there is an ambivalent attitude toward taboos, especially the taboo against incest. There is a strong desire to violate the taboo and a fear and horror of doing so.

Thus far, we have been speaking about the incestuous desire for the mother, but the Oedipus complex is primarily about a male child's relation to his father.

> I should like to insist that the beginnings of religion, morals, society and art converge in the Oedipus complex. This is in complete agreement with the psychoanalytic finding that the same complex constitutes the nucleus of all

neuroses, so far as our present knowledge goes. It seems to me a most surprising discovery that the problems of social psychology too, should prove soluble on the basis of one single concrete point – man's relation to his father. (*SE* XIII, 156)

Still, there is an important link that needs to be clarified. How does this analysis of taboo, which has led us to the Oedipus complex, enable us to understand the phenomenon of totemism? The totemic animal is originally a substitute for the father. When Freud introduces this crucial move in his account of totemism, he tells us that he is repeating what primitive men themselves say. They "describe the totem as their common ancestor and primal father" (*SE* XIII, 131). If the totemic animal is a substitute for the father, then we can understand the emotional ambivalence directed to the totem, and why it is the object of taboos. The totemic festival is a repetition of the devouring of, and identification with, the father.

> Psycho-analysis has revealed that the totem animal is in reality a substitute for the father; and this tallies with the contradictory fact that, though the killing of the animal is as a rule forbidden, yet its killing is a festive occasion – with the fact that it is killed and yet mourned. The ambivalent emotional attitude, which to this day characterizes the father-complex in our children and which often persists into adult life, seems to extend to the totem animal in its capacity as substitute for the father. (*SE* XIII, 141)

Let us pause and reflect on what Freud describes as a "fantastic" tale. We may admire (or condemn) Freud for his audacity, but how seriously are we to take this speculative account of incest, taboo, totemism, and the murder of the primal father? How seriously are we to take Freud's claim that we find here the origin of social organization, morality, and religion? And, the key question for us is: What does any of this have to do with evil? Let me anticipate what Freud is showing in his moral psychology. The very core of human life is ambivalent – an ambivalence that penetrates the deepest layers of our unconscious. Ambivalence in psychoanalysis is not a vague general term expressing some sort of conflict. It has a much more precise trenchant meaning. As Laplanche and Pontalis tell us:

> The novelty of the notion of ambivalence as compared to earlier evocations of the complexity of the emotions and the fluctuations of attitudes consists on the one hand in the maintenance of an opposition of the yes/no type, *wherein affirmation and negation are simultaneous and inseparable*; and, on the other hand, in the acknowledgement that this basic opposition is to be found in different sectors of mental life.[13]

They also point out that the "Oedipal conflict, in its instinctual root, is conceived of as a conflict of ambivalence (*ambivalenz Konflict*), one of whose principal dimensions is 'a well grounded love and a no less justifiable hatred towards one and the same person'."[14] This psychic ambivalence is ineradicable and universal. "In almost every case where there is an intense emotional attachment to a particular person we find that behind the tender love there is a concealed hostility in the unconscious. This is the classical example, the prototype, of the ambivalence of human emotions. This ambivalence is present to a greater or less amount in the innate disposition of everyone" (*SE* XIII, 60). We never completely succeed in overcoming this ambivalence. And because it is located in the recesses of our unconscious, we never completely control it. It is probable "that *the psychical impulses of primitive peoples were characterized by a higher amount of ambivalence than is to be found in modern civilized man. It is to be supposed that as this ambivalence diminished, taboo (a symptom of the ambivalence and a compromise between the two conflicting impulses) slowly disappeared*"(*SE* XIII, 66). But Freud stresses that this ambivalence, and the traces of taboo, never disappear fully. The traces of primitive taboo throw light on the nature and origin of conscience. "It is possible, without any stretching of the sense of the terms, to speak of taboo conscience or, after a taboo has been violated, of a taboo sense of guilt. Taboo conscience is probably the earliest form in which the phenomenon of conscience is met with" (*SE* XIII, 67).

> Conscience is the internal perception of the rejection of a particular wish operating within us. The stress, however, is upon the fact that this rejection has no need to appeal to anything else for support, that it is quite 'certain of itself'. This is even clearer in the consciousness of guilt – the perception of the internal condemnation of an act by which we have carried out a particular wish. To put forward any reason for this would seem superfluous: anyone who has a conscience must feel within him the justification for the condemnation, must feel the self-reproach for the act that has been carried out. This same characteristic is to be seen in the savage's attitude towards taboo. It is a command issued by conscience; any violation of it produces a fearful sense of guilt which follows as a matter of course and of which the origin is unknown. (*SE* XIII, 68)

If evil is characterized as the violation of moral prohibitions, as a violation of the dictates of moral conscience, then the *temptation* to evil is ineradicable. An ethic of honesty demands that we recognize this as a constitutive feature of our psychic lives. It might seem that Freud is dressing up in a modern psychoanalytic fashion the old Hobbesian view of man in the state of nature. But Freud is far more radical and disturbing than Hobbes. For Hobbes there is an adequate *rational* response to what we discover (or postulate) about the psychological character of human beings in a state of nature. But this is what Freud is denying. We have to learn to live with this deep, ineradicable ambivalence; we cannot contain or adequately rationally control it. We cannot eliminate our unconscious desires to violate moral prohibitions. It is also a serious distortion to think that Freud's doctrine is a secular version of the Christian doctrine of original sin. The powerful psychic ambivalence that we experience is not the result of some fall or act of a free will. It is certainly not freely chosen. Consequently, it would be totally irrational to blame or morally judge human beings for this psychic ambivalence that is ineradicable and universal.

There is still a fundamental perplexity that we have to confront in this story of primal patricide. There seems to be a curious circularity to Freud's account. On first reading, it seems that he is giving us a historical account of the origin of social organization, religion, and morality, drawing on his psychoanalytic experience with neurotics and children. But the more closely we examine what Freud is actually doing, the more evident it becomes that this is not the deep logic of his narrative construction. Suppose once again, we go over Freud's narrative. Consider the state of affairs *before* the sons rise up and murder the father. The father has taken possession of the females in the horde (including his own daughters) for his own sexual satisfaction. But there is no suggestion in Freud's tale that the father experiences a "horror of incest." Furthermore, since the father threatens to murder or castrate his sons if they infringe upon his female possessions, there doesn't seem to be any taboo against murder. Does this mean that the father does not experience "emotional ambivalence"? But if psychic ambivalence is universal, why doesn't the father (who himself was once a son) experience it? Presumably, Freud's story of the primal horde is supposed to give an account of the origin of taboo. But in order for this "historical" account to work, to *explain* what it purports to explain, Freud has to *presuppose* that the sons experience a psychic ambivalence that is not experienced by the father. But why do the sons experience psychic ambivalence when the father doesn't? There is a crucial gap in his narrative.

Let us bracket this difficulty for the moment, and consider what happens *after* the brothers kill and devour the father. The reason why Freud places so much emphasis on the cannibalistic devouring of the father (the basis for the totemic festival) is because he interprets this act as a form of psychic *identification* with the father. But this inference is itself based on Freud's psychoanalytic understanding of the dynamics of the unconscious. In short, it looks like Freud is already presupposing what he is trying to explain. What happens next? The band of brothers experience a sense of guilt and remorse because of their "criminal" act. But why? And in what sense is this a "criminal" act, especially if the prohibition against murder does not yet exist? Freud says:

> We need only suppose that the tumultuous mob of brothers were filled with the same contradictory feelings which we can see at work in the ambivalent father-complexes of our children and of our neurotic patients. They hated their father, who presented such a formidable obstacle to their craving for power and their sexual desires; but they loved and admired him too. After they got rid of him, had satisfied their hatred and had put into effect their wish to identify themselves with him, the affection which had all this time been pushed under was bound to make itself felt. It did so in the form of remorse. A sense of guilt made its appearance which in this instance coincided with the remorse felt by the whole group. The dead father became stronger than the living one had been – for events took the course we often see them follow in human affairs to this day. What had up to then been prevented by his actual existence was thence forward prohibited by the sons themselves, in accordance with the psychological procedure so familiar to us in psycho-analysis under the name of 'deferred obedience'. They revoked their deed by forbidding the killing of their totem, the substitute for their father; and they renounced its fruits by resigning their claim to the women who had now been set free. They thus created out of their filial sense of guilt the two fundamental taboos of totemism, which for that very reason inevitably corresponded to the two repressed wishes of the Oedipus complex. Whoever contravened those taboos became guilty of the only two crimes with which primitive society concerned itself. (*SE* XIII, 143)

I have cited this passage at length because it makes it eminently clear that the story of the primal horde does not *explain* the origin of the psychic ambivalence that is characteristic of taboo, totemism, and conscience. Rather, Freud presupposes that primitive men experience the *same* psychic dynamics as the children and neurotics whom he has clinically observed. What Freud has actually done is to create a historical myth – one that purports to explain the origin of social organization, morality, and religion – which presupposes our *present* psychoanalytic understanding of ambivalence, identification, guilt, the Oedipal complex, repression, and the psychic dynamics of the unconscious. We can now more fully appreciate the perspicacity of Lévi-Strauss's remark: "With *Totem and Taboo*, Freud constructed a myth, and a very beautiful myth too. But like all myths, it doesn't tell us how things really happened. It tells us how men need to imagine things happened so as to try to overcome contradictions."[15]

In emphasizing that the story of the primal horde is a mythic representation of the psychological truth that Freud takes to be characteristic of human beings, my intention is not to criticize Freud, but to clarify what he is actually doing when he appeals to our archaic heritage. There is a striking similarity here between Freud's constructions of the past and Nietzsche's genealogy. Both thinkers appeal to the past in order to provide – to use Foucault's phrase – "a history of the present." And like Nietzsche with his genealogical forays, Freud seeks to shed light on our present moral prohibitions. Freud differs significantly from Nietzsche in his conviction that the basic psychic dynamics of human beings are universal and ahistorical. The dynamics of ambivalence, repression, guilt, and remorse do not change; only their *manifestations* change in the course of human history. It is, of course true that psychoanalysis is always appealing to past infantile and childhood experiences in order to account for present neuroses. But even this conception of human psychological development is presumably characteristic of all human beings.

In *Moses and Monotheism*, where we find a similar genealogical logic at work, Freud introduces a distinction between what he calls "material truth" and "historical truth." By "material truth" he means a kind of literal truth than can be supported by objective evidence. Freud, the godless Jew, who was critical of the explicit cognitive claims of all religions, steadfastly maintained that they are materially false. But when properly deciphered, it is possible to uncover the "historical truth" of a religion. But by "historical truth" Freud does *not* mean what we ordinarily mean when we use this term; it is not a material truth about the past. Rather, "historical truth" (which might more perspicuously be called "psychological truth" or "psychoanalytic truth") is the truth that psychoanalysis enables us to discover in the historical origins of religion. Using Freud's distinction between material and historical truth, I am claiming that – despite occasional comments to the contrary – the story of the primal horde does not express the material truth about the archaic past. It is a constructed myth intended to express the historical truth – that is, the psychological truth that is concealed and repressed, but which can be recovered by psychoanalytic investigation.[16]

Although Freud is not – and should not be judged as – a moral philosopher since he is not concerned primarily with the meaning and the justification of moral judgments, he is the most significant and disturbing *moral psychologist* of the twentieth century. His claims about the ambivalent contradictory unconscious desires of the human psyche – unconscious desires and motivations that are never *completely* susceptible to rational control – are essential for any adequate account of evil. Freud was not hesitant to speak about evil. In response to the disillusionment that resulted from the First World War, he wrote an essay, entitled "Thoughts for the Times on War and Death" (1915), in which he confronted the troubling issue of "the brutality shown by individuals whom, as participants in the highest human civilization, one would not have thought capable of such behaviour." He explicitly rejects the idea that we can eradicate "evil human tendencies and, under the influence of education and a civilized environment, [replace] them by good ones" (*SE* XIV, 280–1).

> In reality, there is no such thing as 'eradicating' evil. Psychological – or, more strictly speaking, psycho-analytic – investigation shows instead that the deepest essence of human nature consists of instinctual impulses which are of an elementary nature, which are similar in all men and which aim at the satisfaction of certain primal needs. These impulses in themselves are neither good nor bad. We classify them and their expressions in that way, according to their relation to the needs and demands of the human community. It must be granted that all the impulses which society condemns as evil – let us take as representative the selfish and the cruel ones – are of this primitive kind. (*SE* XIV, 281)

Freud consistently warns against the temptation to be seduced by opposing extremes: attaching too much rigidity to the "innate part" of human nature, and "overestimating the total susceptibility to culture in comparison with the portion of instinctual life which has remained primitive" (*SE* XIV, 283). The ethic of honesty demands that we acknowledge that "belief in the 'goodness' of human nature is one of those *evil illusions* by which mankind expect their lives to be beautified and made easier while in reality they only cause damage" (*SE* XXII, 104; emphasis added). This ethic also demands that we avoid the opposing extreme – of thinking that human nature is inherently and irredeemably depraved. Some commentators have thought that Freud's basic message is a pessimistic one, and that he completely abandons any Enlightenment hope regarding the efficacy of reason. But this is unwarranted. Freud seeks an honest enlightenment about reason itself, and urges us to become more realistic about its fragility and limitations. Not pessimism, but a certain realism in the face of uncontrollable contingencies, and an honest appraisal of the ineradicability of evil, constitute the dominant message of Freud's psychoanalytic investigations.

The theory of instincts

If we are to understand why Freud thinks that there is no such thing as eradicating evil, then we need to probe his *late* theory of instincts. In 1915, when he wrote his essay on war and death, he had not yet advanced this theory – that of the struggle between the life and the death instincts (*Triebe*): between *Eros* and *Thanatos*.[17] It is only in *Beyond the Pleasure Principle*

– a book that many believe represents a decisive turning point in Freud's development – that this thesis is speculatively advanced. But what does Freud mean by *Trieb*? [18] In *Instincts and their Vicissitudes* (*Triebe und Triebschicksale*), Freud describes *Trieb* as "a concept on the frontier between the mental and the somatic . . . the psychical representative of the stimuli originating from within the organism and reaching the mind, as a measure of the demand made upon the mind for the work in consequence of its connection with the body" (*SE* XIV, 121–2).[19]

There is also another sense in which *Trieb* is a border, or frontier, concept. It not only marks a frontier concept between the somatic and the mental, but also a border between the unconscious and the conscious. To indicate this *in-between* status, Freud coins the technical expression *Repräsentanz* (representation), and speaks of "psychical representations." *Triebe*, grounded in our biological nature, can have different "psychical representations." This is what enables us to speak of their vicissitudes.[20] This turns out to be especially important for understanding how the life instincts and death instincts have varied psychical representations.[21]

Prior to Freud's speculative introduction of the new dualism of the life and death instincts in *Beyond the Pleasure Principle*, he had distinguished between sexual instincts and ego instincts. But Freud tells us that the "compulsion to repeat" painful traumas that he observed clinically in the dreams of patients who suffered from traumatic neurosis compelled him to revise his understanding of the workings of the pleasure and reality principles, as well as his theory of instincts. Laplanche and Pontalis describe what is new in the dualism of instincts that Freud introduced in 1920, and which he steadfastly maintained until the end of his life.

> The new instinctual dualism introduced in *Beyond the Pleasure Principle* contrasts the life instincts and the death instincts, modifying the function and location of the instincts in the conflict.
>
> a. The topographical conflict (between the defensive agency and the repressed agency) no longer coincides with instinctual conflict: the id is pictured as an instinctual reservoir containing both types of instinct. The energy used by the ego is drawn from this common fund, particularly in the form of "desexualized and sublimated" energy.
>
> b. The two great classes of instincts are postulated in this last theory less as the concrete motive forces of the actual functioning of the organism than as fundamental principles which *ultimately* regulate its activity: "The forces which we assume to exist behind the tensions caused by the needs of the id are called *instincts*." This shift of emphasis is especially clear in a familiar statement of Freud's: "The theory of the instincts is so to say our mythology. Instincts are mythical entities, magnificent in their indefiniteness."[22]

At the conclusion of *Beyond the Pleasure Principle*, Freud (in a final footnote) gives his own description of the shift that has taken place with his new speculative hypothesis.[23]

> We came to know what the 'sexual instincts' were from their relation to the sexes and to the reproductive function. We retained this name after we had been obliged by the findings of psycho-analysis to connect them less closely with reproduction. With the hypothesis of narcissistic libido and the extension of the concept of libido to the individual cells, the sexual instinct was transformed for us into Eros, which seeks to force together and hold together the portions of living substance. What are commonly called the sexual instincts are looked upon by us as part of Eros which is directed towards objects. Our speculations have suggested that Eros operates from the beginning of life and appears as a 'life instinct' in opposition to the 'death instinct' which was brought into being by the coming to life of inorganic substance. These speculations seek to solve the riddle of life by supposing that these two instincts were struggling with each other from the very first. (*SE* XVIII, 60–1)

It may appear that Freud is backing into a psychological version of Manichaeism, where our lives are caught in the battle and struggle of two opposing cosmic forces. But any identification of *Eros* with a cosmological principle of the good, and the death instincts with a principle of evil is simplistic and grossly misleading. It is certainly true that when Freud speculates about the battle between the life and death instincts, he claims that their scope is far wider than the human psyche. The aim of the death instincts is a return to the inorganic (a thesis that fascinated Thomas Mann), whereas the aim of the life instincts is to combine more and more living substance into ever greater unities. He closely associates the death instincts with the tendency to self-destructiveness. In the *New Introductory Lectures*, he advances the following speculation:

> If it is true that – at some immeasurably remote time and in a manner we cannot conceive – life once proceeded out of inorganic matter, then, according to our presumption, an instinct must have arisen which sought to do away with life once more and to reestablish the inorganic state. If we recognize in this instinct the self-destructiveness of our hypothesis, we may regard the self-destructiveness as an expression of a 'death instinct' which cannot fail to be present in every vital process. And now the instincts that we believe in divide themselves into two groups – the erotic instincts, which seek to combine more and more living substance into ever greater unities, and the death instincts, which oppose this effort and lead what is living back into an inorganic state. From the concurrent and opposing action of these two proceed the phenomena of life which are brought to an end by death. (*SE* XXII, 107)

Freud is certainly aware of the objection that he is engaging in wild speculation – speculation that goes far beyond what clinical observation warrants. But he responds by declaring: "You may perhaps shrug your shoulders and say: 'That isn't natural science, it's Schopenhauer's philosophy!' But, Ladies and Gentlemen, why should not a bold thinker have guessed something that is afterwards confirmed by sober and painstaking detailed research?" (*SE* XXII, 107).[24]

Despite the fact that during his lifetime (and up until the present) many critics, and even Freud's most sympathetic defenders, have strongly objected to his speculative hypothesis about the dualism of life and death instincts, Freud himself never hesitated in advocating his late theory of instincts.[25] The most important feature of this duality is Freud's insistence on the inextricable fusion (*Vermischung*) and mingling of these opposing instincts and their psychical representations. We never encounter either of these in its "pure" form, although for analytical purposes we characterize them as if they are distinguishable. This means that we never find the psychical representative of the life instincts without also discovering the psychical representative of the death instincts. It is this *fusion* of these basic instincts that is the source of Freud's conviction that evil is ineradicable. From Freud's psychoanalytic perspective, it is impossible to think that there can be *Eros* without *Thanatos* (or *Thanatos* without *Eros*) – although the psychical representation of these instincts, and the dominance of one of them over the other, may vary.

Actually the extent of the fusion of the life and death instincts is even more intricate and complex than has yet been indicated. If we analyze closely Freud's initial description of the life and death instincts, and follow his subsequent formulations, we discover a subtle, but consequential, shift of emphasis. In *Beyond the Pleasure Principle*, when Freud introduces his new dualism of instincts, he stresses that the aim of *Eros* is to create and maintain ever-greater unities; it is the binding instinct. This is why *Eros* is so vital for the creation of civilized communities. In his final formulation of the theory of instincts presented in *An Outline of Psycho-Analysis* (written in 1938, but published posthumously in 1940), he declares:

> After long hesitancies and vacillations we have decided to assume the existence of only two basic instincts, *Eros* and *the destructive instinct* . . . . The aim of the first of these instincts is to establish ever greater unities and to preserve them thus – in short, to bind together; the aim of the second is, on the contrary, to undo connections and so to destroy things. In the case of the destructive instinct we may suppose that its final aim is to lead what is living into an inorganic state. For this reason we also call it the *death instinct*. (*SE* XXIII, 148)

But in many places, and especially in *Civilization and its Discontents*, Freud also describes how sexual love (one of the manifestations of *Eros*) is disruptive of the *binding* force of civilizing processes. "On the one hand love comes into opposition to the interests of civilization; on the other, civilization threatens love with substantial restrictions" (*SE* XXI, 103). *Eros* in one of its psychical representations is a binding force for greater and greater unities, but in another of its psychical representations, it is violently disruptive of civilizing processes. Consequently, there is not only a dualism between life and death instincts, but also a duality *intrinsic* to *Eros* itself. This basic instinct can have contradictory psychical representations. The same is true of the death instincts. Just as *Eros* is essential for the creation of civilization, but can also be disruptive and destructive, so the death instincts are not simply destructive, but can also be creative. One of the primary manifestations of the aggressive energy of the death instincts is work. Without work, there would be no civilization. And human work can harness this aggressive energy in a nondestructive way. If one deprives the tendency toward aggression of the possibility of manifesting itself in "creative" external ways, there is a danger that this aggressive energy will turn against the self in a neurotic and self-destructive manner. But the death instincts also pose a threat to civilization. They can explode into a fury of destruction and self-destruction. There is also an *intrinsic* duality within the death instincts. Consequently there is not only a warring duality between *Eros* and *Thanatos*; there is an intrinsic duality (ambivalence) within the life and death instincts. *Both* are at once absolutely necessary for the creation and preservation of civilization, and *both* pose the greatest dangers and threats to civilization.

In order to draw out the full significance of Freud's understanding of the ambivalence that is intrinsic to the basic instincts of *Eros* and *Thanatos* for our inquiry into evil, I want to turn to one of the most disturbing and thought-provoking discussions of Freud's late theory of instincts – the discussion in *Civilization and its Discontents*. He begins the sixth section of the book by "confessing" that he has a strong feeling that what he has said so far (in the first five sections of the book) is common knowledge and self-evident. He now turns to explore how a "special, independent aggressive instinct means an alteration of the psycho-analytic theory of the instincts" (*SE* XXI, 117). He acknowledges that his introduction of the duality of the life and death instincts has met with resistance even in analytic circles. But he informs us that in the ten years since he first put forth the hypothesis of the duality of the life and death instincts, "they have gained such a hold upon me that I can no longer think in any other way" (*SE* XXI, 119). The phenomena of sadism and masochism had been important for psychoanalysis long before the introduction of the late theory of instincts, but they had previously been associated with forms of eroticism. Freud now says: "I can no longer understand how we can have overlooked the ubiquity of non-erotic aggressivity and destructiveness and can have failed to give it its due place in our interpretation of life . . . . I remember my own defensive attitude when the idea of an instinct of destruction first emerged in psycho-analytic literature, and how long it took before I became receptive to it" (*SE* XXI, 120). With blatant sarcasm, he dismisses theological and religious attempts to explain away this innate aggressiveness and destructiveness.

> For [in Goethe's words] 'little children do not like it' when there is talk of the inborn human inclination to 'badness', to aggressiveness and destructiveness, and so to cruelty as well. God has made them in the image of His own perfection; nobody wants to be reminded how hard it is to reconcile the undeniable existence of evil – despite the protestations of Christian Science – with His all-powerfulness or His all-goodness. The Devil would be the best way out as an excuse for God; in that way he would be playing the same part as an agent of economic discharge as the Jew does in the world of the Aryan ideal. But even so, one can hold God responsible for the existence of the Devil just as well as for the existence of their wickedness which the Devil embodies. In view of these difficulties, each of us will be well advised, on some similar occasion, to make a low bow to the deeply moral nature of mankind; it will help us to be generally popular and much will be forgiven us for it. (*SE* XXI, 120)[26]

Despite the sarcasm of this passage, Freud's point is perfectly clear. He rejects any view of human nature, whether it has a religious or a secular origin, that fails to recognize the irreducibility of aggressive, destructive, and violent impulses that inhere in the human psyche. Freud is not only emphatic in his insistence "that the inclination to aggression is an original, self-subsisting instinctual disposition in man," but "that it constitutes the greatest impediment to civilization" (*SE* XXI, 122). This original, self-subsisting, aggressive instinct, which opposes the integrative work of *Eros*, is also essential for the development of civilization. Further, it is this aggressive instinct that "is the derivative and the main representative of the death instinct which we have found alongside Eros and which shares world-dominion with it" (*SE* XXI, 122). It is this discovery of the equiprimordial nature of the life and death instincts that illuminates the "meaning of the evolution of civilization."

> And now, I think, the meaning of the evolution of civilization is no longer obscure to us. It must present the struggle between Eros and Death, between the instinct of life and the instinct of destruction, as it works itself out

in the human species. This struggle is what life essentially consists of, and
the evolution of civilization may therefore be simply described as the struggle for life of the human species. And it is this battle of the giants that our
nurse-maids try to appease with their lullaby about Heaven. (*SE* XXI, 122)

I want to draw out the consequences of this understanding of the battle
between *Eros* and *Thanatos* for the moral psychology of evil. Although
Freud does occasionally speak about "good" and "evil" impulses, or even
instincts, in his more careful formulations he makes it clear that the id —
the primary source of instincts — is nonmoral. "From the point of view of
instinctual control, of morality, it may be said of the id that it is totally
nonmoral, of the ego that it strives to be moral, and of the super-ego that
it can be super-moral and then become as cruel as only the id can be" (*SE*
XIX, 54). Moral predicates are applicable to the ego and the superego,
but not to the id. Morality itself, as we have seen, is a cultural invention
that comes into existence with the "criminal deed" of the murder and
devouring of the primal father by the band of brothers. It is not only that
the id is the source of nonmoral instincts, but that these instincts are
contradictory and ambivalent: it is *impossible* to satisfy all our instinctual
desires. Our instinctual drives are at once the source of moral prohibitions
and always stand ready to disrupt moral prohibitions. Civilization is the
site of the never-ending struggle between *Eros* and *Thanatos*. The key term
here is *struggle* — a struggle that can take many different forms, but such
that there is never a final, permanent reconciliation or stabilization. At
times, Freud entertains the possibility that we may neutralize our native
aggressiveness. Indeed, if there is to be any civilization, we must be able to
control and redirect our aggressiveness so that it is not totally destructive.
But this attempt is never completely successful or stable. Even though
there are complex psychic mechanisms for repressing and sublimating our
basic instincts, their primal energy is never really diminished. They can
break out with renewed power in the most unexpected circumstances in
the development of an individual or a civilization. There is no way to
eliminate the psychic ambivalence which is intrinsic to our human nature
and which is manifested in the struggle of our basic instincts.

Freud died on the eve of the Second World War, but he had already
witnessed the cruelty and barbarity of the Nazis. He certainly would not
have been shocked by the subsequent genocide and exterminations that
occurred, or by the massacres that have occurred (and continue to occur)
since the end of the Second World War throughout the world under the
most diverse conditions. We have already seen that in "Thoughts for the
Times on War and Death" he noted the tendency of highly civilized
societies to regress to extreme forms of cruelty and unrestrained orgies of

destructiveness. There are those who think that by keeping alive the memories of barbaric horrors we can prevent them from occurring again. Freud
would agree that it is important to keep these memories alive, but not
because this can prevent such horrors from happening again. What is far
more important is that we remember that the destructive power of our
instinctual nature is *never* obliterated. All talk of some final reconciliation
or harmony is nursery talk. Our most violent primitive instinctual impulses coexist with the very development of moral codes and prohibitions.
We may desperately want to believe that there is something we can do,
some institutionalization of the memory of horrors, some political ar-
rangement that can be brought about, that will finally and *successfully*
contain the aggressive and destructive capacities of human beings. To
succumb to such a wish fulfillment is to succumb to a dangerous illusion.
Freud is in the best tradition of the *Aufklärung* insofar as his ethic of
honesty demands "telling it as it is," even when this requires challenging
Enlightenment prejudices about the goodness, malleability, or rationality
of human nature. What we must never forget is that our so-called primitive instinctual impulses (including our aggressive and destructive impulses)
coexist alongside the development of moral codes and prohibitions and
the development of civilization.

> The earlier mental state may not have manifested itself for years, but none
> the less it is so far present that it may at any time again become the mode
> of expression of the forces in the mind, and indeed the only one, as though
> all later developments had been annulled or undone. This extraordinary
> plasticity of mental developments is not unrestricted as regards direction; it
> may be described as a special capacity for involution – for regression –
> since it may well happen that a later and higher stage of development, once
> abandoned, cannot be reached again. But the primitive stages can always
> be re-established; the primitive mind is, in the fullest meaning of the word,
> imperishable. (*SE* XIV, 285–6)

To complete my analysis of the relevance of Freud's moral psychology
for the problem of evil, I want to examine his genetic account of conscience and the sense of guilt, the character of human responsibility, and
the fragility of reason. In so doing we will see both the similarities and the
striking differences with Nietzsche. Let us begin by recalling what Freud
tells us about the genesis of conscience in *Totem and Taboo.* Taboo conscience is the most primitive form of conscience, and it is the basis for the
more highly developed forms of religious and moral conscience. "Conscience is the internal perception of the rejection of a particular wish
operating within us" (*SE* XIII, 68). It is closely associated with the consciousness of guilt and the remorse experienced by the band of brothers

when they murdered the tyrannical father whom they revered and honored but also feared and hated. We find traces of taboo conscience in civilized moral conscience. Thus, Freud concludes, "it seems probable that conscience arose on a basis of emotional ambivalence . . . that it arose under the conditions which we have shown to apply in the case of taboo and of obsessional neurosis – namely, that one of the opposing feelings involved shall be unconscious and kept under repression by the compulsive domination of the other" (*SE* XIII, 68). Freud frequently refined his views on the origin of conscience. After he introduced his model of the id, ego, and superego in 1923, he enriched and revised his understanding of the origin and formation of conscience.[27]

In his relatively late *New Introductory Lectures* (1933), he describes conscience as arising from the splitting of the ego, where one part observes and judges the other part. Just as the ego arises from the id, so the superego arises from the splitting of the ego. Freud identifies conscience with the superego – or, more accurately, with the *tension* that arises between the ego and the superego. He even refers to Kant's famous statement about the moral law (which Freud associates with moral conscience) in the *Critique of Practical Reason.*

> Following a well-known pronouncement of Kant's which couples the conscience within us with the starry Heavens, a pious man might well be tempted to honour these two things as the masterpieces of creation. The stars are indeed magnificent, but as regards conscience God has done an uneven and careless piece of work, for a large majority of men have brought along with them only a modest amount of it or scarcely enough to be worth mentioning . . . . Even if conscience is something 'within us', yet it is not so from the first. (*SE* XXII, 61)[28]

Just as Freud denies that there is an innate or original aversion to incest or murder, so he does not think that there is any original or innate conscience. This is why we must give a genetic account of the prohibition against incest, murder, and the origin of conscience. Let us see how this unfolds.

The id is the mental province in which the logical laws of thought (including the law of contradiction) do not apply. "Contrary impulses exist side by side, without cancelling each other out or diminishing each other . . . . There is nothing in the id that could be compared with negation . . . . There is nothing in the id that corresponds to the idea of time; there is no recognition of the passage of time, and . . . no alteration in its mental processes is produced by the passage of time . . . . The id of course knows no judgements of value: no good and evil, no morality" (*SE* XXII, 73–4).

There is an ambiguity in this characterization of the id that Freud clears up elsewhere. One may wonder whether if it even makes sense to speak of *contrary* impulses standing side by side if there is nothing in the id that can be compared with negation. When Freud says that there are contrary impulses in the id, he is *already* speaking from the perspective of the ego, for which the concept of negation and "contrary impulses" make sense. In *The Question of Lay Analysis* (1926), Freud describes the id as follows: "In the id there are no conflicts; contradictions and antitheses persist side by side in it unconcernedly, and are often adjusted by the formation of compromises. In similar circumstances the ego feels a conflict which must be decided; and the decision lies in one urge being abandoned in favour of the other. The ego is an organization characterized by a very remarkable trend toward unification, towards synthesis. This characteristic is lacking in the id; it is, as we might say, 'all to pieces'; its different urges pursue their own purposes independently and regardless of one another" (*SE* XX, 196). If we restrict our discussion to the id – or, as we might say, the id *in itself* – there is, strictly speaking, no conflict, ambivalence, contradiction, or negation. Conflict and ambivalence emerge only with the development of the ego, and with the manifestation in the ego of urges that have their original locus in the id. With the formation of the ego, there is no escape from conflict and ambivalence.

Despite Freud's admiration for Kant, he radically departs from Kant. Unlike Kant, he does not think that the source of the moral law and moral conscience is to be found in practical reason. For Kant it makes no sense to speak of the psychological origins of the moral law, but only of the psychological origins of our becoming *aware* of this law. But for Freud the origin of the moral law and moral conscience is to be traced back to the psychic ambivalence that is the basis for taboos. Moral conscience comes into existence from the tension between the superego and the ego. What fascinated Freud about primitive taboos originally is that there did not seem to be any explanation for their existence. The question of the "justification" of taboos does not even arise for those primitives who experience them. This is why Freud seeks a psychoanalytic account of their origin. Just as he thinks that the origin of totem conscience has nothing to do with reason, so he regards this as just as true of its more civilized derivative, moral conscience. To give an adequate account of the function of morality, we have to appeal to the dynamics of the interplay of the id, the ego, and the superego. But what is the source of the harshness and cruelty of the superego – a harshness and cruelty that can become excessive and make it pathologically dysfunctional? Initially, the superego represents the internalization of parental authority. But the development of conscience and the sense of guilt are more complicated than this. The very aggressiveness that is rooted in the id becomes an additional, and more threatening, source of the energy and harshness for the superego.

In *Civilization and its Discontents*, Freud explains how this *introjection* is the source of the severity and threatening power of the superego.

> His aggressiveness is introjected, internalized; it is, in point of fact, sent back to where it came from – that is, it is directed towards his own ego. There it is taken over by a portion of the ego, which sets itself over against the rest of the ego as the super-ego, and which now, in the form of 'conscience', is ready to put into action against the ego the same harsh aggressiveness that the ego would have liked to satisfy upon the other, extraneous individuals. The tension between the harsh super-ego and the ego that is subjected to it, is called by us the sense of guilt; it expresses itself as a need for punishment. Civilization, therefore, obtains mastery over the individual's dangerous desire for aggression by weakening and disarming it and by setting up an agency within him to watch over it, like a garrison in a conquered city. (*SE* XXI, 123–4)[29]

Consequently, there is a three-stage model in the genesis of moral conscience. "First comes renunciation of instinct owing to fear of aggression of *external* authority." Then "comes the erection of an *internal* authority, and the renunciation of instinct owing to the fear of conscience [*Gewissenangst*]." Finally, there is the "double bind" of conscience.

> And here at last an idea comes in which belongs entirely to psycho-analysis, and which is foreign to people's ordinary way of thinking. This idea is of a sort which enables us to understand why the subject-matter was bound to seem so confused and obscure to us. For it tells us that conscience (or more correctly, the anxiety which later becomes conscience) is indeed the cause of instinctual renunciation to begin with, but that later the relationship is reversed. Every renunciation of instinct now becomes a dynamic source of conscience and every fresh renunciation increases the latter's severity and intolerance. (*SE* XXI, 128–9)

There is another extremely important consequence of Freud's genetic account of the formation of conscience. The formation of conscience is, of course essential for the development of morality. Without conscience there is no morality, no control over "evil impulses." But there is no guarantee that conscience will function in a normal way. Freud entertains the hypothesis that there are social circumstances in which there can be a disappearance of conscience. In *Group Psychology and the Analysis of the Ego*, Freud elaborates this possibility.

> For us it would be enough to say that in a group the individual is brought
> under conditions which allow him to throw off the repressions of his uncon-
> scious instinctual impulses. The apparently new characteristics which he
> then displays are in fact the manifestations of this unconscious, in which all
> that is evil in the human mind is contained as a predisposition. We can find
> no difficulty in understanding the disappearance of conscience or of a sense
> of responsibility in these circumstances. (*SE* XVIII, 74)

Freud here opens up a frightening possibility that he never systematically
explored – that there are social circumstances in which there is a "disappearance of conscience" and no repression of "all that is evil in the human
mind." Although Hannah Arendt was deeply suspicious of psychoanalysis,
and rarely ever mentions Freud, she was nevertheless concerned with the
phenomenon of the disappearance of conscience in totalitarian regimes –
or rather, the ways in which it could be so easily manipulated. This
became a major theme in *Eichmann in Jerusalem.*

> And just as the law in civilized countries assumes that the voice of con-
> science tells everybody "Thou shalt not kill," even though man's natural
> desires and inclinations may at times be murderous, so the law in Hitler's
> land demanded that the voice of conscience tell everybody "Thou shalt
> kill," although the organizers of massacres knew full well that murder is
> against the normal desires and inclinations of most people. Evil in the
> Third Reich had lost the quality by which most people recognize it – the
> quality of temptation.[30]

I suspect that Freud might well agree with Arendt, but with one very
important caveat. It is only in a manifest sense that "murder is against the
normal desires and inclinations of most people." Psychoanalysis teaches us
that murderous desires are "normal" and ineradicable. This is precisely
why the renunciation of instincts, and especially the repression of aggressive instincts, are so vital for the development of civilization. It is also why
the development of conscience and morality is so important for sustaining
civilization. And finally, this is why "disappearance of conscience" is such
a dangerous (albeit all too real) possibility that threatens civilization with
outbursts of unrestrained aggressiveness and destruction.

Nietzsche and Freud

The similarity between Nietzsche's genealogical account of the formation
of conscience and Freud's genetic account is striking initially. The very
logic of Nietzsche's *Genealogy of Morals* seems to anticipate Freud. In

Nietzsche's account of the formation of conscience, there is a movement from *external* social circumstances to *internalization*. But the more closely we compare Nietzsche and Freud, the more their fundamental differences emerge. Nietzsche describes the origin of bad conscience as a dialectical development in his genealogical narrative – a stage that is situated between the myth of the aristocratic noble ethic of good and bad and the (*possible*) movement *beyond* good and evil. But the primary thrust of Freud's thinking is to challenge any such dialectical interpretation of the renunciation of the instincts, as well as the internalization that gives rise to conscience. The function of Freud's mythological narrative of the murder of the primal father is the very opposite of Nietzsche's genealogical account. It is intended to show that ever since brothers first killed and devoured the primal father, there has been *no* fundamental change in the psychic dynamics of the formation of conscience and the experience of guilt and remorse. Ineradicable ambivalence is not a dialectical stage in the development of humanity: *it is a permanent feature of the psychic life of humans.* From a depth-psychological (or psychoanalytical) perspective, there is *no* fundamental difference between the emotional life of so-called primitive men and that of contemporary civilized men. Moreover, it is an illusion to think that we can overcome or transform this ambivalence. The vicissitudes of our psychic dynamics (including repression, guilt, and conscience) take place within a very limited range.[31] The ethic of honesty demands that we learn to live with this. Freud would be suspicious of the hypothesis that there was a time when aristocratic nobles did not experience guilt, remorse and bad conscience. Although Freud affirms that aggressive instincts can express themselves creatively in ways that are essential for civilization (for example, productive work), he would challenge the claim that the external discharge of these instincts can *eliminate* psychic ambivalence. There cannot be any final, or even stable, "solution" to the warring between *Eros* and *Thanatos*. To believe that there can be such a solution is to underestimate the depth of irreconcilable instinctual conflicts. Freud is scornful of those who think that there can be some sort of utopian solution to this fundamental psychic ambivalence. And he would be just as scornful of any talk of a transvaluation of values, or a movement beyond good and evil that suggests that men (even only a few gifted free spirits) can achieve an aesthetic harmony that somehow transforms or reconciles these fundamental instinctual conflicts. Freud might even accuse Nietzsche, the great critic of morality, of being infected by the moralism that he deplores. Nietzsche's critique of morality is performed from the perspective of a demand for a higher ethic. The passion and intensity of Nietzsche's critique of morality, his analysis and ultimate condemnation of the "will to nothingness," derive from his demand for a new transvaluation of values, a new higher ethic. But for Freud, this "higher ethic" is a dangerous illusion, because it seduces us into thinking that we can change what cannot be altered – our unconscious instinctual life, which is marked by the perpetual struggle of the life and death instincts.

It is, of course true that both Nietzsche and Freud warn us about what can happen when the aggressive instincts that are bottled up and internalized explode into a fury of destruction. Indeed, they were both prophetic about a possibility, which has become all too *real* in the twentieth century. Neither of them would be surprised by the massacres, sadistic orgies of destruction, and genocides of our time. But the consequences of their thinking concerning the problem of evil are very different. The evil that most concerns Nietzsche is that which results from the triumph of *ressentiment*, the nihilism that is the consequence of the will to nothingness. Only the transvaluation of values achieved by Nietzsche's overman (*Übermensch*) can "redeem" humanity. But Freud is far more cautious and modest in his aims. We must learn to live with the fact that there are no final solutions for the struggle between the life and death instincts, that there is no way to eliminate latent human aggressiveness and ambivalence. Their consequences can be modulated only within a very limited range. We cannot eliminate our "evil impulses." Freud's primary message is deflationary of utopian hopes, but it is not a doctrine of pessimism. It is, rather, a doctrine of *psychological realism* whose intent is to disabuse us of misguided illusions about who we are and who we may become. The ethic of honesty demands constant vigilance against the outbursts of unrestrained aggressiveness.

Responsibility for evil

I want to conclude my interrogation of Freud's moral psychology by exploring human responsibility for evil and the modest, but crucial, role of reason. Because the id is the locus of instincts that are beyond our conscious rational control, it might seem that the very idea of moral responsibility is undermined. Furthermore, there has been a great deal of loose talk about Freud's psychological determinism, which would seem to undermine any positive conception of human freedom and responsibility. But this is a false, distorted picture of Freud (and psychoanalysis), for Freud provides us with a more complex and subtle account of human responsibility. It is, of course true that we are *not* responsible for our instinctual endowment, or for the psychic ambivalence that we experience. Moreover, we are not responsible for the many unpredictable contingencies that can have such a dramatic effect on the formation and the severity of conscience. The ego, which is the primary locus of responsibility, is always in a precarious position, for it must defend itself from three sources – the id, the superego, and external reality. Philip Rieff states this succinctly when he notes that Freud tended to envisage the ego as in permanent crisis where it is "goaded on by the id, hemmed in by the super-ego and rebuffed by reality."[32] The ethic of honesty demands an appreciation of the various factors that condition human responsibility – not abandonment of responsibility. Freud is quite explicit about this. In a little-known note that he intended to add to later editions of *The Interpretation of Dreams*, he raised the question of our responsibility for the latent content of our dreams.[33] He says, "one must hold oneself responsible for the evil impulses of one's dreams. What else is one to do with them? . . . . If I seek to classify the impulses that are present in me according to social standards into good and bad, I must assume responsibility for both sorts; and if in defence, I say that what is unknown, unconscious and repressed in me is not my 'ego,' then I shall not be basing my position upon psychoanalysis" (*SE* XIX, 133). Freud is aware of the objection that "this bad repressed content" belongs to the id, not to the ego, but he reminds us that "this ego developed out of the id, it forms with it a single biological unit, it is only a specially modified peripheral portion of it, and it is subject to the influences and obeys the suggestions that arise from the id. For any vital purpose a separation of the ego from the id would be a hopeless undertaking" (*SE* XIX, 133). To drive home his point about responsibility, he says:

> Moreover, if I were to give way to my moral pride and tried to decree that for the purposes of moral valuation I might disregard the evil in the id and need not make my ego responsible for it, what use would that be to me? Experience shows me that I nevertheless *do* take responsibility, that I am somehow compelled to do so. (*SE* XIX, 133)

It may be objected that Freud is here dealing with the psychological fact that individuals *feel* responsible for their "evil impulses," but that this psychological observation is not to be confused with the *moral* question of whether they *ought* to assume responsibility for these impulses. This objection fails to appreciate the extent to which Freud is calling into question a categorical divide between "is" and "ought." Freud does recognize that there are pathological conditions in which individuals suffer painfully from a sense of guilt over which they have no control. But he is just as insistent in affirming that there is a proper, essential role for conscience, guilt, and a sense of responsibility. He continues the passage I have just quoted as follows:

Psycho-analysis has made us familiar with a pathological condition, obsessional neurosis, in which the poor ego feels itself responsible for all sorts of evil impulses of which it knows nothing, impulses which are brought up against it in consciousness but which it is unable to acknowledge. *Something of this is present in every normal person.* It is a remarkable fact that the more moral he is the more sensitive is his 'conscience'. It is just as though we could say that the healthier a man is, the more liable he is to contagions and to the effects of injuries. This is no doubt because conscience is itself a reaction-formation against the evil that is perceived in the id. The more strongly the latter is suppressed, the more active is the conscience. (*SE* XIX, 133–4; emphasis added)

We can now appreciate the meaning of the famous statement that is frequently quoted (and just as frequently misunderstood). "Where id was, there ego shall be" (*Wo Es war, soll Ich werden*). Freud makes this statement in his *New Introductory Lectures on Psycho-Analysis* (1933), where he warns us about making the distinction between id, ego, and superego too rigid. We must allow them to merge together like "areas of colour melting into one another as they are presented by modern artists" (*SE* XXII, 79). Freud declares that the aim of psychoanalytic therapy is to *strengthen* the ego. He writes: "Its intention is, indeed, to strengthen the ego, to make it more independent of the super-ego, to widen its field of perception and enlarge its organization, so that it can appropriate fresh portions of the id. Where id was, there ego shall be. It is a work of culture—not unlike the draining of the Zuider Zee" (*SE* XXII, 80).

When we consider Freud's analysis of conscience, the sense of guilt, the superego, morality, and responsibility, we realize how strikingly he departs from the Kantian tradition that virtually identifies morality with practical rationality. Conscience – the heart of everyday morality – has little to do with rationality. Its genesis is to be explained as a vestige of taboo conscience. As Philip Rieff notes, "The aim of reason may be either (1) to introduce or to buttress super-ego controls for purposes of efficiency, or (2) to break down rigid and superfluous moral controls . . . . Conscience, not passion, emerges as the last enemy of reason. True self-awareness is impossible until the moralizing voice is restrained, or at least controlled."[34] Freud neither denigrates nor exaggerates the role that reason plays in our lives. Against some of the grandiose claims made about the power and autonomy of reason, Freud is the great debunker. He certainly exposes what he considers the misguided claim that reason is the ground of morality and moral conscience. But it would be the gravest error to think that Freud mocks or underestimates the importance of the rational functions of the ego. It is only by strengthening the rational functions of the ego that we can ever hope to restrain the potential disastrous destructive consequences of our "evil impulses." At times, Freud expresses skepticism about how much success can be achieved in strengthening the ego, and in cultivating a healthy sense of moral responsibility.[35] But at other times, he is cautiously optimistic. In *The Future of an Illusion*, he writes: "We may insist as often as we like that man's intellect is powerless in comparison with his instinctual life, and we may be right in this. Nevertheless, there is something about this weakness. The voice of the intellect is a soft one, but it does not rest till it has gained a hearing. Finally, after a countless succession of rebuffs, it succeeds" (*SE* XXI, 53).[36] When Freud speaks in this manner (as he frequently does), he identifies himself explicitly with the Enlightenment's commitment to reason and science – to *logos*.[37] But he stands in that tradition which demands that Enlightenment itself must be subjected to critique, and that we be honest about the fragility and precariousness of reason. There is not any inconsistency in these opposing emphases; they bring forth the nuances of Freud's position. We must be sensitive to the fragility and limits of reason, but vigilant in strengthening the rational functions of the ego. We must be realistic about the conflicting nature and dynamics of our basic instincts, but aware of the responsibility we bear when we allow our aggressive instincts to manifest themselves in destructive ways.

Yet, despite Freud's skepticism regarding Kantian claims about the significance and role of practical rationality in accounting for morality, there is a sense in which Freud vindicates Kant's doctrine of radical evil. Let us recall that the primary meaning of "radical" for Kant is the etymological sense in which it literally refers to the root of things. When Kant affirms, that "man is evil by nature," he is asserting that human beings, in their very roots, are evil. Ironically, it is Freud who, in his moral psychology, provides grounds for this thesis. Freud, in his analysis of psychic ambivalence, in his myth of the primal horde, in his late theory of instincts, teaches us that there are powerful evil propensities. He provides the psychoanalytic evidence that warrants the key claim made by Kant, but which is never adequately justified by him.

Recently, Freud has come in for a great deal of criticism. Indeed "Freud-bashing" has become an industry. Psychoanalysis as a therapy for curing or alleviating pathological conditions has come under severe attack, and is being rapidly displaced by other forms of therapy. But alongside this, psychoanalysis as a source of insight and fertile speculation in such fields as film studies, feminism, cultural criticism, and even Holocaust studies is flourishing. I have already indicated how even the most sympathetic defenders of Freud reject his speculation about the death instinct. And disputes about the epistemological status of psychoanalysis as a scientific discipline continue to rage just as they did during Freud's lifetime. But even as we subject Freud to the most rigorous criticism, and reject many of his specific claims, I believe that Freud has significantly altered our understanding of human nature and the dynamics of the psyche. This has the utmost significance for our understanding of the human capacity for evil. Freud teaches us that, "in reality, there is no eradicating of evil." We must never underestimate the power and energy of our basic drives and instincts, and the depth of psychic ambivalence. We must never delude ourselves into thinking that our instinctual destructive capacity can be completely tamed or controlled. We must never forget that all sorts of unexpected contingencies can unleash "barbarous" outbursts of aggression and destruction. This is true for individuals, groups, and societies. Unfortunately, the evidence of the massacres and genocides of the twentieth century, which have occurred under the most diverse conditions, "confirms" Freud's warning. Freud's ethic of honesty demands that we learn to recognize and live with this reality without succumbing to ineffectual moralizing. Regression and barbarism can never be laid to rest. This does not mean that we must impotently resign ourselves to them. While recognizing the fragility and limits of reason, we must seek to strengthen those rational ego functions that enable us to mitigate the destructive consequences of our aggressive impulses. The sobering moral to be drawn from Freud is that there are no (and cannot be any) "final solutions" to the problem of evil. The drama of our individual and collective lives is always being played out against a background of ineradicable psychic ambivalence, where "evil impulses" may temporarily be held in check, suppressed, and repressed, but never permanently eliminated.

Part III

After Auschwitz

Prologue

Arendt: You know, what was decisive was not the year 1933, at least not for me. What was decisive was the day we learned about Auschwitz.

Gaus: When was that?

Arendt: That was in 1943. At first we didn't believe it – although my husband and I always said that we expected anything from that bunch. But we didn't believe this because militarily it was unnecessary and uncalled for. . . . And then a half-year later we believed it after all, because we had the proof. That was the real shock. Before that we said: Well, one has enemies? That is entirely natural. Why shouldn't people have enemies? But this was different. It was really as if an abyss had opened. Because we had the idea that amends could somehow be made for everything else, as amends can be made for just about everything at some point in politics. But not for this. *This ought not to have happened.* And I don't mean just the number of victims. I mean the method, the fabrication of corpses and so on – I don't need to go into that. This should not have happened. Something happened there to which we cannot reconcile ourselves. None of us ever can.[1]

This exchange took place on October 28, 1964, in a television interview between Günter Gaus and Hannah Arendt that was broadcast on West German television. But many survivors and witnesses of the Shoah have reiterated the sentiment that Arendt expresses in such a straightforward manner – that it was as if an abyss had opened, that something had happened to which we cannot reconcile ourselves. The Shoah, and indeed the entire Nazi era, have been studied with greater intensity and more detailed scholarship than any other period in history. The fascination, sometimes bordering on obsession, with investigating the minutest details of what happened (and did not happen) shows no signs of diminishing. Yet Arendt's initial shock and judgment still remain. The same judgment has been expressed by Saul Friedlander, the eminent Israeli historian of the Nazis and the Jews, and by Jürgen Habermas, one of Germany's outstanding philosophers and social theorists.

> What turns the "Final Solution" into an event at the limits is the very fact that it is the most radical form of genocide encountered in history: the willful, systematic, industrially organized, largely successful attempt totally to exterminate an entire group within twentieth-century Western society. In Jürgen Habermas' words: "There [in Auschwitz] something happened, that up to now nobody considered even possible. There one touched on something which represents the deep layer of solidarity among all that wears a human face: not withstanding all the usual acts of beastliness of human history, the integrity of this common layer had been taken for granted . . . Auschwitz has changed the basis for the continuity of the conditions of life within history."[2]

In this part of the book I want to explore the reflections of three thinkers who were profoundly affected by the Shoah, and who took it to be an exemplar of the most radical evil. They experienced the shock that Arendt describes. They struggled to comprehend its significance and consequences, and to face up to the fundamental philosophical and religious issues that it posed: Emmanuel Levinas, Hans Jonas, and Hannah Arendt. They have a great deal in common, although – as we shall see – there are fundamental differences among them. Because each of their lives was shaped and transformed by the events of the Nazi period, their biographies are relevant to their confrontation with this evil. They were roughly the same age. Levinas and Arendt were both born in 1906, Jonas in 1903. All three were Jewish. Arendt and Jonas were born in Germany; Levinas grew up in Kovno, Lithuania. As university students, each of them was initiated into the Husserlian phenomenological movement and studied with Martin Heidegger, who had a profound influence upon their intellectual lives. Arendt and Jonas first encountered Heidegger at Marburg in the early 1920s, before he moved to Freiburg, and before he published *Sein und Zeit*. In 1923, Levinas left Kovno to study philosophy at the University of Strasbourg, and in 1928–9 went to Freiburg to further his study of phenomenology and listen to Heidegger. It was Levinas who was primarily responsible for introducing the phenomenology of Husserl and Heidegger into France. He eventually became a French citizen and fought in the Second World War. Because he was a French soldier, his life was spared when the Germans captured him. He spent several years in a German prisoner of war camp.

Both Arendt and Jonas fled Germany in 1933. Arendt made her way to Paris, where she remained until 1941, when she managed to flee to New York. Jonas, who had identified himself with the Zionists, escaped to Palestine in 1935. Subsequently, he fought in the famous Jewish Brigade of the British Army. For both Levinas and Jonas, Auschwitz was not only a symbol of the Nazi horror; their closest relatives were exterminated in Auschwitz. Although Arendt managed to escape from Germany with her mother, she herself came close to being shipped to Auschwitz. Shortly before the Nazis invaded France, she was interned (as a German *émigré*) in the French detention camp at Gurs. In the confusion that arose when the Germans marched into France, she managed to escape. But many of the women who remained in Gurs were eventually shipped to Auschwitz to be exterminated. Jonas returned to Palestine in 1945 and saw combat once again in the Israeli War of Independence. But in 1949, desiring to continue his philosophical career, he accepted a fellowship at McGill University in Canada. In 1955, he was invited to join the graduate faculty of the New School for Social Research. A decade later, Hannah Arendt became his colleague at the New School. Jonas and Arendt were well acquainted with each other's work, but there is little evidence that either of them had more than a superficial acquaintance with Levinas's work. And although Levinas mentions Arendt in a few places, he never engaged in a serious encounter with her work or with that of Jonas.

In this final part of my study, I plan to proceed in a slightly different manner than in the two previous parts. I want to compare and contrast the distinctive understandings and responses to the evil witnessed by Levinas, Jonas, and Arendt. Collectively, their attempts to confront the evils of the twentieth century are even more powerful than their individual voices. Each of them also reopens the question: What does responsibility mean today? I shall begin with Levinas, because he presents the fundamental problem that all three thinkers address – how to think about evil when we no longer have any confidence in traditional theodicies, when the very idea of seeking to "justify" evil is obscene, and when there is no possibility of reconciling ourselves to the brute existence of evil.

6

Levinas: Evil and the Temptation of Theodicy

The metaphor that best captures the movement of Levinas's thinking is the one used by Derrida when he compares it to a wave crashing on a beach: always the "same" wave returning and repeating its movement with a deeper insistence.[1] Regardless of what theme we follow – the meaning of ethics, responsibility, the alterity of the other (*l'autrui*), subjectivity, substitution – there is a profound sense that the "same" wave is crashing. This is just as true when we focus on those moments in philosophy that indicate that there is "something" more (and something more important) than being and ontology. Levinas keeps returning to Plato's suggestion that the Good is beyond Being, and to the moment in Descartes's *Meditations* when he discovers that the *ideatum* of infinity positively exceeds its idea, that infinity transcends any idea of finite substances. Or, to switch metaphors, no matter which of the many pathways we take, pathways that seem to lead off in radically different directions, we always end up in the "same" place, the "same" clearing. This is not the clearing of *Being*, but rather the place where ethics *ruptures* Being. But even when the outlines of Levinas's thinking come into sharper focus, our perplexity and puzzlement increase. We want to know how he arrives at his radical and startling claims. What are the considerations that lead him to insist on our asymmetrical and nonreciprocal relation to the other (*l'autrui*), and our *infinite* responsibility to and for the other? Some have suggested that the place to begin is with the influence of Heidegger on his thinking, with the way in which Levinas is in a continuous critical dialogue with Heidegger. Others have suggested that we must go back to Franz Rosenzweig's *The Star of Redemption*, especially to Rosenzweig's critique of philosophy ("from Iona to Jena") and the very idea of totality that permeates so much of Western philosophy. Still others have argued that the primary source of Levinas's understanding of ethics is to be found in his interpretation of the Hebrew Bible and the Jewish rabbinic tradition of commentary on the Torah. There is something right about all these suggestions (which are not incompatible), but frankly, they do not go deep enough. They do not answer the question: Why does Levinas interpret and use these sources in such a distinctive, unique manner? The thesis I want to advance and defend is that the primary thrust of Levinas's thought is to be understood as his response to the horror of evil that erupted in the twentieth century. Levinas's entire philosophical project can best be understood as an *ethical* response to evil – and to the problem of evil that we must confront after the "end of theodicy."

At first glance such a thesis seems paradoxical, because Levinas does not thematize evil in any of his major works. In the extensive secondary literature dealing with Levinas, evil (*mal*) is barely even mentioned. Yet, like an ever-present, ominous specter, evil casts its shadow over everything he has ever written. It is no exaggeration to assert that Levinas's confrontation with the "unspeakable" evil of the twentieth century – where Auschwitz is the very paradigm of this evil – has not only elicited his fundamental *ethical* response, but has led him directly to his distinctive understanding of ethics.

I can illustrate what I mean by turning to the opening provocative sentence of *Totality and Infinity*:[2] "Everyone will readily agree that it is of the highest importance to know whether we are not duped by morality." (*On conviendra aisément qu'il importe au plus haut point de savoir si l'on n'est pas le dupe de la morale.*) (*TI* 21; p. ix). What does it mean to be duped by morality?[3] In the paragraphs that follow this dramatic opening, Levinas speaks of politics, war, and violence, and introduces the theme of totality. "War does not manifest exteriority and the other as other; it destroys the identity of the same. The visage of being that shows itself in war is fixed in the concept of totality, which dominates Western philosophy" (*TI* 21; p. ix). But the possibility of being duped by morality means more than this. Consider Levinas's response to a question about the Greek and Jewish elements in his thinking that he was asked in an interview.[4] He insists that his thought is Greek (that is, philosophical): "[E]verything that I say about justice comes from Greek thought, and Greek politics as well. But what I say, quite simply, is that it is ultimately based on the relationship to the other, on the ethics without which I would not have sought justice. Justice is the way in which I respond to the fact that I am not alone in the world with the other" (PM 174). But what about the Jewish moment in his thinking? He tells us:

If there is an explicitly Jewish moment in my thought, it is the reference to Auschwitz, where God let the Nazis do what they wanted. Consequently, what remains? Either this means that there is no reason for morality and hence it can be concluded that everyone should act like the Nazis, or the moral law maintains its authority. Here is freedom; this choice is the moment of freedom.

It still cannot be concluded that after Auschwitz there is no longer a moral law, as if the moral or ethical law were impossible, without promise. Before the twentieth century, all religion begins with the promise. It begins with the "Happy End." (PM 175–6)

It is not a rhetorical question to ask whether we can still believe in morality after Auschwitz. It is the most serious question to be asked. "The essential problem is: can we speak of an absolute commandment after Auschwitz? Can we speak of morality after the failure of morality" (PM 176)? Perhaps we really have been duped by morality. Arendt and Jonas both raise similar questions – and were troubled by the same anxiety. Nihilism – the type of nihilism that questions the very possibility of ethics and morality – is no longer just a philosophical or theoretical issue. Auschwitz makes the question of nihilism all too real and concrete. Arendt (like Levinas) believes that the evil that burst forth in the Nazi period indicates a rupture with tradition, and reveals the inadequacy of traditional accounts of morals and ethics to deal with evil. She declares, "We have witnessed the total collapse of all established moral standards in public and private life during the thirties and forties." "Without much notice all this collapsed almost overnight and then it was as though morality suddenly stood revealed . . . as a set of mores, customs and manners which could be exchanged for another set with hardly more trouble than it would take to change the table manners of an individual or a people."[5] And in her posthumously published *The Life of the Mind*, she says "The fact that we usually treat matters of good and evil in courses in 'morals' and 'ethics' may indicate how little we know about them, for morals comes from *mores* and ethics from *ethos*, the Latin and the Greek words for customs and habit, the Latin word being associated with rules of behavior, whereas the Greek is derived from habitat, like our habits."[6]

The end of theodicy

The question raised by Levinas is one not only about morality, but also about religion – specifically, the question of theodicy. In his essay "Useless Suffering," Levinas explicitly takes up the question of theodicy, and it is here that he declares that we are now living in a time after "the end of theodicy."[7] "Perhaps the most revolutionary fact of our twentieth century consciousness . . . is that of the destruction of all balance between explicit and implicit theodicy of Western thought and the forms of suffering and its evil take in the very unfolding of this century" (US 161). But what does Levinas mean by theodicy, and in what sense are we now living in a time after "the end of theodicy"? When Levinas speaks of theodicy, he is not only referring to the specific sense of theodicy introduced by Leibniz in 1710. Theodicy, in its broad sense, is "as old as a certain reading of the Bible." Levinas speaks of theodicy as a *temptation*. This seductive temptation consists "in making God innocent, or in saving morality in the name of faith, or in making suffering – and this is the true intention of the thought that has recourse to theodicy – bearable" (US 161).

Theodicy in this broad sense is not only evidenced in the Christian doctrine of original sin, but is already implicit in the Jewish Bible, "where the drama of the Diaspora reflects the sins of Israel" (US 161). Lest we think that theodicy is restricted to religious faith, Levinas emphasizes that, in a secular age, theodicy has persisted "in a watered-down form at the core of atheist progressivism which was confident, nonetheless, in the efficacy of the Good which is immanent to being, called to visible triumph by the simple play of natural and historical laws of injustice, war, misery, and illness" (US 161). In short, theodicy, in both its theological and secular forms, is the temptation to find some sort of justification, some way to reconcile ourselves to useless, unbearable suffering and evil. But intellectual honesty demands that we recognize that theodicy – in this broad sense – is over. "The philosophical problem then, which is posed by the useless pain (*mal*) which appears in its fundamental malignancy across the events of the twentieth century, concerns the meaning that religiosity and the human morality of goodness can still retain after the end of theodicy" (US 163).

We can appreciate the radicalness of Levinas's claim by comparing him with Kant. The latter criticized theodicy as a *theoretical* problem, because it presupposes that we can have some knowledge (no matter how partial or inadequate) of God's attributes (for example, that God is – or is not – omnipotent, omniscient and beneficent). But such theoretical knowledge is impossible. Furthermore, Kant begins his *Religion within the Limits of Reason Alone* by categorically affirming that morality "stands in need neither of the idea of another Being over him, for him to apprehend his duty, nor of an incentive other than the law itself, for him to do his duty . . . . Hence for its own sake morality does not need religion at all."[8] Yet, from Levinas's perspective, Kant does not resist the temptation of theodicy. He affirms a *practical* need to postulate a beneficent God. Lurking in the background here is still the idea of reconciliation; the "promise" of being worthy of what Levinas calls "the Happy End." This is what we must now give up. The phenomenon of Auschwitz demands (if we are not duped by morality) that we conceive of "the moral law independently of the Happy End."

Auschwitz (where most of Levinas's family were murdered) is the "paradigm of gratuitous human suffering, where evil appears in its diabolical horror" (US 162). But it is not exclusively the Jewish catastrophe that Levinas singles out. Levinas is explicit about this.

> This is the century that in thirty years has known two world wars, the totalitarianisms of right and left, Hitlerism and Stalinism, Hiroshima, the Gulag, and the genocides of Auschwitz and Cambodia. This is a century which is drawing to a close in the haunting memory of the return of everything signified by these barbaric names: suffering and evil are deliberately imposed, yet no reason sets limits to the exasperation of a reason become political and detached from all ethics. (US 162)

He also says, "I think that all the dead of the Gulag and all the other places of torture in our political century are present when one speaks of Auschwitz" (US 167). His emphasis on Auschwitz as an exemplar of the evil that has burst forth in the twentieth century enables us to understand better the interweaving of Greek and Jewish elements in Levinas's thinking. Sometimes the contrast between the Greek and the Jew is overdrawn (even by Levinas himself). I have already quoted the passage in which Levinas insists that his philosophical thought is essentially Greek. (To assert that philosophical thought is Greek is redundant.) But it is just as important to realize that when Levinas weaves "Jewish" elements into his thinking, he is primarily concerned to highlight their *universal* significance.

> I do not preach for the Jewish religion. I always speak of the Bible, not the Jewish religion. The Bible, including the Old Testament, is for me a human fact, of the human order, and entirely *universal*. What I have said about ethics, about the *universality* of the commandment in the face, of the commandment which is valid even if it doesn't bring salvation, even if there is no reward, is valid independently of any religion. (PM 177; emphasis added)

For all the distinctiveness of the evils of the twentieth century, we can also hear the voices of Nietzsche and Dostoevsky speaking through Levinas. Nietzsche is the most brilliant diagnostician of the human need to "justify" suffering. And it was Nietzsche who radically criticized theodicy in the very sense in which Levinas intends it – where the aim is to "justify" unbearable suffering.

What really arouses indignation against suffering is not suffering as such but the senselessness of suffering: but neither for the Christian, who has interpreted a whole mysterious machinery of salvation into suffering, nor for the naïve man of more ancient times, who understood all suffering in relation to the spectator of it or the causer of it, was there any such thing as *senseless* suffering. So as to abolish hidden, undetected, unwitnessed suffering from the world and honestly to deny it, one was in the past virtually compelled to invent gods and genii of all the heights and depths . . . . For it was with the aid of such inventions that life knew how to work the trick which it has always known how to work, that of justifying itself, of justifying its "evil."[9]

There is a similar theme in Dostoevsky. Levinas tells us that his first introduction to philosophy came from reading Russian novels when he was an adolescent in Kovno. When he speaks about our essentially asymmetrical relation with the other, and the responsibility that we have to the other, he frequently cites the famous statement of Aloysa Karamazov: "'Everyone is guilty [responsible] in front of everyone else and me more than all the others.' That is the idea of dissymmetry. The relationship between me and the other is unsurpassable" (PM 179). But we can also hear the voice of Ivan Karamazov's diatribe against the suffering of innocent children. When Levinas speaks about the scandal of useless suffering, he sounds as if he is uttering the very words of Ivan.

Western Humanity has none the less sought for the meaning of this scandal by invoking the proper sense of a metaphysical order, an ethics, which is invisible in the immediate lessons of moral consciousness. This is the kingdom of transcendent ends, willed by a benevolent wisdom, by the absolute goodness of a God who is in some way defined by this supernatural goodness; or a widespread, invisible goodness in Nature and History, where it would command the paths which are, to be sure painful, but which lead to the Good. Pain [*mal*] is henceforth meaningful, subordinated in one way or another to the metaphysical finality envisaged by faith or by a belief in progress. These beliefs are presupposed by theodicy! . . . The evil which fills the earth would be explained in a 'plan of the whole': it would be called upon to atone for a sin, or it would announce, to the ontologically limited consciousness, compensation or recompense at the end of time. (US 160–1)

Levinas's response to useless suffering is neither that of Nietzsche, who calls for the "transvaluation of values," nor the self-laceration of Ivan Karamazov, who refuses to accept a world in which there is useless suffering of innocent children. Levinas's response is an *ethical* response – one that leads to his distinctive understanding of the asymmetrical, nonreciprocal responsibility to and for the other, a response to the suffering of the other (*l'autrui*), my neighbor.

But does not this end of theodicy, which obtrudes itself in the face of this
century's inordinate distress, at the same time in a more general way reveal
the unjustifiable character of suffering in the other person, the scandal
which would occur by my justifying my neighbor's suffering? So that the
very phenomenon of suffering in its uselessness is, in principle, the pain of
the Other. For an ethical sensibility – confirming itself, in the inhumanity
of our time, against this inhumanity – the justification of the neighbor's
pain is certainly the source of all immorality. (US 163)

We see why Levinas's understanding of our ethical relation and responsibility to the other (*l'autrui*) is so demanding, and yet so appealing. When
confronted with those exemplars of extreme evil in the twentieth century,
we tend to focus on the actions of the perpetrators and the suffering of the
victims. We are much more uneasy and ambivalent about the responsibility of the so-called bystanders, by those who allow such actions to take
place, and who justify their complicity by excusing themselves from any
direct responsibility. Despite the voluminous literature about the Nazi era,
and the many explanations offered, this still remains one of the most
troublesome unresolved questions. How are we to account for the fact
that so many people, who were for the most part decent, law-abiding
citizens, could be unmoved when their neighbors and even friends were
suffering, disappearing, being deported, brutalized, and murdered? Of
course, one cannot underestimate blatant anti-Semitism or the effectiveness of Nazi terror and propaganda. The most insignificant gesture of
support for the victims could lead to incarceration, torture, or death.
Although it may sound hyperbolical to assert, that "the justification of the
neighbor's pain is certainly the source of all immorality," think how different the history of the twentieth century might have been if more individuals had felt responsible for the suffering of their neighbors and fellow
human beings. Levinas's understanding of ethics and "the infinite responsibility" that we bear *to* and *for* other persons is poignantly illustrated by a
passage from Hannah Arendt's *Eichmann in Jerusalem*. She tells the story of
Anton Schmidt, whose name was brought up in the course of the trial by
the prosecution. Anton Schmidt was a German soldier in charge of a
patrol in Poland that collected German soldiers who were cut off from
their units. For five months, from October 1941 until March 1942, Schmidt
helped Jewish partisans by supplying them with forged papers and trucks.
He was then arrested by the Germans and quickly executed. That's almost all we know about Anton Schmidt, except that "He did not do it for
money." When Anton Schmidt's story was told in the Jerusalem court, it
was as if those present observed a two-minute silence in honor of this
German soldier who saved Jewish lives. Arendt's comment is certainly in

the spirit of Levinas's understanding of ethics and responsibility for the suffering of one's fellow human beings.

> And in those two minutes, which were like a sudden burst of light in the midst of impenetrable unfathomable darkness, a single thought stood out clearly, irrefutable, beyond question – how utterly different everything would be today in this courtroom, in Israel, in Germany, in all of Europe, and perhaps in all countries of the world, if only more such stories could have been told.[10]

Hans Jonas tells a very different story, but one that also makes the point that Levinas stresses. On January 30, 1993, just six days before his death, Jonas gave a talk in the Italian town of Udine. He was there to receive the Premio Nonino, an award honoring the Italian translation of *The Imperative of Responsibility*. Udine had a special significance for Jonas, a town that "denotes a milestone in my life and enshrines one of its most unforgettable memories."[11] In the early summer of 1945, Jonas, who was still a soldier, went to Udine. During the previous five years, he had fought in the Jewish Brigade. In defiance of the Nazis, the Jewish Brigade was proud to display the Star of David on their uniforms. Consequently, as they marched through Italy, Jewish survivors frequently sought them out. One day in Udine, two elderly Austrian-Jewish sisters from Trieste approached Jonas to tell their story. When the Germans were rounding up Jews in Trieste for deportation, the sisters managed to escape and to find their way to Udine as a place of refuge "where nobody knew them and they knew nobody." Shortly after they arrived, a van stopped in front of the house where they had an attic apartment and delivered two beds with a message from the local archbishop who had heard of their situation and wished to make them more comfortable. In the succeeding months they survived by selling off their jewelry to buy food on the black market because, as nonregistered strangers, they had no ration cards. They told Jonas about an incident that occurred when they purchased a kilogram of lard from a black-marketer at an exorbitant price. It is what happened next that so moved Jonas.

> Late at night that same day, there was a knock at their door. Fearfully they opened it – and there stood the hard-boiled black-market operator who said, "Forgive me, please. I didn't know who you were when I sold you that lard this morning. I was told later and have come to apologize. From you I will take no money." He thrust an envelope stuffed with their banknotes into their hands, turned, and fled down the stairs.[12]

Jonas carried this story with him throughout his life, "like a sacred trust," and he concludes his tale by saying, "Incidentally, you will not have

missed the lovely irony in the reassuring phrase, 'Nobody knows us here.'
Many, it seems, knew of them without their knowing it, and it is to the
lasting glory of Udine that this did not imperil them but, on the contrary,
protected them."[13] This story beautifully illustrates Levinas's understanding of one's responsibility to the other (*l'autrui*).

The phenomenology of evil

But let us return to the question of how Levinas understands evil "after
the end of theodicy." One of the few places in which he deals directly with
evil is in his article "Transcendence and Evil."[14] The occasion for writing
it was the appearance of Philippe Nemo's *Job et l'excès du mal*, a philosophical meditation on the question of evil in the book of Job. Levinas is
primarily concerned with the "philosophical perspective opened by this
work" (TE 157). He focuses on three moments of the phenomenology of
evil: evil as excess, evil as intention, and the hatred or horror of evil.

Evil as excess initially suggests an excess of its quantitative intensity, "of
a degree surpassing measure." But Levinas stresses how "evil is an excess
in its very quiddity" (TE 158). Evil is not an excess because suffering can
be terrible and unendurable. "The break with the normal and the normative, with order, with synthesis, with the world, already constitutes its
qualitative essence" (TE 158). Levinas is not simply calling attention to
the unbearable torture and suffering that evil deeds inflict, he wants to
underscore that we cannot "synthesize" evil; it cannot be integrated into
our categories of understanding or reason.

> It is as though to synthesis, even the purely formal synthesis of the Kantian
> "I think," capable of uniting the data however heterogeneous they may be,
> there would be opposed, in the form of evil, the nonsynthesizable, still more
> heterogeneous than all heterogeneity subject to being grasped by the for-
> mal, which exposes heterogeneity in its very malignancy . . . . In the ap-
> pearing of evil, in its original phenomenality, in its *quality*, is announced a
> *modality*, a manner: not finding a place, the refusal of all accommodation
> with – a counternature, a monstrosity, which is disturbing and foreign of
> itself. *And in this sense transcendence!* (TE 158)

I want to bring out the nuances of Levinas's meaning when he speaks of
the "transcendence" of evil, and the sense in which it cannot be synthesized. He seeks to describe how evil is *experienced*. But phrasing the issue in
this way suggests that there is something paradoxical about the excess, the
transcendence of evil. If we think of *experience* in a Kantian way, it is
precisely what *can be* synthesized. There is no experience without synthe-

sis. And if "something" is literally beyond experience or transcends experience, then we cannot know it. But against this Kantian understanding of experience and transcendence, Levinas indicates that the malignancy of evil is *experienced* as "something" that cannot be synthesized, as something that is at once experienced and yet *defies* categorization, as something that is more heterogeneous than the heterogeneity that can be grasped by formal synthesis. We would misinterpret Levinas if we thought he was claiming that we can have *no* knowledge or understanding of evil. After all, he is telling us a great deal about what he takes to be the distinguishing marks of evil. But, at the same time, he wants to emphasize that there is something about evil that eludes *total* comprehension. He also wants to claim that this transcendence of evil is experienced directly and intimately. Although Levinas makes his point with reference to the Kantian idea of synthesis, the experience of the transcendence of the excess of evil can be approached in other ways. What Levinas seeks to show us is closely related to what Arendt intends when she speaks about comprehension at the beginning of *The Origins of Totalitarianism*:

> Comprehension does not mean denying the outrageous, deducing the unprecedented from precedents, or explaining phenomena by such analogies and generalities that the impact of reality and the shock of experience are no longer felt. It means, rather, examining and bearing consciously the burden which our century has placed on us – neither denying its existence nor submitting meekly to its weight. Comprehension, in short, means the unpremeditated, attentive facing up to, and resisting of, reality – what ever it may be.[15]

Ironically – or perhaps not so ironically – Levinas's claims about the excess of evil and its transcendence parallel some of the claims that Kant makes about the sublime in the *Critique of Judgment*. Kant too is attempting to articulate the awareness that we can have of "something" that defies our categories of understanding and comprehension. The major difference, Levinas might argue, is that ultimately Kant treats the sublime as if it can be integrated with ideas of reason (*Vernunft*). But for Levinas, "evil is not only nonintegratable, it is also the nonintegratability of the nonintegratable" (TE 158). Evil, we might say, is a malignant sublime.

When evil is understood as "an excess in its very quiddity," then we can better understand why it not only resists all forms of theodicy, but *opposes* theodicy. Theodicy, whether in its religious or secular form, is based on the presupposition that there is some way of integrating the existence of evil within a coherent, comprehensible economy of good and evil. This is what is required if we are to reconcile ourselves to the appearance or existence of evil. What is so striking about Levinas's discussion of evil as nonintegratable excess is the way in which his reasoning parallels his critique of totality and his critique of the dialectic of the same and the other. Just as infinity *ruptures* totality, so too does evil. Just as the dialectic of the same and the other is *disrupted* because of the nonintegratable excess of the otherness of the other (*l'autrui*), so comprehension and synthesis are disrupted by the transcendence of evil. I do not think that this formal parallel is accidental. On the contrary, it is because of the transcendence of evil, because it cannot be integrated or totally comprehended, that the only adequate response to the malignancy of evil is a response that is "commensurate" with this transcendence of evil. This is precisely the *ethical* response which recognizes that the otherness of the other can never be totally comprehended, that I am infinitely responsible for and to the other person, whose suffering is ethically more important than my own suffering.

The second moment in this phenomenology is the intentionality of evil. "Evil reaches me as though it sought me out; evil strikes me as though there were an aim behind the ill lot that pursues me, as though someone were set against me, as though there were malice, as though there were someone" (TE 159–60). Evil is not just some misfortune that happens to me. I am a *victim* of evil that is directed to me. Even if we consider a natural disaster such as the Lisbon earthquake, it is not the earthquake *per se* that is taken to be evil. It is taken to be an example of natural evil because (explicitly or implicitly) it is assumed that a supreme being allowed it to happen, or caused it to happen. Or if we consider Job's lot, it is not just because terrible things happen to him, but because he believes that it is within God's power to have prevented them from happening, that he questions the justice of God. It is because of the *intentionality* of evil – the presupposition that evil reaches me as though it sought me out and is the result of someone's malice – that the temptation to theodicy arises. This is the point that Nietzsche understood so well when he declared, "what really arouses indignation against suffering is not suffering as such but the senselessness of suffering." But we must resist the temptation of theodicy; we must resist the temptation to justify useless suffering. It is the transcendence of evil that leads us to recognize that the first metaphysical question (*pace* Leibniz and Heidegger) is not "Why is there something rather than nothing?" but "Why is there evil rather than good?" (TE 160). This second moment in the phenomenology of evil provides a glimpse of what is beyond Being, beyond ontology. "The ontological difference is preceded by the difference of good and evil" (TE 160). There is a *priority* of the ethical over the ontological; the ontological presupposes the ethical. Once again it is evil that leads us to ethics as first philosophy, to the primacy of the ethical.

Throughout Levinas's discussion of the phenomenology of evil there is a subtext: his ongoing quarrel with Heidegger. Levinas's thinking, as he himself frequently acknowledges, would not be possible without Heidegger. It is Heidegger's understanding of fundamental ontology that is Levinas's starting point. But when Levinas objects to Heidegger's understanding of Being as the ultimate horizon, when in the language of *Totality and Infinity* he claims that ontology itself is dependent upon, and presupposes, ethics as first philosophy, he is criticizing Heidegger for his failure to confront evil, and for his failure to appreciate what is distinctive about the ethical response to evil. This criticism is reflected even in the terms that Levinas uses to make his point. Heidegger uses the term "metaphysics" (especially in his late philosophy) to name the forgetfulness of Being, to indicate the way in which the tradition has confused the ontic with the ontological. For Heidegger, it is metaphysics that at once presupposes and obscures fundamental ontology. But when Levinas contrasts ontology with metaphysics and asserts the primacy of metaphysics, he does so in order to show that there is "something" beyond Heidegger's fundamental ontology, "something" beyond the horizon of Being. Levinas's ethical thinking rejects "ontological imperialism" (*impérialisme ontologique*) (*TI* 44; 15). Levinas's fundamental claim, that "Western philosophy [including Heidegger's philosophy] has most often been an ontology: a reduction of the other to the same by interposition of a middle and neutral term that ensures the comprehension of being" (*TI* 43; 13). The logic and economy of this reduction, this assimilation of the other to the same, *is* the logic of imperialism that seeks to colonize the nonintegratable integrity of the other. When Levinas speaks of "ontological imperialism," he is not using a "dead" metaphor. For at the core of what we normally call imperialism – whether political or economic imperialism – the same "logic" is at work: the logic of colonizing what is foreign, different, and other.[16] "Metaphysics, transcendence, the welcoming of the other by the same, of the Other by me, is concretely produced as the calling into question of the same by the other, that is as the ethics that accomplishes the critical essence of knowledge. And as critique precedes dogmatism, metaphysics precedes ontology" (*TI* 43; 13). Levinas's critique of Heidegger is primarily a *philosophical* critique.[17] Heidegger's ontological thinking lacks the resources to deal with evil and the ethical response to evil. Despite Heidegger's strenuous efforts to distinguish his thinking from that of his predecessors, he never escapes from the limitations of ontology.

Levinas's third moment is the hatred or horror of evil. This is at once the source of the greatest temptation to ontologize evil, to seek an (impossible) reconciliation with evil, and at the same time the occasion for opening us to the ethical relation with another person: "Evil strikes me in my horror of evil, and thus reveals – or is already – my association with the Good. The excess of evil by which it is a surplus in the world is also our impossibility of accepting it" (TE 161). Everything depends on precisely how one interprets this horror of evil. If I interpret it as meaning that there is an economy whereby evil *must* be counterbalanced by good, then once again I am being seduced by the temptation of theodicy. I am still operating in a framework where there is an economy of relationships that are symmetrical. I am still thinking that good is the dialectical negation of evil, and/or evil is the dialectical negation of good. But Levinas categorically asserts, "There can be no question of a passage from Evil to the Good through the attraction of contraries. That would make but one more theodicy" (TE 161).

But there is another way (the Levinasian way) of interpreting how the "horror of evil" leads to the intimation of the Good – the Good that is beyond Being. The horror of evil opens me up and invites an ethical response to evil. The excess of evil, its malignancy that resists integration, solicits a transcendence that shines "forth in the face of the other man: an alterity of the nonintegratable, of what cannot be assembled into a totality" (TE 163). The following passage eloquently summarizes the movement of Levinas's thinking (the "same" wave that keeps breaking with renewed insistence).

> This is no longer a transcendence absorbed by my knowing. The face puts into question the sufficiency of my identity as an ego; it binds me to an infinite responsibility with regard to the other. The original transcendence signifies in the concreteness, from the first ethical, of the face. That in the evil that pursues me, the evil suffered by the other man afflicts me, that it touches me, as though from the first the other was calling to me, putting into question my resting on myself and my *conatus essendi*, as though before lamenting over my evil here below, I had to answer for the other – is not that a breakthrough of the Good in the "intention" of which I am in my woe so exclusively aimed at? . . . The horror of the evil that aims at me becomes horror over the evil in the other man. Here is a breakthrough of the Good which is not a simple inversion of Evil but an elevation. This Good does not please, but commands and prescribes. (TE 163–4)

We deepen our understanding of Levinas's phenomenological description of evil by considering what he means by the *conatus essendi*. This expression is taken from Spinoza, but it has a much more general significance for Levinas. The *conatus essendi* is the "law of being."

> A being is something that is attached to being, to its own being, which is always a persistence of being. That is Darwin's idea. The being of animals is a struggle for life. A struggle without ethics. It is a question of might.

> Heidegger says at the beginning of *Being and Time* that *Dasein* is a being who in his being is concerned for this being itself. That's Darwin's idea: the living being struggles for life. The aim of being is being itself. (PM 172)

Whatever we may think of this association of Heidegger with Darwin, Levinas's point is clear. The law of being, the *conatus essendi*, is the drive of being to preserve itself. We as human beings are, of course, beings. Consequently, *qua* beings, this law is also our law. But – and this is the crucial point – we are not *exclusively* beings. We are not exclusively what Heidegger calls *Dasein* (being there). We are *human* beings. Levinas declares that "the human breaks with pure being, which is always a persistence in being. This is my principal thesis" (PM 172). Levinas – as if he were summing up his philosophy in a single sentence – tells us: "However, with the appearance of the human – and this is my entire philosophy – there is something more important than my life, and that is the life of the other" (PM 172). He is fully aware that there is something "unreasonable" about this, for it is reasonable to look after oneself – to follow the law of one's being. "But we cannot not admire saintliness. Not the sacred, but saintliness: that is, the person who in his being is more attached to the being of the other than to his own. I believe that it is in saintliness that the human begins; not in the accomplishment of saintliness, but in the value. It is the first value, an undeniable value" (PM 172–3).

We can clarify Levinas's meaning by pursuing a formal analogy with Kant. Just as Kant argues (counterfactually) that if we were exclusively *natural* beings, there would be no *categorical* imperative, and consequently no morality, so Levinas argues that if we were exclusively *beings*, there would be no *ethical* imperative. And just as Kant claims that nature has its own laws, so Levinas claims that being has its own law. For Kant, there is nothing intrinsically good or evil about the laws of nature; for Levinas the law of being is itself neither good nor evil. According to Kant, to acknowledge the moral law does not mean that we always follow it. Nevertheless, we *can* obey the moral law; we can recognize its authority and do what it requires. So too for Levinas, to acknowledge the supreme ethical imperative does not mean that we always follow it; but we *can* obey this command. Ethics presupposes saintliness not as an accomplishment, but as a value or an ideal. I can always act in such a manner as will give ethical priority to the life of the other (*l'autrui*). I stress that this analogy is a "formal" analogy, because, unlike Kant, Levinas does not think that morality is "grounded" in practical reason. Kantian autonomy and responsibility *presuppose* a more primordial heteronomy whereby I am responsible to and for the other. "The presence of the Other [*d'Autrui*], a privileged heteronomy does not clash with freedom but invests it" (*TI* 88; 60).

But how do these reflections about being, the law of being, and the *conatus essendi* further our understanding of evil? We are told, "It is in the human being that a rupture is produced with being's own law, with the law of being. The law of evil is the law of being. Evil is, in this sense, very powerful" (PM 175). The categories of good and evil do not apply to all beings, but only to human beings – to those beings who are *capable* of responding to ethical imperatives. It is because we, as human beings, are aware of the suffering of others that we can respond in an ethical manner. If we fail to respond to the suffering of others, then we are succumbing to the law of evil, the law of being. For Kant, evil arises when we willfully disregard the moral law and succumb to the temptations of self-love. For Levinas, evil arises when we deliberately violate the ethical imperative that binds us to the other (*l'autrui*).

> In the *conatus essendi*, which is the effort to exist, existence is the supreme law. However, with the appearance of the face on the inter-personal level, the commandment 'Thou shalt not kill' emerges as a limitation of the *conatus essendi*. It is not a rational limit. Consequently, interpreting it necessitates thinking it in moral terms, in ethical terms. It must be thought of outside the idea of force. (PM 175)

There is no evil (or good) in a world of pure being. This is why there is not, and cannot be, any place for ethics in a philosophy whose ultimate horizon is Being. Heidegger treats humanism as if it were limited to the horizon of (what Heidegger calls) "metaphysics" – a metaphysics that conceals the horizon of being. But from Levinas's perspective, Heidegger fails to realize that a true humanism – an *ethical humanism* – requires a rupture with Being and the law of being, the *conatus essendi*. To become human is to transcend my own law of being, and to respond ethically to the evil that afflicts my neighbor.

Infinite responsibility

To complete my discussion of the transcendence of evil and the ethical response to evil, I want to consider the distinctive way in which Levinas appeals to infinity, and what he means when he speaks of our infinite responsibility. Levinas departs from the way in which Kant and Hegel appeal to the notion of infinity. Both Kant and Hegel – and Levinas would say most Western philosophers – have explicitly or implicitly identified infinity with totality. In Kant, infinity names a type of totality of the unconditioned that we may *think*, but cannot *know*. This is what Hegel called the bad infinite (*die schlechte Unendlichkeit*). The true infinite lies beyond this bad infinite; it overcomes the dichotomy between the finite and the bad infinite. Hegel brings out the hidden dialectic of the same and the other, the dialectic that culminates in the identification of totality with infinity. Levinas's philosophical starting point is that neither Kant nor Hegel (nor even Heidegger) fully appreciate that infinity cannot be integrated into totality or being. Concerning the Kantian idea of infinity, Levinas tells us: "The Kantian notion of infinity figures as an ideal of reason, the projection of its exigencies in a beyond, the ideal completion of what is given incomplete – but without the incomplete being confronted with a privileged *experience* of infinity, without it drawing limits of its finitude from such a confrontation" (*TI* 196; 170). Concerning the Hegelian idea of infinity, Levinas tell us: "[Hegel] posits the infinite as the exclusion of every 'other' that might maintain a relation with the infinite and thereby limit it. The infinite can only encompass all relations. Like the god of Aristotle it refers only to itself, though now at the term of a history" (*TI* 196; 170).

For Levinas, the infinite is what *ruptures* totality and being; what is *beyond* totality and being, what opens the space for the ethical relation to the other that resists and opposes any assimilation to totality and being. It is just this nonintegratable, radically heterogeneous infinite that is the warrant for Levinas to speak of our "infinite responsibility" to and for the other. "*Infinite* responsibility" is not to be understood in a Kantian manner as a type of responsibility that is an idea of reason, a regulative idea that can never be realized fully. Nor is it to be understood in a Hegelian manner as the infinity that is truly and actually realized in a totality. Rather, it is the type of responsibility that *precedes*, and is more primordial than, my own autonomous freedom. I can never totally fulfill my responsibilities to the other (*l'autrui*). But this is neither a doctrine of despair nor an ethic of heroism. It is an ethic of everyday life, because in the simplest act or gesture of welcoming I can act in an ethically responsible way. Levinas was once asked how he would respond to the objection that his notion of infinite ethical responsibility is "entirely utopian and unrealistic." This is how he responded:

> This is the great objection to my thought. 'Where did you ever see the ethical relation practised?' people say to me. I reply that its being utopian does not prevent it from investing our everyday actions of generosity or goodwill towards the other: even the smallest and most commonplace gestures, such as saying 'after you' as we sit at the dinner table or walk through a door, bear witness to the ethical. The concern for the other remains utopian in the sense that it is always out of place (*u-topos*) in this world,

always other than the 'ways of the world'; but there are many examples of it in the world. I remember meeting once with a group of Latin American students, well versed in the terminology of Marxist liberation and terribly concerned by the suffering and unhappiness of their people in Argentina. They asked me rather impatiently if I had ever actually witnessed the utopian rapport with the other which my ethical philosophy speaks of. I replied: 'Yes, indeed, here in this room.'[18]

In his essay, entitled "Signature," which begins with a brief (one paragraph) account of his life, Levinas concludes by telling us that it has been "dominated by the presentiment and memory of the Nazi horror."[19] The Nazi horror – symbolized by Auschwitz – is, as I have previously observed, the paradigm or exemplar of the evil so characteristic of the twentieth century, the evil that ruptures all categories of knowledge and comprehension. We may well be reminded of what Levinas's good friend and admirer, Maurice Blanchot, said in *The Writing of the Disaster*. He tells the story of the young prisoner of Auschwitz who had suffered the worst, led his family to the crematorium, attempted to hang himself, but was "saved" at the last minute. He was then compelled by the Nazis to hold the heads of victims so that when the SS shot them the bullets would more easily be lodged in their necks. "When asked how he could bear this, he is supposed to have answered that 'he observed the comportment of men before death'." But Blanchot declares: "I will not believe it . . . . His response . . . was not a response, he could not respond."

> What remains for us to recognize in this account is that when he was faced with an impossible question, he could find no other alibi than the search for knowledge, the so-called dignity of knowledge: that ultimate propriety which we believe will be accorded us by knowledge. And how, in fact, can one accept not to know? We read books on Auschwitz. The wish of all in the camps, the last wish: know what has happened, do not forget, and at the same time never will you know.[20]

Levinas would certainly agree with this moving and perceptive statement. We can never adequately know or comprehend this evil, even though we cannot give up the desire and the attempt to comprehend it. It transcends and ruptures our categories of understanding. But this is not the transcendence that signifies some "other realm." Oxymoronically, it is an *immanent* transcendence – one that we encounter in all its overwhelming horrible concreteness. When Blanchot says that the survivor's answer is "not a response," Levinas would agree. It is not a response, because there is nothing that can be *said* or *known* that would be an adequate response. To think that this evil can be fully grasped and known is to delude ourselves – to be seduced by the temptation of theodicy, the temptation to find some explanation, some justification that is commensurate with this evil. But we *can* respond – not by more refined knowledge, not by finding out more details about Auschwitz, not by reading more books about the Shoah, but in the only way that is *commensurate* with the excess of evil that we encounter. This is the *ethical response* in which I recognize my infinite responsibility for the unjustifiable suffering of others, for the evil they suffer. The same wave keeps breaking with renewed and deafening insistence. The only response to the evil that has erupted in the twentieth century is to acknowledge "my responsibility for the other person, without concern for reciprocity, in my call to help him gratuitously, in the asymmetry of the relation *one* to the *other*" (US 165).

7

Jonas: A New Ethic of Responsibility

Hans Jonas shares many of the concerns and anxieties of Levinas. He also studied with, and was deeply influenced by, Heidegger. Like Levinas, he thought that the great failing of Heidegger was most evident in Heidegger's inability to provide any basis for ethics. Heidegger ineluctably leads us down the path to ethical nihilism, undermining the objectivity of any and all moral norms. Like Levinas, Jonas draws upon the Jewish tradition in seeking to confront the evil exemplified by Auschwitz. Also like Levinas, Jonas insists on the need to distinguish philosophical argumentation – even in its speculative mode – from religious faith and theological convictions. Jonas too had little patience with philosophical and theological attempts to explain away or justify evil.

Yet, when we examine the way in which Jonas conceives of ethics and its relation to ontology, we find that his approach not only differs from that of Levinas, but appears flatly to contradict it. Jonas does not think that ethics is somehow beyond ontology and being, or that it *ruptures* being. On the contrary, what ethics requires – and what he attempts to do – is that we rethink what we mean by being, especially animate and human being, in a way that will enable us to *ground* a new ethic in a proper understanding of being.[1] Although Jonas elaborates a new imperative of responsibility, he does not speak of an infinite responsibility that precedes human freedom. The fundamental Levinasian themes of a rupture with being that opens the space for ethics and the ethical relation as an asymmetrical, nonreciprocal relation to the other (*l'autrui*) are foreign to Jonas's philosophical thinking. Furthermore, although Jonas, like Levinas, is dubious about traditional theodicies, he does not totally reject the theological framework in dealing with the problem of evil. He accepts the idea of a personal, caring God who is beneficent, but he categorically rejects the idea of an omnipotent God. As we shall see, Jonas claims that the very idea of omnipotence is incoherent. Without minimizing the striking differences between Levinas and Jonas, I want to argue that, when we work through what Jonas is saying, we see how his philosophic insights complement those of Levinas. Interweaving their philosophic strengths provides a richer, more nuanced account of evil and responsibility "after Auschwitz."

Let me begin with Jonas's philosophical starting point – his encounter with Heidegger. Jonas, like Levinas, testifies to the mesmerizing power of Heidegger as a teacher. He acknowledges that Heidegger is "perhaps the most important philosopher of [the twentieth] century."[2] Yet, after 1933 Jonas became disillusioned with Heidegger both as a person and as a philosopher. He was shocked by Heidegger's "infamous" 1933 rector's address delivered at Freiburg under the Nazi regime. Unlike Hannah Arendt, who thought that Heidegger's ten-month term as rector was an "error" from which he quickly recovered, Jonas came to a very different conclusion.[3] When asked whether he thought there was a connection between Heidegger "the magnificent thinker" and the person who actively supported the Nazis, Jonas did not hesitate to answer affirmatively – although he admitted that it had taken him a long time to realize this.

> In 1933, when he gave that infamous rectoral address, justifiably called treacherous in a philosophical sense and actually deeply shameful for philosophy, I was simply appalled and spoke with friends about it and said: "That from Heidegger, the most important thinker of our time." Whereupon I heard the reply: "Why are you so surprised? It was hidden in there. Somehow it could already be inferred from his way of thinking." That was when I realized, for the first time, certain traits in Heidegger's thinking and I hit myself on the forehead and said: "Yes, I missed something there before."[4]

Jonas came to the conclusion that the very abstractness of the Heideggerian concepts of resoluteness (*Entschlossenheit*) and authenticity (*Eigenlichheit*) was what enabled Heidegger to endorse the Nazis enthusiastically. The characteristic of authenticity, which Heidegger distinguishes from the anonymous "One" (*Das Man*), is resoluteness. "Resoluteness as such, not *for what* or *against what* one resolves oneself, but *that* one resolves oneself becomes the *authentic* signature of *authentic* Dasein. Opportunities to resolve oneself are, however, offered by historicity." With a sad bitterness, Jonas adds:

> In any case, in January 1933, when the moment had arrived, history offered the opportunity for resoluteness. One should throw oneself into this new destiny. One should finally take the leap way from the whole compro-

mising, weak, civilized, subdued negotiations of the intellect at the German universities (particularly in philosophy but also in general), and leap into the events of a new beginning. Suddenly the tremendous questionability of Heidegger's entire approach indeed became clear to me . . . .

But in Hitler and in National Socialism and in the new departure, in the will to begin a new Reich, even a thousand-year Reich, he saw something he welcomed . . . . He identified the decisiveness as such (of the Führer and the Party) with the principle of decisiveness and resoluteness as such. When I realized, appalled, that this was not only Heidegger's personal error but also somehow set up in his thinking, the questionability of existentialism as such became apparent to me: namely, the nihilistic element that lies in it. That went together with what I had recognized as an essential feature of the Gnostic agitation at the beginning of the Christian age, which also contained a strongly nihilistic element.[5]

These allusions to the nihilism of Gnosticism and existentialism provide a basis for understanding Jonas's philosophical project. Jonas was not only a student of Heidegger, but also a student of the great theologian Rudolf Bultmann. It was under their mutual influence and with their mutual encouragement that he was led to undertake his path-breaking study of Gnosticism. Jonas eventually came to realize that there is a very close affinity between the nihilistic dualism of the Gnostic tradition and the nihilism so characteristic of existentialism, especially that of Heidegger. In his essay "Gnosticism, Existentialism and Nihilism," Jonas explores the affinity between these two disparate movements, separated by centuries in historical time.[6] He tells us that in Gnosticism, "the subversion of the idea of law, of *nomos*, leads to ethical consequences in which the nihilistic implications of Gnostic acosmism . . . become even more obvious than in the cosmological aspect" (GEN 224). Both Gnosticism and existentialism deny the existence of any objective moral norms. There are, of course, vastly different grounds for this denial. The "antinomian Gnosis appears crude and naïve in comparison with the conceptual subtlety and historical reflection of its modern counterpart" (GEN 224). This nihilism is intimately related to a dualism whereby there is an ontological split between "man and *physus*." "Gnostic man is thrown into an antagonistic, antidivine, and therefore antihuman nature, modern man into an indifferent one" (GEN 233). Modern nihilistic dualism is far more radical and desperate than Gnostic dualism. According to Gnosticism, nature is hostile, antagonistic, and demonic. But modern nihilism no longer thinks of nature as hostile, but rather as *indifferent* to human concerns.

This makes modern nihilism infinitely more radical and more desperate than Gnostic nihilism ever could be for all its panic terror of the world and its defiant contempt of its laws. That nature does not care, one way or the other, is the true abyss. That only man cares, in his finitude facing nothing but death, alone with his contingency and the objective meaningless of his projecting meanings, is a truly unprecedented situation. (GEN 233)

The response to nihilism

Jonas combats this modern nihilism – a nihilism that is the ineluctable consequence of Heidegger's philosophy. Jonas's entire philosophy, including his reflections on the phenomenon of life and his defense of a new ethic and a new imperative of responsibility, and his theological speculations about the concept of God after Auschwitz are his response to this radical nihilism.[7] In contemporary philosophy there has been an oscillation between a reductionist naturalism that would abolish the idea of man as man and a conception of isolated selfhood that is at once groundless, rootless, and stripped of any moral mooring. The primary philosophical problem of our time is to escape the twin disasters of this Scylla and Charybdis – to find a "third way", one whereby "the dualistic rift can be avoided and yet enough of the dualistic insight saved to uphold the humanity of man" (GEN 234).

Before turning to what Jonas means by this "third way," I want to consider the similarities between Jonas's and Levinas's understanding of our contemporary predicament. Levinas is not concerned with the affinity between Gnosticism and existentialism. Nor does he speak of "nihilistic dualism." Nevertheless, there is a basic agreement between Levinas and Jonas in their understanding of our modern predicament. They both argue that the most pressing philosophical task of our time is to probe the meaning of ethics and responsibility in the face of the unprecedented evil of the twentieth century. The reason why Levinas is so critical of a philosophical orientation that is limited to the horizon of Being and ontology is because he thinks that in such a world there is no legitimate place for ethics. It is the ethical nihilism implicit in the ontological tradition that so disturbs and provokes him. To assert that "it is of the highest importance to know whether we are not duped by morality" is another way of saying that we must inquire whether there is an escape from ethical nihilism. Levinas agrees with Jonas that there is no place for ethics in Heidegger's philosophy. Heidegger's failure is not a localized philosophical omission. If ethical nihilism prevails, then there is no basis for condemning evil. There is no basis for condemning what happened at Auschwitz.

The responses of Levinas and Jonas to ethical nihilism differ. We have seen that for Levinas ethical nihilism is a consequence of ontology, of taking Being as the ultimate horizon, of failing to appreciate the transcendence of ethics as first philosophy. A rupture with being is required in the ethical relation to the other (*l'autrui*). But the primary issue for Jonas is to *rethink* our ontology in such a manner that we can ultimately provide a metaphysical ground for a new ethical imperative, a new ethics of responsibility. Jonas is concerned not only with the dualism implicit in Gnosticism and existentialism, but also with the dualism that has been so dominant in modern philosophy. He argues that once we accept the Cartesian dichotomy of *res extensa* and *res cogitans*, or the dichotomy between body and mind, there is no escape from nihilism. The problem is not just dualism, but the entire framework of thinking that a dualism spawns. Even materialists and idealists are operating in a framework that accepts this mode of dichotomous thinking, though they differ in which extreme of this binary opposition they deny. So if one is to meet the challenge posed by ethical nihilism, one must critique the ontological and epistemological dualism that underlies it.

This is precisely what Jonas does in *The Phenomenon of Life*, his rethinking of the meaning of organic life. He realizes that his philosophical project goes against many of the deeply embedded prejudices and dogmas of contemporary philosophy. He challenges two well-entrenched dogmas: that there is no metaphysical truth, and that there is no path from the "is" to the "ought". To escape from ethical nihilism, we must show that there is a metaphysical ground of ethics, an objective basis for value and purpose in being itself. These are strong claims; and, needless to say, they are extremely controversial. In defense of Jonas, it should be said that he approaches this task with both boldness and intellectual modesty. He frequently acknowledges that he cannot "prove" his claims, but he certainly believes that his "premises" do "more justice to the total phenomenon of man and Being in general" than the prevailing dualist or reductionist alternatives. "But in the last analysis my argument can do no more than give a rational grounding to an *option* it presents as a choice for a thoughtful person – an option that of course has its own inner power of persuasion. Unfortunately I have nothing better to offer. Perhaps a future metaphysics will be able to do more."[8]

To appreciate how Jonas's philosophical project unfolds, we need to examine his philosophical interpretation of life. This is the starting point of his grounding of a new imperative of responsibility. It also provides the context for his speculations concerning evil. In the foreword to *The Phenomenon of Life*, Jonas gives a succinct statement of his aim.

Put at its briefest, this volume offers an "existential" interpretation of biological facts. Contemporary existentialism, obsessed with man alone, is in the habit of claiming as his unique privilege and predicament much of what is rooted in organic existence as such: in so doing, it withholds from the organic world the insights to be learned from the awareness of self. On its part, scientific biology, by its rules confined to the physical, outward facts, must ignore the dimension of inwardness that belongs to life: in so doing, it submerges the distinction of "animate" and "inanimate." A new reading of the biological record may recover the inner dimension – that which we know best – for the understanding of things organic and so reclaim for psycho-physical unity of life that place in the theoretical scheme which it had lost through the divorce of the material and the mental since Descartes. (*PL*, p. ix)

Jonas, in his existential interpretation of *bios*, pursues "this underlying theme of all of life in its development through the ascending order of organic powers and functions: metabolism, moving and desiring, sensing and perceiving, imagination, art, and mind – a progressive scale of freedom and peril, culminating in man, who may understand his uniqueness anew when he no longer sees himself in metaphysical isolation" (*PL*, p. ix). The way in which Jonas phrases this theme recalls the Aristotelian approach to *bios*, and it is clear that Aristotle is a major influence on Jonas. There is an even closer affinity with the philosophy of nature that Schelling sought to elaborate in the nineteenth century. Schelling (like many post-Kantian German thinkers) was troubled by the same fundamental dichotomy that underlies the problem for Jonas. The dichotomy that Kant introduced between the realm of "disenchanted" nature and the realm of freedom leads to *untenable* antinomies. Jonas differs from both Aristotle and Schelling in taking into account Darwin and contemporary scientific biology. A proper philosophical understanding of biology must always be compatible with the scientific facts. But at the same time, it must also root out misguided materialistic and reductionist *interpretations* of those biological facts. In this respect, Jonas's naturalism bears a strong affinity with the evolutionary naturalism of Peirce and Dewey. At the same time, Jonas is deeply skeptical of any theory of evolutionary biology that introduces mysterious "vital forces" or neglects the contingencies and perils of evolutionary development.[9]

Jonas seeks to show "that it is in the dark stirrings of primeval organic substance that a principle of freedom shines forth for the first time within the vast necessity of the physical universe" (*PL* 3). Freedom, in this broad sense, is not identified exclusively with human freedom; it reaches down to the first glimmerings of organic life, and up to the type of freedom manifested by human beings. "'Freedom' must denote an objectively discernible mode of being, i.e., a manner of executing existence, distinctive of the organic *per se* and thus shared by all members but by no nonmembers of the class: an ontologically descriptive term which can apply to mere physical evidence at first" (*PL* 3). This coming into being of freedom is not just a success story. "The privilege of freedom carries the burden of need and means precarious being" (*PL* 4). It is with biological metabolism that this principle of freedom first arises. Jonas goes "so far as to maintain that *metabolism*, the basic stratum of all organic existence, already displays freedom – indeed that it is the first form freedom takes."[10] With "metabolism – its power and its need – not-being made its appearance in the world as an alternative embodied in being itself; and thereby being itself first assumes an emphatic sense: intrinsically qualified by the threat of its negative it must affirm itself, and existence affirmed is existence as a concern" (*PL* 4). This broad, ontological understanding of freedom as a characteristic of *all* organic life serves Jonas as "an Ariadne's thread through the interpretation of Life" (*PL* 3).

The way in which Jonas enlarges our understanding of freedom is indicative of his primary argumentative strategy. He expands and reinterprets categories that are normally applied exclusively to human beings so that we can see that they identify objectively discernible modes of being characteristic of everything animate. Even *inwardness*, and incipient forms of *self*, reach down to the simplest forms of organic life.[11] Now it may seem as if Jonas is guilty of anthropomorphism, of projecting what is distinctively human onto the entire domain of living beings. He is acutely aware of this sort of objection, but he argues that even the idea of anthropomorphism must be rethought.[12] We distort Jonas's philosophy of life if we think that he is projecting *human* characteristics onto the nonhuman animate world. Earlier I quoted the passage in which Jonas speaks of a "third way" – "one by which the dualistic rift can be avoided and yet enough of the dualistic insight saved to uphold the humanity of man" (GEN 234). We avoid the "dualistic rift" by showing that there is genuine continuity of organic life, and that such categories as freedom, inwardness, and selfhood apply to everything that is animate. These categories designate objective modes of being. But we preserve "enough dualistic insight" when we recognize that freedom, inwardness, and selfhood manifest themselves in human beings in a distinctive manner. I do not want to suggest that Jonas is successful in carrying out this ambitious program. He is aware of the tentativeness and fallibility of his claims, but he presents us with an understanding of animate beings such that we can discern both continuity and difference.[13]

It should now be clear that Jonas is not limiting himself to a regional philosophy of the organism or a new "existential" interpretation of biological facts. His goal is nothing less than to provide a new metaphysical understanding of being, a new ontology. And he is quite explicit about this.

Our reflections [are] intended to show in what sense the problem of life, and with it that of the body, ought to stand in the center of ontology and, to some extent, also of epistemology. . . . The central position of the problem of life means not only that it must be accorded a decisive voice in judging any given ontology but also that any treatment of itself must summon the whole of ontology. (*PL* 25)

The philosophical divide between Levinas and Jonas appears to be enormous. For Levinas, as long as we restrict ourselves to the horizon of Being and to ontology (no matter how broadly these are conceived), there is no place for ethics, and no answer to ethical nihilism. For Jonas, by contrast, unless we can enlarge our understanding of ontology in such a manner as would provide an objective grounding for value and purpose within nature, there is no way to answer the challenge of ethical nihilism. But despite this initial appearance of extreme opposition, there is a way of interpreting Jonas and Levinas that lessens the gap between them. In Levinasian terminology, we can say that Jonas shows that there is a way of understanding ontology and the living body that does justice to the nonreducible alterity of the other (*l'autrui*).[14]

Still, we might ask how Jonas's "existential" interpretation of biological facts and the new ontology he is proposing can provide a metaphysical grounding for a new ethics. Jonas criticizes the philosophical prejudice that there is no place in nature for values, purposes, and ends. Just as he maintains that freedom, inwardness, and selfhood are objective modes of being, so he argues that values and ends are objective modes of being. There is a basic value *inherent* in organic being, a basic affirmation, "The 'Yes' of Life" (*IR* 81).[15] "The self-affirmation of being becomes emphatic in the opposition of life to death. Life is the explicit confrontation of being with not-being. . . . The 'yes' of all striving is here sharpened by the active 'no' to not-being" (*IR* 81–2). Furthermore – and this is the crucial point for Jonas – this affirmation of life that is in all organic being has a binding *obligatory* force upon human beings.

This blindly self-enacting "yes" gains obligating force in the seeing freedom of man, who as the supreme outcome of nature's purposive labor is no longer its automatic executor but, with the power obtained from knowledge, can become its destroyer as well. He must adopt the "yes" into his will and impose the "no" to not-being on his power. But precisely this transition from willing to obligation is the critical point of moral theory at which attempts at laying a foundation for it come so easily to grief. Why does now, in man, that become a duty which hitherto "being" itself took care of through all individual willings? (*IR* 82)

We discover here the transition from "is" to "ought" – from the self-affirmation of life to the binding *obligation* of human beings to preserve life not only for the present but also for the future. But why do we need a *new* ethics? The subtitle of *The Imperative of Responsibility* – *In Search of an Ethics for the Technological Age* – indicates why we need a new ethics. Modern technology has transformed the nature and consequences of human action so radically that the underlying premises of traditional ethics are no longer valid. For the first time in history human beings possess the knowledge and the power to destroy life on this planet, including human life. Not only is there the new possibility of total nuclear disaster; there are the even more invidious and threatening possibilities that result from the unconstrained use of technologies that can destroy the environment required for life. The major transformation brought about by modern technology is that the consequences of our actions frequently exceed by far anything we can envision. Jonas was one of the first philosophers to warn us about the unprecedented ethical and political problems that arise with the rapid development of biotechnology. He claimed that this was happening at a time when there was an "ethical vacuum," when there did not seem to be any effective ethical principles to limit or guide our ethical decisions. In the name of scientific and technological "progress," there is a relentless pressure to adopt a stance where virtually anything is permissible, including transforming the genetic structure of human beings, as long as it is "freely chosen." We need, Jonas argued, a new categorical imperative that might be formulated as follows:

> "Act so that the effects of your action are compatible with the permanence of genuine human life"; or expressed negatively: "Act so that the effects of your action are not destructive of the future possibility of such a life"; or simply: "Do not compromise the conditions for an indefinite continuation of humanity on earth"; or again turned positive: "In your present choices, include the future wholeness of Man among the objects of your will." (*IR* 11)

Even if we are in sympathy with Jonas's plea for a new imperative, we must understand that the *need* for such an imperative does not mean that it can be rationally justified. Furthermore, we must understand what Jonas means by the imperative of *responsibility*.

Jonas distinguishes between two widely differing senses of responsibility: formal responsibility and substantive responsibility. Formal responsibility means "responsibility as being accountable 'for' one's deeds, whatever they are"; whereas substantive responsibility means "responsibility 'for' particular objects that commits an agent to particular deeds concerning them" (*IR* 90). Substantive responsibility presupposes formal responsibility, but the heart of Jonas's ethics concerns our new substantive responsibility. Like Levinas, Jonas emphasizes that a substantive responsibility involves a "nonreciprocal relation" (*IR* 94). The nonreciprocal, "vertical" caring relation of parent and child is a paradigm for substantive responsibility. The parent has a responsibility and an obligation to care for the well-being of the child. Our new technological situation demands that we extend the scope of our substantive responsibility. We, as human beings, have a responsibility for preserving the conditions for life, especially human life, for the indefinite future.

> Man's distinction that he alone can *have* responsibility means also that he *must* have it for others of his like – that is, for such that are themselves potential bearers of responsibility – and that in one or another respect he, in fact, always has it . . . . In this sense an "ought" is concretely given with the very existence of man . . . . Put epigrammatically: the possibility of there being responsibility in the world, which is bound to the existence of men, is of all objects of responsibility the first. (*IR* 99)[16]

There are many questions that can be raised about Jonas's argumentation and the adequacy of his understanding of our collective responsibility for the preservation of those (human) beings that are capable of responsibility, but we can now grasp the overall structure of his philosophical project.[17] Nihilism, especially the ethical nihilism so prevalent in the contemporary world, is the problem for Jonas. It has created an "ethical vacuum." The nihilism that most concerns him is not the nihilism of philosophers, but the nihilism of everyday life – such that there is no longer any confidence that there are *any* secure objective norms to guide our decisions and actions. What makes this situation potentially disastrous is the new technological age. Human agents are capable of destroying the very conditions for the possibility of life on this planet. It is not the failure of technology, but its fantastic success, that makes this situation so threatening. There is a relentless pressure to develop and apply ever-new technologies that affect the very conditions of life itself. (Long before the recent debates about cloning and stem cell research, Jonas anticipated the troublesome ethical and political issues that would arise with technologies that enable us to alter radically the conditions of living organisms.) The philosophical task in this potentially catastrophic situation is to provide a vivid and lucid understanding of our situation. But this is not sufficient. It must also show how a proper understanding of the phenomenon of life can enable us to develop and justify a new ethics – one whose starting point is the self-affirmation of life itself. Our first priority must be to act in such a manner that we preserve the conditions by which human beings will continue to exist in the future. Because there are no limits to this new responsibility, Jonas might well have said – following Levinas – that this is an "infinite responsibility." A theory of responsibility must have its objective and subjective sides.

> But the two sides are mutually complementary and both are integral to ethics itself. Without our being, at least by disposition, responsive to the call of duty in terms of feeling, the most cogent demonstration of its right, even when compelling theoretical assent, would be powerless to make it a motivating force. Conversely, without some credentials of its right, our *de facto* responsiveness to appeals of this kind would remain at the mercy of fortuitous predilections (variously preconditioned themselves), and the options made by it would lack justification. (*IR* 85)

Evil and our apocalyptic situation

Like a specter, the theme of evil hovers in the background of Jonas's search for a new ethics – just as it does with Levinas. "We live in an apocalyptic situation, that is under the threat of a universal catastrophe if we let things take their present course" (*IR* 140). If Jonas had been in dialogue with Levinas, he might have said: "Without a new ethic of responsibility, a new ethic for the future, the very possibility of the continued *existence* of those others for whom we are responsible is itself threatened." Jonas echoes Levinas's phenomenological description of evil when he writes:

> The perception of the *malum* is infinitely easier to us than the perception of the *bonum*; it is more direct, more compelling, less given to differences of opinion and taste, and, most of all, obtruding itself without our looking for it. An evil forces its perception on us by its mere presence, whereas the beneficial can be present unobtrusively and remain unperceived, unless we reflect on it. . . . We are not unsure about evil when it comes our way, but of the good we become sure only via the experience of its opposite. (*IR* 27)

This observation – that an evil forces itself upon us – provides a transition to Jonas's confrontation with the evil epitomized by "Auschwitz." In words that virtually repeat what Levinas wrote, Jonas speaks of himself as "one who had gone through the horrors of the thirties and forties and had to live the rest of his days under the shadow of Auschwitz."[18] In 1984, when Jonas was already past his eightieth birthday, he delivered a remarkable lecture at Tübingen University, entitled "The Concept of God after Auschwitz: A Jewish Voice."[19]

Jonas consistently acknowledged that he could not offer any *proof* for his metaphysical speculations, or for his attempt to ground a new ethic of responsibility in the ontological self-affirmation of living beings. But, as a philosopher, he sought to give the strongest *reasons* to support his claims. When he speculates about theology, he is even more tentative. He describes himself as engaged in "a piece of frankly speculative theology." He accepts the Kantian warning that in this domain one cannot claim knowledge.[20] But Jonas poses the following questions.

> What did Auschwitz add to that which one could always have known about humans and from times immemorial have done? And what has it added in particular to what is familiar to us Jews from a millennial history of suffering and forms so essential a part of our collective memory? The question of Job has always been the main question of theodicy – of general theodicy because of the existence of evil as such in the world, and of particular theodicy in its sharpening by the riddle of election, of the purported covenant between Israel and its God. (CGA 132)

The reference to theodicy should not mislead us, because Jonas is just as critical of traditional (religious or secular) theodicies as Levinas is. No theodicy is adequate if it seeks to deny, "explain away," or justify the brute reality of evil of Auschwitz. These questions are even more poignant for a Jew than a Christian, because "to the Jew, who sees in 'this' world the locus of divine creation, justice, and redemption, God is eminently the Lord of *history*, and in this respect 'Auschwitz' calls, even for the believer, the whole traditional concept of God into question. . . . What God could let it happen?" (CGA 133).

In order to deal with these emotionally charged questions, Jonas elaborates a *myth* of his own – "that vehicle of imaginative but credible conjecture that Plato allowed for the sphere beyond the knowable" (CGA 134).[21] The details of this myth are at once moving and eloquent, but let me present a condensed version.

In the beginning the Divine, the ground of being, "chose to give itself over to the chance and risk and endless variety of becoming." But once the world has been created, its laws "brook no interference," and are not "softened by any extramundane providence." In order for the world to be for itself, an immanent domain, "God renounced his being, divesting himself of his deity – to receive it back from the odyssey of time weighted with the chance harvest of unforeseeable temporal experience: transfigured or possibly even disfigured by it." In the course of eons of cosmic chance and probability, there arise the first stirrings of life. This is the "world-accident for which the becoming deity had waited and with which its prodigal stake begins to show signs of being redeemed." With life

comes death, the adventure in mortality, and the beginning of the evolutionary process. "The divine landscape bursts into color and the deity
comes to experience itself." Initially, in its simplest organic forms, this is a
world of innocence. But something new arises with the evolutionary development of human beings. There is the "advent of knowledge and freedom, and with this supremely double-edged gift the innocence of the
mere subject of self-fulfilling life has given way to the charge of responsibility under the disjunction of good and evil." "With the appearance of
man, transcendence awakened to itself and henceforth accompanies his
doings and with bated breath of suspense, hoping and beckoning, rejoic-
ing and grieving, approving and frowning – and I dare say, making itself
felt to him even while not intervening in the dynamics of his worldly
scene: for can it not be that by the reflection of its own state as it wavers
with the record of man, the transcendent casts light and shadow over the
human landscape." (See CGA, 134–6 for the complete statement of the
myth.)

This is Jonas's myth; a myth that he confesses may appear to be "a
willful private fantasy." But, as he draws out its consequences, it becomes
apparent that it is neither willful nor private. When Jonas first presented
it in his essay "Immortality and the Modern Temper," he wrote: "Such is
the tentative myth which I would like to believe 'true' – in the sense in
which myth may happen to adumbrate a truth which of necessity is
unknowable and even, in direct concepts, ineffable, yet which, by intima-
tions to our deepest experience, lays claim upon our powers of giving
indirect account of it in revocable, anthropomorphic images."[22]

It is the truth implicit in this myth that Jonas seeks to convey. In his
commentary on it, he stresses several important features. First, the God
that he is speaking of is a *suffering God*, though not in the Christian sense
of a God who allowed himself to be crucified. From the moment of
creation, and certainly from the time of the creation of human beings,
there is suffering on the part of God. Secondly, the God of Jonas's myth
is a *becoming God*. "It is a God emerging in time instead of possessing a
completed being that remains identical with itself throughout eternity"
(CGA 137). Jonas admits that this conception of God departs from the
Hellenic tradition in theology, which assigns priority to eternal being
over becoming, but he thinks that the concept of *divine becoming* can be
more readily reconciled with the portrayal of God in the Hebrew Bible.
This is a God who is affected and indeed *altered* by what happens in the
world. We are not only dependent on God, but God is *dependent on us*, on
what we human beings do. "God's own destiny, his doing or undoing, is
at stake in this universe to whose unknowing dealings he committed his
substance, and man has become the eminent repository of this supreme

and ever betrayable trust. In a sense, he holds the fate of deity in his hands."[23] Bound up with the idea of a *suffering* and *becoming* God is a *caring God.* "God's caring about his creatures is, of course, among the most familiar tenets of Jewish faith. But my myth stresses the less familiar aspect that this caring God is not a sorcerer who in the act of caring also provides the fulfillment of his concern: he has left something for other agents to do and thereby has made his care dependent on them" (CGA 138). Consequently, this is a God who is endangered and runs a real risk.

The most significant claim in Jonas's theological speculations is his insistence that this God is *not* an omnipotent God. Jonas rejects this time-honored doctrine of absolute, unlimited power. In its place he makes a much stronger claim: "From the very concept of power, it follows that omnipotence is a self-contradictory, self-destructive, indeed senseless concept."[24] The attributes traditionally ascribed to God – "absolute goodness, absolute power, and intelligibility" – form an incoherent triad. The conjunction of any two of these attributes excludes the third. "The question then is: Which are truly integral to our concept of God, and which, being of lesser force, must give way to their superior claim? Now, surely, goodness is inalienable from the concept of God, and not open to qualification" (CGA 139).[25]

Despite the apparently idiosyncratic features of Jonas's myth, it is not just "a private willful fantasy." Jonas himself notes that there is an affinity between his myth and the Kabbalah.

> There we meet highly original, very unorthodox speculations in whose company mine would not appear so wayward after all. Thus, for example, my myth at bottom only pushes further the idea of the *tzimtzum*, that cosmogonic center concept of the Lurianic Kabbalah. *Tzimtzum* means contraction, withdrawal, self-limitation. To make room for the world the *En-Sof* (infinite: literally, No-End) of the beginning had to contract himself so that, vacated by him, empty space could expand outside of him: the "Nothing" in which and from which God could then create the world. Without this retreat into himself, there could be no "other" outside God, and only his continued holding-himself-in preserves the finite things from losing their separate being again into the divine "all in all." (CGA 142)[26]

But how does this myth enable us to deal with the question: How could God let it happen? How can we face the full horror of the evil of Auschwitz and still maintain a faith in God? This is just the sort of question that Dostoevsky might well have raised, had he witnessed Auschwitz. Initially, it seems as if Jonas is still operating within a traditional framework of theodicy, at least insofar as he wants to show that we can reconcile the existence of evil – even the evil of Auschwitz – with the concept of a beneficent God. Jonas "solves" the theological problem by affirming God's intelligibility and his goodness, but denying his omnipotence. "But if God is to be intelligible in some manner and to some extent (and to this we must hold), then his goodness must be compatible with the existence of evil, and this it is only if he is not all powerful. Only then can we uphold that he is intelligible and good, and there is yet evil in the world" (CGA 140).

To interpret Jonas's myth in this manner, while not incorrect, is to miss its *primary* thrust. Jonas's myth is intended to underscore man's over-whelming – we might even say, infinite – responsibility. And Jonas is just as emphatic as Levinas in insisting that "responsibility is first and foremost of men and for men, and this is the archetype of all responsibility" (*IR* 98). Human beings – and human beings alone – are responsible for the evil that exists in the world, and have a supreme obligation to combat it. This responsibility transcends a "merely" human responsibility; it is our re-sponsibility to and for the *suffering, becoming, caring* God. Jonas, like Levinas, does not take "Auschwitz" to name just one place and one series of horrendous events, but to stand for all genocides of our time. When Jonas first introduced his myth, he asked:

> What about those who never could inscribe themselves in the Book of Life with deeds either good or evil, great or small, because their lives were cut off before they had a chance, or their humanity was destroyed in degrada-tions most cruel and most thorough such as no humanity can survive? I am thinking of the gassed and burnt children of Auschwitz, of the defaced, dehumanized phantoms of the camps, *and of all the other, numberless victims of the other man-made holocausts of our time.* [27]

To dramatize his understanding of a suffering, becoming, caring God whose very destiny is dependent on us, Jonas declares:

> And this I like to believe: that there was weeping in the heights at the waste and despoilment of humanity; that a groan answered the rising shout of ignoble suffering, and wrath – the terrible wrong done to the reality and possibility of each life thus wantonly victimized, each one a thwarted at-tempt of God . . . . Should we not believe that the immense chorus of such cries that has risen up in our lifetime now hangs over our world as a dark and accusing cloud? that eternity looks down upon us with a frown, wounded itself and perturbed in its depths?[28]

Neither providence nor the dialectical necessity of history is responsible for Auschwitz.

The disgrace of Auschwitz is not to be charged to some all-powerful providence or to some dialectically wise necessity, as if it were an antithesis
demanding a synthesis or a step on the road to salvation. *We* human beings
have inflicted this on the deity, we who have failed in the administering of
his things. It remains on our account, and it is we who must again wash
away the disgrace from our own disfigured faces, indeed from the very
countenance of God.[29]

Jonas's "speculative experiment" is not merely an intellectual exercise. "I
was impelled to the view, which every doctrine of faith would probably
find heretical, that it is not God who can help us, but we who must help
God."[30] But he tells us that this heretical conception of a Jewish God
became "more valid with the confession of an actual witness, sealed with
her own life, of whom I learned much later. These words of a confessor
are found in the preserved diaries of Etty Hillesum, a young Jewish woman
from the Netherlands, who in 1942 voluntarily reported to the camp at
Westerbork in order to be of help there and to take part in the destiny of
her people. In 1943 she was sent to the gas chamber in Auschwitz."[31]

> I will go to any place on this earth where God sends me, and I am ready in
> every situation and until I die to bear witness . . . that it is not God's fault
> that everything has turned out this way, but our fault.
> . . . and if God does not continue to help me, then I must help God . . .
> I will always endeavor to help God as well as I can.
> I will help you, O God, that you do not forsake me, but right from the
> start I can vouch for nothing. Only this one thing becomes more and more
> clear to me: that you cannot help us, but that we must help you, and in so
> doing we ultimately help ourselves. That is the only thing that matters: to
> save in us, O God, a piece of yourself. Yes, my God, even you in these
> circumstances seem powerless to change very much . . . . I demand no
> account from you; you will later call us to account. And with almost every
> heartbeat it becomes clearer to me that you cannot help us, but that we
> must help you and defend up to the last your dwelling within us.[32]

"Demythologizing" Jonas's myth

Jonas confesses that these words of Etty Hillesum, which he discovered in
1984, more than 40 years after they were written, are emotionally overwhelming for him. They sum up his own heretical understanding of the
suffering, becoming, caring God – a limited God whom we must help.
Jonas does not hestitate to express his own passionately held convictions.
But he, like Levinas, also believes that philosophers must always strive to
meet the most rigorous norms of philosophical argumentation, and must

not allow philosophical claims to be based on religious faith. Although both are committed, religious Jews, they claim that the truth of what they are saying has *universal* significance. So our task is to stand back and see to what extent Jonas's myth contains claims that can be defended philosophically. To do this, I want to take what might seem to be a slight detour, but one that will actually bring us to the heart of the matter.

I have spoken of Jonas's original attraction to, and subsequent disillusionment with, Heidegger as both a person and a philosopher. But the other great teacher who had a formative influence on Jonas was Rudolf Bultmann. Indeed, it was a report that Jonas prepared for Bultmann's seminar on the New Testament that eventually led to his interest in Gnosticism.[33] Jonas maintained a lifelong personal and intellectual friendship with Bultmann, a thinker he always respected. Bultmann was the only one of Jonas's professors with whom he paid a farewell visit when he left Germany in 1933. And Bultmann was one of the first people he visited when he returned to Germany in 1945 as a soldier in the Jewish Brigade. In 1977, a year after Bultmann's death, Jonas was invited to participate in a memorial symposium that enabled him to reflect on the philosophical aspects of Bultmann's work.[34]

Bultmann's great theological contribution was his elaboration of the method of demythologizing – "'a method of interpretation' . . . 'a hermeneutical procedure that interrogates statements . . . about their reality content' . . . namely, that which concerns human existence." According to Bultmann, myth at once reveals and conceals. The true meaning of myth " – in the case of Scripture at least – [is]'to speak of the essential reality of man'."[35] Jonas is at once sympathetic with, yet sharply critical of this understanding of myth.

I want to show both the applicability – and the *limits* – of this method of interpretation when applied to Jonas's own myth. To begin with, employing metaphorical language, Jonas's myth is at once consistent with, and expresses, the substance of his own understanding of the emergence of life and the evolutionary process.[36] Indeed, it is consistent with the evolutionary naturalism that he advocates in *The Phenomenon of Life* and related writings – texts that employ exclusively philosophical arguments. In his myth, Jonas eschews any suggestion of supernatural intervention in the course of evolution. (God is not a sorcerer.) Furthermore, he acknowledges that it was a naturalistic "world accident" when life first appeared. With the origins of living organisms, there was a quickening of the evolutionary process. At a certain stage of this evolutionary process, human beings arose – beings capable of assuming responsibility for other human beings. In short, there is nothing in this part of Jonas's myth that cannot be stated adequately in nonmythological terms. Jonas's philosophical understanding of nature, life, and the evolutionary ascent of man guide his construction of the myth. But the myth also underscores Jonas's understanding of responsibility. Freedom, inwardness, and selfhood in its incipient forms reach down to all living creatures, but it is only with humans that a being emerges who is capable of being responsible.

It might seem that, following out the "logic" of this procedure for interpreting Jonas's myth, we could think of it as a vivid metaphorical way of portraying what can be expressed and translated (without remainder) in conceptual terms.[37] But this is just the conclusion that Jonas *resists*. When he introduces his myth, he cites Plato, and alludes to the subtle interplay between *mythos* and *logos* in Plato. *Mythos* becomes relevant precisely when one seeks to conjecture about what cannot be known. Jonas claims that myth cannot be "translated" or reduced to "the self-understanding of Man" – a form of demythologizing already advocated by Feuerbach. "On the pain of immanentism or mere anthropologism, the understanding of God is not to be reduced to the self-understanding of man."[38] This is the *limit* of demythologizing.[39] Jonas treads a fine and delicate line. He insists that his myth must be compatible with what can be established philosophically, and that it must also be compatible with our scientific knowledge; but he resists the suggestion that myth is just a lively metaphorical way of stating what can be translated in purely conceptual terms. Myth does not lend itself to complete objectification in human discourse. What Jonas writes in the conclusion of his essay "Heidegger and Theology" is perfectly applicable to his own myth of the suffering, becoming, caring God whom we are obligated to help.

> The final paradox [of divinity] is better protected by the symbols of myth than by the concepts of thought. Where the mystery is rightfully at home, "we see in a glass darkly." What does "in a glass darkly" mean? In the shapes of myth. To keep the *manifest opaqueness* of myth transparent for the ineffable is in a way easier than to keep the seeming transparency of the concept transparent for that to which it is in fact as opaque as any language must be.
>
> Myth taken *literally* is crudest objectification.
> Myth taken *allegorically* is sophisticated objectification.
> Myth taken *symbolically* is the glass through which we darkly see.[40]

Jonas and Levinas

The differences between Jonas and Levinas are as striking as their similarities. It is disingenuous to try to smooth out their differences and underestimate their conflicting – and at times – contradictory claims. Jonas would never accept Levinas's deep skepticism regarding the philosophical enterprise of ontology. The task of a proper metaphysics, as Jonas understands it, is to develop a more *adequate* understanding of being – especially animate being – in a way that can ground ethics. Jonas would also criticize Levinas's emphasis on "ruptures" – and especially the presumed rupture with being that opens the space for the good and for the ethical relation to the other (*l'autrui*). I suspect that Jonas would detect here the vestiges of a type of dualistic thinking that he has been at great pains to criticize and overcome. And, given the rhetorical construction of *Totality and Infinity* with its reiterated dichotomies of totality and infinity, ontology and metaphysics, being and ethics, there is plenty of evidence of dualistic thinking. The primary goal of Jonas – to develop a new ethic for our technological age wherein we seek to protect the environment and organic life – is marginal to Levinas.[41] Despite the poetic and ethical eloquence with which Levinas describes the face, the alterity of the other (*l'autrui*), and our infinite responsibility to and for the other, Jonas might see Levinas's understanding of ethics as tainted by anthropocentric bias that he takes to be characteristic of traditional ethics. Levinas fails to acknowledge "the altered nature of human action" that has resulted from our contemporary technological knowledge and power.

Even these differences might well serve as the basis for a fruitful dialogue – one in which their different emphases and claims might help to correct shortcomings in their respective philosophies. Levinas comes close to caricaturing traditional philosophy and ontology, and he exaggerates his differences with the philosophical tradition. Derrida made this point in his famous article on Levinas that brought the latter's thought to international attention.[42] Levinas does not sufficiently consider the possibility that the ontological enterprise opens itself to the type of reform and revision that Jonas develops. Jonas's attempt to provide an evolutionary account of the advent of human life that does justice to both *continuity* and the emergence of *difference* – especially the differences that arise with the evolutionary development of human beings – shows that not all ontology can be interpreted as committed to the totality that Levinas criticizes. There is a tendency in Levinas to focus on the domain of ethics as if its exclusive concern with the asymmetrical, nonreciprocal interhuman relationship between the other and ourselves. Levinas might well have benefited from exposure to the more global and cosmological concern of Jonas that seeks to take account of how contemporary technology alters the way in which we must think about ethics. At the same time, there are lessons that Jonas might well learn from Levinas. Sometimes Jonas comes close to neglecting the particularity and concreteness of the ethical relation that are so prominent in Levinas. In Jonas's anxiety about our "endangered future," he sometimes neglects our ethical relationship with our contemporaries. His concern with preserving the conditions for the possibility of a future humanity becomes extremely abstract. Is our responsibility primarily to "humanity" or to individual unique human beings – to the alterity of concrete others?

Yet, despite these tensions and conflicts, we should not underestimate how much the two thinkers have in common in their confrontations with the evil epitomized by Auschwitz. Both are painfully aware of the "ethical vacuum" and ethical nihilism that so pervade the modern age. Both seek to address the question of whether we have been "duped by morality" – whether it still makes sense to speak of ethical imperatives that can guide our actions. Both categorically reject any philosophical or religious attempt to "reconcile" us to evil. They would agree that we must give up both vulgar and sophisticated forms of "the Happy End." There is something brute, unsurpassable, and "transcendent" about evil, which challenges and defies philosophical concepts and categories. Both men speak from the depth of their own Jewish faith and convictions. For them the problem of evil is not just an ethical problem; it is also a religious one, and raises the most profound questions about whether faith is still possible after Auschwitz – and if so, what kind of faith. They both highlight the *ethical* significance of their Jewish heritage – not that Judaism can be *reduced* to its ethical content, but rather that it can *inform* one's understanding of ethics and responsibility.

The most original and distinctive feature of their responses to evil is the way in which each seeks to rethink the very meaning and scope of responsibility. At first the Levinasian idea of "infinite responsibility" seems hyperbolic, and even offensive – insofar as we may think that a responsibility that is infinite (and consequently can never be completely fulfilled) undermines the very idea of responsibility. But the more closely we examine what Levinas means, the more we can appreciate the intelligibility of his claim. As human beings we find ourselves in a world where responsibility is thrust upon us – responsibility *to* and *for* the others whom we encounter. When Levinas stresses that the ethical relation is asymmetrical and nonreciprocal, his primary point is to underscore that ethical responsibility is not based on some form of expectation or calculation that others will act towards me in a way in which I act toward them. Levinas is at his most forceful in showing what it means to be responsive and responsible to the otherness of the other (*l'autrui*) – to refuse the temptation to assimilate the other to the type of ontological imperialism and colonization whereby I allow myself to violate the other's integrity. But there is a corresponding sense of "infinite responsibility" in Jonas's thinking, although he does not use this expression. This is evident in the centrality he gives to our responsibility to our fellow human creatures – even those who are not yet born. This is also a responsibility – "an infinite responsibility" that cannot be completely fulfilled. Nevertheless, it can guide our finite actions. Jonas intensifies his understanding of responsibility in his myth of a limited God *for whom* we are also responsible. Our responsibility for combatting evil is further intensified in the heightened wake of evil symbolized by Auschwitz. This is a responsibility thrust upon us by virtue of our humanity. Both Jonas and Levinas argue that the autonomy that is so cherished by Kant – what Jonas calls "formal responsibility," where we are accountable "for" our deeds – *presupposes* a more substantive responsibility for our fellow human beings, including those not yet born. There is no escape from the threat of evil, which can assume ever-new forms and confront us in the most unexpected ways. Nor is there any escape from our infinite responsibility to combat evil wherever it occurs.

8

Arendt: Radical Evil and the Banality of Evil

This inquiry began with my reflections on Hannah Arendt. Arendt once remarked that thinking is communicated by infecting others with one's own perplexities. Dealing with her perplexities led to my own interrogations. Specifically, it was her thoughts about Kant and radical evil that led me back to Kant, and to follow the vicissitudes of the encounters with the multifaceted aspects of evil in subsequent thinkers. I want to conclude my interrogations by returning to Arendt. Like Levinas and Jonas, Arendt believed that it was Auschwitz and Gulag – more generally, Hitler's and Stalin's totalitarianism – that demanded a rethinking of the very meaning of evil in our time.[1]

Despite differences in temperament, emphasis, and concern from Levinas and Jonas, Arendt has a great deal in common with them. As with them, her decisive formative philosophical experience was her encounter with Heidegger. At the age of 18 she went to study with him when he was teaching at Marburg.[2] Born in the same year as Levinas (1906), she came from a German-Jewish assimilated family. She tells us that Judaism as a religion and Jewish issues were of little concern to her as a child and an adolescent.[3] As a young student, she was much more interested in Christian thinkers such as Kierkegaard, and she wrote her dissertation with Karl Jaspers on St Augustine. Her friendship with Hans Jonas, whom she met as a university student, provided the occasion for her first awakening to Zionism. In 1926, when both Arendt and Jonas were at Heidelberg, Jonas invited Kurt Blumenfeld, the chief spokesman of the Zionist Organization of Germany, to give a lecture to the Zionist student club. As Elizabeth Young-Bruehl, Arendt's biographer, tells us, "The lecture did not convert Hannah Arendt to Zionism, but it did convert her to Kurt Blumenfeld" – who became her life long friend.[4] Arendt's interest in the Jewish question was further stimulated when she started working on her book *Rahel Varnhagen: The Life of a Jewess*. She began this manuscript in the late 1920s, and completed it in Paris after she fled Germany in 1933.[5] Initially, Arendt was not interested in politics or history, but by 1933 she felt that she had been hit over the head by history. That year she was asked by her Zionist friends to do some "illegal" research on German anti-Semitism at the Prussian State Library. Subsequently she was apprehended and interrogated for eight days. Shortly after her release, she fled Germany – to Prague, Geneva, and finally to Paris. Reflecting on this period of her life, she tells us, "I realized what I then expressed time and again in the sentence: If one is attacked as a Jew, one must defend oneself as a Jew. Not as a German, not as a world-citizen, not as an upholder of the Rights of Man, or whatever."[6] Arendt – unlike so many others in similar situations – was "lucky." Twice she managed to escape from threatening situations. The first time was when she was interrogated in Berlin in 1933; the second when she escaped from Gurs, the French internment camp to which she was sent from Paris in 1940 as a German *émigré*. Her good luck continued, and she found a safe haven in France with friends. Rejoined by her husband, Heinrich Blücher, they made their way to Lisbon, where they sailed for New York in the spring of 1941.

Arendt believed that all genuine thinking is grounded in personal experience, and as with Levinas and Jonas, the primary experience that shaped virtually all her thinking was living through the Nazi period. In 1945 she already declared, "The problem of evil will be the fundamental question of postwar intellectual life in Europe."[7] It is the problem (or, more accurately, the cluster of problems) to which she returned over and over again until the end of her life. In the preface to *The Origins of Totalitarianism*, she wrote, "And if it is true that in the final stages of totalitarianism an absolute evil appears (absolute because it can no longer be deduced from humanly comprehensible motives), it is also true that without it we might never have known the truly radical nature of Evil."[8]

Before turning to an examination of what she means by radical evil, and to the much more famous (and misunderstood) idea of the banality of evil, I want to say something about Arendt's style of thinking. The expression that best captures this distinctive style is one that she used many times, "thought-trains." These thought-trains, grounded in one's experiences, energize thinking and provide it with concrete specificity. They crisscross, interweave, reinforce each other, and sometimes conflict with each other. Following these different thought-trains requires some delicacy in distinguishing them from each other and seeing how they are interrelated. This is why I now think that categorizing Arendt's thinking about evil under the rubrics of "radical evil" and "the banality of evil" can be misleading, because they do not do justice to her complex thought-trains. I want to orient my discussion of Arendt's reflections (*Nachdenken*) on evil by distinguishing these thought-trains – these strands that make up the complex fabric of her thinking.

Let me begin with an exchange that took place between Arendt and Jaspers in 1951. Arendt sent Jaspers one of the first copies of *The Origins of Totalitarianism* so that it would arrive in time for his birthday. After reading the preface and the final chapter, Jaspers immediately acknowledged this gift from his former student (who used a quotation from him as the epigraph to the book).[9] He added a cryptic last sentence to his short letter, "Hasn't Jahwe faded too far out of sight?"[10] In her next letter to Jasper (March 4, 1951), she replied:

> Your question "Hasn't Jahwe faded too far out of sight?" has been on my mind for weeks now without my being able to come up with an answer to it. No more than I've been able to find one to my own demand from the final chapter . . . . Evil has proved to be more radical than expected. In objective terms modern crimes are not provided for in the Ten Commandments. Or: the Western tradition is suffering from the preconception that the most evil things human beings can do arise from the vice of selfishness. Yet we know that the greatest evils or radical evil has nothing to do anymore with such humanly understandable, sinful motives. What radical evil really is I don't know, but it seems to me it somehow has to do with the following phenomenon: making human beings as human beings superfluous (not using them as means to an end, which leaves their essence as humans untouched and impinges only on their human dignity; rather, making them superfluous as human beings). This happens as soon as all unpredictability – which, in human beings, is the equivalent of spontaneity – is eliminated. And all this in turn arises from – or better, goes along with – the delusion of the omnipotence (not simply the lust for power) of an individual man. If an individual man qua man were omnipotent, then there is in fact no reason why men in the plural should exist at all – just as in monotheism it is only God's omnipotence that makes him ONE. So, in this same way, the omnipotence of an individual man would make men superfluous.[11]

These remarks are in a letter that was not intended for publication, and Arendt is aware of their tentativeness. Later in the same letter, she confesses, "None of it is thought through at all." Yet, if we analyze carefully what she says here against the background of what she says about radical evil in her published writings, these remarks already indicate several of her most characteristic thought-trains.

1 There is the dominant theme that radical evil "has to do with the following phenomenon: making human beings as human beings superfluous." This is closely related to the next two themes.
2 The elimination of human unpredictability and spontaneity. This, in turn, is connected to what she later called natality, as well as to human freedom.
3 The idea that the delusion of omnipotence (which is not to be confused with the lust for power) of an individual man is incompatible with the existence of *men* in the plural. This is intimately related to her claim in *The Human Condition* that "plurality is specifically the condition – not only the *conditio sine qua non*, but the *conditio per quem* – of all political life."[12]
4 Traditional moral prohibitions, as represented in the Ten Commandments, are no longer adequate to characterize modern crimes.
5 The most evil deeds that human beings perform do not arise from the vice of selfishness. And more generally, "radical evil has nothing to do with such humanly understandable, sinful motives."

I want to pursue each of these thought-trains, and the ways in which they are interrelated. But it is worth noting how significantly Arendt departs from Kant, despite her admiration for him, and his influence on her own thinking. In *Religion within the Limits of Reason Alone*, Kant explicitly stated that self-love (selfishness) is the source of evil. This is just what Arendt denies in regard to what *she* calls radical evil. Making human beings as human beings superfluous is more radical than disobeying the Kantian categorical imperative – the imperative that forbids us to treat individuals as *means* only, and forbids us to violate their *dignity*. It is no accident that Arendt uses the Kantian term "spontaneity." According to Kant, spontaneity is the essential characteristic of our human rationality and freedom. From a Kantian perspective, it makes no sense to suggest that human spontaneity can be eliminated. For this would mean that we were no longer human rational agents. But twentieth-century totalitarianism shows that we must now live with the all too *real* possibility that human spontaneity can be eliminated. Stated another way, Arendt does not disagree with Kant that spontaneity is a necessary condition for the very possibility of a rational human life. Where she differs from him is in thinking that even this apparently *transcendental* condition of a human life *can* be eliminated *empirically*, by totalitarian means. This, as we shall see, stands at the heart of her understanding of radical evil.

Superfluousness, spontaneity, and plurality

Let me begin by exploring the first three related, but distinguishable, thought-trains: superfluousness, the elimination of unpredictability and spontaneity, and how omnipotence threatens plurality. Superfluousness is a pervasive theme in *The Origins of Totalitarianism*. It takes a variety of forms, and Arendt explores its significance in a variety of contexts. She notes that the major political events of the twentieth century, from the First World War on, have created millions of people who are not only homeless and stateless, but are treated as if they were completely superfluous and dispensable. Arendt's apprehension regarding the sudden creation of masses of superfluous people was prophetic. A remark she makes towards the end of *The Origins of Totalitarianism* has a chilling poignancy: "Totalitarian solutions may well survive the fall of totalitarian regimes in the form of strong temptations which will come up whenever it seems impossible to alleviate political, social, or economic misery in a manner worthy of man" (*OT* 459). The theme of superfluousness also shapes her critical discussion of abstract universal claims about the "Rights of Man."

> The calamity of the rightless is not that they are deprived of life, liberty, and the pursuit of happiness, or of equality before the law and freedom of opinion – formulas which were designed to solve problems *within* given communities – but that they no longer belong to any community whatsoever. Their plight is not that they are not equal before the law, but that no law exists for them; not that they are oppressed but that nobody wants even to oppress them. Only in the last stage of a rather lengthy process is their right to live threatened; only if they remain perfectly "superfluous," if nobody can be found to "claim" them, may their lives be in danger. (*OT* 295–6)

It is because of the threat of superfluousness that Arendt insists that the most fundamental right is "the right to have rights," the right to belong to a community that protects one's rights – a community in which one can exercise these rights. She also calls attention to the feature of totalitarian ideology whereby the allegedly "universal laws of Nature and History" transcend individual human aspirations, so that *all* individuals can be sacrificed for the cause of the movement. In this sense the manipulators of totalitarian regimes are most dangerous, because they not only treat their victims as if they were superfluous, they also treat themselves as superfluous – as vehicles for carrying out the laws of Nature and History.[13]

But the deepest and most shocking sense of superfluousness – the one that reveals what she means by radical evil – is epitomized in the concentration and death camps, the "laboratories" of totalitarian regimes. It is in these laboratories that the most radical experiments were conducted of changing the character of human beings – that is, in "making human beings as human beings superfluous." "The horror of the concentration and extermination camps can never be fully embraced by the imagination, for the very reason that it stands outside of life and death."[14] Appeals to common sense, utilitarian categories, and liberal rationalizations break down when confronted with the phenomenon of the death camps. In her perceptive reconstruction of the "logic" of total domination, Arendt distinguishes three analytical stages.

"The first essential step on the road to total domination is to kill the juridical person in man" (*OT* 447). This started long before the Nazis established the death camps. Arendt is referring to the legal restrictions that stripped Jews (and other marginalized groups) of their juridical rights. The highly effective and humiliating way in which these juridical restrictions were enacted has been graphically recorded in that remarkable document, the diaries of Victor Klemperer, *I Will Bear Witness*.[15] Arendt tells us that "The aim of an arbitrary system is to destroy the civil rights of the whole population, who ultimately become just as outlawed in their own country as the stateless and homeless. The destruction of man's rights, the killing of the juridical person in him, is a prerequisite for dominating him entirely" (*OT* 451). In the camps, there is not even the pretense of any civil or human rights – no inmates have any rights.

"The next decisive step in the preparation of living corpses is the murder of the moral person in man. This is done in the main by making martyrdom, for the first time in history, impossible" (*OT* 451). The SS, who supervised the camps, were perversely brilliant in corrupting any and all forms of human solidarity. They succeeded in making decisions of conscience questionable and equivocal.

> When a man is faced with the alternative of betraying and thus murdering his friends or of sending his wife and children, for whom he is in every sense responsible, to their death; and when even suicide would mean the immediate murder of his own family – how is he to decide? The alternative is no longer between good and evil, but between murder and murder. Who could solve the moral dilemma of the Greek mother, who was allowed by the Nazis to choose which of her three children should be killed? (*OT* 452)

It is the third stage of this "logic" of total domination that brings us closest to what Arendt means by "making human beings as human beings superfluous" – to the core and horror of radical evil. It is the extraordinary attempt to transform human beings, to destroy any vestige of human individuality and spontaneity – and consequently, any vestige of human freedom and solidarity.

> After the murder of the moral person and annihilation of the juridical person, the destruction of individuality is almost always successful . . . . For to destroy individuality is to destroy spontaneity, man's power to begin something new out of his own resources, something that cannot be explained on the basis of reactions to environment and events. (*OT* 455)

We detect here the importance of the second thought-train – the elimination of individuality and spontaneity. The point that she is making takes on an added significance when we relate it to her discussion of *natality* in *The Human Condition*. This is the human capacity to initiate, to begin something new, something unpredictable. It is a capacity that comes into existence with each new life. She associates this capacity with spontaneity, and it is the source of human freedom. The final paragraph of *The Origins of Totalitarianism* indicates the centrality of this thought-train.

> But there remains also the truth that every end in history necessarily contains a new beginning; this beginning is the promise, the only "message" which the end can ever produce. Beginning, before it becomes a historical event, is the supreme capacity of man; politically, it is identical with man's freedom. *Initium ut esset homo creatus est* – "that a beginning be made man was created" said Augustine. This beginning is guaranteed by each new birth; it is indeed every man. (*OT* 479)[16]

It is in *The Human Condition* that Arendt turns to a full-scale analysis of natality and its relation to the web of concepts – spontaneity, individuality, freedom, plurality – that are characteristic of human action. These are the features that make a human life *human*. In this sense, her phrase "making human beings as human beings superfluous" has a much more horrifying and specific meaning. It means literally the attempt to transform human beings in such a way so that they are no longer *human*.

> The camps are meant not only to exterminate people and degrade human beings, but also to serve the ghastly experiment of eliminating, under scientifically controlled conditions, spontaneity itself as an expression of human behavior and transforming the human personality into a mere thing, into something that even animals are not; for Pavlov's dog, which as we know, was trained to eat not when it was hungry but when a bell rang, was a perverted animal. (*OT* 438)

Arendt's thought-train concerning the totalitarian attempt to eliminate natality, spontaneity, and individuality is also related to her reflections on omnipotence and plurality. "Plurality" is the predominant theme in Arendt's political thinking. Margaret Canovan, in her extremely perceptive study of Arendt's political thought, concludes her study with the following observation.

> Lecturing in 1955 on the history of political thought, she remarked that each of the key political thinkers of the past 'has thrown one word into our world, has augmented it by this one word, because he responded rightly and thoughtfully to certain decisively new experiences of his time'. After following her thought-trains we must, I think, concede that in the course of her own response to the experiences of her time, Arendt also 'augmented' the world by one word: the word 'plurality'. [17]

Plurality, for Arendt, means much more than "otherness" and "difference," although it shares some of the features that Levinas ascribes to the other (*l'autrui*). Both Levinas and Arendt want to highlight the *singularity* of each individual, a singularity that resists reduction to a common essence. There is a structural parallel between Levinas's critique of the dialectic of the same and the other, a dialectic that seeks to colonize and reduce the other to the same, and Arendt's critique of the tradition of political philosophy that seeks to ignore or obliterate the irreducibility of human plurality.[18] It is because of this plurality that each of us has a different perspective on a common world. And because we have different perspectives, the space of political life is one in which there is (or ought to be) a contest – an *agon* – of competing opinions (*doxai*). "Men in the plural, that is men in so far as they live and move and act in this world, can experience meaningfulness only because they can talk with and make sense to each other and themselves" (*HC* 4).[19]

Arendt's reflections on plurality help to illuminate what she means when she writes in her letter to Jaspers that "if an individual man qua man were omnipotent, then there is in fact no reason why men in the plural should exist at all." Later in the same letter she says: "Western philosophy has never had a clear concept of what constitutes the political, and couldn't have one, because, by necessity, it spoke of man the individual and dealt with the fact of plurality tangentially."[20] The Nazi leaders believed in their own omnipotence, and thought "everything is possible"; they sought to eliminate the plurality of their victims. This provides still another gloss on the phrase "making human beings as human beings superfluous." "Total domination, which strives to organize the infinite plurality and differentiations of human beings as if all of humanity were just one individual is possible only if each and every person can be reduced to a never-changing identity of reactions, so that each of these bundles of reaction can be exchanged at random for any other" (*OT* 438).

Arendt's interweaving thought-trains about superfluousness, the elimination of spontaneity, and pluralism have consequences that go beyond her attempt to explain what she means by radical evil. Many scholars and critics have been perplexed about the relation between *The Origins of Totalitarianism*, which focuses on the constellation of elements that crystallized into the phenomenon of totalitarianism, and *The Human Condition*, which appears to be inspired by Arendt's interpretation of the Greek *polis*. The two books seem to be entirely different in subject matter, as well as in the way Arendt treats issues. But too little attention has been paid to the thought-trains that led her to take up the issues that stand at the heart of *The Human Condition*. I have argued that the shadow of twentieth-century evil shaped the intellectual projects of Levinas and Jonas, but this is just as true of Arendt. Specifically, it was her attempt to understand what seemed to defy comprehension, the radical evil manifested in the "logic" of totalitarian domination, that was a primary motivation to thematize the basic characteristics of human life – spontaneity, natality, action, freedom, and plurality. It was the totalitarian attempt to eliminate these, to make human beings superfluous by transforming them into something other than (and less than) human, that led her to the themes and questions that are so prominent in *The Human Condition*. I fully agree with Margaret Canovan, one of the few interpreters of Arendt who traces in detail the trains of thought that led from *The Origins of Totalitarianism* to *The Human Condition*, when she writes: "Not only is *The Human Condition* itself much more closely related to *The Origins of Totalitarianism* than it appears to be, but virtually the entire agenda of Arendt's political thought was set by her reflections on the political catastrophes of the mid-century."[21] Arendt would certainly agree with Jonas's claim that we perceive evil more directly than we perceive good, just as she would agree with Levinas's characterization of evil as an *excess* that cannot be integrated into our normal categories of understanding and reason.

Levinas and Jonas identified themselves as religious Jews, but Arendt, although never hesitant to affirm her identity as a Jew, was not committed to Judaism as a religion.[22] In the same letter in which she responded to Jaspers's question about Jahwe, she wrote, "All traditional religion as such, whether Jewish or Christian, holds nothing whatsoever for me anymore."[23] Yet, when we reflect on what she says about radical evil and superfluousness, we can discern a theological aura to her thinking.[24] What is it about superfluousness that makes this evil so distinctive and so radical? It is not exclusively the humiliation, torture, and systematic murder of millions (Jews and non-Jews). It is also the *hubris* of those totalitarian leaders who think they are omnipotent, that they can *rival* a God who created a plurality of human beings.

Evil intentions and motivations?

But there is still something vital missing from these reflections on radical evil. However sympathetic we may be to Arendt's description of radical evil as making human beings as human superfluous by liquidating sponta- neity, freedom, natality, individuality, and plurality, we cannot avoid the troubling questions about intention and motivation. Throughout Western thought, the very "grammar" of evil has involved the idea of evil *intentions*. Kant is perhaps the outstanding modern representative of this tradition; it is central to his very understanding of morality. Evil, for Kant, is the intentional adoption of evil maxims. Even when he speaks of radical evil as an innate propensity, he tells us that it involves "the ultimate subjective ground of the adoption of maxims" which must be adopted by free choice (*Willkür*). Arendt began questioning the role of evil motives and intentions in the committing of evil deeds *before* she wrote *The Origins of Totalitarianism*, and it became a central issue in *Eichmann in Jerusalem*. Her introduction of the controversial notion of the banality of evil must be understood in the context of her thought-trains about the meaning of the intentionality in- volved in committing evil deeds.

I want to pursue these trains of thought (on page 208) by going back to an earlier exchange between Jaspers and Arendt – one that occurred in 1946, shortly after they reestablished their correspondence at the end of the Second World War. Jaspers, the most prominent German philosopher to raise the issue of German guilt, sent Arendt a copy of his book *Die Schuldfrage*. In a long letter dated August 17, 1946, Arendt (who had dis- cussed the book thoroughly with her husband, Heinrich Blücher) com- mented on it, and indicated her reservations about Jasper's treatment of Nazi policy as a crime.

> Your definition of Nazi policy as a crime ("criminal guilt") strikes me as questionable. The Nazi crimes, it seems to me, explode the limits of the law; and that is precisely what constitutes their monstrousness. For these crimes, no punishment is severe enough. It may be essential to hang Göring, but it is totally inadequate. That is, this guilt, in contrast to all criminal guilt, oversteps and shatters any and all legal systems. . . . We are simply not equipped to deal, on a human, political level, with a guilt that is beyond crime and an innocence that is beyond goodness or virtue.[25]

In his reply to Arendt, Jaspers wrote:

> You say that what the Nazis did cannot be comprehended as "crime" – I'm not altogether comfortable with your view, because a guilt that goes beyond all criminal guilt inevitably takes on a streak of "greatness" – of satanic

greatness – which is, for me, as inappropriate for the Nazis as all the talk about the "demonic" element in Hitler and so forth. It seems to me that we have to see these things in their total banality (*in ihrer ganzen Banalität*), in their prosaic triviality, because that's what truly characterizes them. Bacteria can cause epidemics that wipe out nations, but they remain merely bacteria. I regard any hint of myth and legend with horror, and everything unspecific is just such a hint. . . .The way you do express it, you've almost taken the path of poetry. And a Shakespeare would never be able to give adequate form to this material – his instinctive aesthetic sense would lead to falsification of it – and that's why he couldn't attempt it.[26]

Arendt was impressed by Jaspers's reply, and acknowledged that she was half convinced by him, because she too *totally* rejected any suggestion of mythical or "satanic greatness" being ascribed to the Nazi leaders. In her response, we see already how she was anticipating her own understanding of radical evil.

I found what you say about my thoughts on "beyond crime and innocence" in what the Nazis did half convincing; that is, I realize completely that in the way I've expressed this up to now I come dangerously close to that "satanic greatness" that I, like you, totally reject. But still, there is a difference between a man who sets out to murder his old aunt and people who without considering the economic usefulness of their actions at all (the deportations were very damaging to the war effort) built factories to produce corpses. One thing is certain: We have to combat all impulses to mythologize the horrible, and to the extent that I can't avoid such formulations, I haven't understood what actually went on. *Perhaps what is behind it all is only that individual human beings did not kill individual other human beings for human reasons, but that an organized attempt was made to eradicate the concept of the human being.*[27]

There are several points that I want to underscore in this illuminating exchange. Arendt, like Jaspers, rejected any suggestion of "satanic greatness," and any mythological or aesthetic attempt to characterize the intentions of the perpetrators of radical evil. Jaspers' reference to Shakespeare has special relevance. Much later, when Arendt sought to understand the phenomenon of the banality of evil, she frequently *contrasted* the mentality exhibited by Eichmann with that of the great Shakespearean evil characters.[28] We can also detect the germ of the thought-train that led her to question the adequacy of the traditional catalogue of evil or sinful intentions to account for Nazi crimes – such as selfishness, lust for power, greed, and sadism. These, of course, as she frequently acknowledged, played a role in Nazi crimes, but she felt that they were not sufficient to explain what happened. Even the appeal to anti-Semitism was not suffi-

cient to account for the death camps.[29] Arendt was perfectly aware of the
bestiality of the Nazis, especially the SA, and she well understood the evil
of unrestrained *ressentiment*.[30] "Behind the blind bestiality of the SA, there
often lay a deep hatred and resentment against all those who were socially, intellectually, or physically better off than themselves, and who
now, as if in fulfillment of their wildest dreams, were in their power. This
resentment, which never died out entirely in the camps, strikes us as a last
remnant of humanly understandable feeling" (*OT* 454). What troubled
Arendt was the fact that totalitarianism went beyond this. Bestiality,
ressentiment, sadism, humiliation have a long history – yet they are still
distinctively *human* categories. But something new and different arose with
totalitarianism, and was epitomized in the concentration and death camps.

> The real horror began, however, when the SS took over the administration
> of the camps. The old spontaneous bestiality gave way to an absolutely cold
> and systematic destruction of human bodies, calculated to destroy human
> dignity: death was avoided or postponed indefinitely. The camps were no
> longer amusement parks for beasts in human form, that is, for men who
> really belonged in mental institutions and prisons: the reverse became true:
> they were turned into "drill grounds" on which perfectly normal men were
> trained to be full-fledged members of the SS.[31]

This is the phenomenon that raised the most difficult and troubling problems for Arendt: how to account for the fact that "perfectly normal men"
were trained not only to be members of the SS, but also to accept the
murder of innocent victims as if it were the most "normal" state of affairs.
As she tells us in *Eichmann in Jerusalem*, "Evil in the Third Reich had lost
the quality by which most people recognize it – the quality of temptation"
(*EJ* 150).

When Arendt wrote *The Origins of Totalitarianism*, she forcefully stated
that Nazi crimes should not be assimilated to traditional crimes, and that
radical evil could not be deduced from "humanly comprehensible motives." But she was less clear when it came to providing an alternative
account of these crimes and the motives for committing them. What
categories were appropriate for understanding Nazi crimes, and more
generally the crimes of totalitarian regimes? To be told that radical evil
has something to do with "making human beings as human beings superfluous" is not yet to answer questions regarding the intentions and
motivations of the individuals responsible for this radical evil. Arendt
returned to these questions in her controversial *Eichmann in Jerusalem*, although in a very different context. After Eichmann's capture in Argentina
in May of 1960, and before his trial began on April 11, 1961, Arendt
engaged in a lengthy correspondence with Jaspers about the appropriate-

ness of trying Eichmann in Jerusalem and the legal characterization of the crimes that he had committed. Jaspers did not think that an Israeli court should try Eichmann, but, although Arendt favored the idea of an international tribunal for such crimes, she defended the right of Israel to try Eichmann.[32] In one of her exchanges with Jaspers, she affirmed that "the concept of *hostis humani generis* . . . is more or less indispensable to the trial. The crucial point is that although the crime at issue [a crime against humanity] was committed primarily against the Jews, it is in no way limited to the Jews or the Jewish Question."[33] She reaffirmed these ideas in the epilogue of *Eichmann in Jerusalem* where she said that Eichmann (and others like him) is "a new type of criminal, who is in actual fact *hostis generis humani*." This new type of criminal "commits his crimes under circumstances that make it well-nigh impossible for him to know or to feel that he is doing wrong" (*EJ* 276).[34] This appeal to a new type of criminal and a new type of crime – a crime against humanity – enables us to categorize the Nazi crimes without any suggestion of "satanic greatness;" but we still have to face the difficult issues of the intention and motivation of the perpetrators. When Arendt introduced her controversial epithet "the banality of evil" in *Eichmann in Jerusalem,* she was struggling to confront questions concerning the *motives* of those desk murderers who committed those crimes against humanity.

Before turning to what Arendt means by the banality of evil, we must confront a stumbling block that has misled many interpreters of Arendt. On February 16, 1963, the first installment of her five-part report on the Eichmann trial was published in the *New Yorker*. Even before the first installment appeared, she was criticized, attacked, and vilified. Moreover, the controversy over *Eichmann in Jerusalem* raged long after her death in 1975. Arendt was accused of exonerating Eichmann and blaming the Jews for their own extermination. She was condemned as being "soulless," "malicious," "arrogant," and "flippant." She distorted the facts, and was a "self-hating" Jew.[35] Gershom Scholem wrote the most notable critique. In a letter to Arendt he wrote:

> I remain unconvinced by your thesis concerning the "banality of evil" – a thesis which, if your sub-title is to be believed, underlies your entire argument. This new thesis strikes me as a catchword: it does not impress me, certainly, as the product of profound analysis – an analysis such as you gave us so convincingly, in the service of a quite different, indeed contradictory thesis, in your book on totalitarianism . . . . Of that "radical evil," to which your then analysis bore such eloquent and erudite witness, nothing remains but this slogan .[36]

In her reply to Scholem, Arendt wrote:

> In conclusion, let me come to the only matter where you have not misun-
> derstood me, and where indeed I am glad that you have raised the point.
> You are quite right: I changed my mind and do no longer speak of "radical
> evil." . . . It is indeed my opinion now that evil is never "radical," that it is
> only extreme, and that it possesses neither depth nor any demonic dimen-
> sion. It can overgrow and lay waste the whole world because it spreads like
> a fungus on the surface. It is "thought-defying," as I said, because thought
> tries to reach some depth, to go to the roots, and the moment it concerns
> itself with evil, it is frustrated because there is nothing. That is its "banal-
> ity."[37]

It is certainly true that Arendt no longer spoke of "radical evil," but
this reply to Scholem is extremely misleading. Arendt *never* repudiated the thought-trains that went into her original discussion of radical evil, especially her claim that radical evil involves making human
beings as human beings superfluous, as well as a systematic attempt
to eliminate human spontaneity, individuality, and plurality.[38] On
the contrary, the phenomenon that she identified as the banality of
evil *presupposes* this understanding of radical evil. It is true that she
rejects the idea that such evil "has depth or any demonic dimension." But, as we have seen from her earlier exchange with Jaspers,
she had repudiated the idea of the demonic and "satanic greatness"
of Nazi crimes already in 1946.[39] The very words she uses in her
reply to Scholem echo Jaspers's earlier words when he objected to
speaking about the "demonic" element in Hitler, and declared: "It
seems to me that we have to see these things in their total banality,
in their prosaic triviality, because that's what truly characterizes them.
Bacteria can cause epidemics that wipe out nations, but they remain
merely bacteria."[40] When she now says that evil is extreme but not
radical, that it lacks depth, she is calling attention to the fact that evil
is on the *surface*. Insofar as "radical" suggests digging to roots that are
hidden, she no longer thinks that evil is radical in *this sense*. It is
"thought-defying" because thought seeks something that has depth.
But this meaning of "radical" is quite independent of the sense of
"radical" that she associates with superfluousness.

   Although Arendt's remark is misleading, she did change her mind
about one crucial aspect of evil – the *motivation* for committing these crimes.
Or perhaps it is more accurate to say that she clarified an ambiguity that
was present in her earlier reflections. Previously, she had insisted that
radical evil could not be explained or deduced from humanly comprehensible motives. When confronted with Eichmann in the Jerusalem court,
she came to the conclusion that he committed monstrous deeds without
being motivated by monstrous evil intentions.

> When I speak of the banality of evil, I do so only on the strictly factual level, pointing to a phenomenon which stared one in the face at the trial. Eichmann was not Iago and not Macbeth, and nothing would have been farther from his mind than to determine with Richard III "to prove a villain." Except for an extraordinary diligence in looking out for his personal advancement, he had no motives at all. . . . He *merely*, to put the matter colloquially, *never realized what he was doing. (EJ* 287)[41]

Arendt does not mean that Eichmann failed to realize that he was sending millions of people to their death. He was not stupid. He was extremely intelligent and efficient in knowing how to keep the deportations operating, even under the most adverse conditions of fighting a war on several fronts.[42] But this does not mean that his motives themselves were wicked or demonic. One of the clearest statements of what Arendt means by the "banality of evil" appears in an essay that she wrote ten years after the trial, "Thinking and Moral Considerations."

> Some years ago, reporting the trial of Eichmann in Jerusalem, I spoke of "the banality of evil" and meant with this no theory or doctrine but something quite factual, the phenomenon of evil deeds, committed on a gigantic scale, which could not be traced to any particularity of wickedness, pathology, or ideological conviction in the doer, whose only personal distinction was a perhaps extraordinary shallowness. However monstrous the deeds were, the doer was neither monstrous nor demonic, and the only specific characteristic one could detect on his part as well as in his behavior during the trial and the preceding police examination was something entirely negative: it was not stupidity but a curious, quite authentic inability to think.[43]

Arendt was relentless (and even offensive) in ridiculing what she took to be the melodramatic case presented by the chief prosecutor, Gideon Hauser, who portrayed Eichmann as a sadistic monster, and claimed that he was the chief architect of the "final solution."[44] But she was raising profound issues. She was questioning a long and deep tradition in theological, philosophical, moral, and legal discourse – that evil deeds presuppose evil intentions and evil motives, and that the degree of evil manifested in the deeds corresponds to the degree of wickedness of the motives. This is a tradition that can be traced back to St Augustine. Kant himself makes it perfectly clear that evil is ultimately to be accounted for by the evil will and intentions of the agent.[45] But the phenomenon that Arendt confronted was one in which monstrous deeds were committed without monstrous motives. Arendt went further, because she was concerned not only with Eichmann, but with "the moral collapse" of those "respectable" people who accepted and participated in a policy of racial murder. Margaret Canovan succinctly states what so troubled Arendt:

Although these [ordinary respectable] people would never have dreamed of committing crimes as long as they lived in a society where such activities were not usual, they adapted effortlessly to a system in which blatant crimes against whole categories of people were standard behaviour. In the place of 'thou shalt not kill' which had seemed the most indisputable rule of civilian existence, such people had no difficulty in accepting the Nazis' rule according to which killing was a moral duty for the sake of the race. Principles which had been self-evident, moral behaviour which had been 'normal' and 'decent' could not be taken for granted any more.[46]

Eichmann: human-all-too-human

Arendt's earlier insistence that radical evil could not be explained by humanly comprehensible motives might easily lead one to think that the motives involved were either incomprehensible or – in some unspecified sense – nonhuman. But her portrait of Eichmann revealed him to be *human-all-too-human*. According to her account, neither blind anti-Semitism, sadistic hatred, nor even deep ideological convictions motivated him. He was motivated by the most mundane, and petty considerations of advancing his career, pleasing his superiors, demonstrating that he could do his job well and efficiently. *In this sense*, his motives were at once banal and all too human.[47]

I do not think that we should underestimate the disturbing significance of what Arendt reveals about the face of evil in the twentieth century. Let us recall that when Kant introduced his concept of radical evil, he distinguished three degrees of evil. The first is due to the *frailty* of human nature, the second to *impurity* ("mixing unmoral and moral motivating causes"), and the third – the most extreme – to the *wickedness* of human nature or the human heart. This last reflects the cast of mind that is "corrupted at its root."[48] But this is what Arendt questions. Her portrayal of Eichmann is much more damning than simply characterizing him as some sort of demonic monster. One of the deeper reasons for the controversy over *Eichmann in Jerusalem* is that Arendt compels her readers to question their deeply held moral convictions about good and evil. It is much easier, as well as more conventional, to think that anyone who did what Eichmann did *must* be some sort of demonic monster. But totalitarianism, whose legacy still haunts us, shows that very ordinary people motivated by the most mundane, banal considerations can commit horrendous crimes.

Arendt was not satisfied just to describe what she took to be the phenomenon of the banality of evil; she wanted to understand what it was about Eichmann that allowed him to commit such crimes. Eichmann seemed to be trapped in clichés and accepted "language rules."

The longer one listened to him, the more obvious it became that his inability to speak was closely connected with an inability to *think*, namely *to think from the standpoint of someone else.* No communication was possible with him, not because he lied but because he was surrounded by the most reliable of all safeguards against the words and the presence of others, and hence against reality as such. (*EJ* 49; emphasis added)

In her subsequent attempts to account for the banality of evil, Arendt kept returning to Eichmann's inability to *think* and make independent *judgments.* She was convinced that such thoughtlessness, such an inability to think from the standpoint of someone else, "can wreak more havoc than all the evil instincts taken together, which perhaps are inherent in man – that was, in fact, the lesson one could learn in Jerusalem" (*EJ* 288).[49] In the introduction to *The Life of the Mind*, she informs us that the phenomenon of the banality of evil was one of the occasions for writing the book.

The question that imposed itself was: Could the activity of thinking as such, the habit of examining whatever happens to come to pass or to attract attention, regardless of results and specific content, could this activity be among the conditions that make men abstain from evil-doing or even actual "condition" them against it? . . . To put it differently and use Kantian language: after having been struck by a fact that, willy-nilly, "put me in possession of a concept" (the banality of evil), I could not help raising the *questio juris* and asking myself "by what right I possessed and used it." (*LM* 5)

Just as Arendt was about to begin the third part of *The Life of the Mind*, "Judging" – the section that would be most relevant to answer the questions she raised – she suddenly died. The title page, "Judging," was left in her typewriter.[50] But during the last decade of her life she increasingly focused her attention on those mental activities that might enable human beings to abstain from committing evil deeds.[51]

Although Arendt's thoughts about the relation between thinking and evil were still very tentative and inconclusive at the time of her death, I want to pursue one central theme –a theme that will allow us to join issue again with Levinas and Jonas. All three believed that one of the most important challenges of Auschwitz – perhaps the most important philosophical challenge – was to rethink the meaning of responsibility. We have already seen how central to Levinas's thinking is the understanding of the responsibility *to* and *for* the other that is thrust upon us before we can even speak of our autonomous responsibility. And in the case of Jonas, we have seen how he seeks to elaborate a new imperative of responsibility, where we bear a responsibility for future generations of humankind. Arendt's primary focus is different. Her main concern was the "total moral collapse" that she had witnessed. This was not just an intellectual, but also a deeply personal problem. Speaking about her experiences in 1933, she said, "The problem, the personal problem, was not what our enemies did but what our friends did. In the wave of *Gleischschaltung* (co-ordination), which was relatively voluntary – in any case, not yet under the pressure of terror – it was as if an empty space formed around one."[52]

The problem that dominated Arendt's reflections was the inadequacy of the traditional disciplines of morals and ethics to shed light on this new face of evil. These traditional disciplines focused on customs, habits, and rules.[53] But totalitarianism revealed how easily such habits, customs, and rules could be exchanged for another opposing set. Yet there were some individuals (albeit all too few) from all walks of life who were able to resist evil and act in a decent manner. She raised this issue in the postscript to *Eichmann in Jerusalem*: "Those few who were still able to tell right from wrong went really only by their own judgments, and they did so freely; there were no rules to be abided by, under which the particular cases with which they were confronted could be subsumed. They had to decide each instance as it arose, because no rules existed for the unprecedented" (*EJ* 295). What enabled those few to resist? What saved them from the collapse of moral standards that surrounded them? It was their capacity to judge what is right and wrong, their capacity to judge the evil they confronted without having to rely on preexisting general rules. This was one of the primary reasons why Arendt became so preoccupied with the faculty of judgment and its relation to thinking, and why she turned to Kant, who "discovered an entirely new human faculty, namely judgment."[54] Kant, in his *Critique of Judgment*, dealt with reflective judgment in connection with the problem of aesthetic judgment. But Arendt argued that Kant's understanding of reflective judgment had important moral and political consequences. The faculty of judgment, as she conceived it, does not require sophisticated theoretical knowledge; it is exhibited by individuals who cut across all walks of life – educated and uneducated. In her essay entitled "Thinking and Moral Considerations," she drew upon Socrates as an individual who eminently illustrated this capacity to think and to judge.[55] At times she suggested that judging was itself a form of thinking, although in *The Life of the Mind* she emphasized that thinking and judging are independent mental activities. We can only speculate about what Arendt might have said in the final, unwritten part of *The Life of the Mind*, but she does give a preliminary sketch of the relation between thinking and judging.

When everybody is swept away unthinkingly by what everybody else does and believes in, those who think are drawn out of hiding because of their refusal to join in is conspicuous and thereby becomes a kind of action. In such emergencies, it turns out that the purging component of thinking (Socrates' midwifery, which brings out implications of unexamined opinions and thereby destroys them – values, doctrines, theories, and even convictions) is political by implication. For this destruction has a liberating effect on another faculty, the faculty of judgment, which one may call with some reason the most political of man's mental abilities. It is the faculty that judges particulars without subsuming them under general rules which can be taught and learned until they grow into habits that can be replaced by other habits. . . . The manifestation of the wind of thought is not knowledge: it is the ability to tell right and wrong, beautiful from ugly. And this, at the rare moments when the stakes are on the table, may indeed prevent catastrophes, at least for the self. (*LM* 193)

In attempting to illuminate the distinctive characteristic of judging, Arendt developed an original interpretation of Kant's *Critique of Judgment*. Her thinking comes close to one of Kant's deepest insights in *Religion within the Limits of Reason Alone*. Suppose we raise the question of how we are to explain the fact that there are always some persons who judge the particular manifestations of evil and resist them. To use her own example, how are we to account for the difference between an Adolf Eichmann and an Anton Schmidt, the German soldier who helped Jews in Poland by providing forged papers and trucks, and who was caught by the Nazis and executed?[56] No doubt if we knew more about this simple soldier, we would discover aspects of his background that might help explain why he did what he did. But Arendt, like Kant, would say that, in the *final analysis*, this is a question that we cannot answer satisfactorily. We reach the limits of understanding because – to use Kant's expression – the matter is inscrutable (*unerforschlich*). Nevertheless, we can hold individuals responsible for their failure to think and judge. Arendt was skeptical and critical of the idea of "collective guilt." In a draft of her essay "Personal Responsibility under Dictatorship," she writes: "The point I wish to raise here goes beyond the well-known fallacy of the collective-guilt first applied to the German people and its collective past – all of Germany stands accused and the whole of German history from Luther to Hitler – which in practice turned into a highly effective white-wash of all those who had actually done something; *where all are guilty, no one is.*"[57] Arendt also strongly objected to the "cog" theory – that Eichmann was simply a cog in a death machine, and consequently should not be held responsible for his actions.

When I went to Jerusalem to attend the Eichmann trial, I felt it was the great advantage of the court-room procedure that this whole cog business makes no sense in its setting, and therefore forces us to look at all these questions from a different point of view. To be sure, that the defense would try to plead in this sense was predictable – Eichmann was but a small cog – that the defendant himself would think in these terms was probable – he did up to a point – whereas the attempt of the prosecution to make out of him the biggest cog ever – worse and more important than Hitler – was an unexpected curiosity. The judges did what was right and proper: they discarded the whole notion, *and so incidentally, did I* – all blame and praise to the contrary notwithstanding. For, as the judges took pains to point out, in a court-room there is no system on trial, no history or historical trend, no 'ism,' anti-Semitism for instance, but a person: and if the defendant happens to be a functionary, he stands accused precisely because even a functionary is still a human being, and it is in this capacity that he stands trial.[58]

In response to the excuse that one is merely a cog or a wheel in a system, it is always appropriate to ask: "And why did you become a cog or continue to be a wheel in such circumstances?"[59]

Levinas, Jonas, and Arendt, all of whom witnessed the unprecedented radical evil of Auschwitz, and whose lives and thinking were shaped by it, felt the need to *rethink* the very meaning of evil. Their approaches and emphases differ, but all three would agree that this evil was an "excess" that cannot be adequately assimilated to our categories of understanding and comprehension. Nevertheless, all three sought to bring some illumination to this black hole. In rethinking the meaning of evil, all three realized that one must also rethink what responsibility means. Despite their many substantive differences, Levinas, Jonas, and Arendt were engaged in a common project. Each of them highlights aspects of responsibility – our primordial responsibility to and for the other (*l'autrui*); our responsibility to act in a manner that will insure the existence of future generations of responsible beings; our personal responsibility that demands the imaginative ability "to think from the standpoint of somebody else," to have the courage to exercise our personal reflective judgment when there are no rules to guide us in resisting evil.

Conclusion

It is time to stand back and ask what we have learned from these interrogations. I want to do this by enumerating and commenting on a number of theses.

1. *Interrogating evil is an ongoing, open-ended process.* Throughout I have indicated my skepticism about the very idea of a *theory* of evil, if this is understood as a complete account of what evil *is*. I do not think that such a theory is possible, because we cannot anticipate what new forms of evil or vicissitudes of evil will appear. I can illustrate what I mean with reference to Levinas, Jonas, and Arendt. Their philosophical investigations are haunted by their experience of twentieth-century evils – especially the evil epitomized by Auschwitz. Each of them seeks to characterize what is distinctive about twentieth-century evils, what new problems arise from confronting these evils, and what ought to be our response to them. Levinas claims that the evil of Auschwitz is so extreme that it compels us to ask whether we have been "duped" by morality. His entire philosophical project can be viewed as an ethical response to this unprecedented evil. Jonas argues that the technological age has so transformed the conditions and consequences of human actions that many actions which were previously taken to be ethically neutral can now be seen to have potentially evil consequences – especially the destruction of the environmental conditions required to support life. And he argues that this new form of evil demands a new ethics of responsibility. Arendt argues that with the emergence of twentieth-century totalitarianism, we are confronted with an unprecedented type of evil – radical evil – whereby a systematic attempt is made to make human beings superfluous as *human* beings. We must also confront the

phenomenon of the banality of evil whereby monstrously evil deeds can be performed by "normal" human beings who are neither monsters nor demonic. Each of them is claiming that something unprecedented (and something that could not have been anticipated) has happened in our time, and that this demands *new* thinking about evil. Traditional concepts are no longer adequate in helping us to understand what appears so incomprehensible. Each of these thinkers warns us that there is no reason to think that in the future we will not face new forms of evil and new questions. The truth is that we do not have to wait for the future. For we are constantly being confronted with unanticipated forms of brutal ethnic cleansing, militant religious fanaticism, terrorist attacks, and murderous varieties of nationalism.

But there is also another way of appreciating the intrinsic openness of any inquiry about evil. I agree with Jonas when he says that our perceptions and judgments of evil are more immediate and insistent than those regarding what we take to be good. We do not have to be persuaded that the deliberate infliction of unbearable suffering on innocents is evil. Our judgments of what we take to be exemplars of evil deeds are historically conditioned, but this does not diminish their painful insistence. Of course, the direct experience or witnessing what we take to be evil is just the *beginning* of our questioning. It is the occasion for asking what it is about this phenomenon that makes it evil. What features does it exhibit? What is our warrant for classifying and condemning it as evil? Such an investigation demands that we support our judgments with reasons that we are prepared to articulate and defend. (This is true even if we think that there are no ultimate rational foundations to justify our "final vocabularies.") In short, the investigation of evil is a hermeneutic activity in which we "begin" with our prejudgments about evil, and then critically reflect upon these. There is a movement here wherein we test our prejudgments and deepen our understanding of evil. This process is essentially open-ended, and new experiences may require us to revise and transform our judgments in light of a better understanding.[1]

2. *There is a plurality of types of evil, with no common essence.* This thesis is a corollary to the first thesis. Nevertheless, it must be clearly stated because a great deal of confusion and needless controversy arises from ignoring it. Wittgenstein's insights about "family resemblances" and how they function, are persuasive because he had an appreciation of the seductive temptation to search for essences – the temptation to think that there *must* be such essences. Even when we think we have abandoned the search for essences, there is something uncanny about the way in which this desire and need expresses themselves in devious ways. This is especially evident

in the discourse about evil. There is something deep in us that desires a reassuring closure. It is not only Wittgenstein's therapy that is intended to help us to resist this temptation. Nietzsche, with his understanding of perspectival knowing, explodes the myth of a single essence of evil. The priestly class designates the "good" of the noble aristocrats the very quintessence of "evil." But there is also the "evil" of the priests themselves –– the evil that the narrator of the *Genealogy of Morals* calls *ressentiment*. The assumption that evil is reducible to a common denominator or that there is single essence of evil has plagued contemporary discussions of evil. Let me illustrate this with reference to the debates that have raged about Arendt's notion of "the banality of evil." One reason why this concept has generated so much controversy (in addition to blatant misunderstandings) is that Arendt has been (mis)understood to be defining the *essence* of Nazi evil. She herself bears some responsibility for this misunderstanding. The controversy might have been avoided if she had been clearer and more forceful in stating that what she calls the "factual" phenomenon of the banality of evil was only *one* aspect of Nazi evil. It is not a thesis about the essential character of evil. In her responses to her many critics, she tried to clarify this key point. She was perfectly aware that the expression "the banality of evil" was not appropriate to describe Hitler and other Nazi leaders, and she was certainly not naïve regarding the barbarous sadism and rabid anti-Semitism of many Nazis. She rejected the claim that she had a *theory*, or even a general *thesis*, about evil. But localizing her claims to "desk murderers" like Eichmann does not diminish the significance of these claims. She wants to make us acutely aware that individuals who commit monstrous deeds do not necessarily have monstrous evil motives. She never intended to exonerate Eichmann, but rather to expose and underscore a new and more horrifying form of evil. With the acknowledgment that there is an irreducible plurality of evils, and with an awareness that new forms of evil do emerge in differing historical circumstances, Arendt's insights about the banality of evil enrich and complicate our contemporary discourse about evil.

3. *Evil is an excess that resists total comprehension.* I have used the language of Levinas to express this thesis. Levinas describes "evil as excess in its very quiddity," as being "the nonsynthesizable," and "still more heterogeneous than all heterogeneity."[2] In light of these comments about the "quiddity" of evil, it may seem that this third thesis conflicts with my second thesis about the plurality of evils and the lack of a common essence. But I do not think that the Levinasian point loses any of its relevance if we limit ourselves to the claim that this excess is characteristic of extreme evils. From the context in which Levinas makes these claims, it is clear that Auschwitz

is the paradigm of the evil he is speaking about. This is the type of evil that resists what Kant calls "synthesis." It defies what Kant took to be essential for experience – that it can be synthesized, conceptualized, and categorized. This is what Levinas calls the "transcendence of evil," but it is an *experienced* transcendence. Consequently, we find ourselves in a paradoxical situation in interrogating evil. We seek to understand it, to find the concepts that are adequate to describe and comprehend it. Yet the more rigorously we interrogate it, the more we realize that there is something about the most extreme and radical forms of evil that eludes us. We ineluctably come up against the limits of comprehension.

Levinas's claim about the excess of evil is closely related to Arendt's understanding of comprehension. She declares, "Comprehension does not mean denying the outrageous, deducing the unprecedented from precedents, or explaining phenomena by such analogies and generalities that the impact of reality and the shock of experience are no longer felt. It means, rather, examining and bearing consciously the burden which our century has placed on us – neither denying its existence nor submitting meekly to its weight."[3] Levinas and Arendt, although deeply affected by Auschwitz, were not themselves survivors of concentration or death camps. But the point they make about the character and limits of comprehension, and the experienced sense of evil as *excess*, has been given eloquent testimony by survivors such as Primo Levi, Jean Améry, and Jorge Semprum who have written about their experience in the camps. At crucial points in their works of recollection, they confess to the disparity between what they actually experienced and their persistent attempts to describe and understand it. My thesis about the excess, or transcendence, of evil is perhaps best epitomized by the passage from Blanchot that I quoted earlier: "And how, in fact, can one accept not to know? We read books in Auschwitz. The wish of all in the camps, the last wish: know what has happened, do not forget, and at the same time never will you know."[4] Interrogating evil falls in the space between two extremes. We cannot give up the desire to know, to understand, to comprehend the evil we confront. If we did, we would never be able to decide how to respond to its manifestations. But we must avoid the extreme of deluding ourselves that *total* comprehension is possible. At the same time, we must also avoid the extreme of thinking that because there are limits to comprehension, because we experience the incomprehensibility of the most extreme forms of evil, we must remain silent before it. Total comprehension *or* complete silence is a specious dichotomy. There is a place for silence – a silence that reveals more than any conceptualization – but it comes only at those moments when we most directly experience the limits of comprehension.

4. Evil resists all attempts to justify it; it resists theodicy. I here use "theodicy" in the broad sense described by Levinas, where it may take either a religious or a secular form. We may seek to justify and reconcile the existence of evil with the religious faith in a benevolent God. Or we may seek to justify evil by showing that it is a necessary moment in the development of humanity. Both are varieties of theodicy. I agree with Nietzsche and Levinas that the true purpose of any theodicy is to find a "justification" for unbearable suffering. Nietzsche, more trenchantly than any other previous thinker, understood the psychological need to try to find some justification for suffering. It is not suffering *per se* that we find so unacceptable and offensive, but suffering that is utterly meaningless. Nietzsche's claims are closely allied to the Levinasian claim that, after Auschwitz, we must give up any idea of the "Happy End," the idea of some sort of ultimate cosmic harmony in which extreme evil and suffering have their proper place. After Auschwitz, it is obscene to continue to speak of evil and suffering as something to be justified by, or reconciled with, a benevolent cosmological scheme.

Hegel can be interpreted as the culmination of the Western philosophical and theological tradition of theodicy. This is true regardless of whether we emphasize the religious or the secular character of his thought. At the heart of his thinking was the dialectical development from finitude through the spurious infinite to the true infinite. This means that evil is a *necessary* moment in the actualization of Spirit. But to affirm that evil is a *necessary* moment in the development of Spirit is to *justify* evil. Beginning with Hegel's contemporary, Schelling, and in all the subsequent thinkers that I have interrogated – Nietzsche, Freud, Levinas, Jonas, and Arendt – there is a sharp critique of this Hegelian drive to an *Aufhebung* that heals the wounds of Spirit without leaving any scars. There are ruptures, breaks, wounds, abysses, and evils that are so profound that complete healing is impossible. There are wounds that do not heal, that cannot be sublated. There is *no* "After Auschwitz."

5. The temptation to reify evil must be avoided. This is the temptation to think that evil is a fixed ontological feature of the human condition, and there is nothing to be done except to learn to live with it and resign ourselves to its brute existence. This can lead to an overwhelming sense of pessimistic impotence when we are confronted with concrete evils. Ever since the early days of the Enlightenment, there has been an oscillation between utopian visions of a future, in which all evils are eliminated, and periods of disillusionment, when it is thought that attempts to combat evil are useless. There has been an alternation between grand narratives of moral progress and those of moral decline. We are living in a time – in part due to the horrors witnessed in the twentieth century – when vulgar and sophisticated declension narratives have become intellectually fashionable. But both extremes must be rejected. My criticism of Hegel's attempts to explain and justify evil notwithstanding, there is an important lesson to be learned from him – especially when we read Hegel against Hegel. For Hegel is perhaps the greatest critic of all attempts to reify evil – to ontologize evil in such a manner that we fail to appreciate the dynamic ways in which we can overcome specific concrete evils. Evil may be a "permanent" feature of the human condition, in the sense that there will always be new, concrete evils to be overcome and combated. In Hegelian terms, there will always be ruptures and diremptions that break out in the course of history and need to be overcome, but evil is not a fixed, static, existential condition of human life. Implicit (*an sich*) in the spurious infinite is the promise of the true infinite – even if we think (against Hegel) that this goal is regulative and never fully constitutive. Understanding evil in this way has important practical consequences. It means that when we are confronted with specific evils, whether they are ethical, social, or political, the challenge is always to search for ways to combat and eliminate them.

6. *The power of evil and the human propensity to commit evil deeds must not be underestimated.* We have seen that Kant firmly believed that it is always in our power to resist evil and to adopt good maxims (maxims in conformity with the moral law). At the same time he claimed that there is an inborn tendency, or propensity, to evil. In my critique of Kant, I argued that there are deep tensions in his analysis of the character of this propensity (*Hang*). There is a disparity between his intentions and the details of his analysis. My critique of Kant was directed to his *specific* understanding of this propensity, not to his *general* claim that there *is* such a propensity. Schelling perceived the source of these difficulties in Kant, and sought to provide a more adequate understanding of the *continuity* between causality and freedom. Schelling also emphasized the psychological power of the temptation to commit evil deeds, and thereby opened the way for a richer, more complex moral psychology than we find in Kant.

Nietzsche and Freud pursued this moral psychology of evil with much greater subtlety and finesse. Nietzsche's critique of morality is ultimately based on what he took to be the evil destructiveness of *ressentiment*, which he claimed, underlies our contemporary morality. In his account of how *ressentiment* originates and festers, he provided us with a warning about the dark side and dangers of modernity. But Nietzsche also held out the promise of the possibility of overcoming this morality of *ressentiment*, of imagining a new transvaluation of values. Freud's analysis of the dynamics of repression bears a close affinity with Nietzsche's understanding of "bad conscience," but there is also a major, consequential difference between Nietzsche and Freud. *Ressentiment* – or rather, the psychological truth that underlies *ressentiment* – is not just a dialectical stage in the historical development of human beings. It is an illusion to think that there ever was a time when psychological ambivalence did not exist or that there will ever be a time when it passes away. It is an illusion to think that there was a stage in history when aristocratic nobles did not experience repression, just as it is a dangerous illusion to think that there will be a time when it can be completely overcome. Of course, there are times in the life of individuals and societies when there are greater and lesser dangerous manifestations of repression. Freud rejected what might be labeled the "utopian" traces that still marked Nietzsche's thinking. It would be wrong to say that Freud was more "pessimistic"; it is more accurate and perceptive to speak of his psychological *realism*, which is a consequence of his ethic of honesty. The most important lesson to be learned from Freud concerns the depth and inescapability of psychological ambivalence – an ambivalence ultimately rooted in the unconscious. Freud's reflections on civilization and its discontents serve as a warning against the idea that as civilization develops, so this powerful psychic ambivalence decreases. On the contrary, civilization leads to greater repression and an increased sense of guilt. And Freud well understood how, as a consequence of this psychic ambivalence, we are always threatened by the possibility of destructive and self-destructive outbursts of repressed aggressiveness. This is the sense in which we must understand Freud's claim that: "In reality, there is no such thing as 'eradicating' evil." Freud is not making a philosophical claim about the ontological or existential condition of human beings. He is making a psychological claim about human beings based, on his clinical psychoanalytic investigations – one that reveals the threatening power of psychic ambivalence. Freud probes the moral psychological basis for what Kant *intended* when he spoke of the propensity to evil, and he helps us to better understand the sources of the power of this tendency – one which was already anticipated by Schelling and Nietzsche.

7. Radical evil is compatible with the banality of evil. I want to highlight one aspect – one thought-train – in Hannah Arendt's reflections on radical evil. Arendt affirmed that radical evil had emerged in connection with a system in which all men are equally superfluous, a system that makes human beings as *human* superfluous. "Superfluous" is perhaps not the most perspicuous term for expressing what she means, but the point she is making is insightful and sound. This becomes clear in her discussion of the "logic" of total domination, where she distinguishes three analytic stages – the killing of the juridical person, the killing of the moral person, and ultimately the attempt to eliminate any trace of human spontaneity, unpredictability, plurality, and individuality. Torture, humiliation, massacres, pogroms, sadistic orgies, even genocide, have had a long history. Arendt singles out something that was unprecedented – the systematic attempt to transform human beings so that they no longer exhibit the characteristics of a distinctively human life. "The concentration camps are the most consequential institution of totalitarian rule."[5] The concentration and the extermination camps of totalitarian regimes serve as the laboratories in which the fundamental belief of totalitarianism that everything is possible is being verified.

According to Kant, spontaneity is the most fundamental characteristic of human beings. Without spontaneity, there would be no rationality and no freedom. But Kant never really considered the possibility that spontaneity might be eliminated. Arendt does not disagree with Kant's understanding of spontaneity, but she claims that totalitarianism has shown us that this presumably "transcendental" condition of our humanity can be eliminated. "What totalitarian ideologies therefore aim at is not the transformation of the outside world or the revolutionizing transmutation of society, but the transformation of human nature itself."[6] This *new* possibility – the possibility of "radically" transforming human nature so that human beings become superfluous – does not disappear with the passing away of totalitarian regimes. It is an all too real possibility that remains with us. The expression "radical evil" is intended to designate what is distinctive about this evil of total domination. But this concept of radical evil (by itself) does not tell us anything about the motives or intentions of the perpetrators of radical evil. When Arendt introduced the notion of the banality of evil, she was concerned primarily with issues of intention and motivation – specifically the motivations of Adolf Eichmann. I have argued that, rather than displacing the concept of radical evil, the banality of evil *presupposes* it.

We must be more careful than Arendt was in speaking about the banality of evil. The banality of evil is a phenomenon exemplified by only *some* of the perpetrators of radical evil – desk murderers like Eichmann. Even if we set aside the controversial historical issue of the accuracy of her description of Eichmann, we should recognize her contribution to our contemporary understanding of evil. She is identifying a new, frightening aspect of twentieth-century evil. In our common moral discourse (as well as in the philosophical tradition) there has been a well-entrenched belief that those who commit evil deeds *must* have evil motives. The more evil the deeds, the more wicked are the motives. This is the belief that Arendt is critiquing. Individuals who are neither monsters, perverts, sadists, nor ideological fanatics, individuals who are motivated by little more than ambition, the desire to please their superiors and advance their careers, can – in the circumstances of totalitarianism – commit the most horrendous evil deeds. In a different society and in different historical circumstances, Eichmann might well have been an innocuous petty bureaucrat. Or, stated in a different way, perfectly ordinary people who are motivated by the most mundane desires can – in extraordinary circumstances – commit monstrous deeds. What is so frightening about the bureaucratic conditions of modernity is that they increase the potential for this sort of evil. And just as Arendt claims that radical evil remains a live possibility even after the end of totalitarian regimes, so this is true of the banality of evil.

8. *There is no escape from personal responsibility for committing evil deeds.* Throughout these interrogations we have seen an inextricable link between concepts of evil and concepts of responsibility. Kant's lasting contribution to moral discourse is his laudable, uncompromising position vis-à-vis our responsibility for moral evil. Our sensuous nature and our natural inclinations are not intrinsically evil. Neither is human reason corrupt in itself. Evil always comes back to *willing* evil. And, according to Kant, it is always within our power to choose between evil and good maxims. Kant never considered the type of case that Arendt mentions, of the mother who was asked by the Nazis which of her three children should be murdered. Such cases might lead us to qualify Kant's rigorism. But, as Arendt herself points out, this extreme situation is one that arises in the systematic attempt to kill the moral person. The Kantian emphasis on personal responsibility and accountability is important at a time when it has become fashionable to undermine moral responsibility, to deny that there is an agent who bears responsibility, to find "excuses" for what we do – to say that we are only "cogs" in a system.

There are some critics and defenders of Freud who think that he undermines the concept of responsibility by showing that we are causally determined by unconscious motives over which we have no conscious control. But this is a serious misinterpretation of Freud and of psychoanalysis. It is certainly true that Freud shows that unconscious dynamics play a significant role in shaping our behavior, and that human reason – including what Kant called practical reason – is limited and fragile. It is also true that Freud (like Nietzsche) seeks to understand the psychological genealogy of our moral sense of guilt and responsibility. But Freud's investigations do not undermine the concept of responsibility. On the contrary, Freud enables us to gain a better understanding of personal responsibility. Like his Enlightenment predecessors, he is committed to exposing illusions in order to enable us to live freer, more humane, and more realistically responsible lives.

9. *Affirming personal responsibility is not enough: after Auschwitz, we must rethink the very meaning of responsibility.* Levinas, Jonas, and Arendt contribute to this rethinking of responsibility. Initially, it may seem that Levinas's understanding of responsibility flatly contradicts the Kantian concept of responsibility. Levinas characterizes his understanding of responsibility as heteronomy whereby we have a responsibility to and for the other (*l'autrui*) that is ethically prior to our freedom and autonomy. But he is not denying Kantian autonomy. Rather, he is seeking to show that this autonomy already presupposes a more fundamental commitment, an infinite responsibility to and for the other (*l'autrui*). Jonas contributes to a new understanding of responsibility when he draws the distinction between formal responsibility and substantive responsibility. Formal responsibility means being accountable for our deeds – which is the core of the Kantian idea of responsibility. But there is also substantive responsibility for particular persons and objects, which commits an agent to particular deeds concerning them. Employing Jonas's distinction between formal and substantive responsibility, we may say that Levinas wants to show that Kantian formal responsibility is based on our substantive responsibility to others. But for Jonas, our substantive responsibility goes beyond this; we have a responsibility to preserve the conditions for life (including the life of responsible human beings) on this planet. This is why a new ethic of responsibility is required. Jonas's myth about a suffering, becoming, caring, and limited God emphasizes the human responsibility we now bear to combat the type of radical evil epitomized by Auschwitz. The disgrace of Auschwitz is not to be blamed on an all-powerful deity. Arendt illuminates another aspect of personal responsibility that has become important "after Auschwitz." The shock that Arendt experienced and witnessed during the Nazi era was the widespread collapse of accepted civilized moral standards. In this she saw a rupture with tradition. Like Levinas and Jonas, she felt that we needed to raise the question of whether we have been duped by morality. She too was haunted by the question of ethical nihilism, not merely as a theoretical possibility but as an all too ominous reality. Totalitarianism revealed how effortlessly traditional ethical and moral habits and customs could be replaced and displaced by new habits and customs that not only permitted evil, but also encouraged it. The issue that obsessed Arendt was what human beings could rely on – in extreme limit situations – when all else failed. She was impressed by those few individuals who managed to avoid – or actively resisted evil – when everyone around them "tolerated" it. They had nothing to rely on except their own *judgment*. Arendt was drawn to Kant's *Critique of Judgment* because she felt that Kant's understanding of reflective judgment provided the basis for understanding this capacity to judge that was exercised in those critical

situations of coming face to face with evil. Although Kant was interested primarily in aesthetic judgment based on taste, Arendt argued that Kant's understanding of the faculty of judgment had important political and ethical consequences. Eichmann, she claimed, lacked the ability to think and to judge. The only notable characteristic that she could detect in Eichmann was something negative – not stupidity, but thoughtlessness and an inability to think and to judge. Arendt's reflections on thinking and its relation to judging were still very tentative and sketchy at the time of her death. She left us with many unanswered questions. But she opened a rich train of thought concerning judging and its relevance for understanding personal responsibility. In sum, Levinas, Jonas, and Arendt all contribute to rethinking the meaning of responsibility after Auschwitz.

10. *The ultimate ground for the choice between good and evil is inscrutable.* We initially encountered this thesis in Kant's reflections on radical evil, when he claimed that the ultimate subjective ground of the adoption of moral maxims is inscrutable. I consider this to be one of Kant's most profound and important insights about morality. I also think that everything that we have learned by "dwelling on the horrors" of the twentieth-century confirms and testifies to this "black hole." This is where we come face to face dramatically with the limits of any interrogation of radical evil. We seek to comprehend the meaning of evil, its varieties and vicissitudes. We want to know why it is that some individuals choose evil and others resist it. We want to know why some individuals adopt good maxims and others adopt evil maxims. There is much we can say about someone's background, training, education, character, circumstances, etc. The social disciplines and psychology all contribute to this understanding. But it never adds up to a *complete* explanation of why individuals make the choices they do. There is always a gap, a "black hole," in our accounts. We have learned "after Auschwitz" how insightful Kant was about the ultimate inscrutability of the moral choices that individuals make. In the final analysis, it is inscrutable why some individuals like Anton Schmidt were able to exercise the type of judgment required to resist evil. This inscrutability is – as Kant has taught us – at the core of what it means to be a free, responsible person.

Notes

Introduction

1 Hannah Arendt, "Nightmare and Flight," in *Hannah Arendt: Essays in Understanding, 1930–1954*, ed. Jerome Kohn (New York: Harcourt, Brace & Co., 1994), p. 134.

2 Hannah Arendt, "'What Remains? The Language Remains': A Conversation with Günter Gaus," in *Essays in Understanding*, p. 14.

3 Andrew Delbanco, *The Death of Satan* (New York: Farrar, Straus, and Giroux, 1995), p. 3.

4 *Hannah Arendt/Karl Jaspers: Correspondence 1926–1969*, ed. Lotte Kohler and Hans Saner (New York: Harcourt Brace Jovanovich, 1992), p. 69.

5 Emmanuel Levinas, "Useless Suffering," in *The Provocation of Levinas: Rethinking the Other*, ed. Robert Bernasconi and David Wood (London: Routledge, 1988), p. 163.

6 Ibid., p. 162.

7 See chapter 7, "From Radical Evil to the Banality of Evil: From Superfluousness to Thoughtlessness," and chapter 8, "Evil, Thinking, and Judging," in Richard J. Bernstein. *Hannah Arendt and the Jewish Question* (Cambridge: Polity, 1996).

8 An English translation of this essay is published as an appendix to Michael Despland, *Kant on History and Religion* (Montreal: McGill–Queen's University Press, 1973).

9 Hans Jonas, *The Imperative of Responsibility: In Search of an Ethics for the Technological Age* (Chicago: University of Chicago Press, 1984), p. 27.

10 Emmanuel Levinas, "Transcendence and Evil," tr. A. Lingis. In *The Phenemenology of Man and of the Human Condition*, ed. A-T. Tymieniecka, Analecta Husserliana, 14, (Dordrecht: D. Reidel, 1983), p. 158.

Chapter 1   Radical Evil: Kant at War with Himself

1   Hannah Arendt, *The Origins of Totalitarianism*, 3rd edn revised (New York: Harcourt Brace Jovanovich, 1968), p. 459; Hannah Arendt, *Essays in Understanding, 1930–54*, ed. Jerome Kohn (New York: Harcourt Brace & Co., 1994), p. 14.

2   T. M. Greene and H. H. Hudson translate *Die Religion innerhalb der Grenzen der blossen Vernunft* as "Religion within the Limits of Reason Alone." In the new *Cambridge Edition of the Works of Immanuel Kant*, George di Giovanni translates the title in a more literal manner, "Religion within the Boundaries of Mere Reason." My references are to the Greene and Hudson translation, which is still the standard one. This edition contains an Introduction by John R. Silber, "The Ethical Significance of Kant's Religion." References to this translation (*Rel.*) are followed by page numbers in *Die Religion innerhalb der Grenzen der blossen Vernunft*, ed. Karl Vorländer (Hamburg: Felix Meiner Verlag, 1990).

3   See the discussion of Reinhold's criticism of Kant (and a similar recent criticism by Gerald Prauss) in Henry E. Allison, *Kant's Theory of Freedom* (Cambridge: Cambridge University Press, 1990), pp. 133–6.

4   Kant sometimes uses the word *Wille* in a broad sense and sometimes in a narrow, more technical sense. When used broadly, it refers to the entire faculty of volition. In the narrow, more technical sense, it refers exclusively to the norm – the moral law – that is the incentive for our free choice [*Willkür*]. For a discussion of the *Wille/ Willkür* distinction, see Allison, *Kant's Theory of Freedom*, pp. 129–36; also Silber's "Ethical Significance of Kant's Religion," pp. xciv–cvi. I have followed the procedure of always adding the appropriate German word to the English translation in order to indicate clearly when Kant uses *Wille* and *Willkür*. For a discussion of the English translations of these terms (and their cognates) see Ralf Meerbote, "*Wille* and *Willkür* in Kant's Theory of Action," in *Interpreting Kant*, ed. Moltke S. Gram (Iowa City: University of Iowa Press, 1982), pp. 69–89.

5   For a discussion of what Allison calls the "Incorporation Thesis," see Allison, *Kant's Theory of Freedom*, pp. 5–6.

6   Ibid., p. 129.

7   Silber, "Ethical Significance of Kant's Religion," p. civ. Such expressions as "strong," "strong enough," and "pressure" can be misleading insofar as they suggest a (natural) causal efficacy. For Kant the *Wille* as the "law of freedom" can be a sufficient *rational* incentive for adopting a good maxim. See also Yirmiyahu Yovel's discussion of the relation of *Wille* and *Willkür* in "Kant's Practical Reason as Will: Interest, Recognition, Judgment, and Choice," *Review of Metaphysics*, 52/3 (1998), pp. 267–94. Yovel writes: "because *Wille* spells out the structure and terms of autonomy, it sets the conditions for coherent self-determination to take place, as opposed to the vacuous and incoherent form implied in *Willkür*. This gives *Wille* normative priority, but also vindicates *Willkür's* role, because one of the main conditions for genuine

self-determination is *Willkür's* activity at the base. *Wille* must serve to universalize *Willkür* and thereby transform (and realize it), but never to discard or replace it. . . . Coherent self-determination requires the free act of choosing, personalizing, and self-universalizing performed by *Willkür*, no less than the universal structure implied in *Wille*" (pp. 292–3).

8	Yovel, "Kant's Practical Reason as Will," p. 281.

9	Allen W. Wood, *Kant's Moral Religion* (Ithaca, N.Y.: Cornell University Press, 1970), p. 211.

10	Christine Korsgaard, *Creating the Kingdom of Ends* (Cambridge: Cambridge University Press, 1996), pp. 55–67. I have used her translations of Kant's *Groundwork.*

11	Ibid., p. 55.

12	Ibid., p. 58.

13	Ibid., p. 60.

14	According to this "rigorist" analysis, Kant would not hesitate to condemn those philosophers from Hume to Annette Baier to Richard Rorty who argue that in moral situations we *ought* to be guided by our sense of benevolence and our sympathy for our fellow human beings. They are not simply misguided; they are recommending the adoption of evil maxims.

15	Allison, *Kant's Theory of Freedom*, pp. 147–8.

16	Several of Kant's contemporaries (including Goethe and Schiller) were extremely critical of Kant's introduction of the concept of radical evil. They took it to be a misguided concession to Christian orthodoxy. Schiller called Kant's essay on radical evil "scandalous," and Goethe wrote: "Kant required a lifetime to purify his philosophical mantle of many impurities and prejudices. And now he has wantonly tainted it with the shameful stain of radical evil, in order that Christians too might be attracted to kiss its hem." For these references and a discussion of these criticisms, see Emile Fackenheim, "Kant and Radical Evil," *University of Toronto Quarterly*, 23 (1954), p. 340.

17	Arendt, *Origins of Totalitarianism*, p. 459.

18	Ibid. For an analysis of what Arendt means by "radical evil," see pp. 209–17 below.

19	Silber, "The Ethical Significance of Kant's Religion," p. xcvii.

20	Korsgaard, *Creating the Kingdom of Ends*, p. 160. See also Henry E. Allison, *Kant's Transcendental Idealism* (New Haven: Yale University Press, 1983); and Wood, *Kant's Moral Religion.*

21	Wood, *Kant's Moral Religion*, pp. 210–11.

22	It is very difficult to find proper English equivalents for Kant's German expressions: *Gesinnung*, and *Hang*, and *Anlage*. These expressions have been translated, respectively, as "disposition," "propensity," and "predisposition". But the differences among these concepts are absolutely crucial for understanding radical evil.

23	Silber, "Ethical Significance of Kant's Religion," p. cxv.

24	Ibid., p. cxxvii.

25	See Daniel O'Connor, "Good and Evil Dispositions," *Kant-Studien*, 76 (1985), pp. 288–302. O'Connor brings out many of the tensions and difficulties in

Kant's analysis of *Gesinnung* and its relevance for understanding evil. I am in basic agreement with him when he writes: "There is something odd about Kant's whole discussion of evil, for even if we accepted Kant's contradictory notion of an evil disposition which is freely chosen outside of time, we would by his own admission gain nothing in the way of understanding. 'The rational origin of the perversion of the will . . . remains inscrutable to us, because this propensity itself must be set down to our account and because, as a result, that ultimate ground of all maxims would in turn involve the adoption of an evil maxim [as its basis]'" (p. 299). See Allison, *Kant's Theory of Freedom*, pp. 136–45, where he attempts to answer O'Connor's criticisms and to give a plausible account of *Gesinnung*. See also Gordon E. Michalson Jr's helpful discussion of the difficulties and instabilities in Kant's understanding of radical evil as an innate propensity, in *Fallen Freedom* (Cambridge: Cambridge University Press, 1990), pp. 40–51 and 62–70.

26   Here we touch upon one of the most complex and intensely controversial topics in Kant scholarship: the precise meaning and role of maxims. Here I simply want to note that in the *Religion*, Kant clearly commits himself to the idea of a hierarchy of maxims – to the idea of a "supreme maxim" that somehow governs more specific maxims. This raises the difficult issue concerning the precise relation between these different levels of maxims. If all maxims are freely chosen, if they are manifestations of the "exercise of freedom," then the precise relation between a supreme maxim and the more specific maxims that it presumably governs is not entirely clear. Radical evil is a "corrupt propensity" – that is, a supreme maxim that corrupts more specific maxims – but it is not clear precisely how this corruption manifests itself. How does one freely chosen maxim (no matter how supreme or ultimate it may be) corrupt another freely chosen maxim? For discussions of the meaning and role of maxims, see Allison, *Kant's Theory of Freedom*; Onora O'Neill, *Acting on Principle: An Essay on Kantian Ethics* (New York: Columbia University Press, 1975); *idem*, "Kant After Virtue," *Inquiry*, 26 (1983), pp. 387–405; *idem*, "Universal Laws and Ends in Themselves," *Monist*, 73 (1989), pp. 341–61; Barbara Herman, *The Practice of Moral Judgment* (Cambridge, Mass.: Harvard University Press, 1993); and Christine Korsgaard, *Creating the Kingdom of Ends*.

27   Although Yovel gives a helpful description of *Gesinnung*, which is compatible with my interpretation, he does not explain the disparity (and asymmetry) between *Gesinnung* and *Hang*. He writes: "Kant in the *Religion* distinguishes two kinds of choice: singular and long-term. The first is involved in ordinary, one-time acts, and the second stands at their base, as a global moral life-strategy, which Kant calls 'disposition' (*Gesinnung*). The latter is the ground (always non-deterministic) of one-time choices. In acting from that disposition, my new one-time choice ratifies and, in a certain sense, re-enacts the original global choice. . . . The originary choice which sets up the global disposition is the true 'inscrutable' in Kant" (Yovel, "Kant's Practical Reason as Will," p. 283). But if one accepts this understanding of *Gesinnung* whereby the originary choice is the true "inscrutable," then one ought to be

committed to a complete symmetry where there is an "originary choice" between good and evil dispositions.

28 I do not consider it appropriate to either ignore or exaggerate Kant's prejudices. Kant, who always insisted on public criticism, would expect one to expose unfounded prejudices – even when he himself expresses them. He does not give any evidence for his claim that "all savage peoples have a propensity for intoxicants." He seems to think it an obvious truth. A careful reading of the *Religion* shows how he exhibits numerous anthropological and religious prejudices, some of which are very damaging. Kant displays his ignorance of, and prejudice about, religions other than Christianity when he claims that the Christian religion is the one true natural and learned religion: i.e., the religion that possesses "the prime essential of the true church, namely the qualification for universality" (*Rel.* 145; 175). Furthermore, he declares that "of all the public religions that have ever existed, the Christian alone is moral" (*Rel.* 47; 57).

29 One might think that although the *Willkür* is not determined, it is at least influenced by the propensity to evil. No doubt Kant sometimes seems to be saying this. But if "influenced" means "causally influenced," then this suggestion is incompatible with Kant's understanding of freedom and free choice (*Willkür*).

30 Sharon Anderson-Gold, in her discussion of radical evil, says: "there is a certain parallel between Kant's concept of radical evil and Hannah Arendt's concept of 'banal' evil in *Eichmann in Jerusalem* . . . although Arendt would not treat evil as a species character" ("Kant's Rejection of Devilishness: The Limits of Human Volition," *Idealistic Studies*, 14 (1984), p. 48, n. 30).

31 In the litany of examples that Kant gives to show why we do *not* need a formal proof that "man is evil by nature," we once again find evidence of his prejudices, based upon limited and highly selective anthropological sources.

> If we wish to draw examples from the state in which various philosophers hoped preeminently to discover the natural goodness of human nature, namely from the so-called state of nature, we need but compare with this the hypothesis the scenes of unprovoked cruelty in the murder-dramas enacted in Tofoa, New Zealand, and in the Navigator Islands, and the unending cruelty (of which Captain Hearne tells) in the wide wastes of northwestern America, cruelty from which, indeed, not a soul reaps the smallest benefit, and we have vices of barbarity more than sufficient to draw us from such an opinion. (*Rel.* 28; 34)

32 Allison, *Kant's Theory of Freedom*, p. 154. I have several problems with Allison's attempt to justify – that is, to give a deduction of – what he characterizes as the *synthetic a priori* postulate that human beings are radically evil. There is not the slightest indication that Kant himself ever thought that such a deduction was necessary or even possible. Of course, there can be no objection to trying to improve upon Kant, as long as we recognize that this is not what Kant says or implies. Turning to Allison's attempted proof, he tells us that "the key to this deduction is the impossibility of attributing a propensity to good to finite,

sensuously affected agents such as ourselves (either to the race as a whole or to particular individuals)" (p. 155). But, given the way in which Kant understands a propensity (*Hang*), I fail to find Allison's reasoning persuasive. If a propensity is a supreme maxim, "a subjective determining ground of the will" that "springs from our freedom," then why can't there be a propensity to good? After all, possessing such a propensity does not mean that we will become morally good unless we deliberately adopt good maxims in specific circumstances, just as the propensity to evil does not mean that we will actually become evil unless we adopt specific evil maxims. This reinforces a point I made earlier. Kant frequently reiterates that a disposition (*Gesinnung*) may be good or evil, but he does not explain why a propensity (*Hang*) is only a propensity towards evil. Daniel O'Connor, in his critique of Kant, also asks: "Why not a propensity towards good?" He says, "The lack of symmetry in the two aspects of moral motivation must arouse suspicions about the very notion of a moral propensity" ("Good and Evil Dispositions," p. 297).

There is an unresolved tension that runs through Kant's discussion of *Gesinnung* and *Hang*. When he discusses these concepts and draws upon empirical evidence, he himself suggests that there are good and evil characters, dispositions, and propensities. And this is what we would expect insofar as these terms are intended to designate features of our moral character for which we are responsible. But when Kant turns explicitly to radical evil as a propensity (*Hang*), he drops any suggestion of symmetry between good and bad propensities.

There is still another serious problem lurking here. Consider the following claims that Kant makes or implies: (a) radical evil is the propensity to moral evil; (b) this propensity is innate (*angeboren*) and universal in the human species; (c) this propensity "must spring from freedom" – i.e., from "the exercise of freedom whereby the supreme maxim . . . is adopted by the will [*Willkür*]." But these three claims entail what (on Kantian grounds) is an absurd – indeed, a self-contradictory – conclusion. All human beings (the human race or species) *necessarily* freely choose the propensity to moral evil.

33 John R. Silber, "Kant at Auschwitz," in *Proceedings of the Sixth International Kant Congress*, ed. Gerhard Funke and Thomas Seebohm (Washington, D.C.: Center for Advanced Research in Phenomenology and University Press of America, 1991), p. 180.

34 It is uncanny how close Eichmann came to getting Kant right. Before his actual trial, in an interview with Avner Less, the Israeli police interrogator, Eichmann said that he had done his duty according to the categorical imperative, "the demand by Kant I long assumed as my guiding principle. I fashioned my life according to this demand." At the trial, when Judge Raveh asked Eichmann what he meant by this statement, he replied: "That the basis of my will and the pattern of my life should be such that at all times I should be a universal example of lawfulness. This is what I more or less understood by it." Judge Raveh then asked, "Would you say, then, that your activities within the framework of the deportation of the Jews were consistent with Kant?" Eichmann then gave a very sophisticated Kantian answer. "No, certainly not. For I did not mean as I was living then, under the pressure of

a third party. When I talked of the categorical imperative, I was referring to the time when I was my own master, with a will and aspirations of my own, and not when I was under the domination of a supreme force." And he added, "Then I could not live in accordance with this principle [the categorical imperative]. But I could include in this principle the concept of obedience to authority. This I must do, for this authority was then responsible for what happened." These passages from Eichmann's testimony are cited and discussed by Silber in "Kant at Auschwitz."

35   Ibid., p. 185.
36   Ibid., p. 191.
37   Both these passages are cited by Silber, "Kant at Auschwitz," pp. 186, 189. See Silber's discussion of these and other closely related passages. See also Thomas Seebohm's discussion of Kant's uncompromising position in "Kant's Theory of Revolution," *Social Research*, 48/3 (Fall 1981), pp. 557–87. Hannah Arendt also discusses how Kant, despite his initial enthusiasm for the French Revolution, argues that there is never a right to revolution or rebellion. See her *Lectures on Kant's Political Philosophy*, ed. Ronald Beiner (Chicago: University of Chicago Press, 1982). See also her comments on Eichmann's appeal to Kant in *Eichmann in Jerusalem: A Report on the Banality of Evil*, 2nd edn. (New York: Viking Press, 1965), p. 136.
38   This assertion is from Kant's famous essay. "What is Enlightenment?," where he distinguishes between the public and the private use of one's reason: in *Practical Philosophy: The Cambridge Edition of the Works of Immanuel Kant* (Cambridge: Cambridge University Press, 1996), pp. 18–19.
39   When Kant argues that there is a duty to obey "a supreme lawmaking power," he is primarily concerned with civil society and its basis for legitimation. He was *not* dealing with a fanatical *Führer* who was a mass murderer.
40   Silber claims that "Kant's theory can comprehend the motivations of an Eichmann, a functionary whose efficiency and zeal were motivated almost entirely by careerist concerns, but it cannot illuminate the conduct of a Hitler" ("Kant at Auschwitz," p. 194).
41   Allison, *Kant's Theory of Freedom*, p. 310.
42   In this context, I am not questioning the status of this claim – one that is basic to Kant's moral philosophy. Kant, of course, is not making an empirical claim but an a priori claim. Nevertheless, I do think we should reflect on what Hannah Arendt says happened in Nazi Germany.

And just as the law in civilized countries assumes that the voice of conscience tells everybody "Thou shalt not kill," even though man's natural desires and inclinations may at times be murderous, so the law of Hitler's land demanded that the voice of conscience tell everybody: "Thou shalt kill," although the organizers of the massacres knew full well that murder is against the moral desires and inclinations of most people. Evil in the Third Reich had lost the quality by which most people recognize it – the quality of temptation. (Arendt, *Eichmann in Jerusalem*, p. 150)

43   Silber, "Kant at Auschwitz," pp. 198–9. In this passage, Silber seems to identify "the deliberate rejection of the moral law" with "knowingly doing evil for its own sake." But these need to be carefully distinguished, especially in light of Silber's claim that "Kant's ethics is inadequate to the understanding of Auschwitz." To say that Nazi leaders deliberately rejected the moral law does not entail that they knowingly did evil for its own sake. There is a danger here of ascribing to the Nazi leadership the type of "satanic greatness" that we sometimes ascribe to fictional characters, especially in Shakespeare and Dostoevsky. See my discussion of this in relation to Hannah Arendt's exchange with Karl Jaspers, p. 214 below.

44   Wood, *Kant's Moral Religion*, pp. 212–13.

45   Silber, "Ethical Significance of Kant's Religion," p. cxxix.

46   I think that Wood also obscures the basic issue that Silber is addressing when he writes: "Kant is sometimes criticized for rejecting the possibility of an impulse to evil in man, and inclination to rebel against the law or to disobey the law simply for the sake of disobedience" (*Kant's Moral Religion*, p. 212). If "impulse" and "inclination" are understood to refer to our sensuous nature, then, of course, there is not, and cannot be, a natural inclination to moral evil. Evil results only from an act of the will (*Willkür*). And (human) *Willkür* cannot be identified with (or reduced to) our sensuous nature. But Silber is not referring to a natural inclination or impulse, but rather to an incentive that is consciously adopted in an evil maxim. The brunt of Silber's criticism of Kant is that he fails to acknowledge that there can be such an incentive.

47   Sharon Anderson-Gold has also attempted to defend Kant against Silber's criticism. She does this by emphasizing that radical evil is a "species character." But insofar as Silber is concerned primarily with those individuals who become demonic or diabolical, I do not think she adequately meets his challenge. See Anderson-Gold, "Kant's Rejection of Devilishness."

48   The expression "radically free" is my term and not Kant's. But I am using "radical" here in the sense in which Kant uses it – as that which goes to the very root. *Willkür*, at its very root, is unconstrained free choice (including the choice to defy the moral law, and even the choice to do evil for its own sake).

49   Kant describes several different types of self-love, but these do not include the full range of nonmoral human incentives. (See *Rel.* 41; 49).

50   Consider the catalogue of evil incentives in Ivan Karamazov's diatribe that serves as a prelude to "The Grand Inquisitor" in *The Brothers Karamazov*. Many of the incidents he cites are based upon news clippings that Dostoevsky collected.

51   From a different perspective, Slavoj Žižek raises questions about Kant's restrictions on the types of incentive involved in the adoption of evil maxims and the performance of evil deeds. He also questions Kant's rejection of 'diabolical evil.' "By rejecting the hypothesis of 'diabolical' evil, Kant retreats from the ultimate paradox of radical Evil, from the uncanny domain of those acts which, although 'evil' as to their content, thoroughly fulfill the formal criteria of an ethical act. Such acts are not motivated by any pathological considerations, i.e. their sole motivating ground is Evil as a principle, which

is why they can involve the radical abrogation of one's pathological interests, up to the sacrifice of one's life" (Slavoj Žižek, *Tarrying with the Negative: Kant, Hegel, and the Critique of Ideology* (Durham, N.C.: Duke University Press, 1993), p. 95).

52　In the chapters dealing with Nietzsche and Freud, I will try to show the importance of a more complex (and darker) moral psychology for coming to grips with the problem of evil.

53　There is a reason why I have qualified this statement by saying, "*insofar* as humans have spontaneous free choice." When I examine Hannah Arendt's understanding of radical evil, we will see that she argues that it is this free spontaneity that totalitarian regimes seek to destroy in their victims.

Chapter 2　Hegel: The Healing of the Spirit?

1　For a detailed discussion of Hegel's speculative philosophy of religion, its historical background, and the controversy that it provoked, see Walter Jaeschke, *Reason in Religion: The Foundations of Hegel's Philosophy of Religion*, tr. J. M. Stewart and P. C. Hodgson (Berkeley: University of California Press, 1990).

2　See Stephen Crites's discussion of the conflicting interpretations of Hegel's conceptions of God and religion. The quotations from Stirling and Solomon come from Stephen Crites, *Dialectic and Gospel in the Development of Hegel's Thinking* (University Park: Pennsylvania State University Press, 1998), p. xvi.

3　For a history of the editing of Hegel's lectures, and the principles used in the reconstruction of the four sets thereof, see the "Editorial Introduction" to *Hegel's Lectures on the Philosophy of Religion*, ed. Peter C. Hodgson, 3 vols. (Berkeley: University of California Press, 1984–5). This introduction also contains a lucid analysis of the changes introduced in the different series of lectures. This three-volume edition includes English translations of the four lecture series. In addition, Hodgson has prepared a one-volume edition of the lectures of 1827: *Hegel's Lectures on the Philosophy of Religion: One-Volume Edition, The Lectures of 1827* (Berkeley: University of California Press, 1988). I refer to passages in both of these editions. I have drawn upon Hegel's own lecture manuscript, as well as on the different series of lectures. When I refer to passages in the comprehensive edition, I cite volume number followed by page number, for example, i. 77. When I refer to passages in the one-volume edition, I use the abbreviation *L* followed by the page number, for example, *L* 99. These English translations indicate the German sources for the reconstruction of these lectures.

4　For a discussion of the distinction between representation and thought, see "Hegel's Lecture Manuscript" (i. 247–52).

5　Harold Bloom, *Agon: Towards a Theory of Revisionism* (New York: Oxford University Press, 1982), p. viii.

6　Immanuel Kant, *Critique of Pure Reason*, tr. Norman Kemp Smith (New York: St Martin's Press, 1965), p. 29.

7 See the discussion of the finite and the infinite in Hegel's *Science of Logic*, tr. A. W. Miller (New York: Humanities Press, 1969), pp. 116–56. When I refer to the *Science of Logic*, I use the abbreviation *SL*.

8 In the *Science of Logic*, Hegel introduces a number of important distinctions concerning different types of reflection. See especially the first section of the second book, "The Doctrine of Essence" (*SL*, 389–478).

9 See Hans-Georg Gadamer, "Hegel's 'Inverted World,' " in *Hegel's Dialectic*, tr. P. Christopher Smith (New Haven: Yale University Press, 1971), pp. 35–53.

10 G. W. F. Hegel, *Phenomenology of Spirit*, tr. A. W. Miller (Oxford: Clarendon Press, 1977), p. 49. When I refer to *The Phenomenology of Spirit*, I use the abbreviation *PS*.

11 See the preface to the *Phenomenology*, where Hegel says that the life of Spirit "is not the life that shrinks from death and keeps itself untouched by devastation, but rather the life that endures it and maintains itself in it. . . . It is this power, not as something positive, which closes its eyes to the negative, as when we say of something that it is nothing or is false, and then, having done with it, turn away and pass on to something else; on the contrary, Spirit is this power only by looking the negative in the face, and tarrying with it" (*PS* 19).

12 The one factor that remains constant in the successive changes in Hegel's lecture series is the main division into "Concept of Religion," "Determinate Religion," and "Consummate Religion."

13 G. W. F. Hegel, *Lectures on the Philosophy of World History*, tr. H. B. Nisbet (Cambridge: Cambridge University Press, 1975), pp. 90–1.

14 We can also interpret this passage as an implicit criticism of Kant's doctrine of radical evil. According to Kant, there is an asymmetry between good and evil, in that he affirms that humanity is evil by nature ("Der Mensch ist von Nature böse"), but denies that humanity is (morally) good by nature.

15 Hodgson makes the following comment about the translation of *Erkenntnis*: "In deference to familiar biblical language . . . the term *Erkenntnis* is sometimes translated as 'knowledge' rather than as 'cognition.' For Hegel himself, 'cognition' is a particular form of 'knowing' (*Wissen*) to be distinguished from other such forms" (iii. 205).

16 See Stephen Crites's discussion of the fall in *Dialectic and Gospel*, pp. 501–4.

17 This is another example of Hegel's agonistic relationship with Kant. Hegel, like Kant, emphasizes the element of choice and will that is involved in evil, even though for Hegel there is a much more intimate relationship between will and knowledge. So both Hegel and Kant start from a similar starting point in their analyses of evil. But Hegel also maintains that Kant, who insists on a rigid distinction between the finite and the infinite, and who refuses to acknowledge the reconciliation brought about in the dialectical movement to the true infinite, actually *reifies* the precondition for evil.

18 Crites, *Dialectic and Gospel*, pp. 289–90.

19 See William Desmond's perceptive discussion of evil in *Beyond Hegel and Dialectic: Speculation, Cult, and Comedy* (Albany, NY: State University of New York Press, 1992), pp. 189–357. Desmond distinguishes three strains in Hegel's

discussion of evil: existential, logicist, and world-historicist. Desmond is extremely critical of Hegel's attempt to "justify" evil as a necessary stage in the development of spirit. More generally, he argues that evil *resists* the sublation of dialectical thought. He declares, that "Hegel's claim to systematic completeness stands or falls on how we understand evil" (p. 244). Desmond is also incisive in pointing out the ambiguities of Hegel's discussion of forgiveness and evil (see pp. 192–2; and 238–41).

20 For an overview of the various traditional attempts to reconcile the existence of evil with the existence of God, see Ronald M. Green, "Theodicy," in *Encyclopedia of Religion*, editor-in-chief Mircea Eliade (New York: Macmillan, 1987), vol. 14, pp. 430–41.

21 Jean Hippolyte, *Genesis and Structure in Hegel's Phenomenology of Spirit*, tr. S. Cheniak and J. Heckman (Evanston: Ill: Northwestern University Press, 1974), p. 190.

22 In the background here is another set of deep problems and ambiguities concerning the relation of temporality, history, and eternity. Right Hegelians focus on the aspect of eternity in Hegel's system, where Hegel's *Science of Logic* is taken to articulate the eternal structure of the *logos*. Left Hegelians tend to focus more on the dynamics of history and temporality, where the realization of spirit (or humanity) is seen as a strenuous and painful historical achievement. As one might suspect, Hegel thinks that a rigid distinction between temporality and eternity is another false dichotomy.

23 Hegel, *Lectures on the Philosophy of World History*, pp. 42–3.

24 Desmond, *Beyond Hegel and Dialectic*, p. 241.

25 This is the translation that appears in Hippolyte's *Genesis and Structure*, p. 525.

26 Ibid., p. 527.

27 Ibid.

28 Ibid. I do not know if Jean Améry, the survivor of Auschwitz and Nazi torture, was familiar with this passage from Hippolyte. But this is precisely what he is contesting and challenging in the passage cited as my second epigraph to this chapter.

29 Jürgen Habermas, *The Philosophical Discourse of Modernity* tr. Frederick Lawrence (Cambridge, Mass.: MIT Press and Cambridge, Polity, 1987) pp. 21–2.

30 Ibid., p. 21.

31 See below, pp. 168–74.

32 There are many other thinkers who question Hegel's understanding of sublation (*Aufhebung*), and reconciliation (*Versöhnung*) including Marx, Kierkegaard, Heidegger, Sartre, and Derrida, but Schelling was one of the first to do so.

33 Desmond, *Beyond Hegel and Dialectic*, pp. 222–3.

34 See my essay, "Reconciliation/Rupture," in *The New Constellation: The Ethical-Political Horizons of Modernity/Postmodernity* (Cambridge: Polity, 1991), pp. 293–322.

35 This reading of Hegel is very close to how Michel Foucault interprets Kant's essay "What is Enlightenment?" See my discussion of Foucault, in "Foucault: Critique as a Philosophic Ethos," in *New Constellation*, pp. 142–71.

36 See Bernstein, "Reconciliation/Rupture," p. 309.

Chapter 3   Schelling: The Metaphysics of Evil

1   My interpretation of Schelling is based primarily on his monograph *Philosophische Untersuchungen über das Wesen der menschlichen Freiheit und die damit zusammenhängenden Gegenstände*, published in 1809. A literal translation would be "Philosophical Investigations into the Nature of Human Freedom and Matters Connected Therewith." An English translation by James Gutmann was published in 1936 entitled *Schelling: Of Human Freedom* (Chicago: Open Court Publishing Co.). A more recent translation by Priscilla Hayden-Roy is included in *Philosophy of German Idealism*, ed. Ernst Behler (New York: Continuum, 1987). I have used the Gutmann translation because it is more widely known, includes page references to the standard German edition of Schelling's works, and also contains helpful notes by the translator. Occasionally, I have altered this translation. I signal my changes by placing them in curly brackets. Words and phrases in square brackets are those added by Gutmann. Page references in the text are to the Gutmann translation (abbreviated *HF*). I have also included the corresponding page numbers in the recent German text, *Philosophische Untersuchungen über das Wesen der menschlichen Freiheit und die damit zusammenhängenden Gegenstände*, ed. T. Buchheim (Hamburg: Felix Meiner Verlag, 1997).

In the summer semester of 1936, Martin Heidegger gave a lecture course on this work. A transcription of this lecture course was later published, entitled *Schelling: Abhandlung über das Wesen der menschlichen Freiheit* (Tübingen: Max Niemeyer Verlag, 1971). An English translation of this edition by Joan Stambaugh was subsequently published with the title *Schelling's Treatise on the Essence of Human Freedom* (Athens, Oh: Ohio University Press, 1985). All page references to Heidegger's lectures are indicated by the abbreviation *ST* followed by page numbers in the English translation then page numbers in the 1971 German text. A more recent German edition with some emendations and corrections has been published in Heidegger's *Gesamtausgabe, Schelling: vom Wesen der menschlichen Freiheit (1809)* (Frankfurt am Main: Vittorio Klostermann, 1988). Although Heidegger's lectures focus on themes that are close to his own philosophical thinking, they are extremely illuminating in demonstrating the novelty and power of Schelling's investigation of freedom and evil.

2   See Heidegger's discussion of the meaning of "system" and the idea of a "system of freedom" in *ST*, 22–42; 27–50.

3   In the final analysis, Schelling is also haunted by the specter of theodicy. He wants to reconcile the ontological *reality* of evil with the existence of the Christian God. Nevertheless there is a subtle but crucial difference between Schelling and Hegel. Hegel also affirms the reality of evil, and insofar as evil (as self-diremption) is ascribed to God, Hegel ascribes evil to "infinite Substance." But Hegel, unlike Schelling, maintains that evil is a *moment*, a stage in the dialectical development of Spirit. This is just where Schelling digs in and challenges him. According to Schelling, there is something specious

about the way in which Hegel affirms *and* denies the brute reality of evil. Schelling is laying the groundwork for what in his late philosophy became a full-scale critique of Hegel, a critique that rejects Hegel's understanding of the dialectical activity of Spirit such that there is sublation of all diremptions.

4   See Gutmann's discussion of disputes concerning how many periods should be distinguished in Schelling's philosophical development in the introduction to his translation (*HF*, xxvii–xxix). Gutmann wrote his introduction in 1936; but these disputes about Schelling's shifts of emphasis and development have persisted right up to the present.

5   A list of the relevant publications of Dieter Henrich and Manfred Frank is contained in the bibliography of Andrew Bowie's book; *Schelling and Modern European Philosophy: An Introduction* (London: Routledge, 1993), pp. 204–7. Bowie's bibliography also lists many of the best recent discussions of Schelling. Bowie has been influenced by Frank, with whom he studied, and has sought to show the significance of Schelling for contemporary philosophy. See also Alan White, *Schelling: Introduction to the System of Freedom* (New Haven: Yale University Press, 1983); Peter Dews, *The Limits of Disenchantment* (London: Verso, 1995); and Slavoj Žižek, *The Indivisible Remainder: An Essay on Schelling and Related Matters* (London: Verso, l996). Recent interpretations of Schelling in English have been facilitated by some excellent translations in the series, Texts in German Philosophy published by Cambridge University Press. These include *F. W. J. Schelling, Ideas for a Philosophy of Nature*, tr. E. E. Harris and P. Heath, with an introduction by R. Stern (Cambridge: Cambridge University Press, 1988); and, F. W. J. von Schelling, *On the History of Modern Philosophy* (Cambridge: Cambridge University Press, 1994). For a very helpful discussion of the philosophical disputes that set the context for Schelling's philosophy, see Frederick C. Beiser, *The Fate of Reason: German Philosophy from Kant to Fichte* (Cambridge, Mass.: Harvard University Press, 1987).

6   See chapter 6, "Schelling or Hegel?," in Bowie, *Schelling and Modern European Philosophy*, pp. 127–91. See also Heidegger's brief discussion of Schelling and Hegel (*ST* 12–13: 14–16).

7   In his preface, Schelling tells us that the "old contrast" between nature and spirit has been dislodged, and he declares "that the time has come for the higher distinction or, rather, for the real contrast, to be made manifest, the contrast between Necessity and Freedom, in which alone the innermost center of philosophy comes to view" (*HF* 3; 3).

8   Although there are many unresolved difficulties in the way in which Schelling sought to work out the details of his "higher realism," nevertheless his project of developing an enriched, nonreductive naturalism bears a strong family resemblance to the nonreductive naturalism of John Dewey and other classic American philosophers. Even more striking are the affinities between Schelling's project and the enriched naturalism based on the idea of a second nature that has been advanced by John McDowell. McDowell, like Schelling, wants to rethink the idea of nature so that it is compatible with the Kantian idea of spontaneity. Schelling decries what he takes to be a dead, mechanistic idea of nature. And McDowell thinks that we must reject the disenchanted concep-

tion of nature that has been so prominent in modern philosophy. Both
Schelling and McDowell reject what McDowell calls "bald naturalism."
Schelling would certainly endorse McDowell's suggestion that: "If we can
rethink our conception of nature so as to make room for spontaneity . . . we
shall by the same token be rethinking our conception of what it takes for a
position to deserve to be called 'naturalism' " (John McDowell, *Mind and
World* (Cambridge, Mass.: Harvard University Press, 1994), p. 77). I do not
want to exaggerate the similarities between Schelling and McDowell, because their differences are as philosophically significant as anything they
have in common. Furthermore, they both have to confront numerous serious
obstacles in working out the details of such an enriched, nonreductive naturalism. My primary point in drawing the comparison is to warn against a
dismissive attitude towards Schelling's project of a philosophy of nature.

Schelling is both fascinating and frustrating because of his naturalistic
(even materialistic) and theological (even theosophical) resonances. Given his
basic conviction that there is an ultimate unity between living nature and
embodied spirit in his higher system of realism, we can understand the
source of this double character of his work. It is this Janus-faced character of
his writings that invites the most diverse interpretations. For an imaginative
and provocative reading of Schelling as a materialist thinker see Slavoj Žižek,
The Indivisible Remainder. Žižek himself emphasizes that his "dialectical materialist" interpretation cannot be divorced from the "theosophico-mytho-
logical" aspects of Schelling's system.

9 See Bowie's discussion of the controversies surrounding pantheism and
Spinozism in *Schelling and Modern Philosophy*, pp. 15–29. See also Heidegger's
discussion of Schelling's interpretation of pantheism (*ST* 62–90).

10 Heidegger offers the following explication of the meaning of these fundamental expressions; "being," "ground," and "existence":

> "Being" [*Wesen*] is not meant here in the sense of the "essence" of a thing, but
> in the sense in which we speak of a "living being," of "household affairs," of
> "educational matters." What is meant is the individual, self-contained being as a
> whole. In every being of this kind, we must distinguish its "ground" and its "exist-
> ence." This means that beings must be comprehended as existing and as ground-
> giving.
>
> "Ground" [*Grund*] always means for Schelling foundation, substratum, "basis,"
> thus not "ground" in the sense of "ratio," not with the counter concept "conse-
> quence" insofar as the *ratio* says why a statement is true or not true. "Ground" is
> for Schelling precisely the nonrational. On the other hand, however, we must
> avoid throwing this ground into the primeval swamp of the so-called irrational.
>
> "Existence" [*Existenz*] does not really mean the manner of Being; but, rather,
> beings themselves in a certain regard – as existing; as we speak of a dubious
> "existence" and mean the existing person himself. Schelling uses the word exist-
> ence in a sense which is closer to the literal etymological sense than the usual long
> prevalent meaning of "existing" as objective presence. Existence, *what emerges from
> itself* and in *emerging reveals itself*. (*ST* 107; 129)

Schelling does not make a systematic distinction between *Sein* and *Wesen*. Depending on the context, Stambaugh sometimes translates *Wesen* as "essence," sometimes as "being." Heidegger insists on following Schelling's archaic spelling of *Seyn*. Throughout his lectures he speaks of *Seyn* and the *Seynsfrage*.

11 For a discussion of the use of metaphors and analogies in Schelling, see Bowie, *Schelling and Modern European Philosophy*, pp. 5–11.

12 See Heidegger's discussion of Schelling's "anthropomorphic" language in *ST* 163–4; 194.

13 Schelling anticipates what will become of one of his major criticisms of Hegel. For Schelling will argue that the Hegelian conception of negation fuses together (and therefore systematically confuses) what must be carefully distinguished – the difference between differentiation and antithetical opposition.

14 The priority of ground to existence in God is neither a temporal nor merely a logical or conceptual priority. For a discussion of this priority as it relates to Schelling's understanding of eternity and temporality, as well as the sense in which "the Being of God is a *Becoming* to himself out of himself," see Heidegger, *ST* 112–18; 135–42.

15 At this point, I cannot help remarking that Heidegger, who shows his deep understanding of the movement of Schelling's questioning – and especially Schelling's understanding of the reality of evil – delivered these lectures in 1936, at a time when he was surrounded not merely by the possibility of evil, but by its reality. Yet, in the entire course of lectures (at least in their original *published* version) there is not a single reference to what was going on in Nazi Germany at the time.

16 Žižek, *The Indivisible Remainder*, p. 65. Žižek adds a perceptive footnote to this passage. He writes:

> In this respect Heidegger's procedure in *Being and Time* is the very opposite of Schelling's. Schelling . . . proposes an *'ethical'* *reading of ontology* (the very fact of reality, the fact that the universe exists, involves an ethical decision; it is proof that, in God, Good got the upper hand over Evil, expansion over contraction); whereas Heidegger is in the habit of taking a category whose 'ethical' connotation in our common language is indelible (guilt [*Schuld*], the opposition of 'authentic' and 'unauthentic' existence) and then depriving it of this connotation i.e. offering it as a neutral description of man's ontological predicament (*Schuld* as the designation of the fact that man, due to his finitude, has to opt for a limited set of possibilities, sacrificing all the others, etc.) (p. 88, n. 6).

Although Žižek makes this point with respect to *Being and Time*, the same point applies to Heidegger's lectures on Schelling. Schelling's own text, and especially his understanding of being, ground, and existence, are saturated with ethical connotations. Yet Heidegger not only de-emphasizes this aspect of Schelling's *Untersuchungen*, he mocks those who think that Schelling's understanding of freedom has anything to do with what is normally called "free will." It is certainly true that Schelling is placing the discussion of the essence of human freedom in a broader metaphysical context. But this does not mean that Schelling is screening out the ethical implications of his concerns. On the contrary, Schelling's approach to being, ground, existence, God, and human beings is saturated with an ethical orientation. In this respect, there is a greater affinity of Schelling with Franz Rosenzweig, and Emmanuel Levinas.

17 Later we shall see how a similar conception of the relation between God and human beings becomes central to Hans Jonas's speculations about God "after Auschwitz." Both Schelling and Jonas are influenced by the legacy of Kabbalistic sources whereby God *withdraws* in order to create the world and the creatures living within it. See my discussion of Jonas, pp. 194–9.

18 The distinction between ground and existence is applicable to all beings, including nonhuman animals, but it is only human beings who can *will* the dominance of ground over existence, darkness over light. "The dark principle is indeed effective in animals too, as in every other natural being; but in them it has not yet been born to light as in man, it is not *spirit* and understanding but blind passion and desire; in short no degeneration, no division of principles is possible here where there is as yet no absolute or personal unity" (*HF* 49; 44).

19 This quotation comes from notes that Heidegger prepared for an advanced Schelling seminar in the summer semester of 1941. It is included as an appendix to *ST*.

20 Žižek, *The Indivisible Remainder*, p. 61.

21 Ibid., p. 68.

22 Ibid., p. 64.

23 Ibid., pp. 64–5. Žižek adds the following footnote to this passage. "The clearest example, of course, was the good old 'totalitarian' Communist Party, which claimed to stand directly for the liberation of the whole of humanity (in contrast to all other political agents, who stood for narrow class interests); any attack on it equaled an attack on all that was progressive in the entire cumulative history of humankind" (p. 88).

24 See Vittorio Hösle, *Praktische Philosophie in der modernen Welt* (Munich: Beck, 1992), pp. 166–97.

25 Žižek, *The Indivisible Remainder*, p. 63.

26 See Heidegger's remarks about "anthropomorphism," and the other questions that need to be asked about it in *ST* 161–4; 194–8.

27 This has not always been so. Schelling had a major influence on Coleridge, who has even been accused of plagiarizing Schelling. Most of the classic American philosophers, including Peirce, James, Dewey, and Royce, were not only acquainted with Schelling, also considered him to be a major nineteenth-century philosopher.

Chapter 4   Nietzsche: Beyond Good and Evil?

1 Page references to *On the Genealogy of Morals* are the translation by Walter Kaufman and R. J. Hollingdale (New York: Vintage Books, 1979) abbrevi-

ated *G*. Page references to *Beyond Good and Evil* are to the translation by
Walter Kaufmann (New York: Vintage Books, 1989) abbreviated *BGE*. These
references are followed by the page number of the German text in the
edition of *Nietzsche Werke* edited by Giorgio Colli and Mazzino Montinari.
Jenseits von Gut und Böse and *Zur Genealogie der Moral* are contained in Volume
vi (2) (Berlin: Walter de Gruyter & Co., 1968).

2 Page references are to the selections from *Ecce Homo* (abbreviated *EH*), published in the Kaufmann and Hollingdale edition of *Genealogy*.

3 For an illuminating analysis of Nietzsche's complex attitudes to the Jews, see
Yirmihayu Yovel, *Dark Riddle* (Cambridge: Polity, 1999).

4 The *Genealogy* is the most aesthetically coherent, musical book in Nietzsche's
corpus. As in a great Mozart opera, the preface serves as an overture, introducing the major themes of the work and anticipating the final denouement.
Like the overpowering, ominous notes of the final scene of *Don Giovanni*,
which are heard at the very beginning of the overture (the musical notes that
mark the Don's descent into the fires of hell), the final section of the *Genealogy*
brings us back to the beginning of Nietzsche's preface. Nietzsche subtly
introduces motifs that are developed throughout the three essays. These
essays, which are integrated with each other, can be heard as variations of
the same theme. The motif of *ressentiment*, introduced in section 10 of the first
essay, becomes dominant in the second essay, and returns again in the third
essay.

5 We can appreciate how closely related the *Genealogy* is to *Beyond Good and Evil*
when we realize that *Beyond Good and Evil* begins by raising the problem of the
value of truth, which structurally parallels the problem raised initially in the
Genealogy, the value of morality. These are not separate problems, but the
same problem approached from different perspectives. Just as he asks at the
beginning of the *Genealogy* whether the value judgments good/evil have hin-
dered or promoted human prosperity, so at the beginning of *Beyond Good and
Evil*, he asks, concerning the true/false distinction, "to what extent it is life-
promoting, life-preserving, perhaps even species-cultivating" (*BGE* 11; 21).
Nietzsche's master question concerning any set of value distinctions is whether
they are "life-enhancing" and "life-affirming."

6 "On the Uses and Disadvantages of History for Life," in *Untimely Meditations*,
tr. R. J. Hollingdale (Cambridge: Cambridge University Press, 1983), pp.
57–124. This essay is abbreviated UD.

7 For a detailed, informative account of these three kinds of history, how they
are related to each other, how each can be used and abused, see Peter
Berkowitz, *Nietzsche: The Ethics of an Immoralist* (Cambridge, Mass.: Harvard
University Press, 1995), pp. 25–43.

8 Ibid., pp. 37–8.

9 This is one of the many respects in which Nietzsche is very close to Hegel, a
philosopher with whom he is all too frequently contrasted. For a perceptive
exploration of the similarities between Nietzsche and Hegel (as well as their
differences), see Eliot L. Jurist, *Beyond Hegel and Nietzsche: Philosophy, Culture,
and Agency* (Cambridge, Mass.: MIT Press, 2000).

10   Typically, when Nietzsche uses the term "morality" (*Moralität*), he means the morality of good and evil (or some variation of it). Occasionally, he uses the term in a more general sense to refer to a comprehensive scheme of values. Thus, for example, in section 10 of the *Genealogy*, he says, that "every noble morality develops from a triumphant affirmation of itself" (*G* 36; 284); and in Section 202 of *Beyond Good and Evil*, he speaks of "*higher* moralities" (*BGE* 115; 126). As Peter Berkowitz notes, "although for the most part he uses the term 'morality' to designate forms of life he detests – as in Christian, democratic, herd, or slave morality – on occasion he uses 'morality' in the ordinary sense as a general category referring to comprehensive schemes of right conduct. The main point is that when Nietzsche attacks the '*moral* interpretation and significance of existence' . . . , when he seeks to determine the 'value of morality' . . . , when he declares war on Christianity because it has waged war against a 'higher type of man' by revaluing the 'supreme values of the spirit as something sinful' . . . , he speaks in the name of a higher morality or ethic, a particular vision of the best life" (*Nietzsche*, p. 48).

11   Although I am making use of some distinctions that Rorty introduces in *Contingency, Irony, and Solidarity*, I am not *endorsing* Rorty's use of these distinctions or his interpretation of Nietzsche. I suspect that Nietzsche would detest Rorty's democratic "liberal ironist," and would condemn him as a mere variation on the desperate ideology of the "last man" – the ideology that Nietzsche so scathingly condemns in *Zarathustra*.

12   The above quotations are from Richard Rorty, *Contingency, Irony, and Solidarity* (Cambridge: Cambridge University Press, 1989), p. 73.

13   Rorty's first condition is that the ironist "has radical and continuing doubts" about her own final vocabulary, because she has been impressed by other vocabularies; the second condition is that the ironist realizes that arguments put forth in her own vocabulary can neither "underwrite or dissolve these doubts." But Nietzsche doesn't seem to have "radical and continuing doubts" about his own final vocabulary, *except* in the sense that he affirms that great spirits are skeptics.

14   Rorty, *Contingency, Irony, and Solidarity*, p. 73.

15   Ibid., p. 74.

16   Ibid.

17   Ibid.

18   Harold Bloom's imaginative description of the "strong poet," and Rorty's extension of this idea to other strong thinkers, are appropriated from their readings of Nietzsche. See Harold Bloom, *The Anxiety of Influence* (Oxford: Oxford University Press, 1973), and Rorty's comments on Bloom in *Contingency, Irony, and Solidarity*, pp. 24–5.

19   For my own attempt to show what is wrong with this dichotomy: either objective rational foundations or self-defeating relativism, see Richard J. Bernstein, *Beyond Objectivism and Relativism* (Oxford: Basil Blackwell, 1983).

20   See Alexander Nehamas, *Nietzsche: Life as Literature* (Cambridge, Mass.: Harvard University Press, 1985) pp. 13–41.

21   Peter Berkowitz (in *Nietzsche*) makes a strong case for claiming that Nietzsche

is not a relativist; he shows that Nietzsche does not call into question the concepts of knowledge, truth and objectivity. On the contrary he challenges what he takes to be false understandings of knowledge, truth, and objectivity.

22   It almost seems as if Nietzsche is describing Shakespeare's Iago, who personifies the man of *ressentiment*.

23   It is striking how Nietzsche anticipates Freud's late theory of instincts – how when the energy of these instincts is not discharged, it is directed inward. This how Freud accounts for the internalization of the superego (which initially gains its power from external authority) and "sense of guilt." But we must also be sensitive to the differences between Nietzsche and Freud. The most important difference is that Nietzsche thinks of "bad conscience" as a characteristic of a specific class of individuals – men of *ressentiment* – whereas Freud thinks of the internalization of the superego and the development of a sense of guilt as universal characteristics of *all* human beings. Furthermore, Freud is quite emphatic in insisting that it is not possible for all instincts to discharge themselves outwardly. There is no escape from internalization and the development of a sense of guilt. In the next chapter, when I discuss Freud, we will see that the differences between Nietzsche and Freud concerning the dynamics of the instincts has significant consequences for their different perspectives on evil.

24   See Paul Ricoeur's account of the hermeneutics of suspicion in *Freud and Philosophy: An Essay in Interpretation* (New Haven: Yale University Press, 1970), pp. 20–35.

25   Nihilism can take a variety of forms, and Nietzsche distinguishes among them. See Stanley Rosen's discussion of nihilism in *The Mask of Enlightenment: Nietzsche's* Zarathustra (Cambridge: Cambridge University Press, 1995), especially his introduction.

26   In the German text there are no paragraph divisions, but Kaufmann's and Hollingdale's English paragraph divisions provide a convenient way of commenting on this final section.

27   Nietzsche also cannot resist taking a swipe at the Germany of his day when he adds the following parenthetical remark: "(that *no* kind of swindle fails to succeed in Germany today is connected with the undeniable and palpable stagnation of the German spirit; and the cause of that I seek in too exclusive a diet of newspapers, politics, beer, and Wagnerian music, together with the presuppositions of such a diet: first, national constriction and vanity, the strong but narrow principle '*Deutschland, Deutschland über alles*,'" and the *paralysis agitans* of 'modern ideas') (*G* 158–9; 425–6).

28   Hannah Arendt, some 60 years after the publication of the *Genealogy*, and after the tumultuous events of the first half of the twentieth century, invokes Nietzsche in her "Concluding Remarks" to *The Origins of Totalitarianism*, where she speaks of the dangers of resentment (with an obvious allusion to Nietzsche's *ressentiment*). She writes: "For the first disastrous result of man's coming of age is that modern man has come to resent everything given, even his own existence – to resent the very fact that he is not the creator of the universe and himself. In this fundamental resentment, he refuses to see rhyme or

reason in the given world. In his resentment of all laws merely given to him, he proclaims openly that everything is permitted and believes secretly that everything is possible. And since he knows that he is a law-creating being, and that his task, according to all standards of past history, is 'super-human', he resents even his nihilistic convictions, as though they were forced upon him by some cruel joke of the devil. (*Origins of Totalitarianism*, 1951 edn, p. 438).

Chapter 5   Freud: Ineradicable Evil and Ambivalence

1   Yovel, "Kant's Practical Reason as Will," p. 294.
2   See Philip Rieff, *Freud: The Mind of the Moralist* (New York: Viking Press, 1959), esp. ch. 9, "The Ethic of Honesty."
3   All references to Freud are to the *Standard Edition of the Complete Psychological Works of Sigmund Freud*, ed. J. Strachey (London: Hogarth Press, 1974), abbreviated *SE*. I give the volume and page number.
4   Ilse Grubrich-Simitis cites both of these passages in *Back to Freud's Texts: Making Silent Documents Speak* (New Haven: Yale University Press, 1996), p. 125. She adds: "But a more sober mood soon prevailed. 'I have retreated far from my initial high opinion of the work,' he told Ferenzi on 12 June, 'and am, on the whole, dubious about it'. A fortnight later, on 26 June: 'I consider the matter on the one hand too beautiful, but on the other hand, times and things are too obscure and to a certain extent beyond the pale of sure assessment'."
5   See A. L. Kroeber, "Totem and Taboo in Retrospect: An Ethnological Psychoanalysis," *American Anthropologist*, 22 (1939), pp. 48–55, for an overview of the criticisms of Freud. For a more recent assessment and critique, see Mario Erdheim's Introduction to *Totem und Tabu* (Frankfurt am Main: Fischer Taschenbuch Verlag, 1991), pp. 7–42.
6   After summarizing the basis for his claims about the primal horde, Freud writes:

> To this day I hold firmly to this construction. I have repeatedly met with violent reproaches for not having altered my opinions in later editions of my book [*Totem and Taboo*] in spite of the fact that more recent ethnologists have unanimously rejected Robertson Smith's hypotheses and have in part brought forward other, totally divergent theories. I may say in reply that these ostensible advances are well known to me. But I have not been convinced either of the correctness of these innovations or of Robertson Smith's errors. A denial is not a refutation, an innovation is not necessarily an advance. Above all, however, I am not an ethnologist but a psycho-analyst. I had a right to take out of ethnological literature what I might need for the work of analysis. (*SE* XXIII, 131)

For a detailed discussion of the relevance of *Totem and Taboo* for *Moses and Monotheism*, see my book, *Freud and the Legacy of Moses* (Cambridge: Cambridge University Press, 1998).

7   In a footnote to this passage, Freud acknowledges that his hypothesis has a
    "monstrous air." He also says: "The lack of precision in what I have written
    in the text above, its abbreviation of the time factor and its compression of
    the whole subject-matter, may be attributed to the reserve necessitated by
    the nature of the topic. It would be as foolish to aim at exactitude in such
    questions as it would be unfair to insist upon certainty" (*SE* XIII, 142–3).
8   Freud qualifies his myth of the primal horde by telling us that the murder of
    the primal father should not be interpreted as a single, datable event, but
    rather one that was repeated many times. He even entertains the possibility
    that such a murder never actually took place. "Accordingly, the mere hostile
    impulse against the father, the mere existence of a wishful *phantasy* of killing
    and devouring him, would have been enough to produce the moral reaction
    that created totemism and taboo. In this way we should avoid the necessity
    for deriving the origin of our cultural legacy, of which we justly feel so proud,
    from a hideous crime, revolting to all our feelings. No damage would thus be
    done to the causal chain stretching from the beginning to the present day,
    for psychical reality would be strong enough to bear the weight of these
    consequences" (*SE* XIII, 159–60). See my discussion of why Freud enter-
    tains, but finally rejects, this possibility in *Freud and the Legacy of Moses*, pp.
    101–3.
       Ilse Grubrich-Simitis notes that Freud did express doubts about the story
    of the primal horde and the murder of the father by the band of brothers.

> Throughout his life, however, Freud remained dubious as to whether his theory of
> the murder of the primal father and the constitution of the archaic heritage should
> be assigned any reality value. This vacillation is revealed by a number of emotive
> variants observable already in the fair copy of "The Return of Totemism in
> Childhood." Where the printed version refers to "the great primeval tragedy," the
> fair copy originally read as follows, before the author deleted and replaced the
> second adjective: "the great mythological tragedy." He thus seems to have clearly
> recognized, even if he was unwilling to admit it to himself, what Claude Lévi-
> Strauss has recently noted again: "With *Totem and Taboo* Freud constructed a
> myth, and a very beautiful myth too. But like all myths, it doesn't tell us how
> things really happened. It tells us how men need to imagine things happened so as
> to try to overcome contradictions." (*Back to Freud's Texts*, p. 173)

9   The solidarity of the band of brothers also has political significance for
    Freud. He even refers to "the original democratic equality that had prevailed
    among all the individual clansmen." But this democratic equality became
    untenable, "and there developed at the same time an inclination, based on
    veneration felt for particular human individuals, to revive the ancient pater-
    nal ideal by creating gods" (*SE* XIII, 148–9).
10 Although Freud typically explores group, social, and cultural phenomena by
    drawing upon his psychoanalytic understanding and clinical experience with
    individuals, he is also sensitive to important differences. He does not uncritically
    assume that what is characteristic of individuals can be generalized to apply

to groups and societies. Thus, for example, he concludes *Totem and Taboo* by examining some of the key differences between individual and social psychology (see *SE* XIII, 157–61).

11 Freud has frequently been criticized for his references to "savages" and "primitive people." But Freud does not refer to "primitive people" in order to demonstrate our superiority over them. Rather, his intention is to show that the psychic dynamics of individuals in "civilized" societies are actually quite close to those in "primitive" and "savage" tribes.

12 When Freud introduces his discussion of taboo, he writes:

> Why, it may be asked at this point, should we concern ourselves at all with this riddle of taboo? Not only, I think, because it is worthwhile trying to solve *any* psychological problem for its own sake, but for other reasons as well. It may begin to dawn on us that the taboos of the savage Polynesians are after all not so remote from us as we were inclined to think at first, that the moral and conventional prohibitions by which we ourselves are governed may have some essential relationship with these primitive taboos and that an explanation of taboo might throw a light upon the obscure origin of our own 'categorical imperative.' (*SE* XIII, 22)

In his preface to *Totem and Taboo*, Freud is even more explicit in suggesting a connection between primitive taboos and Kant's categorical imperative: "taboos still exist among us. Though expressed in a negative form and directed towards another subject-matter, they do not differ in their psychological nature from Kant's 'categorical imperative', which operates in a compulsive fashion and rejects any conscious motives" (*SE* XIII, p. xiv).

There is a significant parallel between Freud's investigation of taboo and Nietzsche's genealogy. Both of them are searching for the "origin" of the psychic dynamics of our present prohibitions and morality. Both invent "myths" about an archaic past to "explain" these origins. Yet the construction of these myths is guided by insights into the psychic dynamics of our present taboos.

13 J. Laplanche and J-B. Pontalis, *The Language of Psychoanalysis*, tr. D. Nicholson-Smith (New York: W.W. Norton, 1973), p. 26, emphasis added.

14 Ibid., p. 28.

15 C. Lévi-Strauss and D. Eribon, *De près et de loin* (Paris: Editions Odile Jacob, 1988). p. 150. See n. 8 above.

16 See my discussion of the distinction between material and historical truth in *Freud and the Legacy of Moses*, (pp. 66–74) where I write: " Despite appearances to the contrary, the primary evidence [for Freud's claims about historical truth] is not some real discovery that Freud has made about what happened in the *past*. It is rather his *present* psychoanalytic understanding of the unconscious dynamics of individuals that provides Freud with evidence that he has discovered the 'historical truth'" (p. 71).

In the 1935 postscript to his "Autobiographical Study," Freud makes it clear that his claims regarding the historical origins of religion and morality are based upon present psychoanalytic hypotheses.

My interest, after making a lifelong *detour* through the natural sciences, medicine and psychotherapy, returned to the cultural problems which had fascinated me long before, when I was a youth scarcely old enough for thinking. At the very climax of my psycho-analytic work, in 1912, I had already attempted in *Totem and Taboo* to make use of the newly discovered findings of analysis in order to investigate the origins of religion and morality . . . . I perceived ever more clearly that the events of human history, the interactions between human nature, cultural development, and the precipitates of primeval experiences (the most prominent example of which is religion) are no more than a reflection of the dynamic conflicts of the ego, the id and the super-ego, which psycho-analysis studies in the individual – are the very same processes repeated upon a wider stage. (*SE* XX, 72)

17 *Thanatos* is not a term that appears in Freud's writings, although it is reported that he used it in conversation to refer to the death instinct. For a concise analysis of the changes in Freud's theory of instincts and drives, see the editor's note to *Instincts and their Vicissitudes* (*SE* XIV, 111–16). See also the entries for "Instinct (or Drive)," "Life Instincts," and "Death Instincts," in Laplanche and Pontalis, *Language of Psychoanalysis*.

18 Many commentators have noted that the word "instinct" in the English translations of Freud is used to translate two different German words and two different concepts: *Instinkt* and *Trieb*. Although Freud vacillates between these two words, Jonathan Lear gives a helpful description of the major difference between them.

> An *Instinkt*, for Freud, is a rigid, innate behavioral pattern, characteristic of animal behavior: e.g., the innate ability and pressure of a bird to build a nest. It is the essence of an *Instinkt* that it could not have a vicissitude: the pattern of behavior that it fuels and directs is preformed and fixed. A *Trieb*, by contrast, has a certain plasticity: its aim and direction is to some extent shaped by experience. To conceive of humans as powered by *Triebe*, as Freud did, is in part to distinguish humanity from the rest of the animal world. (Jonathan Lear, *Love and its Place in Nature* (New York: Farrar, Straus & Giroux, 1990), pp. 123–4).

See also the discussion of *Instinkt* and *Trieb* in Laplanche and Pontalis, *Language of Psychoanalysis*, pp. 214–16. To avoid confusion, I have followed the *SE* practice of translating *Trieb* as "instinct." I want to emphasize that when I use the word "instinct" I am referring to what Freud calls *Trieb*.

19 Freud previously described a *Trieb* in a similar way on at least two other occasions. In his discussion of the Schreber case, "Psycho-analytic Notes on an Autobiographical Account of a Case of Paranoia," he writes: "We regard instinct [*Trieb*] as being a concept on the frontier-line between the somatic and the mental, and see in it the psychical representative of organic forces" (*SE* XII, 74). And in a passage added to the third edition of *Three Essays in Sexuality*, he speaks of a *Trieb* as "the psychical representative of an endosomatic, continuously flowing source of stimulation . . . . The concept of instinct [*Trieb*] is thus one of those lying on the frontier between the mental and the

physical . . . . What distinguishes the instincts [*Triebe*] from one another and endows them with specific qualities is their relation to their somatic sources and to their aims" (*SE* VII, 168).

20 An *Instinkt*, as a fixed pattern of behavior, does not have vicissitudes, even though it can be expressed in a variety of ways. For example, birds can instinctively build their nests in a great variety of ways and adapt themselves to local environmental conditions, but this variation is not to be identified with the plasticity of human *Triebe*.

21 See Paul Ricoeur's perceptive discussion of *Repräsentanz* in *Freud and Philosophy*, pp.134–51.

22 Laplanche and Pontalis, *Language of Psychoanalysis*, p. 216. The final sentence of this passage is a citation from the *New Introductory Lectures on Psychoanalysis* (*SE* XXII, 95).

23 For a provocative analysis of the meaning of speculation in Freud, see Jacques Derrida, "To Speculate – on Freud," in *The Post Card: From Socrates to Freud and Beyond*, tr. Alan Bass (Chicago: University of Chicago Press, 1987). For a contrasting analysis and evaluation of Freud's speculative audacity, see Paul Ricoeur, *Freud and Philosophy*, pp. 281–309.

24 Freud comments that what he is saying is "not even genuine Schopenhauer. We are not asserting that death is the only aim of life; we are not overlooking the fact that there is life as well as death. We recognize two basic instincts and give each of them its own aim. How the two of them are mingled in the process of living, how the death instinct is made to serve the purposes of Eros, especially by being turned outwards as aggressiveness – these are tasks which are left to future investigation" (*SE* XXII, 107).

25 Most practicing psychoanalysts are critical of Freud's postulation of the death instinct. For a recent criticism of the death instinct, see Jonathan Lear, *Happiness, Death, and the Remainder of Life* (Cambridge, Mass.: Harvard University Press, 2000).

26 In a footnote to this passage, Freud cites two passages from Faust to show that "in Goethe's Mephistopheles we have a quite exceptionally convincing identification of the principle of evil with the destructive instinct" (*SE* XXI, 120–1).

27 See the Editor's Introduction to *The Ego and the Id* (*SE* XIX, 3–11) for an explanation of Freud's reasons for introducing "his new account of the anatomy of the mind."

28 Freud is referring to the following passage from the conclusion of Kant's *Critique of Practical Reason*.

Two things fill the mind with ever new and increasing admiration and reverence, the more often and more steadily one reflects on them: the starry heavens above me and the moral law within me. . . . The first begins from the place I occupy in the external world of sense and extends the connection in which I stand in an unbounded magnitude with worlds upon worlds and systems of systems, and moreover into the unbounded times of their periodic motion, their beginning and their duration. The second begins from my invisible self, my personality, and presents me in a world which has true infinity but which can be discovered only by the understanding, and I cognize that my connection with the world (and thereby with all those visible worlds as well) is not merely contingent, as in the first case, but universal and necessary. (Immanuel Kant, *Critique of Practical Reason*, in *Cambridge Edition*, p. 269.)

29   In *The Ego and the Id*, Freud writes:

It is remarkable that the more a man checks his aggressiveness towards the exterior the more severe – that is, aggressive – he becomes in his ego ideal. The ordinary view sees the situation the other way round: the standard set up by the ego ideal seems to be the motive for the suppression of aggressiveness. The fact remains, however, as we have stated it: the more a man controls his aggressiveness, the more intense becomes his ideal's inclination to aggressiveness against his ego. (*SE* XIX, 54)

30   Arendt, *Eichmann in Jerusalem*, p. 150.
31   In *Eros and Civilization* (Boston: Beacon Press, 1955), Herbert Marcuse who accepts Freud's later theory of instincts as the battle between *Eros* and *Thanatos*, nevertheless challenges Freud's claim that the dynamics between the life and death instincts cannot be transformed. In this respect, Marcuse develops what can be interpreted as a Nietzschean critique of Freud. But Marcuse's challenge to Freud has its own problems. See my discussion of Marcuse, "Negativity: Theme and Variations," in *Philosophical Profiles* (Cambridge: Polity, 1986) pp. 176–96. For a sophisticated psychoanalytic critique of Marcuse see Joel Whitebook, *Perversion and Utopia: A Study of Psychoanalysis and Critical Theory* (Cambridge, Mass.: MIT Press, 1995), pp. 24–41.
32   Rieff, *Freud*, p. 62.
33   For the bibliographical history of this note, see the Editor's Introduction to "Some Additional Notes on Dream-Interpretations as a Whole" (*SE* XIX, 125–6).
34   Philip Rieff, *Freud*, pp. 70–1.
35   Freud's late essay "Analysis Terminable and Interminable" is frequently cited as evidence of Freud's skepticism about what can be achieved through psychoanalytic therapeutic treatment. But even here he affirms: "Our aim will not be . . . to demand that the person who has been 'thoroughly analysed' shall feel no passions and develop no internal conflicts. The business of the analysis is to secure the best possible psychological conditions for the functions of the ego; with that it has discharged its task" (*SE* XXIII, 250).
36   *The Future of an Illusion* is the book in which Freud identifies himself most explicitly with the Enlightenment commitment to reason and *Logos*. "We believe that it is possible for scientific work to gain some knowledge about the reality of the world, by means of which we can increase our power and in accordance with which we can arrange our life" (*SE* XXI, 55).
37   See *The Future of an Illusion* (*SE* XXI, 54–5), where Freud speaks of "Our God, Logos" and contrasts this with the God of the religious believer.

Prologue

1 Hannah Arendt, " 'What Remains? The Language Remains': A Conversation with Günter Gaus," in *Essays in Understanding, 1930–54* , pp. 13–14.
2 Saul Friedlander (ed.), *Probing the Limits of Representation: Nazism and the "Final Solution"* (Cambridge, Mass.: Harvard University Press, 1992), p. 3.

Chapter 6 Levinas: Evil and the Temptation of Theodicy

1 Jacques Derrida, "Violence and Metaphysics," in *Writing and Difference*, tr. Alan Bass (Chicago: University of Chicago Press, 1978), p. 312.
2 Emmanuel Levinas, *Totality and Infinity: An Essay on Exteriority*, tr. Alphonso Lingis (Pittsburgh: Duquesne University Press, 1969); *Totalité et infini: essai sur l'extériorité* (The Hague: Martinus Nijhoff, 1961). References are abbreviated *TI*, followed by the page number in the English edition, then the page number in the French edition. Levinas normally distinguishes *l'autre* from *l'autrui*. The former (*l'autre*) is used when he is speaking about the "other" in an abstract manner – for example, when he speaks about the dialectic of the same and the other. The latter (*l'autrui*) is used to refer to the personal other, the other human being. Levinas is not always consistent in his terminology, but from the context we can discern his meaning. Some English translators have sought to note this difference by capitalizing "Other" when it is used to translate *l'autrui*.
3 Levinas frequently uses the expressions "morality" and "ethics" interchangeably, although he prefers "ethics," which is derived from the Greek *ethos*. Sometimes he distinguishes ethics from morality, when he wants to distinguish ethics as first philosophy from the specific rules of morality.
4 "The Paradox of Morality: An Interview with Emmanuel Levinas," in *The Provocation of Levinas: Rethinking the Other*, ed. Robert Bernasconi and David Wood (London: Routledge, 1988), pp. 168–80. References to this interview are abbreviated PM, followed by the page number.
5 Hannah Arendt, "Some Questions of Moral Philosophy," *Social Research*, 61/4 (Winter 1994).
6 Hannah Arendt, *The Life of the Mind*, 2 vols (New York: Harcourt, Brace, Jovanovich, 1978), vol. 1, p. 5.
7 Levinas, "Useless Suffering." References to this article are abbreviated US, followed by the page number.
8 Kant, *Religion within the Limits of Reason Alone*, p. 3.
9 Nietzsche, *Genealogy of Morals*, p. 68.
10 Arendt, *Eichmann in Jerusalem*, p. 231.
11 Hans Jonas, "Epilogue: The Outcry of Mute Things" in *Mortality and Morality* p. 198.
12 Ibid., p. 199.
13 Ibid., p. 200.

14 Levinas, "Transcendence and Evil." References to this article are abbreviated TE, followed by the page number.
15 Arendt, *Origins of Totalitarianism*, 1968, 3rd edn, p. viii.
16 See my discussion of this logic of colonization, "Serious Play: The Ethical-Political Horizon of Jacques Derrida," in *New Constellation*, pp. 172–98.
17 For a lucid statement of Levinas's indebtedness and critique of Heidegger, see his interview with Richard Kearney in Richard Kearney, *Dialogues with Contemporary Continental Philosophers* (Manchester: Manchester University Press, 1984), pp. 49–69.
18 Ibid., p. 68.
19 Levinas, "Signature," in *Difficult Freedom*, tr. S. Hand (Baltimore: Johns Hopkins University Press, 1990), p. 291.
20 Maurice Blanchot, *The Writing of the Disaster*, tr. Ann Smock (Lincoln: University of Nebraska Press, 1986), p. 82. Carol L. Bernstein called this passage by Blanchot to my attention.

Chapter 7   Jonas: A New Ethic of Responsibility

1 Jonas typically speaks about metaphysics rather than ontology, but by "metaphysics" he does *not* mean what Levinas means when he uses the term. "Metaphysics" for Jonas is what Levinas calls "ontology," the study of Being.
2 Hans Jonas, "Heidegger's Resoluteness and Resolve," in *Martin Heidegger and National Socialism*, ed. G. Neske and E. Kettering, tr. L. Harries (New York: Paragon House, 1990), p. 197.
3 See Hannah Arendt, "For Martin Heidegger's Eightieth Birthday," reprinted in *Martin Heidegger and National Socialism*, pp. 207–18. For my critique of Arendt, see my article, "Heidegger's Silence?," in *New Constellation*, p. 81.
4 Jonas, "Heidegger's Resoluteness and Resolve," pp. 200–1. In one of his last public lectures Jonas repeats his disillusionment with Heidegger. "Therefore, when the most profound thinker of my time fell into step with the thundering march of Hitler's brown battalions, it was not merely a bitter personal disappointment for me but in my eyes a debacle for philosophy. Philosophy itself, not only a man, had declared bankruptcy." "Philosophy at the End of the Century: Retrospect and Prospect," in *Mortality and Morality*, p. 49.
5 Jonas, "Heidegger's Resoluteness and Resolve," pp. 202–3. Jonas's most passionate and devastating critique of Heidegger is contained in his essay "Heidegger and Theology," reprinted in *The Phenomenon of Life* (New York: Harper & Row, 1966), pp. 235–61. It was originally delivered as an address to a conference of theologians. References to *The Phenomenon of Life* are abbreviated *PL* followed by the page number. In the United States, it was theologians who were originally most sympathetic to Heidegger, and sought to explore the theological implications of *Sein und Zeit*. Jonas argues that this was a catastrophic mistake, a failure to appreciate the pagan and anti-theological character of this work. He condemns Heidegger for his "false humility," and claims that Heidegger is guilty of "the most enormous hubris in the whole history of thought. For it is nothing less than the thinker's claiming that

through him speaks the essence of things itself, and thus the claim to an authority which no thinker should ever claim" (*PL* 257).

6 Jonas, "Gnosticism, Existentialism, and Nihilism," in *PL* 224. References are abbreviated GEN, followed by the page number in *PL*.

7 Lawrence Vogel, in the introduction to his excellent anthology of Jonas's essays, *Mortality and Morality*, provides a perceptive overview of Jonas's philosophy as an antidote to the "nihilistic character of modern thought." Vogel says: "Because [Jonas] sees this nihilism crystallized in *Being and Time* – the master work of his *Doctorvater*, Martin Heidegger – Jonas's fundamental project can be seen as no less than an overcoming of his intellectual father-figure, whose behavior during the Third Reich Jonas diagnoses as a symptom of the ethical weakness of Heidegger's nihilistic ideas" (p. 4).

8 Jonas, "Toward an Ontological Grounding of an Ethics for the Future," in *Mortality and Morality*, p. 108.

9 Jonas clearly dissociates himself from the "evolutionary optimism" represented by Teilhard de Chardin. For Jonas, life is "an experiment with mounting stakes and risks which in the fateful freedom of man may end in disaster as well as in success" (*PL* p. x).

10 Jonas, "Evolution and Freedom: On the Continuity among Life-Forms," in *Mortality and Morality*, p. 60.

11 One might think that the concept of self is applicable only to human beings. But Jonas says, "The introduction of the term 'self,' unavoidable in any description of the most elementary instance of life, indicates the emergence, with life as such, of internal identity – and so, as one with that emergence, its self-isolation too from all the rest of reality. Profound singleness and heterogeneousness within a universe of homogeneously interrelated existence mark the selfhood of organism" (*PL* 82–3).

12 See Jonas, "Note on Anthropomorphism," in *PL* 33–7.

13 Jonas sharply distinguishes his understanding of continuity and "emergent novelty" from those theories of emergent evolution that maintain that there are "leaps" in the course of evolution which bring with them totally new levels of causality. In his critique of the theory of emergent evolution (*PL* 67–9) he writes: "Thus we can say that the – theoretically valuable – principle of emergent *novelty*, if it is not to be totally arbitrary and hence irrational, must be tempered by that of continuity: and a substantive continuity, not a merely formal one – so that we must let ourselves be *instructed by what is highest and richest concerning everything beneath it*" (*PL* 69).

14 From Jonas's perspective, there is good reason to claim that Levinas is committed to some version of dualism. Levinas, as we have already noted, affirms, "I do not know at what moment the human appears, but what I want to emphasize is that the human breaks with pure being, which is always a persistence in being. This is my principal thesis" (PM 172).

15 Jonas, *Imperative of Responsibility*. References to this book are abbreviated *IR*, followed by the page number.

16 When Jonas insists that the primary responsibility is *for* those beings that have the capacity to be responsible, it looks as if he is slipping into a type of

anthropocentrism that he criticizes in traditional ethics. But Lawrence Vogel claims that "Jonas's metaphysics undercuts the very distinction between anthropocentrism and nonanthropocentrism. He thinks we can, and indeed must, have it *both* ways. While living nature is a good-in-itself commanding our reverence, and while all organisms participating in this goodness are vulnerable ends-in-themselves who exhibit concern for their own being, humans have special dignity as moral agents, for our will is responsive to ends beyond our own vital ones . . . . Our first duty is to preserve the noble presence of moral responsibility in nature: of a being who is able to recognize the good-in-itself as such" (Introduction to *Mortality and Morality*, p. 17).

17 For a perceptive explication and critique of Jonas's theory of responsibility, see Dimitri Nikulin, "Reconsidering Responsibility: Hans Jonas's Imperative for a New Ethics," in the *Graduate School Philosophy Journal* 23/1 (2002). See also my article, "Hans Jonas: Rethinking Responsibility," *Social Research*, 61/4 (Winter 1994), pp. 833–52.

18 Jonas, Introduction, to *Philosophical Essays: From Ancient Creed to Technological Man* (Chicago: University of Chicago Press, 1974), p. xv. In this introduction, Jonas gives a brief autobiographical sketch of his life and work. See also "A Retrospective View," in Hans Jonas, *On Faith, Reason and Responsibility* (Claremont, Calif.: The Institute for Antiquity and Christianity, Claremont Graduate School, 1981), pp. 107–22. It was only in 1945 at the end of the Second World War that Jonas discovered that his mother had been exterminated at Auschwitz.

19 In a footnote to the English translation of this lecture, Jonas indicates the sources for this lecture, which date back to the early 1960s. See "The Concept of God after Auschwitz: A Jewish Voice," in *Mortality and Morality*, p. 131. References to this text are abbreviated CGA.

20 Jonas sharply distinguishes Kant's warning about the impossibility of achieving *knowledge* of metaphysical truths (which he accepts) from the much more restrictive positivist claim that metaphysical and speculative questions lack any sense (which he rejects). (See CGA 131–2.)

21 Jonas first presented this myth in his essay "Immortality and the Modern Temper," in *Mortality and Morality*. Although he offered this myth originally to deal with the question of immortality, he tells us that "the specter of Auschwitz already played its part" (CGA 134).

22 Jonas, "Immortality and the Modern Temper," pp. 127–8.

23 Ibid., p. 124.

24 Jonas gives logical, ontological, and theological arguments to challenge the coherence of the idea of divine omnipotence. See CGA 138–9.

25 Jonas never seeks to "justify" this fundamental claim, or even to offer reasons to support it. Ironically, he knows that this is precisely the claim that many of the Gnostics denied. Jonas is speaking from a Jewish perspective, and he takes it to be fundamental to Judaism that goodness is an essential attribute of God.

26 There are also some striking similarities between Jonas's mythical account of God and his relation to the world and Schelling. See Peter Dews' discussion

of Schelling and Jonas in " 'Radical Finitude' and the Problem of Evil: Critical Comments on Wellmer's Reading of Jonas," in *Rethinking Evil*, ed. María Pía Lara (Berkeley: University of California Press, 2001), pp. 27–45.

27   Jonas, "Immortality and the Modern Temper," p. 129 (emphasis added).

28   Ibid.

29   Hans Jonas, "Matter, Mind, and Creation: Cosmological Evidence and Cosmogonic Speculation," in *Mortality and Morality*, p. 188.

30   Ibid., p. 191.

31   Ibid., pp. 191–2.

32   Ibid., p. 192. The quotations from Hillesum cited by Jonas are from *An Interrupted Life: The Diaries of Etty Hillesum, 1941–43* (New York: Pantheon Books, 1989).

33   Jonas relates the story of how his participation in Bultmann's seminar led to his own study of Gnosticism in "A Retrospective View," pp.111–15.

34   See Jonas, "Is Faith Still Possible?: Memories of Rudolf Bultmann and Reflections on the Philosophical Aspects of his Work," in *Mortality and Morality*, pp. 144–64.

35   Ibid., p. 149.

36   See Jonas's comments on the relation of metaphor and myth, in ibid., pp. 149–50.

37   Albrecht Wellmer suggests that we interpret Jonas's speculations as the "metaphorical expression of an ethical self-understanding, rather than as its possible foundation." See Albrecht Wellmer, "Der Mythos vom leidenden und werdenden Gott: Fragen an Hans Jonas," in *Endspiele: Die unversöhnliche Moderne* (Frankfurt am Main: Suhrkamp, 1993), p. 253. See also Peter Dews' discussion and critique of Wellmer in " 'Radical Finitude' and the Problem of Evil."

38   "Heidegger and Theology," p. 261.

39   This is the basis of Jonas's disagreement with Bultmann. The symbolic speech of myth cannot be completely translated into philosophical concepts. "The danger of 'appropriateness' of a conceptual scheme is that it may blunt the sense of paradox and create a familiarity where none is permitted" (ibid., p. 260).

40   Ibid., p. 261.

41   Levinas was once asked in an interview, "If animals do not have faces in an ethical sense, do we have obligations towards them? And if so where do they come from?" He answered: "It is clear that, without considering animals as human beings, the ethical extends to all living beings. We do not want to make an animal suffer needlessly and so on. But the prototype of this is human ethics" (PM 172). Jonas would certainly agree that we do not want to make animals suffer needlessly, but *his* concern with nonhuman animals presupposes a more primary obligation to preserve the conditions for the very *possibility* of animal and human life in the future.

42   See Jacques Derrida, "Violence and Metaphysics: An Essay on the Thought of Emmanuel Levinas," in *Writing and Difference*, pp. 79–153.

Chapter 8 Arendt: Radical Evil and the Banality of Evil

1 In my book *Hannah Arendt and the Jewish Question*, I devoted a chapter each to Arendt's reflections on the meaning of radical evil and the banality of evil. Since the publication of the book, I have changed my mind on several issues – in part, as a result of my present inquiry. Although I have not altered my understanding substantively, I now think that her reflections are more subtle, nuanced, and complex than I originally indicated. I will be repeating some of the points that I made originally, but placing them in a new context.

2 Arendt's early love affair with Heidegger is now well known. For a discussion of the intellectual influence of Heidegger on Arendt, see Dana Villa, *Arendt and Heidegger: The Fate of the Political* (Princeton: Princeton University Press, 1996), and Jacques Taminiaux, *The Thracian Maid and the Professional Thinker: Arendt and Heidegger* (Albany: State University of New York Press, 1997). See also my article, "Provocation and Appropriation: Hannah Arendt's Response to Martin Heidegger," *Constellations*, 4/2 (October 1997), pp. 153–71.

3 In her interview with Günter Gaus, she said:

> I come from an old Königsberg family. Nevertheless, the word "Jew" never came up when I was a small child. I first met up with it through anti-Semitic remarks – they are not worth repeating – from children on the street. After that I was, so to speak, "enlightened." . . . as a child – a somewhat older child then – I knew that I looked Jewish. I looked different from other children. I was very conscious of that. But not in a way that made me feel inferior, that was just how it was . . . . [My mother] would never have baptized me! I think she would have boxed my ears right and left if she had ever found out that I had denied being a Jew. It was unthinkable, so to speak. Out of the question. (" 'What Remains? The Language Remains': A Conversation with Günter Gaus," in *Arendt: Essays in Understanding, 1930–1954*, p.7; subsequent references to this volume are abbreviated *EU*).

4 Elizabeth Young-Bruehl, *Hannah Arendt: For Love of the World* (New Haven: Yale University Press, 1982), p. 71. See Arendt's correspondence with Blumenfeld: Hannah Arendt/Kurt Blumenfeld, *". . . in keinen Besitz verwurzelt": Die Korrespondenz*, ed. Ingeborg Nordmann and Iris Pilling (Hamburg: Rotbuch Verlag, 1995).

5 Although the manuscript was completed in the 1930s, *Rahel Varnhagen* was not published until 1958 in London. Harcourt Brace Jovanovich published the American edition in 1974. Liliane Weissberg edited a new edition in 1997 (Baltimore: The Johns Hopkins University Press, 1997).

6 "What Remains? The Language Remains?," *EU* 11–12.

7 Hannah Arendt, "Nightmare and Flight," *EU* 134.

8 Arendt, *Origins of Totalitarianism*, 3rd edn, pp. viii–ix. References to this book are abbreviated *OT*.

9 The epigraph reads: "Weder dem Vergangenen anheinfallen noch dem Zukünftigen. Es kommt darauf an, ganz gegenwärtig zu sein" (Give yourself

up neither to the past nor to the future. The important thing is to remain wholly in the present).

10 *Hannah Arendt/Karl Jaspers Correspondence*, p. 165.

11 Ibid., p. 166.

12 Hannah Arendt, *The Human Condition* (Chicago: University of Chicago Press, 1958), p. 7. References to this book are abbreviated *HC*.

13 For Arendt's discussion of the totalitarian appeal to "the laws of Nature and History," see ch. 13: "Ideology and Terror: A Novel Form of Government," *OT* 460–79. See also Margaret Canovan's lucid account of Arendt's theory of totalitarianism: "Arendt's Theory of Totalitarianism: A Reassessment," in *The Cambridge Companion to Hannah Arendt*, ed. Dana Villa (Cambridge: Cambridge University Press, 2000), pp. 25–43.

14 Arendt, "The Concentration Camps," *Partisan Review*, 15/7 (July 1948), p. 748. Material from this article was revised and incorporated in *OT*. This is one of the first places in which Arendt speaks of "absolute evil."

15 Victor Klemperer, *I Will Bear Witness: A Diary of the Nazi Years, 1933–41, 1942–45*, 2 vols (New York: Random House, 1998, 1999).

16 We must not think that natality, the capacity to begin something new, always has a positive significance for Arendt. Totalitarianism itself is a consequence of this same capacity – this natality. She says, "Everything we know of totalitarianism demonstrates a horrible originality . . . . The originality of totalitarianism is horrible, not because some new 'idea' came into the world, but because its very actions constitute a break with all our traditions; they have clearly exploded our categories of political thought and our standards for moral judgment" ("Understanding and Politics," *EU* 309–10). Margaret Canovan speaks of the "paradox of totalitarian novelty": "Totalitarianism illustrated the human capacity to *begin*, that power to think and to act in ways that are new, contingent, and unpredictable that looms so large in her mature political theory. But the paradox of totalitarian novelty was that it represented an assault on that very ability to act and think as a unique individual" ("Arendt's Theory of Totalitarianism," p. 27).

17 Margaret Canovan, *Hannah Arendt: A Reinterpretation of her Political Thought* (Cambridge: Cambridge University Press, 1992), p. 281.

18 There is also an important difference between Levinas and Arendt insofar as Levinas (especially in *Totality and Infinity*) makes a sharp distinction between ethics and politics – and suggests that it is ethics, not politics, that recognizes the singularity of the other (*l'autrui*). Arendt claims that in politics too we must acknowledge the plurality of individuals who have a distinctive perspective on a common world.

19 For a detailed account of what Arendt means by plurality, see my article, "Provocation and Appropriation."

20 Arendt develops this theme in her essays, "What is Freedom?," and "Tradition and the Modern Age," in *Between Past and Future* (New York: Viking Press, 1961), pp. 143–72, 17–40 respectively.

21 Canovan, *Hannah Arendt*, p. 7.

22 For a discussion and critique of Arendt's understanding of Judaism and

Jewishness, see my final chapter, "Concluding Remarks: Blindness and Insight," in *Hannah Arendt and the Jewish Question*.

23 *Hannah Arendt/Karl Jaspers: Correspondence*, p. 166.

24 See my discussion of the resonances in Arendt's thought with the tradition of Judaism in *Hannah Arendt and the Jewish Question*, pp. 188–9.

25 *Hannah Arendt/Karl Jaspers: Correspondence*, p. 54.

26 Ibid., p. 62. This may have been one of the sources for the expression "the banality of evil" that Arendt first used in *Eichmann in Jerusalem* 25 years later. But see also Jaspers's letter to Arendt dated December 13, 1963, where he writes: "Alcopley told me that Heinrich suggested the phrase 'the banality of evil' and is cursing himself for it now because you've had to take the heat for what he thought of. Perhaps the report isn't true, or my recollection of it is garbled. I think it's a wonderful inspiration and right on the mark as the book's subtitle. The point is that *this* evil, not evil per se, is banal" (ibid., p. 542).

27 Ibid., p. 69; emphasis added.

28 See Arendt, *Eichmann in Jerusalem*, pp. 287–8, and *idem, Life of the Mind*, vol.1, pp. 3–4. References to *Eichmann in Jerusalem* are abbreviated *EJ*; references to *The Life of the Mind* are abbreviated *LM*. See also my discussion of "satanic greatness" in *Hannah Arendt and the Jewish Question*, pp. 150–1.

29 Arendt distinguishes anti-Semitism as "a secular nineteenth-century ideology" that arose in the 1870s from religious Jew-hatred that has a much more ancient history. See the "Preface to Part One: Antisemitism," *OT*, pp. xi–xvi. See also ch. 2: "Anti-Semitism as a Political Ideology," in Bernstein, *Hannah Arendt and the Jewish Question*.

30 In the "Concluding Remarks," of the original (1951) edition of *The Origins of Totalitarianism*, Arendt speaks of the dangers of resentment. In subsequent editions, she deleted this final chapter, but incorporated some of its claims in other parts of her revised text. It is clear that this is an allusion to Nietzsche's *ressentiment* (*OT*, 1951 edn, p. 438).

31 Arendt, "Concentration Camps," p. 758.

32 In light of the many slanderous claims that have been (and are still being) made about Arendt's views concerning Eichmann and the trial, it is important to note that she defended the kidnapping of Eichmann in Argentina by the Israelis and trying him in an Israeli court. She also agreed with the court's decision to hang Eichmann. She expressed her admiration for the judges who tried Eichmann, and endorsed their judgment about Eichmann's responsibility. She wrote, "What the judgment had to say on this point was more than correct, it was the truth." She then cited the following passage from the court's judgment:

In such an enormous and complicated crime as the one we are now considering, wherein many people participated, on various levels and in various modes of activity – the planners, the organizers, and those executing the deeds, according to their various ranks – there is not much point in using the ordinary concepts of counseling and soliciting to commit a crime. For these crimes were committed en masse, not only in regard to the number of victims, but also in regard to the numbers of those who perpetrated the crime, and the extent to which any one of the many criminals was close to or remote from the actual killer of the victim means nothing, as far as the measure of his responsibility is concerned. On the contrary, in general *the degree of responsibility increases as we draw further away from the man who uses the fatal instrument with his own hands*. (*EJ* 246–7; Arendt's emphasis)

33 *Hannah Arendt/ Karl Jaspers: Correspondence*, p. 423. See my discussion of their correspondence concerning the Eichmann trial in *Hannah Arendt and the Jewish Question*, pp. 156–8.

34 See also her own judgment at the conclusion of the "Epilogue" of her report: "And just as you supported and carried out a policy of not wanting to share the earth with the Jewish people and the people of a number of other nations – as though you and your superiors had any right to determine who should and who should not inhabit the world – we find that no one, that is, no member of the human race, can be expected to want to share the earth with you. This is the reason, and the only reason, you must hang" (*EJ* 279). Seyla Benhabib provides an excellent account of Arendt's understanding of "crimes against humanity" in her article "Arendt's *Eichmann in Jerusalem*," in *The Cambridge Companion to Hannah Arendt*, pp. 65–85. She writes: "Arendt's contribution to moral and legal thought in this century will certainly not be the category of the 'banality of evil.' Rather, I want to suggest, the category that is closest to the nerve of her political thought as a whole, and one which has gained significance with the end of the twentieth century, is that of 'crimes against humanity'" (p. 76).

35 For an account of the controversy over *Eichmann in Jerusalem*, see Young-Bruehl, *Hannah Arendt*, 8: "*Cura Posterior: Eichmann in Jerusalem* (1961–1965)," pp. 328–78. For a balanced statement of the strengths and weaknesses of *Eichmann in Jerusalem*, see Hans Mommsen, "Hannah Arendt and the Eichmann Trial," in *From Weimar to Auschwitz: Essays in German History*, tr. Philip O'Connor (Princeton: Princeton University Press, and Cambridge: Polity, 1991).

36 "Eichmann in Jerusalem: An Exchange of Letters between Gershom Scholem and Hannah Arendt," reprinted in Ron H. Feldman (ed.), *Hannah Arendt, The Jew as Pariah: Jewish Identity and Politics in the Modern Age* (New York: Grove Press, 1978), p. 245.

37 Ibid., p. 251.

38 In *Hannah Arendt and the Jewish Question*, I explore in much greater detail the relation between radical evil and the banality of evil. See chs 7 and 8.

39 I agree with Margaret Canovan when she writes that Arendt "never had thought in terms of 'monsters and demons,' and 'banality' was really a more accurate way of describing the self-abandonment to inhuman forces and the diminution of human beings to an animal species that she had all along placed at the centre of totalitarianism" (*Hannah Arendt*, p. 24, n. 30).

40 *Hannah Arendt/ Karl Jaspers: Correspondence*, p. 62.

41 Although Arendt insists that she is speaking "on the strictly factual level," I think she is being ingenuous. She is not simply describing facts, but making

a controversial judgment about their banality. Nevertheless, her insistence makes it clear that she is not offering a *theory* or general doctrine about the nature of evil. And she is certainly not speaking about Hitler and the Nazis in general. I think that some of the confusion and controversy concerning the "banality of evil" might have been avoided if Arendt had been more emphatic in making it clear that her analysis was limited to Eichmann.

42 Arendt underestimates the ideological fanaticism of Eichmann. To cite one notorious example, it is difficult to reconcile Eichmann's actions in Budapest in the spring of 1944 with Arendt's portrait of him as someone who had "no motives at all" and who "never realized what he was doing." By 1944, the only significant Jewish community that had been unaffected by deportation to death camps was in Hungary, where there were 750,000 Jews. When Eichmann and his staff went to Budapest in March 1944, it was clear that the Germans were losing the war, and it was well known what "deportation" and "resettlement" really meant. But Eichmann quickly and efficiently organized a Budapest Jewish Council to facilitate deportations. When orders were given to stop the deportations, Eichmann schemed to continue them. In November 1944, when railroad facilities were no longer available, Eichmann helped to arrange the infamous death march. Arendt describes this as "one of the most damning pieces of evidence against Eichmann" (*EJ* 201), yet fails to see this as evidence of Eichmann's ideological fanaticism. Nevertheless, I think it is important to distinguish the *historical* issue of the accuracy of Arendt's characterization of Eichmann from the *conceptual* issue – that individuals can commit evil deeds on a gigantic scale without these deeds being traceable to monstrous, demonic, evil motives.

43 Arendt, "Thinking and Moral Considerations: A Lecture," *Social Research*, 38/3 (Fall 1971), p. 417.

44 Seyla Benhabib points out other respects in which Arendt was offensive. "Arendt's thinly disguised and almost racist comments on Chief Prosecutor Gideon Hausner's '*ostjüdish*' background, her childish partisanship for the 'German-educated' judges, her dismay about the 'oriental mob' outside the doors of the courtroom in Jerusalem, all suggest a certain failure of nerve and lack of distance from the topic at hand" ("Arendt's *Eichmann in Jerusalem*," p. 65).

45 See Susan Neiman's perceptive discussion of Arendt's critical reflections on the role of intention in committing evil deeds, in *Evil in Modern Thought: An Alternative History of Philosophy*, forthcoming.

46 Canovan, *Hannah Arendt*, p. 158.

47 Selya Benhabib makes a similar point: Arendt "was taken aback by what she later described as the sheer ordinariness of the man who had been party to such enormous crimes: Eichmann spoke in endless clichés, gave little evidence of being motivated by a fanatical hatred of Jews, and was most proud of being a 'law-abiding citizen'. It was the shock of seeing Eichmann 'in the flesh' that led Arendt to the thought that great wickedness was not a necessary condition for the performance of (or complicity in) great crimes. Evil could take a 'banal' form, as it had in Eichmann" ("Arendt's *Eichmann in Jerusalem*," p. 67).

48 Kant, *Religion within the Limits of Reason Alone*, pp. 24–5.
49 Mary McCarthy, who frequently "Englished" Arendt's manuscripts, objected to the term "thoughtlessness." She thought it was an infelicitous expression to designate what Arendt meant by "the inability to think." But Arendt persisted in using it.
50 For a reproduction of this page, and a discussion of the two epigraphs on it, see the interpretive essay by Ronald Beiner in Arendt, *Lectures on Kant's Political Philosophy*, pp. 89–156.
51 For critical discussions of what Arendt means by thinking and judging, and some of the unresolved problems in her reflections, see my articles, "Judging – the Actor and the Spectator," in *Philosophical Profiles*, pp. 221–37. "Arendt on Thinking," in *Cambridge Companion to Hannah Arendt*, pp. 277–92, and "Responsibility, Judging, and Evil," *Revue Internationale de Philosophie*, 2 (1999). See also Beiner's interpretative essay in Arendt, *Lectures on Kant's Political Philosophy*; Seyla Benhabib, "Judgment and the Moral Foundations of Politics in Hannah Arendt's Thought," *Political Theory*, 16/1 (1988); Maurizio Passerin D'Entrèves, "Arendt's Theory of Judgment," in *Cambridge Companion to Hannah Arendt*, pp. 245–60; Robert Dostal, "Judging Human Action: Hannah Arendt's Appropriation of Kant," *Review of Metaphysics*, 37/4 (1984), pp. 125–55. Concerning Arendt's reflections about willing see Suzanne Jacobitti, "Hannah Arendt and the Will," *Political Theory*, 16/1 (1988), pp. 53–76.
52 Arendt, "What Remains? The Language Remains," pp. 10–11.
53 In an unpublished manuscript that served as a basis for a lecture course that she gave at the New School, she wrote:

> We . . . have witnessed the total collapse of all established moral standards in public and private life during the thirties and forties. . . . Without much notice all this collapsed almost overnight and then it was as though morality suddenly stood revealed . . . a set of mores, customs, and manners which could be exchanged for another set with hardly more trouble than it would take to change the table manners of an individual or a people. ("Some Questions of Moral Philosophy," Arendt Archives, Library of Congress)

54 Arendt, *Lectures on Kant's Political Philosophy*, p. 10.
55 For a discussion of the significance of Socrates as a thinker and a citizen, see Canovan, *Hannah Arendt*, ch. 7: "Philosophy and Politics."
56 For Arendt's account of the story of Anton Schmidt, see *Eichmann in Jerusalem*, pp. 230–3.
57 Arendt, draft of "Personal Responsibility under Dictatorship," Arendt Archives, Library of Congress. See also "Organized Guilt and Universal Responsibility," *EU* 121–32.
58 Arendt, "Personal Responsibility under Dictatorship," *Listener*, August 6, 1964, p. 186; emphasis added.
59 Ibid.

Conclusion

1   The events of September 11, 2001, painfully illustrate why I am skeptical of
     a *theory* of evil – a theory that claims universality and completeness – and
     why new unprecedented and unpredictable eruptions of evil demand open-
     ness to rethinking the vicissitudes and proper responses to evil. Unfortunately
     these events have also elicited what I have called "vulgar Manichaeism,"
     where opponents unreflectively demonize each other as epitomizing absolute
     evil.
2   Levinas, "Transcendence of Evil," p. 158.
3   Arendt, *Origins of Totalitarianism*, p. viii.
4   Blanchot, *Writing of the Disaster*, p. 82.
5   Arendt, *Origins of Totalitarianism*, p. 441.
6   Ibid., p. 458.

Bibliography

Allison, Henry E. *Kant's Transcendental Idealism*. New Haven: Yale University Press, 1983.
—— *Kant's Theory of Freedom*. Cambridge: Cambridge University Press, 1990.
Améry, Jean. *At the Mind's Limits: Contemplations by a Survivor on Auschwitz and its Realities*, tr. Sidney and Stella P. Rosenfield. Bloomington: Indiana University Press, 1980.
Anderson-Gold, Sharon. "Kant's Rejection of Devilishness: The Limits of Human Volition." *Idealistic Studies* 14 (1984).
Arendt, Hannah. "The Concentration Camps" *Partisan Review*, 15/7 (July 1948).
—— *The Origins of Totalitarianism*. New York: Harcourt Brace and Co., 1951. 3rd edn revised, New York: Harcourt Brace Jovanovich, 1968.
—— *The Human Condition*. Chicago: University of Chicago Press, 1958.
—— *Between Past and Future*. New York: Viking Press, 1961.
—— "Personal Responsibility under Dictatorship." *The Listener* (August 6, 1964).
—— *Eichmann in Jerusalem: A Report on the Banality of Evil*, 2nd edn. New York: Viking Press, 1965.
—— "Thinking and Moral Considerations: A Lecture." *Social Research*, 38/3 (Fall 1971).
—— *The Life of the Mind*, 2 vols. New York: Harcourt, Brace, Jovanovich, 1978.
—— *Lectures on Kant's Political Philosophy*, ed. Ronald Beiner. Chicago: University of Chicago Press, 1982.
—— "For Martin Heidegger's Eightieth Birthday." In *Martin Heidegger and National Socialism*, ed. G. Neske and E. Kettering, tr. L. Harries. New York: Paragon House, 1990.
—— "Some Questions of Moral Philosophy," *Social Research*, 61/4 (Winter 1994).
—— *Essays in Understanding, 1930–1954*, ed. Jerome Kohn. New York: Harcourt, Brace & Co., 1994.
—— *Rahel Varnhagen: The Life of a Jewess*, ed. Liliane Weissberg. Baltimore: Johns

Hopkins University Press, 1997.

Hannah Arendt/Kurt Blumenfeld, *"in keinen Besitz verwurzelt": Die Korrespondenz*, ed. Ingeborg Nordmann and Iris Pilling. Hamburg: Rotbuch Verlag, 1995.

Hannah Arendt/Karl Jaspers. Correspondence 1926-1969, ed. Lotte Kohler and Hans Saner. New York: Harcourt Brace Jovanovich, 1992.

Beiser, Frederick C. *The Fate of Reason: German Philosophy from Kant to Fichte.* Cambridge, Mass.: Harvard University Press, 1987.

Benhabib, Seyla. "Judgment and the Moral Foundations of Politics in Hannah Arendt's Thought" in *Political Theory* 16/1 (1988).

—— "Arendt's *Eichmann in Jerusalem*." In *The Cambridge Companion to Hannah Arendt*, ed. Dana Villa. Cambridge: Cambridge University Press, 2000.

Berkowitz, Peter. *Nietzsche: The Ethics of an Immoralist.* Cambridge, Mass.: Harvard University Press, 1995.

Bernasconi, Robert, and David Wood, eds. *The Provocation of Levinas: Rethinking the Other.* London: Routledge, 1998.

Bernstein, Richard J. *Beyond Objectivism and Relativism.* Oxford: Basil Blackwell, 1983.

—— *Philosophical Profiles.* Cambridge: Polity, 1986.

—— *The New Constellation: The Ethical-Political Horizons of Modernity/Postmodernity.* Cambridge: Polity, 1991.

—— "Hans Jonas: Rethinking Responsibility." *Social Research*, 61/4 (Winter 1994).

—— *Hannah Arendt and the Jewish Question.* Cambridge: Polity, 1996.

—— "Provocation and Appropriation: Hannah Arendt's Response to Martin Heidegger." *Constellations*, 4/2 (October 1997).

—— *Freud and the Legacy of Moses.* Cambridge: Cambridge University Press, 1998.

—— "Responsibility, Judging, and Evil." *Revue Internationale de Philosophie*, 2 (1999).

—— "Arendt on Thinking." In *The Cambridge Companion to Hannah Arendt*, ed. Dana Villa. Cambridge: Cambridge University Press, 2000.

Blanchot, Maurice. *The Writing of the Disaster*, tr. Ann Smock. Lincoln: University of Nebraska Press, 1986.

Bloom, Harold. *The Anxiety of Influence.* Oxford: Oxford University Press, 1973.

—— *Agon: Towards a Theory of Revisionism.* New York: Oxford University Press, 1982.

Bowie, Andrew. *Schelling and Modern European Philosophy: An Introduction.* London: Routledge, 1993.

Canovan, Margaret. *Hannah Arendt: A Reinterpretation of her Political Thought.* Cambridge: Cambridge University Press, 1992.

—— "Arendt's Theory of Totalitarianism: A Reassessment." In *The Cambridge Companion to Hannah Arendt*, ed. Dana Villa. Cambridge: Cambridge University Press, 2000.

Crites, Stephen. *Dialectic and Gospel in the Development of Hegel's Thinking.* University Park: Pennsylvania State University Press, 1998.

Delbanco, Andrew. *The Death of Satan.* New York: Farrar, Straus, and Giroux, 1995.

D'Entrèves, Maurizio Passerin. "Arendt's Theory of Judgment." In *The Cambridge Companion to Hannah Arendt*, ed. Dana Villa. Cambridge: Cambridge University

Press, 2000.

Derrida, Jacques. *Writing and Difference*, tr. Alan Bass. Chicago: University of Chicago Press, 1978.

—— *The Post Card: From Socrates to Freud and Beyond*, tr. Alan Bass. Chicago: University of Chicago Press, 1987.

Desmond, William. *Beyond Hegel and Dialectic: Speculation, Cult, and Comedy.* Albany, NY: State University of New York Press, 1992.

Despland, Michael. *Kant on History and Religion.* Montreal: McGill–Queen's University Press, 1973.

Dews, Peter. *The Limits of Disenchantment.* London: Verso, 1995.

—— " 'Radical Finitude' and the Problem of Evil: Critical Comments on Wellmer's Reading of Jonas." In *Rethinking Evil*, ed. María Pía Lara. Berkeley: University of California Press, 2001.

Dostal, Robert. "Judging Human Action: Hannah Arendt's Appropriation of Kant." *Review of Metaphysics*, 37/4 (1984).

Erdheim, Mario. *Totem und Tabu.* Frankfurt am Main: Fischer Taschenbuch Verlag, 1991.

Fackenheim, Emile. "Kant and Radical Evil," in *University of Toronto Quarterly*, 23 (1954).

Feldman, Ron H., ed. *Hannah Arendt, The Jew as Pariah: Jewish Identity and Politics in the Modern Age.* New York: Grove Press, 1978.

Freud, Sigmund. *Standard Edition of the Complete Psychological Works of Sigmund Freud*, ed. J. Strachey. London: Hogarth Press, 1974.

Friedlander, Saul, ed. *Probing the Limits of Representation: Nazism and the "Final Solution."* Cambridge, Mass.: Harvard University Press, 1992.

Gadamer, Hans-Georg. *Hegel's Dialectic*, tr. P. Christopher Smith. New Haven: Yale University Press, 1971.

Gram, Moltke S., ed. *Interpreting Kant.* Iowa City: University of Iowa Press, 1982.

Green, Ronald M. "Theodicy." In *Encyclopedia of Religion*, editor-in-chief Mircea Eliade, New York: Macmillan, 1987.

Grubrich-Simitis, Ilse. *Back to Freud's Texts: Making Silent Documents Speak.* New Haven: Yale University Press, 1996.

Habermas, Jürgen. *The Philosophical Discourse of Modernity*, tr. Frederick Lawrence. Cambridge, Mass.: MIT Press, and Cambridge: Polity, 1987.

Hegel, G. W. F. *Science of Logic*, tr. A. W. Miller. New York: Humanities Press, 1969.

—— *Lectures on the Philosophy of World History*, tr. H. B. Nisbet. Cambridge: Cambridge University Press, 1975.

—— *Phenomenology of Spirit*, tr. A. W. Miller. Oxford: Clarendon Press, 1977.

—— *Hegel's Lectures on the Philosophy of Religion*, 3 vols, ed. Peter C. Hodgson. Berkeley: University of California Press, 1984–5.

—— *Hegel's Lectures on the Philosophy of Religion: One Volume Edition, The Lectures of 1827*, ed. Peter C. Hodgson. Berkeley: University of California Press, 1988.

Heidegger, Martin. *Schelling: Abhandlung über das Wesen der menschlichen Freiheit.* Tübingen: Max Niemeyer Verlag, 1971.

—— *Schelling's Treatise on the Essence of Human Freedom*, tr. Joan Stambaugh. Athens,

Oh.: Ohio University Press, 1985.

—— *Gesamtausgabe, Schelling: vom Wesen der menschlichen Freiheit (1809).* Frankfurt am Main: Vittorio Kostermann, 1988.

Herman, Barbara. *The Practice of Moral Judgment.* Cambridge, Mass.: Harvard University Press, 1993.

Hillesum, Etty. *An Interrupted Life: The Diaries of Etty Hillesum, 1941–43.* New York: Pantheon Books, 1989.

Hippolyte, Jean. *Genesis and Structure in Hegel's Phenomenology of Spirit,* tr. S. Cheniak and J. Heckman. Evanston, Ill.: Northwestern University Press, 1974.

Hodgson, Peter C. "Editor's Introduction." In *Hegel's Lectures on the Philosophy of Religion,* vol. 1, ed. Peter Hodgson. Berkeley: University of California Press, 1984.

Hösle, Vittorio. *Praktische Philosophie in der modernen Welt.* Munich: Beck, 1992.

Jacobitti, Suzanne. "Hannah Arendt and the Will." *Political Theory,* 16/1 (1988).

Jaeschke, Walter. *Reason in Religion: The Foundations of Hegel's Philosophy of Religion,* tr. J. M. Stewart and P. C. Hodgson. Berkeley: University of California Press, 1990.

Jonas, Hans. *The Phenomenon of Life.* New York: Harper & Row, 1966.

—— *Philosophical Essays: From Ancient Creed to Technological Man.* Chicago: University of Chicago Press, 1974.

—— *On Faith, Reason and Responsibility.* Claremont, Calif.: The Institute for Antiquity and Christianity, Claremont Graduate School, 1981.

—— *The Imperative of Responsibility: In Search of an Ethics for the Technological Age.* Chicago: University of Chicago Press, 1984.

—— "Heidegger's Resoluteness and Resolve." In *Martin Heidegger and National Socialism,* ed. G. Neske and E. Kettering, tr. L. Harries. New York: Paragon House, 1990.

—— *Mortality and Morality: A Search for the Good after Auschwitz,* ed. Lawrence Vogel. Evanston, Ill.: Northwestern University Press, 1996.

Jurist, Eliot L. *Beyond Hegel and Nietzsche: Philosophy, Culture, and Agency.* Cambridge, Mass.: MIT Press, 2000.

Kant, Immanuel. *Religion within the Limits of Reason Alone,* tr. T. M. Greene and H. H. Hudson. New York: Harper Torchbooks, 1960.

—— *Critique of Pure Reason,* tr. Norman Kemp Smith. New York: St Martin's Press, 1965.

—— "On the Failure of All Attempted Philosophical Theodicies." In Michael Despland, *Kant on History and Religion.* Montreal: McGill–Queen's University Press, 1973.

—— *Die Religion innerhalb der Grenzen der blossen Vernunft,* ed. Karl Vorländer. Hamburg: Felix Meiner Verlag, 1990. Originally published 1793.

—— *Practical Philosophy,* tr. Mary J. Gregor, ed. Allen W. Wood. In *The Cambridge Edition of the Works of Immanuel Kant.* Cambridge: Cambridge University Press, 1996.

—— *Religion and Rational Theology,* tr. and ed. Allen W. Wood and George P. Giovanni. In *The Cambridge Edition of the Works of Immanuel Kant.* Cambridge: Cambridge University Press, 1996.

Kearney, Richard. *Dialogues with Contemporary Continental Philosophers.* Manchester: Manchester University Press, 1984.

Klemperer, Victor. *I Will Bear Witness: A Diary of the Nazi Years, 1933–41, 1942–45,* 2 vols. New York: Random House, 1998, 1999.

Korsgaard, Christine. *Creating the Kingdom of Ends.* Cambridge: Cambridge University Press, 1996.

Kroeber, A. L. "Totem and Taboo in Retrospect: An Ethnological Psychoanalysis." *American Anthropologist,* 22 (1939).

Laplanche, J., and J-B. Pontalis. *The Language of Psychoanalysis,* tr. D. Nicholson-Smith. New York: W. W. Norton, 1973.

Lara, María Pía, ed. *Rethinking Evil.* Berkeley: University of California Press, 2001.

Lear, Jonathan. *Love and its Place in Nature.* New York: Farrar, Straus & Giroux, 1990.

——— *Happiness, Death and the Remainder of Life.* Cambridge, Mass.: Harvard University Press, 2000.

Lévi-Strauss, Claude, and Daniel Eribon. *De prés et de loin.* Paris: Editions Odile Jacob, 1988.

Levinas, Emmanuel. *Totalité et infini: Essai sur l'extériorité.* The Hague: Martinus Nijhoff, 1961.

———. *Totality and Infinity: An Essay on Exteriority,* tr. A. Lingis. Pittsburgh: Duquesne University Press, 1969.

——— "Transcendence and Evil," tr. A. Lingis. In *The Phenomenology of Man and of the Human Condition,* ed. A-T. Tymieniecka, Analecta Husserliana, 14. Dordrecht: D. Reidel, 1983.

——— "The Paradox of Morality: An Interview with Emmanuel Levinas." In *The Provocation of Levinas: Rethinking the Other,* ed. Robert Bernasconi and David Wood. London: Routledge, 1988.

———. "Useless Suffering." In *The Provocation of Levinas: Rethinking the Other,* ed. Robert Bernasconi and David Wood. London: Routledge, 1988.

——— *Difficult Freedom,* tr. S. Hand. Baltimore: Johns Hopkins University Press, 1990.

Marcuse, Herbert. *Eros and Civilization.* Boston: Beacon Press, 1955.

McDowell, John. *Mind and World.* Cambridge, Mass.: Harvard University Press, 1994.

Meerbote, Ralf. "*Wille* and *Willkür* in Kant's Theory of Action." In *Interpreting Kant,* ed. Moltke S. Gram. Iowa City: University of Iowa Press, 1982.

Michalson, Gordon E. Jr., *Fallen Freedom.* Cambridge: Cambridge University Press, 1990.

Mommsen, Hans. *From Weimar to Auschwitz: Essays in German History,* tr. Philip O'Connor. Princeton: Princeton University Press, and Cambridge: Polity, 1991.

Nehamas, Alexander. *Nietzsche: Life as Literature.* Cambridge, Mass.: Harvard University Press, 1985.

Neiman, Susan. *Evil in Modern Thought: An Alternative History of Philosophy.* Forthcoming.

Neske, G., and E. Kettering, eds. *Martin Heidegger and National Socialism,* tr. L. Harries. New York: Paragon House, 1990.

Nietzsche, Friedrich. *Nietzsche Werke*, ed. Giorgio Colli and Mazzino Montinari. Berlin: Walter de Gruyter & Co., 1968.

—— *On the Genealogy of Morals and Ecce Homo*, tr. Walter Kaufmann and R. J. Hollingdale. New York: Vintage Books, 1979.

—— *Beyond Good and Evil*, tr. Walter Kaufmann. New York: Vintage Books, 1989.

—— "On the Uses and Disadvantages of History." In *Untimely Meditations*, tr. R. J. Hollingdale. Cambridge: Cambridge University Press, 1983.

Nikulin, Dmitri. "Reconsidering Responsibility: Hans Jonas's Imperative for a New Ethics." *Graduate School Philosophy Journal*, 23/1 (2002).

O'Connor, Daniel. "Good and Evil Dispositions." *Kant-Studien*, 76 (1985).

O'Neill, Onora. *Acting on Principle: An Essay on Kantian Ethics*. New York: Columbia University Press, 1975.

—— "Kant After Virtue." *Inquiry*, 26 (1983).

—— "Universal Laws and Ends in Themselves." *Monist*, 73 (1989).

Philosophy of German Idealism, ed. Ernst Behler. New York: Continuum, 1987.

Ricoeur, Paul. *Freud and Philosophy: An Essay in Interpretation*. New Haven: Yale University Press, 1970.

Rieff, Philip. *Freud: The Mind of the Moralist*. New York: Viking Press, 1959.

Rorty, Richard. *Contingency, Irony, and Solidarity*. Cambridge: Cambridge University Press, 1989.

Rosen, Stanley. *The Mask of Enlightenment: Nietzsche's Zarathustra*. Cambridge: Cambridge University Press, 1995.

Schelling, F. W. J. *Schelling: Of Human Freedom*, tr. James Gutmann. Chicago: Open Court Publishing Co., 1936.

—— *Philosophische Untersuchungen über das Wesen der menschlichen Freiheit und die damit zusammenhängenden Gegenstande*, ed. T. Buchheim. Hamburg: Felix Meiner Verlag, 1997.

Seebohm, Thomas. "Kant's Theory of Revolution." *Social Research*, 48/3 (Fall 1981).

Silber, John R. "The Ethical Significance of Kant's Religion." In Kant, *Religion Within the Limits of Reason Alone*, tr. T. M. Greene and H. H. Hudson. New York: Harper Torchbooks, 1960.

—— "Kant at Auschwitz." In *Proceedings of the Sixth International Kant Congress*, ed. Gerhard Funke and Thomas Seebohm. Washington, D.C.: Center for Advanced Research in Phenomenology and University Press of America, 1991.

Smith, Gary, ed. *Hannah Arendt Revisited: "Eichmann in Jerusalem" und die Folgen*. Frankfurt: Suhrkamp, 2000.

Taminiaux, Jacques. *The Thracian Maid and the Professional Thinker: Arendt and Heidegger*. Albany: State University of New York Press, 1997.

Villa, Dana. *Arendt and Heidegger: The Fate of the Political*. Princeton: Princeton University Press, 1996.

—— ed. *The Cambridge Companion to Hannah Arendt*. Cambridge: Cambridge University Press, 2000.

Vogel, Lawrence. "Introduction." In Hans Jonas, *Mortality and Morality: A Search for the Good after Auschwitz*, ed. Lawrence Vogel. Evanston, Ill.: Northwestern University Press, 1996.

Wellmer, Albrecht. *Endspiele: Die unversöhnliche Moderne*. Frankfurt am Main:

Suhrkamp, 1993.

White, Alan. *Schelling: Introduction to the System of Freedom*. New Haven: Yale University Press, 1983.

Whitebook, Joel. *Perversion and Utopia: A Study in Psychoanalysis and Critical Theory*. Cambridge, Mass.: MIT Press, 1995.

Wood, Allen W. *Kant's Moral Religion*. Ithaca, N.Y.: Cornell University Press, 1970.

Young-Bruehl, Elizabeth. *Hannah Arendt: For Love of the World*. New Haven: Yale University Press, 1982.

Yovel, Yirmiyahu. "Kant's Practical Reason as Will: Interest, Recognition, Judgment, and Choice." *Review of Metaphysics*, 52/3 (1998).

—— *Dark Riddle*. Cambridge: Polity, 1999.

Žižek, Slavoj. *Tarrying with the Negative: Kant, Hegel, and the Critique of Ideology*. Durham, N.C.: Duke University Press, 1993.

—— *The Indivisible Remainder: An Essay on Schelling and Related Matters*. London: Verso, 1996.

Subject Index

Index of Names

CPSIA information can be obtained
at www.ICGtesting.com
Printed in the USA
BVOW06s0335060617

486109BV00016B/156/P